Cane Fires

The Anti-Japanese Movement in Hawaii, 1865–1945

In the series

Asian American History and Culture

edited by Sucheng Chan

Cane Fires

The Anti-Japanese
Movement in Hawaii,
1865–1945

Gary Y. Okihiro

Temple University Press

Philadelphia

The epigraph to Chapter 9 is from a poem by Muin Otokichi Ozaki, and the epigraph to Chapter 11 from a poem by Sojin Takei. Both are included in a collection of *tanka* poems edited by Jiro Nakano and Kay Nakano, *Poets Behind Barbed Wire* (Honolulu: Bamboo Ridge Press, 1983), and are used here with permission.

Temple University Press, Philadelphia 19122
Copyright © 1991 by Temple University. All rights reserved
Published 1991
Printed in the United States of America

The paper used in this publication meets the minimum requirements of American National Standard for Information Sciences—Permanence of Paper for Printed Library Materials, ANSI Z39.48-1984 ∞

LIBRARY OF CONGRESS CATALOGING-IN-PUBLICATION DATA
Okihiro, Gary Y., 1945–
    Cane fires : the anti-Japanese movement in Hawaii, 1865–1945 / Gary Y. Okihiro.
        p.   cm. — (Asian American history and culture series)
    Includes bibliographical references and index.
    ISBN 0-87722-799-3 (alk. paper)
    1. Japanese Americans—Hawaii—Social conditions.
2. Japanese Americans—Hawaii—Economic conditions.
3. Hawaii—Ethnic relations.   I. Title.   II. Series.
DU624.7.J3038   1991
996.9'004956—dc20   90-41610
                                                                              CIP

To

my mother and father,

Alice Shizue Kakazu Okihiro

and

Tetsuo Okihiro

Contents

Preface

The idea for this book originated in the summer of 1984; as I reread J. Garner Anthony's *Hawaii under Army Rule*, what immediately struck me was that Hawaii's Japanese and the West Coast Japanese were subjected to much the same treatment at the hands of the U.S. military during World War II. That recognition startled me because I had believed, along with others who had studied the subject, that the wartime experience of Hawaii's Japanese differed markedly from that of the West Coast Japanese, whom the army summarily evicted from their homes and confined in concentration camps for the war's duration following President Franklin D. Roosevelt's signing of Executive Order 9066 on February 19, 1942.

In fact, Hawaii, the melting pot of the Pacific, had been held up as an example of racial harmony even during a time of intense national emergency. In the days following Pearl Harbor, acts of violence against Hawaii's Japanese were exceedingly rare; just over 1,400, or less than 1 percent, of the territory's Japanese were interned; and martial law applied to all, demonstrating, in effect, equal treatment for all of Hawaii's residents. The 1982 Report of the Congressional Commission on Wartime Relocation and Internment of Civilians explained: "Hawaii was more ethnically mixed and racially tolerant than the West Coast. Race relations in Hawaii before the war were not infected with the virulent antagonisms of 75 years of anti-Asian agitation. . . . In Hawaii, the spirit of *aloha* prevailed, and white supremacy never gained legal recognition."[1] Accordingly, most scholars believed that Hawaii's wartime experience had little or no bearing on the West Coast situation.

The predominant view of Hawaii's "unorthodox race doctrine" put forward by sociologists Romanzo Adams and Andrew W. Lind (and others) tended to support the popular image of a racial paradise. While Lind's later work rejected simplistic and uncritical descriptions, he depicted the development of race relations as clearly evolving toward greater interracial harmony and assimilation/homogenization, despite occasional lapses.[2] Earlier, Lind's work had mirrored the race relations cycle idea of his mentor, Robert E. Park, especially in his defense of Japanese loyalty during World War II. Lind expanded his 1942 paper "The Japanese in Hawaii under War Conditions" and in 1946 published *Hawaii's Japanese: An Experiment in Democracy*, which described the wartime proposal for concentrating all the territory's Japanese on some barren island such as Molokai in terms of a distasteful loss of innocence. "The proposed segregation of the Japanese," he wrote, "seemed to symbolize the loss of what the Islanders had sentimentally called the *aloha* spirit of Hawaii, and most people sincerely regretted it." He ventured that there were several reasons that the plan was not implemented, but "none is probably more important than the persistent Hawaiian tradition of interracial amity."[3] Thus, according to Lind, Hawaii's "tradition" of friendly intercourse prevented the excesses of the mainland, where the sentiment "once a Jap, always a Jap" prevailed, and the results of this wartime testing of democracy affirmed the seemliness of Hawaii's race relations experiment.

In contrast, J. Garner Anthony insisted that army rule represented democracy gone awry and stressed the military's trampling of civil liberties of *all* Hawaii's people. Drawing the same conclusion as scholars of the mainland experience had drawn, Anthony, Hawaii's wartime attorney general, wrote: "Nothing is eternal but change, however, and if our democracy is to survive, we must never forget the lessons of military rule in Hawaii and the cornerstone of our democracy, the supremacy of civil power."[4] Anthony's persistent hammering forged connections for me, linking the West Coast anti-Japanese movement and America's concentration camps with martial law in the islands. That coupling, in turn, led me to speculate that the unprecedented imposition of martial law in Hawaii on December 7, 1941, like the army's curfew and restricted zones on the West Coast, surely must have some connection with concern over the resident Japanese in the islands.

My interest in the Hawaiian experience deepened as a result of preliminary research that summer at the University of Hawaii at Manoa, especially in the Hamilton Library's microfilms of National Archives material deposited by scholar–activist John E. Reinecke. In researching his book, *Feigned Necessity: Hawaii's Attempt to Obtain Chinese Contract Labor, 1921–23*, Reinecke uncovered the table of contents of a statement by Major General Charles P. Summerall that enumerated ten "factors bearing on the Japanese situation in relation to our military problem." The general's statement accompanied the 1923 report of the federal Hawaiian Labor Commission sent to investigate an alleged labor shortage in the aftermath of the 1920 plantation strike of Japanese and Filipino workers. Reinecke's discovery was the first document to focus my attention on agricultural labor and the agrarian bases of Hawaii's anti-Japanese movement.

The army's "military problem," Summerall had outlined, involved the numbers of Japanese in the territory and their concentration in certain districts of Honolulu, Japanese-language schools, Japanese religious beliefs, their economic penetration of select industries, and the ethnic press. These I knew to have been the same concerns of the Western Defense Command in its justification nearly twenty years later of the mass removal and confinement of the West Coast Japanese under the guise of "military necessity." At the National Archives in Washington, D.C., I located the full text of Summerall's report within the records of the Military Intelligence Division (as opposed to the Labor Department where Reinecke had made his original find).

The Summerall report soon took its place in a long and continuous line of similar intelligence reports and war plans emanating from the army's Hawaiian Department and high command in Washington, including reports from the Office of Naval Intelligence and the civilian Bureau of Investigation (forerunner of the FBI). The accumulated evidence revealed the process that resulted in martial law, demonstrated conclusively that plans were contrived specifically to contain the Japanese, and explained how martial law and the internment of community leaders fit into a comprehensive program designed to render innocuous the "Japanese menace." Most clearly, the evidence pointed to a belief shared by intelligence agencies that the war represented a struggle for dominance in Hawaii and in the Pacific between white America and people of color, led by Imperial Japan. Economic, political, and cultural control (or hegemony), were at stake. The first significant threat to the continued dominance of Hawaii's planters and territorial government were the fires lit by workers in the cane fields of Oahu—the 1909 and 1920 strikes—class struggles in the agricultural arena framed as a race war. Those cane fires threatened to consume not only the owners' private property and the territory's economy but also the heart of white supremacy, as the workers tried to dismantle planter plutocracy and make real the promise of American democracy.

Having established the anti-Japanese character of Hawaii's wartime "experiment in democracy," I sought an understanding of the historical precedents leading to Pearl Harbor to see if a demonstrable anti-Japanese movement might have been the context for the subjugation of the Japanese during World War II. The lesson learned from West Coast historiography prompted that search for continuities. In the words of the historian Roger Daniels, describing the West Coast experience: "The evacuation of 1942 did not occur in a vacuum, but was based on almost a century of anti-Oriental fear, prejudice, and misunderstanding."[5] Departing from the mainland literature, I attempted to order the many facets of anti-Asianism around the relations of production—sugarcane culture—and the race and class alignments created and influenced by one's position either as producer or as expropriator of surplus product.[6]

In my framework, Hawaii's anti-Japanese movement began with America's manifestly destined thrust into the Pacific and Asia, seeking markets for U.S. goods and Pacific and Asian commodities and resources for trade. Christian missionaries followed, accompanied, and paved the way for commerce, carrying the doctrine of capitalism and supplying ideological justifications for conquest and incorporation, themselves participating as major figures in expropriating Hawaiian land, installing the sugar plantation system, and exploiting workers. After depleting the domestic labor supply, the planters instituted a modified system of migrant labor that brought to Hawaii's shores some Europeans but many more Asians—Chinese, Japanese, Filipinos, Koreans. The system of migrant labor was essentially anti-Asian, anti-Japanese, because it was designed to control and exploit the productive labor of Asians and then to expel them when their utility had ended. The period of migrant labor, from 1865 to 1909, constituted the first phase of Hawaii's anti-Japanese movement.

Workers, however, were not simple instruments of the planters but resisted their repression and exploitation by reducing their productivity, depriving owners of their labor by running away, forming permanent communities of settlers, and striking for better conditions and higher wages. In those ways, workers altered the prevailing social relations and compelled new strategies for continued planter dominance. The tremors caused by the sugar plantation strikes of 1909 and 1920 were of such magnitude that they required more sophisticated structures for the maintenance of the status quo. Planter paternalism, racism and racialist meanings given to patriotism, class struggles, ethnic identity, and Americanization were prominent features of the transformed anti-Japanese movement that advanced from a migrant labor system to dependency. Economic, political, and cultural dependency was not instituted to uplift the subordinate group but to produce profits for Hawaii's planters, muzzle dissent, and hinder the development of children of migrant workers. This period of dependency, 1910–1940, was the second phase of Hawaii's anti-Japanese movement.

Those historical precedents served as the staging ground for martial law and the suppression of the Japanese during World War II, the third phase of Hawaii's anti-Japanese movement. As others have shown, the army's defensive posture at Pearl Harbor revealed an expectation of internal subversion rather than invasion.[7] I later discovered that at least as early as World War I, military intelligence saw local Japanese as an implanted "Fifth Column"—a sinister alien presence within the republic's gates—awaiting Japan's command to spring into action. In view of the territory's strategic location in the Pacific, the demographic prevalence of the Japanese in 1940, and the key role of Japanese labor in the territorial economy—in fact, considering the relative threat posed by the Japanese to the internal security of Hawaii compared with the West Coast—the claim of "military necessity" was much more believable in the islands, where one would thus expect a prearranged, thoroughgoing effort to repel the apparent danger.

The historical evidence, I argue, supports that presumption and shows that the military's plans and its implementation of those plans paralleled the planters' strategies to control and exploit Japanese workers. In fact, the "Japanese problem" forged an identity of interest among the planters, the territorial government, and the military. Hawaii's anti-Japanese movement thus spans the entirety of the Japanese experience in the islands, from 1865 when they were first recruited as laborers, to World War II when this narrative ends.

In framing this interpretive history, I owe an intellectual debt to revisionist historians and social scientists of southern Africa for their inquiries into mode of production and social formation, to historians of resistance in Africa and the United States, and to social scientists and historians who have advanced the ideas of migrant labor and international division of labor, dependency and world system, internal colonialism and hegemony.[8]

My reliance on theory and my propensity to generalize individual expressions and behavior, seeking broad, social meanings, might be viewed as unmindful of the unique characteristics of individual events or as an attempt to simplify and decontextualize complex and subtle factors. For example, I contend that Japanese persistence in Hawaii, inasmuch as permanent settlement subverted the system of migrant labor, could be interpreted as resistance to an oppressive form of labor, when, in actuality, a person's decision to remain in Hawaii could have been reached through any number of individual circumstances, such as having no money to return to Japan. I recognize that historical actors, whether planters or workers, individuals or groups, are multidimensional and heterogeneous, and they are often moved by mixed and hidden motives. Accordingly, to speak of "the planters" or "the Japanese" or "the *nisei*" and to see Takie Okumura or the wartime Emergency Service Committee as only serving the purposes of Hawaii's rulers are forms of reductivism. To be sure, the planters were composed of diverse individuals, and Okumura and members of the Service Committee were moved by complex motives, including the desire to fight against racism and injustice.

What I am attempting in this work, nonetheless, is a conceptualization of a social phenomenon, the anti-Japanese movement. I am primarily interested in how individual and group behaviors relate to that movement, rather than personal or particular meanings. Thus, a picture bride might have left Japan for Hawaii because she was bored with school and sought adventure, but she was also a member of a group of women who migrated after the Gentlemen's Agreement of 1908 and who instigated major social changes within the Japanese community and in Japanese relations with Hawaii's white rulers.

I have sought to reproduce faithfully the historical record, with all its complexities and individual variations. At the same time, I have sought out the wider context that I believe adds both perspective and substance to apparently isolated incidents and experiences. Regardless of the motives for loafing or breaking tools, by doing so workers deprived owners of labor and property, and those acts cumulatively were of sufficient gravity as to require rules to punish offenders, thereby preserving the established social order of masters and servants. I am, accordingly, less attentive to individual meanings, divergences, and diffusion than to social meanings, convergences, and overall direction in this historical interpretation of Hawaii's anti-Japanese movement. My aim is to order and explain the nature of social relations in Hawaii, and, in a reflexive way, the Japanese experience in America.

Cane Fires suggests that Hawaii's race relations are connected to those of the U.S. mainland. Asians in Hawaii, like those in California, generally arrived sequentially and after the previous group had been excluded (Chinese, Japanese and Korean, Filipino and Asian Indian); among the migrants, one gender (men) predominated, and these men labored primarily in agriculture. That pattern alone argues for the appropriateness of the migrant labor theory in framing the movement of Asians to Hawaii and California. Once they had settled and had produced a second generation in possession of citizenship, Asians were confronted with economic, political, and cultural dependency. Asians in Hawaii and California struggled for decent wages and better working conditions, sought to secure their civil rights, and created cultural communities that preserved their ethnic identity. But within this wide framework, Asian American history is also diverse and complex because of the regional differences between Hawaii and California (including land, labor, and demography), the evolving needs of capitalism and changing social relations, the international relations between the United States and Asian countries, and the dynamics of American race and class relations.

Cane Fires also suggests a kinship with the history of other minority groups in America. Hawaiians, like American Indians, were dispossessed of their land by white expansion. Asian migrant labor followed and in some instances replaced African bonded labor, and Mexican migrant laborers succeeded Asians in the fields of California. Economic, political, and cultural dependency faced all minorities. In their efforts to liberate themselves, both Japanese and African Americans were subjected to government surveillance and strategies to repress their movements. Their persistent resistance to hegemony was not a matter of mere survival but a struggle that resulted in a more democratic America.

In this work I merely suggest those comparisons, pointing the way to the full inclusion of Hawaii in Asian American and U.S. history. Such a history will go a long way toward demystifying the exoticism of Hawaii's race relations and the Asian American experience, and it will help reshape our thinking about the nature of American society.

A Note on Terminology

A brief word must be included on the terminology employed in this book. I use *Japanese* as inclusive of both *issei* and *nisei*, alien and citizen, of that ethnic group in Hawaii and on the mainland. Where greater precision is required, I specify the generation that is being referred to. Similarly, *military* is used to denote both the army and the navy, as opposed to military parlance that equates "military" with the army. By *planters*, I refer to those who control the means of production; and by *territorial government*, I mean those who hold political power. Generally, the planters and the territorial government acted as a single entity, but they were also sometimes at odds. I use *oligarchy* to denote the unitary rule of the planters and the territorial government, indicative of the concentration of capital and power in the hands of a few. *White supremacy* is the ideology and practice of white dominance over people of color and as such is a form of racial oppression that cuts across class divisions. The way in which the "planters," mainly whites, came to wield economic and political power and the extent of that power, however, deserve fuller explication, which I provide in Chapter 1.

Acknowledgments

This sojourn was not a solitary endeavor. The constant encouragement and support of our nuclear family—Libby, Sean, and Colin—over the course of six years have been immeasurable. My mother and late father provided insights into the *nisei* experience and helped translate documents; my sister, Faith Lebb, searched archives for additional clues; and my late maternal grandparents, who reared me, reminisced about life as *issei* and *uchinanchu* (Okinawans) among *naichi* (Japanese). My family, in truth, exemplifies much of the Japanese experience described in these pages. My grandfather, Kashin Kakazu, worked on Ewa and Waipahu plantations; my grandmother, Kame Chinen, was a picture bride and plantation worker; together they tried pig and pineapple farming in Kipapa Gulch. My mother attended plantation grade school, but had to quit to work and support her younger brothers and sisters as a barber, maid, and worker at the navy's laundry in Aiea; my father was a *kibei* and Aiea plantation worker, member of the 100th Battalion, city and county garbage collector, and "yard boy" and janitor. I am, just as surely as my intellectual descent, a product of that ancestry.

The following librarians and archivists were especially helpful: Timothy K. Nenninger of the Navy and Old Army Branch, and Frederick W. Pernell of the Military Field Branch, National Archives; Terrence J. Gough of the Army's Center of Military History; David Kittelson of the Hawaii War Records Depository, and Michaelyn P. Chou of Special Collections, University of Hawaii at Manoa; and Michael Slackman of the USS *Arizona* Memorial, Pearl Harbor. Dennis M. Ogawa and Edward D. Beechert of the University of Hawaii at Manoa generously shared the fruits of their labor, Ogawa from his research project, "Japanese Internment and Relocation: The Hawaii Experience," and Beechert, plantation records and Bureau of Investigation microfilms. Beechert also commented on portions of the manuscript, Sucheng Chan sharpened my writing and thinking, John M. Liu and Michael Omi added precision to my theoretical frame, Roger Daniels offered sound advice, Chalsa Loo encouraged my progress, and Franklin Odo and Ronald Takaki reminded me that history should also be viewed from the bottom up. Their collegial advice was warming, helped correct my errors and clarify my vision, and stirred me to emulate the high scholarly standards they embody and put forth. I stand in their debt. My students Kelly Blunden, David Drummond, Romelle Mross, and Cindie Nakashima gave valuable research assistance, and a Thomas Terry Grant from Santa Clara University funded most of the research portion of my work for this book, for which I am grateful. Finally, Sucheng Chan, as general editor of the series in which this book appears, was tireless in her effort to improve the manuscript, offering cogent criticism of both the theories that inform my writing and the organization of the text. I am most grateful to her for her meticulous readings and insistence on clarity of thought and expression.

In the end, however, errors of historical interpretation and fact are mine alone, much to my regret.

Part I

Years of Migrant

Labor, 1865–1909

Chapter 1

So Much Charity,
So Little Democracy

*I do not think there is any contest as to who shall
dominate; the white race, the white people, the
Americans in Hawaii are going to dominate.*
                              —Royal D. Mead

*I can see little difference between the importation
of foreign laborers and the importation of jute
bags from India.*
                              —Richard A. Cooke

Precapitalist Social Relations

Sugarcane was introduced to Hawaii by the original caretakers of the land and, like taro and sweet potatoes, was
cultivated in family gardens primarily for the benefit of the
producers. The family or kin group (*'ohana*) was physically
and psychically identified with the land (*'aina*), as shown in
the etymologies of both words. *'Ohana*, derived from *'oha*,
the bud or sprout of the taro plant whose roots provided
poi, the staple food, connotes an agricultural people. *'Aina*
comes from *'ai*, "to feed," and indicates that the homeland
sustained not only the group's bodily needs but its psychic
needs as well, because ancestors (*'aumakua*), with whom
the living identified and to whom they prayed for guidance
and protection, resided on the land.[1] Hawaiian horticulture
was complex, involving plant and soil selection, irrigation,
terracing, wet and dry farming, and fertilizing and mulch-
ing. It was a preeminent occupation for men; boys were
dedicated to Lono, the god of rain and agriculture, during
their initiation into manhood.[2]

Hawaiian society, established about the second century
C.E., became increasingly stratified. The *ali'i* ("chiefs") dis-

tributed land, levied taxes on labor and goods, and settled disputes. They ruled over the *maka'ainana* ("workers"), who produced surpluses sufficient to support the chiefs and to trade. Chiefs neither accumulated wealth nor were they completely autocratic; instead, they were trustees, not owners, of the land and ruled by consent of the people, who commonly removed oppressive chiefs and transferred their allegiance to rulers who promoted the welfare of the *maka'ainana*. During the eighteenth century, warfare dissolved and consolidated many chiefdoms, leading to greater political concentrations and to dramatic changes in land-tenure patterns and labor practices.[3] Kamehameha I, the most successful practitioner of the arts of Ku, the god of war, completed the conquest of all the islands before his death in 1819.

The European and American traders who followed Captain James Cook's 1778 "discovery" of the islands introduced Hawaiians to a market economy and hastened the demise of kin-based production and the rise of a peasantry and a class of wage laborers. The traders introduced manufactured goods in exchange for natural resources such as sandalwood, supplied arms for warfare, and stimulated the chiefs' accumulation of wealth through additional taxes on *maka'ainana* labor and income and a monopoly over the provisions and sandalwood trade. The chiefs demanded a percentage of all market transactions and diverted labor away from subsistence agriculture to producing for a world market that determined the terms of trade. As a result, by 1841, commoners received an estimated one-third of the fruits of their labor, providing little incentive for independent farming under the chiefs. Commoners entered the service of wealthy whites. Isaac Davis, an Englishman and a long-time Kamehameha I adviser, had 400 to 500 commoners working his Oahu lands on a rental basis; Oliver Holmes, an American and the king's governor of Oahu, employed 180 retainers in Honolulu to serve him and his guests.[4]

Missionaries, sent by the American Board of Commissioners for Foreign Missions in 1819, shared with the Yankee traders values rooted in mercantile capitalism and the Protestant work ethic. They equated leisure with vice and subsistence with improvidence. As one missionary, Samuel N. Castle, co-founder of the firm of Castle and Cooke, declared, "As it is true that indolence begets vice, so it is true that industry promotes virtue. All successful efforts taken to produce industry by proper means tend to promote virtue and must be beneficial to that people on whom they are bestowed."[5] That economic creed, presented to Hawaiians from the pulpit and in the classroom, supplied the justification for the capitalist transformation of Hawaiian precapitalist social relations.

Large and Unfamiliar Fishes

Despite their diverse national origins and personal agendas, Hawaii's whites shared European and American ideas of politics and economy. The newcomers imposed these notions on a population decimated by introduced diseases and a government weakened by an unfavorable trade relationship and foreign ideologies. Missionaries such as William Richards and Gerrit P. Judd became advisers to Hawaiian kings; other whites (*haoles*, "foreigners") served the Hawaiian monarchy and chiefs in various capacities. With Richards as his "chaplain, teacher, and translator," King Kauikeaouli (Kamehameha III) announced religious freedom and a declaration of rights in 1839. The following year, Hawaiians, educated for the most part by missionaries, drew up a constitution that limited the arbitrary power of the king by establishing a constitutional monarchy with a hereditary House of Nobles and an elective House of Representatives. Both the 1839 declaration and the 1840 constitution recognized capitalist property rights (in opposition to Hawaiian use rights), which clearly benefited the owners of capital. "Protection is hereby secured to the persons of all people," stated the 1839 declaration, "together with their lands, their building lots and all their property, and nothing whatsoever shall be taken from any individual, except by express provision of the law."[6] These revolutionary changes, together with laws passed during the 1840s that established a cabinet dominated by whites, a civil service, and an independent judiciary, curtailed the power of the king and chiefs and enhanced the position of foreigners—the dominant holders of capital—in the kingdom.

Missionaries considered the destruction of the Hawaiian system of land tenure and kin-based production to be crucial to the advancement of industry and virtue. The yeoman farmer or wage laborer in a company organized on "Christian and benevolent principles" would "uplift the Hawaiian," teach useful skills, and reduce indolence and poverty.[7] In 1841, the Hawaiian legislature gave to the governors of the various islands the authority to lease lands to whites for as long as fifty years. In 1846, the government formed a commission to determine the validity of all titles to land and to issue new titles for claims found to be valid. That act reaffirmed the concept of land as property; as such, it logically followed that land could be transferred to others.

The chiefs at first opposed changing the landholding system and its distribution because they realized that land was a source of their power and wealth. Nevertheless, pushed by Gerrit Judd and other advisers, the chiefs yielded to the demand for private property. The powers of the chiefs had been reduced, but their appetite for European luxury goods remained unsated, *haole* influence in the government and economy was too pervasive, and too many steps had already been taken in the direction of capitalist social relations. In the final division of land in 1848, called the Great Mahele, the chiefs argued only for a greater share of the land, instead of trying to prevent its apportionment among the king, the government, and the chiefs.

In 1850, the legislature made land available to commoners and foreigners on a fee-simple basis, ostensibly freeing Hawaii's masses from serfdom but actually undermining the fundamental basis of Hawaiian society—the relationship between *'ohana* and *'aina*—and made possible the loss of land to those who possessed the capital to purchase and hold title to it. The net result of the land division was 9,337 parcels (about 30,000 acres) awarded to commoners, 1.5 million acres each to chiefs and the government, and nearly 1 million acres to the king.[8]

Earlier, in 1835 on Kauai, Ladd & Company, an American firm in Honolulu, had obtained a lease for 980 acres of land, water rights, and permission to hire Hawaiian labor. William Hooper, a partner in the venture, set out with a keen sense of mission to establish the first sugar plantation in the islands. Hawaiian methods of production, he wrote in his diary, retarded the progress of "civilization, industry and national prosperity"; Koloa plantation would "serve as an entering wedge . . . [to] upset the whole system."[9] Hooper's boast, although feeble judged by the first few years of failure at Koloa, would eventually prove prophetic.

By the mid nineteenth century, all the essential elements for *haole* domination of Hawaii were in place. The Hawaiian scholar David Malo predicted in 1837: "If a big wave comes in, large and unfamiliar fishes will come from the dark ocean, and when they see the small fishes of the shallows they will eat them up."[10] After the Great Mahele and the 1850 land act, foreigners eagerly bought and cheated their way into ownership of large estates; by 1886, two-thirds of government land and much of the land of chiefs and commoners had passed into *haole* hands. Missionaries and their families participated in the land speculation, one buying and selling forty-seven parcels in his lifetime. As early as 1852, sixteen Congregationalist missionaries held land titles that averaged 493 acres per man.[11] Eventually, missionaries such as the Rices and Wilcoxes of Kauai and the Baldwins of Maui would dominate entire islands. Together with businessmen and government officials, they formed a *haole* elite that advised and then directed the Hawaiian monarchy.

In a kingdom where the government, laws and the legal system, economic principles, education, language, religion, and culture and social graces were modeled on European and American forms, Hawaiians had to depend on whites, however marginally qualified, to interpret and implement the new social order. In 1844, less than two weeks after his arrival, John Ricord, a New York attorney, was appointed the kingdom's attorney general. Robert Crichton Wyllie, after a brief stay in Honolulu, became the kingdom's foreign minister in 1845. William Little Lee, en route from New York to Oregon in 1846, was named chief justice of the Hawaiian Supreme Court while still in his twenties.[12] A Welshman, Theophilus Harris Davies, was sent to Honolulu by the creditors of a bankrupt merchandising house in 1867, in time for the sugar boom of the 1870s and 1880s that made Theo. H. Davies & Company a major financier of sugar plantations and the Honolulu Iron Works, which manufactured plantation machinery. Others, like Charles Reed Bishop, married into Hawaiian royalty. (Bishop married a princess, Bernice Pauahi Paki, descendant of Kamehameha I and the largest landholder in the islands, and opened Hawaii's first bank in 1848.) Benjamin Dillingham and Joseph Ballard Atherton married daughters of the *haole* elite and through those unions solidified their position within an emerging *haole*–Hawaiian oligarchy.[13]

The Oligarchy

The power of Hawaii's elite from the mid nineteenth century to World War II derived from its control of land, capital, and the government. Declines in the sandalwood trade during the 1820s and whaling in the 1850s, together with America's westward expansion and the California gold rush, brought importance to agriculture, both in staples and in such crops as sugar, coffee, silk, and cotton, which were suitable for export to the burgeoning American communities in Oregon and California. By the 1850s, island planters and investors looked on coffee and especially sugar as promising cash crops, although cultivation was minor and both were subject to cycles of boom and bust. After reaching a low point in 1855, sugar exports climbed in 1857; the price of sugar remained high, and investments in plantations grew. A Honolulu correspondent for the *San Francisco Bulletin* reported in 1860: "All but one of the present plantations are making large profits. Those now in operation, or in process of establishment, are 12 in number—3 on Kauai, 4 on Maui, and 5 on Hawaii." [14] America's Civil War (1861–1865) disrupted the flow of southern sugar to the northern states, opening new markets for Hawaii's sugar and raising prices even higher. On June 17, 1865, the editor of the *Hawaiian Gazette* proclaimed: "But a new era has dawned upon the Islands—the era of sugar—and the cultivation of cane overshadows by far all other agricultural enterprises. A large proportion of the floating capital in the community has been absorbed in new plantation enterprises, and it is considered beyond a doubt that sugar is to be, in the future, as it already is at present, the staple product of our Islands."

Hawaii's sugar industry was built on a land-tenure pattern of large land-holdings, cheap labor, a plantation system that incorporated both field and mill production under one operation, and an agency system by which factors in Honolulu financed and supplied the plantations. Mercantile firms such as Ladd & Company, which established Koloa plantation, and Castle and Cooke provided merchandise and credit to plantations. Eventually they came to manage and serve as factors or trustees for the plantations. C. Brewer and Company held the agency of four plantations in 1866; Castle and Cooke managed four by 1870; and the largest firm, Walker, Allen and Company, served as agent for twelve plantations and mills.[15] Sugar factors reduced the interplantation competition that had existed under the independent planters, systematized financial and marketing arrangements, and brought plantations under the eventual management of five mercantile houses that came to be known as the Big Five: Alexander & Baldwin, American Factors, C. Brewer and Company, Castle and Cooke, and Theo. H. Davies & Company.

This concentration of economic power found similar expression in the political arena during the nineteenth century. The constitution of 1864 provided the legal foundations for centralization in government throughout much of the second half of the century. King Kamehameha V set the stage by dissolving the 1864 constitutional convention, which was dead-locked on the question of the franchise, with these words: "I have told you, and my Ministers also have told you, that in all other monarchi-cal countries suffrage is limited, and it is thought that the possession of property is proof of industry and thrift, therefore in those enlightened countries it is said that the class who possess property are the proper persons to advise their Representatives in regard to the necessities of Government, and the poor, lazy, and ignorant are debarred from this privilege." On August 20, 1864, the king signed a constitution he and his cabinet members had drawn up, which strengthened the powers of the king and cabinet, merged the House of Nobles with the House of Representatives, and imposed property and educational qualifications on elected representatives and voters.[16] Earlier that year, on April 23, 1864, the *Pacific Commercial Advertiser* had argued for elitism in government: "Every reasonable man must be convinced that a *property qualification* of some kind, applicable to representative candidates as well as to voters, has become a necessity and is the only guard that can be established to prevent our Legislature from being filled with men totally unfit to repre-sent at least the foreign population and its capital, or to enact laws for the Kingdom."

The *haole* elite was able to influence the Hawaiian monarchy to make changes that increasingly served the propertied class because the rulers believed that economic stability and growth protected the kingdom's political independence. The question of a reciprocity treaty with the United States tested that belief and highlighted the kingdom's dilemma. Planters and Honolulu businessmen argued that reciprocity was critical for economic prosperity; many in government favored reciprocity, but saw it as a step toward American annexation. Indeed, President Andrew Johnson's annual message to Congress on December 9, 1868, urging ap-proval of the reciprocity treaty, did little to reduce that fear. "It is known and felt by the Hawaiian Government and people," stated the U.S. presi-dent, "that their Government and institutions are feeble and precarious; that the United States, being so near a neighbor, would be unwilling to see the islands pass under foreign control. . . . A reciprocity treaty, while it would not materially diminish the revenues of the United States, would be a guaranty of the good will and forbearance of all nations until the people of the islands shall of themselves, at no distant day, voluntarily apply for admission into the Union."[17] Although Congress failed to approve the treaty, talk of reciprocity and annexation continued undiminished in Hawaii and in Washington, D.C.

American interest in Hawaii arose from its commercial and its military value. Ostensibly on vacation in the islands, Major General John M. Schofield, commander of the U.S. Army's Military Division of the Pacific, and Brigadier General B. S. Alexander of the Corps of Engineers arrived in 1873 under confidential orders from Secretary of War W. W. Belknap "for the purpose of ascertaining the defensive capabilities of the different ports and their commercial facilities, and to examine into any other subjects that may occur to you as desirable, in order to collect all information that would be of service to the country in the event of war with a powerful maritime nation." Schofield and Alexander stayed in Hawaii for two months, gathering the desired information; later, they submitted a report that stressed the value of Pearl Harbor as a potentially excellent port for military and commercial purposes.[18] The view of Hawaii's worth to America as a commercial and military outpost would influence the outcome of deliberations in Congress over reciprocity and annexation and would supply the rationale for the navy's presence at Pearl Harbor and the army's role in defending Oahu.

While the United States secretly surveyed Pearl Harbor's potential, members of the Hawaiian government, the Honolulu Chamber of Commerce, and the English-language newspapers publicly debated the lease or cession of Pearl Harbor as an inducement for a reciprocity treaty with the United States. The Chamber of Commerce, representing sugar and business interests, argued for reciprocity; dissenting voices, such as those of pro-British Theophilus Davies and the Hawaiians, objected to reciprocity if it meant compromising Hawaiian soil. (From the time of Captain Cook and Kamehameha's "cession" of Hawaii to Britain in 1794 to the American annexation of Hawaii, Britain and British subjects were a significant force in the islands and sought to moderate U.S. influence in the kingdom.) Mass sentiment prevailed. Hawaii's reciprocity proposal to Washington in 1873 did not contain any mention of Pearl Harbor.

The public debate solidified antiforeign, anti-American sentiment among Hawaiians, but failed to stop the movement for reciprocity. The treaty terms considered and passed in the U.S. Congress in 1876 included permission to use Pearl Harbor as a military base and, in partial compensation for the kingdom's earlier refusal to cede Pearl Harbor, language that prohibited the Hawaiian government from alienating any territory to a foreign power or granting reciprocity privileges to countries other than the United States for the treaty's duration. The signed agreement boosted Hawaii's slumping sugar industry, strengthened the economic and political power of the *haole* elite, and linked the kingdom more closely to the United States. In 1875 there were twenty plantations; five years later, there were sixty-three. Over the twenty-two years of the treaty, the sugar industry grew about 2,000 percent.[19]

Having witnessed the resurgence of Hawaiian nationalism during the campaign for reciprocity, members of the *haole* elite, including missionary descendants Lorrin A. Thurston and Sanford Dole, entered politics as antigovernment independents. In 1887, they formed the secret Hawaiian League, placed the all-white Honolulu Rifles at the League's service, and discussed armed insurrection and the removal of King Kalakaua. Confronted by the League, its executive Committee of Thirteen, and the Rifles, Kalakaua agreed to all their demands (including a promise to reign, not rule) and signed a constitution drawn up by Thurston and the League. The 1887 constitution made both Houses of the legislature elective, restored the property qualifications for voting abolished by the 1874 constitution (to qualify, voters now had to show an annual income of $600 or taxable property worth $3,000), and enshrined racism by enfranchising residents (not citizens) of American or European ancestry while denying the vote to Asian residents. These voting restrictions disenfranchised two-thirds of Hawaii's potential electorate and nearly all Hawaii's Asians, and gave the Reform party of whites control of the legislature in the special election of 1887.[20]

In November 1887, faced with a Reform cabinet and legislature, Kalakaua signed the "supplementary convention" that gave the United States exclusive use of Pearl Harbor as a naval station. Although the putative 1889 anti-Reform rebellion, led by part-Hawaiian Robert W. Wilcox, was easily squelched, anti-*haole* sentiment continued to grow after Kalakaua's death and Queen Liliuokalani's accession in 1891. Liliuokalani, who promised a new constitution and a restoration of the powers of the monarchy, threatened the white elite's revolution of 1887. Reform partisans formed the Committee of Safety, representing the "intelligent part of the community" and the "public safety," and on January 16, 1893, appealed to U.S. Minister John L. Stevens for protection. With Stevens's support, the guns of the USS *Boston* and its landed troops, and former members of the disbanded Honolulu Rifles, the provisional government, led by Sanford Dole, accepted the surrender of Liliuokalani, the last Hawaiian monarch. Having failed to secure U.S. annexation, the provisional government proclaimed the Hawaiian Republic on July 4, 1894.

Hawaii's annexation was nonetheless simply a matter of time—and the outcome of a debate in Washington that featured the strategic interests of the United States against the liability of an American territory peopled overwhelmingly with Pacific Islanders and Asians.[21] In Hawaii, the planters' fears that U.S. annexation would end the importation of cheap Asian labor—America had passed a Chinese exclusion law in 1882—was ameliorated by the market advantages of annexation. There was also the belief, held by annexationists such as navy undersecretary Theodore Roosevelt, that annexation would repulse the perceived threat of Asian dominance in Hawaii and Japan's imperialist designs on the islands.[22] The U.S. House Committee on Foreign Affairs, in its report on Hawaii's annexation, stated: "The issue in Hawaii is not between monarchy and the Republic. That issue has been settled. . . . The issue is whether, in that inevitable struggle [between East and West], Asia or America shall have the vantage ground of the control of the naval 'Key of the Pacific,' the commercial 'Cross-roads of the Pacific.' "[23] America's manifest destiny in Hawaii was accomplished not by treaty, because annexation lacked the required two-thirds majority, but by a joint resolution of Congress, which required a simple majority. The House passed the resolution on June 15, the Senate on July 6, and President William McKinley signed it on July 7, 1898.

The Territory

The same men who led the *haole* elite to political dominance under the kingdom and republic headed the new territorial government in Hawaii. Sanford Dole, former president of the republic and the territory's first governor, declared his opposition to "irresponsible people" (those not of the propertied class) and Hawaiians voting or holding office under the new government.[24] The Reverend Sereno E. Bishop echoed Dole's opinion of Hawaiians when he wrote: "The common people were not intrusted with rule, because in their childishness and general incapacity, they were totally unfit for such rule." Hawaii's government, Bishop believed, should be in the hands of the few for the benefit of the masses, who were "babes in character and intellect."[25] Nevertheless, Congress held that the political institutions of any new U.S. territory should be based on the forms of American democracy, and Hawaii's Organic Act was passed in 1900 without property qualifications for either voting or holding office. Despite their declining numbers, Hawaiians maintained a majority at the polls until 1924, but they were able to sustain only a brief interlude of Hawaiian control of the territorial legislature through the Home Rule party, led by the resurgent Robert Wilcox. The Republicans, the party of the white elite, regained control in 1902 when their candidate, Prince Jonah Kuhio Kalanianaole, defeated Wilcox in the race for delegate to Congress and carried other Republican candidates into office with him. Between 1910 and 1940, Republicans controlled more than 80 percent of the seats in the territorial legislature, a dominance maintained until 1946 when the Democrats succeeded in electing half of the territorial House.[26]

Despite the democratic form of Hawaii's government, its substance followed in the tradition of preannexation concentrations of power.[27] "When the Organic Act was passed," observed a Department of the Interior official, "it was accepted without question that Hawaii was to be governed by a 'ruling class' of approximately 4,000 Americans and other Anglo-Saxon peoples who were to have dominion over the remaining 145,000 residents of the Islands. Particular provisions of the basic law were specifically described by Senator Platt, who favored those provisions, as aimed at maintenance of the 'governing class.' "[28] Also, although American traditions proclaimed a democratic form of government, American laws denied naturalization to Asian immigrants, thereby disenfranchising the first generation—nearly 60 percent of Hawaii's total population at the time of annexation. Laws also restricted the further immigration of Chinese, then Japanese, Koreans, and Filipinos, thus limiting their numbers in Hawaii and on the U.S. mainland.

Island politics revolved around three axes of power: the delegate to Congress, the governor, and the territorial legislature. Unlike states, territories are governed by Congress, have governors appointed by the president for four-year terms, and have no inherent powers.[29] To maintain political dominance, the *haole* elite thus had not only to control the territorial legislature but also to sway Congress and the president. As a result, besides arranging to elect their candidate as delegate to Congress, elements of Hawaii's "ruling class," such as the Hawaiian Sugar Planters' Association (HSPA), the Honolulu Chamber of Commerce, and magnate Walter F. Dillingham, established offices in Washington for their lobbyists, whose power frequently eclipsed that of the territory's delegate.[30] The elite's success with Congress and the president prompted a student of Hawaiian politics to write in 1935 that it was widely known that since annexation, governors, legislators, and government officials had been "to a large degree determined by and considerate of the sugar leaders."[31]

The concentration of political and economic power in the hands of a few, typical of Hawaii since the days of the kingdom, was a distinguishing feature of the territory. Robert Littler, a political scientist at the University of Hawaii, succinctly described the islands' social relations in 1929: "To think of Hawaii in an economic sense is to think of sugar. That industry is ruled by a financial oligarchy around which is built the business and social structure of the Islands. Hawaii is thus a territory with a very strong and powerful propertied class, and a very numerous and heterogeneous non-propertied class. There are very few middle class people in between."[32] Hawaii's "financial oligarchy," the Big Five, served as agents for thirty-six of the territory's thirty-eight sugar plantations during the 1930s. The group averaged $115 million per year in its production of sugar and pineapple, or about 90 percent of the total value of Hawaiian products, and realized earnings of over $200 million annually from commissions as steamship agents and middlemen for other businesses. The Big Five also controlled businesses associated with the sugar plantations, including banking, insurance, transportation, utilities, and wholesale and retail merchandising. Through interlocking directorates, intermarriages, and social associations, the *haole* elite managed to keep the wealth within a small circle of families. "In short," wrote a commentator on the eve of Japan's attack on Pearl Harbor, "the management and direction of Hawaii's economy is largely in the hands of a dozen or so men who either serve personally or delegate their business associates, frequently relatives, to serve for them."[33]

An exhaustive study of land and power in Hawaii by George Cooper and Gavan Daws, in examining the post–World War II Democratic party years, reviewed the decades of Republican party dominance from annexation to 1954 when the Democrats won control of both Houses of the territorial legislature. "Republican politics in Hawaii," the authors stated, "was little else but the politics of business, big business. In fact it was true enough to say that government in Hawaii in the Republican years functioned avowedly as an arm of local big business, more particularly as an arm of the so-called 'Big Five.' " During the Big Five era, almost half the total land area of Hawaii was owned by fewer than eighty individuals, and most of the rest was owned by the government. "This was an enormous concentration of wealth and power," concluded Cooper and Daws. "Measure for measure there was nothing like it anywhere else in the United States."[34]

Lawrence Fuchs, in his social history of Hawaii, summed up the *haole* elite's version of the white man's burden that guided actions and reached back to missionary origins. "The oligarchy had spun a web of control over every major aspect of Island life," explained Fuchs. "To dominate, in its view, was not a lustful, greedy ambition. The goal was not just power; nor was it wealth or prestige. It was achievement of a way of life in which the ruling haole elite, through its ingenuity, dedication, and charity, had made Hawaii a veritable paradise on earth."[35] To build that city upon the hill, however, the oligarchy required land, which it possessed in abundance, and laborers who were cheap but efficient and responsive to instruction.

Laborers for Hawaii's industrial agriculture were difficult to obtain, as William Hooper had discovered at Koloa plantation in 1835. Despite Hooper's offer of wages of 12½ cents a day for workers and fees of 25 cents per man, paid to the chiefs each month, Hawaiians preferred kin-based production. During the 1840s, the Hawaiian legislature passed laws against idleness and vagrancy that carried penalties of eviction from neglected farms, repossession of those lands, or punishment at hard labor. In outlawing "sluggardness," the government hastened the transition to wage labor. The new laws eroded the prerogative of the chiefs to tax labor by having offenders work for the nation, as specified by the 1846 statute, which declared that "indolence is a crime involving the best interests of the State."[36] Most influential of the labor laws was the Masters and Servants Act of 1850, which defined two kinds of servants, apprentices and wage laborers, and bound both masters (or employers) and servants to the terms of labor contracts for as long as five years. Although the act obliged the master to care for his servants and restrain his corrections, it provided for contract enforcement through imprisonment, fines, and extensions of the contract period. The severity of labor controls generally increased with successive revisions of the law as Hawaii's sugar planters imported greater numbers of foreign workers.[37]

Foreign labor, resisted at first by the Hawaiian monarchy, was indispensable to the planters, whose need for an adequate labor supply escalated even as the Hawaiian population declined precipitously, largely because of introduced diseases against which Hawaiians had no natural immunity. In 1836, the Hawaiian population had numbered 108,579, but it had dwindled to 69,800 by 1860. Meanwhile, sugar production in 1837 had totaled a mere 4,286 pounds, but it had swelled to 17,127,161 pounds by 1867.[38] In 1864, in response to the labor crisis and the monarchy's desire to repopulate the kingdom with a "cognate race," the legislature established a Bureau of Immigration and charged it with the task of finding workers for Hawaii's plantations. Robert Wyllie, foreign minister under Kamehameha IV and Kamehameha V, augmented bureau initiatives by actively promoting labor migration from Asia and the Pacific. The Planters' Labor and Supply Company, formed in 1882, and its successor, the HSPA, organized in 1895, also joined in the recruiting efforts.[39]

The Chinese were the first sizable group of foreign workers imported for Hawaii's plantations. The planters were well aware of Chinese skills in sugar production. According to a paper read before the Royal Hawaiian Agricultural Society in 1852, "the earliest sugar manufacture was in 1802, by a Chinaman, on the Island of Lanai, who came here in one of the vessels trading for sandalwood, bringing with him a stone mill and boilers."[40] Other Chinese migrants followed and produced modest amounts of sugar using wild cane. One such installation was the William French sugar works at Waimea, Kauai. Hooper visited the Waimea mill before building Koloa plantation and later employed Chinese workers who, he reported to Ladd & Company in 1838, would "put the plantation in order . . . sooner and with less trouble than any other class of husbandmen."[41] In 1852, the Agricultural Society succeeded in importing Chinese contract laborers, whereupon the society's president announced to the membership: "On the subject of labor, I am happy to say, there is less to fear than formerly. The enterprise set on foot by our Society for procuring laborers from China, has at last, met with success. . . . To all planters who can afford it, I would say, procure as many laborers as you can."[42] Despite initial optimism, the export market for Hawaii's sugar shrank during the mid 1850s, and no more Chinese were imported until the boom in sugar exports induced by the U.S. Civil War. In 1865, the Bureau of Immigration sent a commissioner to Hong Kong to recruit 521 contract laborers, including 95 women and 13 children.[43]

The year 1865 also marked Hawaiian Foreign Minister Wyllie's bid for Japanese laborers, who were imported like jute bags, in the words of the

HSPA president, Richard A. Cooke, to perform a specific task and serve the proprietor without want or effect. "Up to now," declared the HSPA secretary, Royal D. Mead, in 1910, "the Asiatic has had only an economic value in the social equation. So far as the institutions, laws, customs, and language of the permanent population go, his presence is no more felt than is that of the cattle on the ranges."[44]

Over the course of a hundred years, white traders, missionaries, and sugar planters had gained supremacy over *maka 'ainana* and *ali' i*, imposed their system of economy and government, and presented Hawaii to the United States as a commercial and military base for America's designs in the Pacific. They had installed the plantation system, centralized economic and political power, and built a society described by the journalist Ray Stannard Baker as "a place where there is so much charity and so little democracy."[45] But that dominance of "the white race, the white people, the Americans in Hawaii," so confidently proclaimed by Mead, would be challenged by Japanese workers in Hawaii's cane fields.

Cane Culture

In 1890, Alfred Thayer Mahan published *The Influence of Sea Power upon History*. A collection of lectures, the book argued that a strong navy and overseas colonies were essential to commerce and national greatness and that the annexation of Hawaii would serve to guard the western approaches to the Panama Canal and provide an outpost in the Pacific for the anticipated impending conflict between East and West. Other apologists for expansionism during the late nineteenth century justified U.S. imperialism as manifestly destined by divine sanction, geography, and racial superiority. The "Anglo-Saxon race," they declared, shouldered the white man's burden of civilization and Christianity and was foreordained to fill the earth and govern, beginning with the North American continent, moving down into Mexico and Central and South America, and extending its reach out to the islands of the sea. Josiah Strong, a clergyman and chief propagandist for imperialism, wrote in 1885 that the United States had become "an Asiatic power, close to the Yellow Sea" because of providential design and the requirements of trade.[46]

Hawaii sat at the confluence of those rivers of Christianity and commerce, flowing from industrial New England to the Pacific Northwest to China and other parts of Asia. Yankee clippers bore manufactures, furs, sandalwood, tea, silk, spices, porcelain, and missionaries, who rode the waves spreading the good news of salvation and capitalism, drawing Hawaii into the world economy. White settlers instigated a profound re-ordering of social relations by separating Hawaiian producers from the land—their means of livelihood—thereby requiring them to subsist by selling their labor for wages. In possession of the material means and the ideology for expropriation, the planters drove home the entering wedge—Koloa plantation—in 1835, to "upset the whole system." The require-ments of cane culture thereafter constituted, to a large extent, the material basis of Hawaiian society and determined the social ordering of groups from the mid nineteenth century through World War II. The exploita-tion of Hawaii's natural resources of sandalwood and whales during the first half of the nineteenth century was succeeded by the exploitation of laborers—Hawaiians, Chinese, Japanese, Filipinos, and smaller numbers of Portuguese, Spaniards, Russians, and Norwegians—within a planta-tion system that voraciously consumed workers like crushed cane.[47] The crushing of Japanese migrants, herein presented as Hawaii's anti-Japanese movement, was systematic and endemic to capitalism in Hawaii.

Chapter 2

Hole Hole Bushi

My husband cuts the cane,
I do the hole hole.
By sweat and tears
We get by.

In Much Need of Them

West to Japan they went, these merchants of labor, seeking the strong and supple for Hawaii's sugar plantations. "We are in much need of them," implored Robert Crichton Wyllie, Hawaiian foreign minister and master of Princeville plantation on the island of Kauai. "I myself could take 500 for my own estates." Wyllie's letter, dated March 10, 1865, began the process that brought the Japanese to Hawaii. "Could any good agricultural laborers be obtained from Japan or its dependencies, to serve like the Chinese, under a contract for 6 or 8 years?" he asked Eugene M. Van Reed, an American businessman in Kanagawa. "If so, send me all the information you can and state at what cost per head they could be landed here; and if their wives and children could be induced to come with them. They would be treated well, enjoy all the rights of freemen, and in our fine [islands], under our beautiful and salubrious climate, they would be better off, as permanent settlers than in their own country."[1]

The following year, the Hawaiian government dispatched an envoy to Japan to negotiate a treaty that would place the kingdom's sugar on a par with imports from the United States and Britain.[2] These labor and market initiatives were taken in response to the boost given Hawaii's sugar industry by the expanding market in the American West and by the U.S. Civil War. Thus Wyllie's "we are in much need of them" contained more than a note of eagerness.

Van Reed agreed to procure Japanese laborers. He wrote to Charles de Varigny, Wyllie's successor: "No better class of people for Laborers could be found than the Japanese race, so accustomed to raising Sugar, Rice, and Cotton, nor one so easily governed, they being peaceable, quiet, and of a pleasant disposition."[3] At its March 1868 meeting, the Bureau of Immigration allocated $1,925 to Van Reed to recruit Japanese contract laborers. Bureau members had heard that the Japanese "resembled our native race very much" and that "there was not the slightest doubt that they would most readily amalgamate."[4] With his modest allocation, Van Reed attempted to navigate the tricky waters of Japanese politics during the last days of the Tokugawa Shogunate.

In a letter to de Varigny dated April 27, 1868, Van Reed informed the foreign minister that the Japanese government had granted him permission to send 350 to 400 workers to Hawaii, but with the key provision that the laborers would be returned, at the owners' expense, to Japan after the completion of their term of contract. Knowing that the return stipulation contradicted the Hawaiian government's plans for a permanent citizenry, Van Reed offered: "The clause compelling their return here, I hope to be able to have annulled within a year, thus allowing the people to become subjects of Hawaii if they so elect."[5] The terms of the final agreement specified a three-year contract, monthly wages of $4, and food, lodging, and passage paid for by the employers. On May 17, 1868, the *Scioto* sailed from Yokohama for Honolulu carrying 149 Japanese migrants—141 men, 6 women, and 2 children.[6]

Giving Satisfaction

Included among the *gannenmono,* or "first year people" (so termed because they migrated during the first year of Meiji rule) were Tomisaburo Makino, an armorer to samurai of the Sendai clan and group spokesman, a thirteen-year-old heavy drinker nicknamed "Ichi the Viper," a few samurai, a hairdresser, cooks, potters, printers, saké brewers, tailors, and woodworkers.[7] Described by Van Reed as "mere Laborers who had been picked out of the streets of Yokohama, sick, exhausted, and filthy, and without clothing to cover decency," the *gannenmono* apparently expected a quick crossing. Instead, the journey lasted thirty-three days. A few days out to sea, the ship encountered a storm, "which frightened the passengers so badly that most of them are said to have cut off their topknots and thrown them into the sea in thanks when it ended."[8]

A stowaway, Yonekichi Sakuma, kept a diary of the voyage, providing a glimpse of conditions on board. He counted 500 bags of unpolished rice, 20 bags of polished rice, and plenty of *shoyu*, *miso*, and firewood in the *Scioto*'s hold, but no fish or fowl. Many of the passengers, however, could not eat the first few days because of seasickness. Sakuma noted that the men spent their time in polishing rice and in horseplay, and he reported that those caught smoking were handcuffed for violating the ship's safety code. Twelve days before sighting land, Kodzu Wakichi died and was buried at sea.[9] Finally, on June 19, 1868, the *Scioto* cast anchor in Honolulu harbor.

On shore, a gift of salted fish from the Hawaiian king and clothes and hats greeted the *gannenmono*. The Bureau of Immigration, on advice of the ship's captain, granted the new arrivals a two-week period to recuperate from the long sea voyage. "They are very good natured and lusty looking set of fellows," reported the *Hawaiian Gazette* of June 24, 1868. "They are very polite withal, having picked up our salutation of 'aloha.' . . . They are favorably received by our population, both Hawaiian and foreign, and the impression is prevalent that they will make peaceable and efficient laborers, and give satisfaction." As the migrants were being feted, the Bureau of Immigration sold their contracts to various plantations at $70 per laborer: 71 workers went to Maui, 51 remained on Oahu, 22 went to Kauai, and 4 left for Lanai. Tomi Ozawa was nineteen years old and eight-months' pregnant when she and her husband, Kintaro, boarded the *Scioto*. She recalled that her greatest fear was the prospect of twelve-hour days in the cane fields with only a lunch break to feed her soon-to-be-born baby. Much to her relief, Ozawa and her husband were selected to work as domestic servants.[10]

Group spokesman Makino wrote to Van Reed a week after landing in Honolulu: "On the ship and upon arrival, we received exceptionally courteous treatment and we are overjoyed that this capital city is much better than we were told in Japan," he reported. "There is not a drunkard or . . . ruffian on the street during daytime or at night, and the people have a gentle disposition. So, we are very fortunate."[11] The shrill siren that roused workers must have wakened the *gannenmono* to the reality of plantation labor, and the soft hands of potters, cooks, and tailors hoed the red earth, stripped sharp-edged leaves, and grasped bundles of cane. Besides the physical rigors of laboring under the hot tropical sun, workers were ruled by the master-and-servant relationship and by strict plantation directives. The Nuuanu plantation, for example, exacted ten hours of daily work, with a 9:00 P.M. curfew when the lights were turned off; no visitors, smoking, or talking were allowed. A worker's pay was docked one-fourth of a day's wage for reporting to work ten to fifteen minutes late, and violations of the evening curfew incurred a fine of 25 cents per offense. Other penalties included two days of extra work for each day lost through unexcused absences or through sickness caused by the "laborer's own imprudence"; wage deductions for "carelessly broken, lost, or stolen tools"; and a fine of 25 cents for each stalk of cane taken.[12]

Before the end of the first month of work, both planters and laborers had lodged complaints with the Bureau of Immigration. M. McInerny petitioned for a refund and compensation for a household servant, Nakasuke, who did not work at all because of illness and who required hospitalization. Theophilus H. Davies, agent for Kaalaea plantation, asked for a full refund for a man who had to be aided by his comrades within the first few minutes of stepping into the field and who died shortly thereafter. Davies, in his request, called the bureau's attention to the nuisance created by that worker's collapse, which was "the occasion of much delay as he had to be tended by the men who were greatly needed at their own work." Workers protested the contract provision that enabled planters to withhold half their wages, disputed the transfer of contracts, and requested pay for days lost because of inclement weather and for holidays.[13]

The bureau ruled in favor of the Japanese on wage withholding, and recommended payment in full at the end of each month. Other issues raised by the workers were apparently left to individual plantations, which may account for contentment among some of the *gannenmono* and bitterness among others. Forty of the *gannenmono* returned to Japan before the completion of their contracts, in a settlement arranged between Japan and Hawaii. Thirty-nine of the returnees signed "The Complaint" published in the *Japan Herald* of April 15, 1870, charging planters with unfulfilled contracts and cruelty toward workers. Thirteen of the *gannenmono* completed their three-year contracts before returning to Japan, and the remainder applied to stay in Hawaii.[14]

A number of the men married Hawaiian women. Matsugoro Kuwada, a tailor on Maui, married Meleana Auwekoolani; Tokujiro Sato, of Pahoa on the island of Hawaii, married Kalala Kamekona; and Toyokichi Fuku- mura married Lukia Kaha of Molokai.[15] According to the *Pacific Commercial Advertiser* of July 11, 1868, one of the *gannenmono* committed suicide at Ulupalakua on the island of Maui. The last of the original group, Sentaro Ishii, died on September 18, 1936, at the age of one hundred two.[16]

With Loving Hand and Heart

Because of the failure of the *gannenmono* experiment, the governments of Japan and Hawaii agreed to let the issue of labor migration rest. During the 1870s, however, both governments launched several diplomatic initia- tives toward restoring amicable relations, culminating with the signing of the Convention of 1886, which opened a new era of Japanese labor migra- tion to Hawaii. Robert Walker Irwin, Hawaiian consul general and special agent for immigration in Japan from 1884 to 1894, played a key role in the negotiations; perhaps more than any other person, he was responsible for installing the system of Japanese labor migration to Hawaii. Irwin, like Van Reed, was a businessman in Japan, but, unlike his predecessor, he maintained close relations with high officials of Japan's government and heads of the new economic order, such as Kaoru Inouye, Japan's foreign minister, and Takashi Masuda, president of Mitsui Bussan Company, both of whom were influential in Irwin's success as a labor recruiter.

The Reciprocity Treaty of 1876 that granted Hawaii's sugar duty-free access to the tariff-protected U.S. market ignited wild speculation in cane culture and intensified the need for labor. Meanwhile, many Chinese plantation workers—the mainstay of the industry—refused to renew their contracts, preferring to move to Honolulu or to work in better-paying jobs. In 1882, of Hawaii's 13,500 Chinese, 5,037 worked on sugar plan- tations and constituted 49 percent of the industry's workforce. By 1890, that number had dwindled to 4,517, or 25 percent of the workforce; and by 1892, to 2,617, or 12 percent. In response to the loss of workers, the planters proposed to require unmarried Chinese men to return to China at the end of their contracts, removing the "danger" of Chinese "passing unchecked into our community," and to recruit laborers more inclined to plantation work to replace the Chinese.[17]

In the wake of a state visit to Japan by King Kalakaua in 1881 and two special-envoy missions (led by John M. Kapena in 1882 and Curtis P. Iaukea in 1884), the Hawaiian legislature allocated $50,000 for Japanese migration. Kapena had delivered the message to Emperor Meiji that "Hawaii holds out her loving hand and heart to Japan and desires that your people may come and cast in their lots with ours and repeople our Island home." Iaukea had offered free passage and guaranteed employment to Japanese migrants. Irwin received the legislative allocation to organize the shipment of laborers under terms agreed to by Iaukea and Inouye, which provided for a three-year contract, monthly wages of $9 for men and $6 for women, twenty-six workdays each month, and ten hours per day for field workers and twelve for mill workers.

Recruitment advertisements were distributed throughout Japan, but on the advice of his associates, Inouye and Masuda, Irwin concentrated his efforts on Yamaguchi and Hiroshima prefectures. Both natives of Yamaguchi, Inouye and Masuda selected that prefecture for labor recruitment perhaps because its people, as described by Masuda, were "not timid or afraid to go to far away places . . . even to foreign countries." They favored Hiroshima because its people were sensible and law-abiding, not radical or revolutionary.[18] Masuda not only provided Irwin with advice but also dispatched Mitsui Bussan employees to Yamaguchi, Hiroshima, Fukushima, and Kumamoto prefectures to recruit laborers. Mitsui also supplied foodstuffs and medicines for Japanese in Hawaii and handled the transfer of workers' remittances sent from Hawaii to savings accounts in Japan. Whereas, according to a company history, Mitsui's business in labor migration "could hardly be called profitable," Irwin apparently built a personal fortune from the trade.[19]

During his tenure as exclusive labor recruiter in Japan, Irwin delivered about 29,000 Japanese to Hawaii's plantations. For each adult male, Irwin received $5 (U.S. gold coin) in commission and, perhaps, a portion of the $15 "brokerage fee" to cover recruitment costs in Japan. Irwin apparently participated in other schemes to collect unauthorized fees from the migrants, such as charging women $40 for their transportation to Hawaii and exacting an extra $15 per man.[20] The bureau's special agent for immigration essentially dictated his own terms because of his close ties with influential Japanese leaders at a time when Hawaii needed a labor recruiter who could be trusted by Japan's government, and because of the persistent demand for labor in Hawaii. The Japanese apparently had an equally powerful desire to migrate to *Tenjiku,* or "faraway place," as can be seen by the more than 28,000 applications for the 943 slots for the first shipload of "government-contract migrants," called *kanyaku imin*.

Benevolent Manipulation

On Sunday, February 8, 1885, the *City of Tokyo* arrived in Honolulu with its cargo of 676 men, 159 women, and 108 children. The *Pacific Commercial Advertiser*, hailing the event as historic, comparable to the Reciprocity Treaty of 1876, predicted: "The arrival of the steamer from Japan with the first lot of immigrants will afford great satisfaction, and the arrangements now contemplated should lead to a large immigration in the next few months."[21] The king, seeing not only laborers but future subjects to offset the threat that the white elite posed to an independent monarchy, presented each migrant with a gift of one dollar and joined his guests in a day of music, saké, and a sumó tournament.[22] Irwin, who accompanied the first group on the *City of Tokyo*, issued a circular published by the Bureau of Immigration containing explicit instructions to the planters on the treatment of Japanese workers. Japanese were "not to be driven," he stressed, but to "be led by a silken thread of kindness"; they must not be whipped, and he urged their promotion to *lunas*, or overseers. His counsel failed to impress those planters who believed that workers had to be broken in. On Maui's Paia plantation, for example, five men died from sickness and very likely from cruel treatment before the end of the year.[23]

Joji Nakayama was brought in by Irwin on the first shipload as "inspector" of Japanese migrants. Nakayama and his staff of seven physicians and ten interpreters were hired to alleviate two of the problems that had plagued the *gannenmono*—poor health and an inability to communicate. As head of the Bureau of Immigration's Japanese section from 1885 to 1895, Nakayama received an initial salary of $100 per month, later increased to $250, and finally to $6,000 per year. His staff toured the plantations, resolving conflicts and promoting worker productivity. Nakayama reminded the inspectors that they must "act firmly with the laborers who are generally ignorant men"; the physicians shared in the disciplining of workers by determining whether a laborer who claimed to be sick was really ill or was simply trying to avoid work.[24]

At first, planters were suspicious of Nakayama's inspectors and were frequently antagonistic toward them, predicting that the inspection sys-

tem would "entirely subvert all proper and needful discipline on plantations." The inspectors therefore had a dual job: to be mindful of planters
who believed they "coddled" Japanese workers and, at the same time, to
gain the confidence of workers in order to anticipate and prevent strikes
or other acts of resistance. The situation at Koloa plantation in 1886 illustrated how the inspection system operated. About fifty of the plantation's
ninety-two Japanese workers had been jailed for refusing to work. They
were protesting the plantation's practice of forced labor even when sick,
irregular payment of wages, and a ban on cooking. Nakayama traveled
to Kauai and secured from the strikers a promise to return to work if
management agreed to arbitration by his team of inspectors. While ostensibly representing the workers in the negotiations, Nakayama advised the
employers to exercise "a certain amount of benevolence in manipulating
Japanese, though it is our desire that there be strictness in making them
carry out a proper amount of work."[25]

That the planters eventually accepted the intervention of Nakayama
and his staff supports the contention that the inspection system benefited
the employers more than it did the workers. The Japanese inspectors were
paid by the Hawaiian government to quell worker unrest, but they also ex-
torted fees from laborers. After 1887, all Japanese plantation workers were
required to pay 35 cents a month into a common fund toward the salaries
(including bonuses) of Nakayama and his staff. In 1892, after he helped
to arrange a reduction in the monthly wages of *kanyaku imin* from $15 to
$12.50, Nakayama was rewarded with a $2,000 bonus and a $200 monthly
supplement, retroactive for one year, drawn from the workers' fund.[26]

In 1890, about 170 Japanese workers at Heeia plantation rebelled against
the *lunas*. The workers claimed they had been kicked and beaten, and that
the *lunas* had deducted one-half to a full day's wages from the workers
for not following orders. Three representatives of the strikers walked ten
miles across the rugged Nuuanu Pali to Honolulu and called on Nakayama
to help them. The inspector "showed them no sympathy. He was haughty
and irate. He threw their petition on the floor without even reading it
and berated them for having the temerity to make complaints and told
them that they should realize that they were nothing but mere contract
laborers."[27] Little wonder that, in the fields, Japanese workers sang:

> The laborers keep on coming
> Overflowing these Islands

But it's only Inspector Nakayama
Who rakes in the profits.[28]

Squeezing Sweat and Blood

The government contract period began in 1885 with the departure of the *City of Tokyo* and lasted until 1894 when the Japanese government turned the business of emigration over to private companies licensed and regulated by the government. During the *kanyaku imin*, twenty-six shiploads totaling about 29,000 Japanese made the crossing to Hawaii's plantations under the terms of the Convention of 1886. At first, passage was free, but after 1887, migrants were charged $70 for transportation and handling expenses. Although the bill was credited against the workers' salaries and was payable in monthly installments, and although the charge decreased to $60 in 1888, $65 in 1890, and $13 in 1891, workers had to pay for what originally had been free. And in 1891 they had to accept a cut in monthly wages from $15 to $12.50, losing in wages what they had gained in reduced transportation costs.[29] The declining per capita cost of importing a Japanese migrant, from $69.90 in the first four shipments (1885–1887) to $7.09 in the next seven shipments (1888–1890), indicated a shifting of costs from the government and planters to the workers.[30]

That pattern established during *kanyaku imin* was repeated and actually heightened during the *jiyu imin*, or "free migrant" period, which began in 1894 and ended in 1908. Approximately 125,000 "free migrants" sailed to Hawaii under the auspices of private emigration firms during these years of Japanese migration. Despite safeguards installed by Japan's government to protect the migrants, emigration companies regularly engaged in fraud, broke promises, and charged extortionate fees. In 1902, an *Osaka Asahi Shinbun* editorial accused the companies of looting migrants: "Each emigration company takes advantage of the naiveté of emigrants, charges unreasonably high commissions, robs emigrants of their savings and is only intent in its own self-centered profit making."[31]

Banks and boardinghouses, often associated with emigration companies, also profited from "migration fever." According to a 1905 report, Keihin Bank, organized by three emigration companies, collected a bloated 12½ percent interest on loans advanced to migrants, and boardinghouses charged migrants "big hotel bills" at the port of embarkation while they waited for processing and the required medical examination.[32] The usurious and fraudulent practices of the Keihin Bank were well known and documented, prompting one historian of the period to write that the bank "was set up to squeeze the sweat and blood out of immigrants."[33]

Individuals recalled owing money to the Keihin Bank. "I was from Miirison, Asa-gun, Hiroshima Prefecture, and went to Hawaii as an immigrant worker at the age of 17," recalled Ko Shigeta. "I wanted to save money in Hawaii and go back to Japan as soon as possible. It was 1903 when I arrived at Honolulu with my two comrades. . . . I had borrowed 100 yen from Keihin Bank." Shigeta worked on Oahu's Aiea plantation for $14 a month, working nine hours daily from 6:00 A.M. to 4:00 P.M. "Fifty of us, both bachelors and married couples, lived together in a humble shed—a long ten-foot-wide hallway made of wattle and lined along the sides with a slightly raised floor covered with a grass rug, and two *tatami* mats to be shared among us." For those living quarters, he paid $7 to $8 a month. Tired and overworked, Shigeta contracted pleurisy, but "since I owed 100 yen to the bank, I could not afford to rest. . . . I worked hard, and in two years I was able to pay back the 100 yen. I often wished I was back in Japan instead of enduring this hardship in Hawaii. The lives of all the Japanese working on the sugar farms were the same as mine, more or less," he concluded.[34]

Hawaii's Japanese were divided by class interests. In November 1903, Japanese business groups, including representatives of the Keihin Bank, launched the Central Japanese League, which was led by Japan's consul general in Hawaii, Miki Saito. Claiming a membership of 25,000, the League professed to speak on behalf of Japanese workers, yet it sought to reduce plantation labor disturbances and halt emigration from Hawaii to the mainland. Both issues were beneficial to planters because they restricted the options available to laborers. The League also promised to seek improvements in education for Japanese children born in Hawaii. In May 1905, workers formed the Japanese Reform Association to demand of the Japanese government freedom "from the clutches" of the emigration companies, Keihin Bank, the consulate, and the Central Japanese League. In response, the government recalled Saito for "consultations," closed down Keihin Bank, and restricted the activities of emigration company agents. In September 1906, the association reported: "The Reform Association, formed on May of last year to extricate the 70,000 Japanese from the clutches of the Keihin Bank and the immigration companies, has fulfilled its mission." Although it disbanded voluntarily, the association promised: "We 70,000 strong can easily unite again if the need arises. This is to declare that the dissolution of the Reform Association does not mean the demise of its fighters." [35]

The Hawaiian government was mainly looking for settlers, but the planters wanted cheap and docile workers. Agents from Hawaii courted a cautious Japanese government with promises of free passage and decent wages and working conditions for Meiji men and women. Before the ink had dried on the agreements, however, Hawaii's planters had modified the terms, passing procurement and transportation costs on to the migrants and instituting harsh labor controls to maximize their returns. The Japanese government, whether out of a need for foreign capital or in order to find work for its depressed peasantry, permitted migration to continue despite contractual modifications that were unfavorable to its citizens. Indeed, Japan's government, through its consul general, typically treated the migrants, once abroad, as a lesser class whose chief duty was to fulfill the terms of contract, "giving satisfaction" to the master class. Irwin, Nakayama, Keihin Bank, and the sugar planters shared a common interest in squeezing sweat and blood from Shigeta and the thousands like him who sought in the cane fields of Hawaii dignity and a means of livelihood.

Songs of Pain

As they worked, the Japanese sang songs called *hole hole bushi*, a name derived from combining the Hawaiian *hole hole* (the work of stripping dried cane leaves) with the Japanese *bushi* ("tune"). The music of the songs generally came from Japanese folksongs; the words were the spontaneous feelings and thoughts of workers engaged in plantation labor. Many *hole hole bushi* were composed by women and reflected their experiences and point of view.[36] Misa Toma remembered years of hardship endured on the plantation; she called her songs *setsunabushi*, "songs of pain":

> Starting out so early
> Lunches on our shoulders
> Off to our holehole work
> Never seems to be enough.[37]

Hole hole bushi not only chronicled the struggles of individuals but aptly symbolized a people's story. The coming together of melody and verse in

hole hole bushi paralleled the process whereby Japanese migrants wove two
distinctive traditions into a harmonious whole and in the process came to
see themselves as settlers—the creators and inheritors of a new tradition.
In the words of an Okinawan song, the migrants grew deep roots "with
green leaves."

My Mother Dear

(A Dialogue)

Let me take my leave, my mother.
Earn money and come home, my child,
As I stay home and pray to the gods.
To this Hawaii from the far away Okinawa
We have come all the way for the sake of money.
Thinking it'd only be a few years we came,
But we have now grown our roots deep and with green leaves.[38]

According to a report published in 1900, housing for the Asian migrants
consisted of barracks with six to forty men in each hall. Wooden plat-
forms running the length of the barracks walls, or shelves stacked three
or four tiers high along the walls, were used as beds and were the only
private space for the workers. "These quarters furnish only a shelter and
a place to rest," observed the report. Despite the spartan arrangements,
continued the report, "actual conditions" on the plantations showed every
labor camp to be "a busy hive," humming with activity and contentment.
"The mother works with her babe near at hand, while the older children
are at school. The happy chatter of women's tongues does not evidence
discontent. There is food enough and a place to eat and sleep and live in,
equal in comfort to that they have left behind. Conveniences are multiply-
ing. The laborer returns to his home in the evening, and every repression
is relaxed." On Sunday, a day of rest, workers put on clean clothes, "pipe
and cigarette lend solace," and "no one would dream of hardship to look
in their faces."[39]

The laborers saw plantation life differently. Baishiro Tamashiro remembered his first day of work as a *kachi kane* ("cut cane") man at Lihue
plantation on Kauai: "Since we used knives, our hands were blistered. . . .
It sure was hard work. We had no time to rest. We worked like machines.
For 200 of us workers, there were seven or eight *lunas* and above them
was a field boss on a horse. We were watched constantly."[40] Haruno Sato
described her tasks as a youth on Oahu's Ewa plantation: "I started to

work in the fields at age thirteen by faking my age because I was tall. I helped my father on the contract system with hăpai kō,[41] piling up the heavy cane stalks and helping to load the cane on Otō-san's ["father's"] shoulders. During certain months of the year, I also worked for the plantation as a 'water boy.' We filled the square cans with water at the upper end of the ditches where the water was cleaner. I also delivered the bentō at lunchtime." As she grew older, Sato moved from "water boy" to *hoe hana* (weeding and cultivating with a hoe).[42]

A *hole hole bushi* likened the early morning plantation work call to birds crying and temple bells tolling—both associated with misfortune and death, especially of a family member.

> Worse than the birds crying
> Or the temple bells tolling
> Is the plantation bell
> Calling us to another day.[43]

Women's recollections of plantation life hardships encompassed field labor and domestic work, as well as their relations with men in camps with many men and few women. Picture brides, such as Kame Kakazu and Tsuru Yamauchi, were especially cut off from normal channels of social interaction and support because they were not only separated from their kinfolk but were also strangers, for the most part, to their husbands. Kakazu told of her extreme loneliness at Kipapa irrigation camp on Oahu's Waipahu plantation and of the many nights she spent crying quietly, so as not to disturb her sleeping husband. She missed her mother and father and was distressed over her plight, unable to confide in a husband with whom she had little time to get acquainted because of the rigors of plantation work or in the one other woman in the camp, who was older than and disdainful of Kakazu, a mere teenager.[44] The first impression of both Kakazu and Yamauchi of their new homes was a sense of isolation because of the physical location of the camp, which was almost hidden amid expanses of sugarcane. "You couldn't see anything but cane and some mountains," recalled Yamauchi of her camp on Waipahu plantation. "I felt lost without my parents and sisters. Here you couldn't see anything, no view, no landscape, just fields and hills. Ah, such a place. The sun was already going down. I thought, 'Is Hawaii a place like this?' "[45]

Perhaps most frightening to eighteen-year-old brides Kakazu and Yamauchi was the prospect of giving birth in that sorrowful place. "There was a lady from Niigata in Mill Camp 2 in Waipahu who came to help," Yamauchi remembered of her first childbirth. "In those days a midwife just helped a baby be delivered, come out, you know. She took care of the umbilical cord and cleaned the rest. She bathed the baby and things like that. She would come back the next day to bathe the baby again. But it was far away, so as soon as the umbilical cord fell off, she stopped coming."[46] Women commonly worked in the fields up to the day of delivery, took their babies to work, and left the infants at the field's edge under makeshift shelters to shield them from the sun and from biting insects. Women's hands, alternately hardened by gripping a hoe and softened by washing clothes, cradled their newborn babes, cooked, and sewed, patched, and ironed clothing for their families. "At night after having the children go to bed, and having taken my bath close to bedtime, I did the children's ironing, trying not to make much noise," recalled Yamauchi. "They could hear everything, you know; the walls were so close to each other. It was 10 o'clock when I went to bed."[47] A *hole hole bushi* captured a mother's lament:

> It's starting to pour
> There goes my laundry
> My baby is crying
> And the rice just burned.[48]

Women, in this setting of mainly bachelor men, were at once deprived of sisterly contact and pursued and tormented by men. Yamauchi was so afraid of being harassed by men that she insisted on having her husband accompany her in the early morning darkness to the outdoor kitchen where she prepared their lunch. "That was because it was uncivilized in those days, you know," she explained. "The hardest thing to get used to was the bachelors saying this and that. I hated it."[49] Choki Oshiro told of how he helped rescue a woman who had been kidnapped from a plantation, taken to Honolulu, and locked in a hotel room. After finding her, Oshiro and his companions confronted the kidnapper and promised not to press criminal charges against the man if he released the woman to them. "The guy was tough and violent," recalled Oshiro, but he eventually relented and let the men take the woman back to her husband.[50]

Perhaps in response to abusive treatment, women developed a callousness that essentially neutered men. Ko Shigeta described how women, "the wives of the others," shared the same bathing facilities with men, and how, as he washed himself, they unconcernedly stepped over him "as if I were a dog or cat in their path." Shigeta added the richly evocative: "I remember the cold drops from the ends of their hair falling on my back."[51] At the same time, the abnormal gender disparity provided some latitude for women, such as fleeing an abusive husband or taking on lovers, as suggested by bawdy *hole hole bushi*, composed and sung by women, whose lyrics were described by a young boy as "quite pornographic."[52] One such song asked:

> Tomorrow is Sunday, right?
> Come over and visit.
> My husband will be out
> watering cane
> And I'll be home alone.[53]

Hole hole bushi, although appropriately symbolic and deeply revealing of Japanese life and labor on Hawaii's plantations, clearly were not representative of the range of experience that varied from person to person, plantation to plantation, and time to time. Important nuances—the stuff of history—have been effectively presented in any number of studies of Hawaii's sugar industry and labor history. *Hole hole bushi*, nonetheless, like the "blues" for African Americans, were both looking glass and mirror, clarifying and baring a minority group's experience in America and, in reflection, American society as a whole.[54] Further, the beginnings of *hole hole bushi* locate the germination of a people, neither Japanese nor European American, but uniquely indigenous and American, deeply rooted and "with green leaves."

Like Hell

Before 1900, when U.S. annexation of Hawaii was formalized, Japanese workers usually arrived in the islands by way of labor contracts. Despite the kingdom's 1839 declaration of rights, which guaranteed "life, limb, liberty, freedom from oppression," and Hawaii's 1852 constitution and its revision in 1864, which outlawed slavery and involuntary servitude, workers essentially remained outside the law. The system of contract labor, as governed by the Masters and Servants Act, devolved into a form of bondage. Workers' (servants') contracts were bought and sold, servants were obliged to obey all lawful commands of masters or their overseers, planters and managers prosecuted and defended all labor contract cases, and judges were appointed by the master class and were easily corrupted. A Japanese worker named Mioshi challenged a pillar of the contract labor system in 1891 before the Hawaiian Supreme Court, arguing that the assignment of his contract from the Bureau of Immigration to Hilo Sugar Company constituted a form of involuntary servitude. The court ruled against Mioshi, but Justice Sanford Dole, in his dissent, agreed that Mioshi did not have a choice of employers and that wages for work did not of itself remove the case from "that condition of involuntary servitude or semi-slavery which is inconsistent with our Constitution and laws."[55]

The control of master over servant began at the level of individual plantation manager, or *luna*, and worker in the field, mill, and camp. Despite labor laws, plantations exercised tight controls; numerous restrictions governed work, housing, and social life and were enforced through fines, docking of time and wages, imprisonment, and corporal punishment. Under a system of rules and correction, workers could easily slip into debt or peonage for reporting to work late, breaking or losing tools, or violating curfew. Fear was used to secure subservience and productivity: "We were always on our guard when working," recalled Tsuru Yamauchi. "If we thought the *lunas* were coming, we were afraid. . . . The *lunas* might or might not come once in a day, but we were always scared that they'd come. We couldn't understand their speech, and so we couldn't answer at all. Both men and women worked very hard, because we were scared."[56] A *hole hole bushi* contrasted the dream of "wonderful Hawaii" with its bitter reality:

> Wonderful Hawaii, or so I heard.
> One look and it seems like Hell.
> The manager's the Devil and
> His lunas are demons.[57]

Waihee plantation on Maui offered explicit guidance to workers about what must have been the golden rule for planters generally: "Laborers are expected to be industrious and docile and obedient to their overseers."[58] Worker docility and obedience were not left to choice, however, but coerced through the "strong hand" of authority. An editorial in the July 26, 1904, *Pacific Commercial Advertiser* commented on the psychology of the "plantation coolie": "Yield to his demands and he thinks he is the master and makes new demands; use the strong hand and he recognizes the power to which, from immemorial times, he has abjectly bowed. There is one word which holds the lower classes of every nation in check and that is Authority."

Authority was flexed through the Masters and Servants Act, labor contracts, the courts and police, plantation rules, a system of punishment and fines, physical abuse, and fear. In 1892, in response to a dramatic increase in runaways, the legislature restored the penal section of the Masters and Servants Act, providing punishment of three-months' hard labor and imprisonment for repeated offenders. Mass incarceration of workers labeled troublesome solely on the word of a plantation manager and without the benefit of a trial was employed as a weapon against strikes; for more serious "disturbances," the Citizens Guard stood ready "to check any trouble or uprising that may occur amongst the ever increasing number of Asiatics," assured the attorney general in 1894.[59] Even artistic expression did not escape the purview of Hawaii's rulers. In 1905, five Japanese actors were arrested for performing plays that contrasted the grim lives of plantation workers with the lives of opulence led by a plantation manager and the wife of Japan's consul general. The government newspaper, the *Hawaiian Gazette*, endorsed the sheriff's action as appropriate, although belated: "It was high time that something of this kind was done in the opinion of the official world. Their [the five Japanese actors'] behavior was regarded as decidedly menacing to the labor situation."[60]

Although probably rare, lynching and murder were the most effective forms of violence because they not only silenced the victim but instilled terror among the general population, thereby effectively muzzling mass dissent. On October 28, 1889, the trussed-up body of Hiroshi Goto, a storekeeper and well-known advocate of Japanese workers in the Honokaa area of the island of Hawaii, was found hanging from a telephone pole. The news spread quickly within the Japanese community. Many believed that Goto's lynching was instigated by the planters because of his outspoken defense of Japanese workers in court. Five "foreigners"—*lunas* on a nearby plantation—and a "Hawaiian" were charged with manslaughter. The five whites were found guilty of manslaughter but were released on bail pending an appeal; they promptly vanished from the islands.[61]

In 1896, facing a swelling stream of Chinese and Japanese workers freed from contract, the attorney general urged passage of a "rigid registration law and internal passport system as a means of controlling the movements of these workers." The so-called free workers, including an estimated 17,000 Japanese—were characterized as shiftless and lazy; regulation was required to direct their labor into useful channels. After annexation in 1900, the planters, with the active cooperation of the Japanese consul and Japanese inspector, instituted a passbook system for workers that was intended to function as a blacklist, and the government tried to revive an old vagrancy statute that compelled workers to accept employment or be forced to work on public works projects as prisoners.[62] Both attempts to control the workforce failed, but they indicated the resolve of Hawaii's rulers to exercise strict authority over workers who, by virtue of U.S. annexation and an end to contract labor, were slipping beyond their grasp. To regain their hold, planters began a new policy of evicting from plantation housing intractable laborers and those no longer employed on the plantation, using the widespread housing shortage as an instrument of coercion.[63]

Annexation was a mixed blessing to Asians in Hawaii. The territory was now part of the United States and subject to its laws, which kept the door to Chinese labor migration closed, but it opened the door to a new migration, from the territory to the U.S. mainland. That option was particularly attractive to plantation workers enticed by promises of higher wages and better opportunities on the mainland. A 1905 advertisement pledged: "The laborers will be subjected to no delay upon arriving in San Francisco, but can get work immediately. . . . Employment offered in picking strawberries and tomatoes, planting beets, mining, and domestic service. Now is the time to go! Wages $1.50 a day."[64] Plantation wages stood at about $16 a month, so the prospect of doubling one's salary in labor that seemed less strenuous stimulated a significant exodus. Between 1905 and 1916, 62,647 Japanese arrived in Hawaii, but 30,119 returned to Japan and 28,068 left the islands for the West Coast, representing a net gain of only 4,460.[65] The agent for Laupahoehoe plantation expressed his frustration over the labor situation; the same ship, he explained, that carried 1,300 Portuguese to Hawaii sailed from Honolulu with 1,000 to 2,000 Japanese bound for Vancouver.[66]

Seeking to halt the outflow, planters seized workers' passports, circulated an appeal from Japan's consul general, and provided monetary inducements. The Central Japanese League mounted a campaign directed at laborers on plantations and at West Coast boardinghouses for a boycott of Japanese migrants from Hawaii.[67] In 1905, the legislature required labor recruiters to buy $500 annual permits or face a fine of between $500 and $1,000 for each conviction. Licensing failed because recruiters ignored the law, but, more fundamentally, because the law offered no remedy for the root cause of outmigration—poor conditions on Hawaii's plantations and the human desire to find "more agreeable employment."[68] The planters finally proposed to bypass Japanese laborers and import Chinese migrant workers, who were seen as "far more reliable and more docile" than the unstable and "aggressive" Japanese. In appealing to Congress for a modification of the Chinese Exclusion Act, Hawaii's planters packaged their plan as a way of destroying the Japanese labor monopoly and saving the territory's economy from the Japanese threat.[69]

All these attempts proved unsuccessful. The Japanese migration to the West Coast was finally stopped only because a growing anti-Japanese movement on the mainland sought Japanese exclusion. The Japanese and Korean Exclusion League, later called the Asiatic Exclusion League, formed in 1905, and the San Francisco school board decision of 1906 to segregate Japanese students in public schools indicated the rising anti-Japanese sentiment. In March 1907, President Theodore Roosevelt signed an executive order that prohibited aliens whose passports had been issued for travel to U.S. territories, the Canal Zone, or any foreign country, including Mexico and Canada, from entering the United States, effectively putting an end to Japanese migration from Hawaii to the mainland. In 1906, 12,221 Japanese left Hawaii for the West Coast; in 1907, the number decreased to 5,438. A mere 69 arrived in 1908 and only 28 in 1909.[70] Hawaii's planters hailed Roosevelt; the Japanese denounced the executive order as a sentence to servitude: "It enslaves us permanently to Hawaii's capitalists."[71]

Beginning in the winter of 1907, the American ambassador to Japan negotiated an assurance from the Japanese government that it would refrain from issuing passports to laborers bound for Hawaii and the U.S. mainland. That accord, called the Gentlemen's Agreement, became binding in the summer of 1908, adding to the effectiveness of Roosevelt's executive order. In Hawaii, despite the sentiment voiced for "citizen labor" (as opposed to "coolies," who could not assimilate or be naturalized), pragmatic economic realities moved the planters. The territory's governor, Walter Frear, wrote to his superior in Washington: "We do not wish to lose the Japanese until we can get Europeans or Americans." In fact, the governor held independent discussions with Japan's Ambassador Shuzo Aoki and Consul General Saito for the continued migration of Japanese laborers to Hawaii. Frear's initiative embarrassed the Roosevelt administration, which was at the time conferring over the terms of the Gentlemen's Agreement. The president, wrote his secretary to the governor, "very strongly feels that it is the most unwise possible policy to subordinate the ultimate interests of Hawaii to the present needs of the sugar planters, and to run the island on the theory of treating it primarily for the use of large planters who run their plantations with the labor of Asiatic coolies."[72]

According to the U.S. immigration commissioner, the Gentlemen's Agreement was based on the understanding that Japan would discourage emigration of its subjects to the United States, and both countries would cooperate to make that policy "as effective as possible." The only categories of migrants permitted entrance to Hawaii were "former residents" and the parents, wives, and children of Japanese residents.[73] The impact was immediate and dramatic: in 1906, 17,509 Japanese arrived in Hawaii; in 1907, 14,742; in 1908, 4,202; and in 1909, 1,310.[74] Picture brides were allowed entrance under the terms of the agreement. For example, 755 picture brides arrived in Hawaii in 1908; their numbers dipped during the next two years to 436 and 658, respectively, but rose rapidly to 865 in 1911, 1,285 in 1912, and 1,572 in 1913. Overall, between 1908 and 1915, picture brides constituted more than 58 percent of all women migrants to Hawaii.[75]

The infusion of women, together with natural increase among the Japanese already in the islands, tilted the gender scale toward greater numerical equality between men and women. In 1890, there were 10,219 Japanese men and 2,391 women in Hawaii; in 1900, 47,508 men and 13,603 women; in 1910, 54,784 men and 24,891 women; and in 1920, 62,644 men and 46,630 women.[76] An immigration official commented on the possible meaning of the trend: "This change in the character of Japanese [migration] may indicate that the people of that nationality are beginning to take root in the Territory to a greater extent than heretofore."[77]

Charity and Benevolence

Closing the door to Japanese migration circumscribed Hawaii's planters, who had relied on migrants for cheap labor since the 1850s. At the same time, Japanese plantation workers, like the Chinese before them, sought alternative employment opportunities in family farming and urban trades. Those remaining on plantations grew increasingly impatient with poor conditions and depressed wages. "It is a well known fact," stated a plantation manager in 1906, "that a large proportion of the Japanese around the Islands would rather take subcontracting on any sort of road or ditch construction than do the regular Plantation work."[78]

Meanwhile, the planters were unsuccessful in Europeanizing the workforce. Although whites or "citizen labor" were preferred over Asians, they were difficult to obtain, too expensive to recruit and import, and unwilling to remain on the plantations. Faced with restrictive immigration laws emanating from the national government, the planters experimented with tapping another labor reservoir in the recently conquered Philippines. First attempts to recruit Filipino workers, in 1906 and 1907, were beset with adversity, and the results were disappointing. After six months of wrestling with the American colonial bureaucracy in the Philippines and with Filipino reluctance to go abroad, HSPA agent Albert F. Judd returned to Hawaii with 15 men. By 1907, only 150 Filipinos had been recruited. The HSPA president, E. Faxon Bishop, conceded that the experiment had been "all but a failure."[79]

Planters now faced the prospect of having to fill their labor needs almost entirely from local supplies. That stern reality called for a new approach to planter control over the workforce. A leading HSPA official described the change to a plantation manager: "In times past we got too much into the habit of treating the Japanese and Chinese as if they were more animals than men. We can not do this now, and it is not likely that the Japanese will stand being so treated when they themselves are an extremely polite race. So, while you must not give way to loafers for a moment, it would be well to be firm in a more kindly manner than was the custom ten years ago."[80]

Firmness with kindness—planter paternalism—was fed on a steady diet of Christian charity and benevolence. Indeed, many plantations were begun by missionaries—the Alexanders, Baldwins, Castles, Cookes, Rices, Wilcoxes. These chieftains presumed ownership of workers for their benefit and improvement. "A plantation is a means of civilization," declared an 1886 issue of *Planters' Monthly*. "It has come in very many instances like a mission of progress into a barbarous region and stamped its character on the neighborhood for miles around."[81] A beacon in the

wilderness, the plantation upheld Christianity and civilization; the plantation master, through discipline and paternal affection, cultivated cane and
morality among his impressionable charges. "A Manager's Influence," an
essay in *Planters' Monthly*, lay the "white man's burden" at the doorsteps
of the masters: "Every manager has a grave responsibility in keeping up
discipline and order on his plantation as well as a healthy moral tone."
An occasional social evening with "respectable employees," an invitation
for "an evening's chat or a little music, or a quiet game of an innocent
nature," might show that the manager considered his employees not mere
laborers but fellow human beings "with desires and interests akin to his
own." Finally, and perhaps of greater importance, admonished the essay-
ist, "some attempt should be made at religious instruction and inspiration
of some kind," especially in giving to Sunday "some appearance at least
of a sacred day."[82]

Various plantation rules, such as those of Kohala plantation in 1862,
codified the spirit of the appeal for a moral order. "The laborers and all
belonging to the plantation are requested to attend church on at least
every Sunday and prayer meeting once during the week," read one of its
rules. Other rules, prohibiting card playing, "quarreling with or whipping
wives," and "tittle tattling" revealed the hand of missionaries.[83] The daily
controls exercised over virtually all aspects of workers' lives spawned a
dependency among the recipients of planter benevolence, establishing
the master's claim to obedience while acting as a check against protest.[84]
"My entire family is grateful to my master for his generosity," stated
gannenmono Yonematsu Sakuma in 1917. "Now that I am aged and can no
longer work, he built us this comfortable home and is giving us a generous pension of $25 a month. He put my oldest son through college and
my daughter through normal school. He is also paying for the education
of all my other children."[85] *Issei* (first-generation Japanese) could understand Confucian status ethics, subservience, and heartfelt obligation to
Hawaii's planters. But some sought to create a new tradition, based on
the American proposition that "all men are created equal."

Chapter 3

With the Force of Wildfire

Just as if with the force of wildfire, 7,000 of the compatriots, from each of Oahu's plantations, launched the great strike in the month of May.
— Yasutaro Soga

Demanding Equality

Japanese resistance to oppression on Hawaii's plantations was recurrent, took a variety of forms, and sought the betterment both of individuals and the group. Women who ran away from abusive husbands were examples of individual acts of resistance. Protests at the point of production—breaking or losing tools, feigning illness, working at a slow pace, and running away—were acts of resistance in the workplace, whether or not the actors perceived them as such. Attacks on cruel *lunas* and plantation police, and arson in sugar mills and cane fields, were other worker responses to expropriation and oppression.[1] Collective action by workers was clearly the most impressive form of resistance. Although the participants often did not recognize that their resistance undermined the plantation system, their actions were certainly seen by the planters as a threat to the controls they exercised and, indeed, to their way of life.

The historical record of collective resistance by Japanese workers on plantations before 1900 is unfortunately slender, although it is richly suggestive. In April 1890, at Heeia, 6 men were tried as rioters because they broke the windows of a fellow worker who had refused to join them in a planned strike; in May 1890, at Hakalau, 400 marched to Hilo to protest overwork; in April 1891, at Hana, Maui, 150 walked off, complaining of nonpayment of wages; in June 1891, at Ewa, 200 marched into Honolulu to voice various grievances; in October 1891, at Makaweli, Kauai, 275 struck for unspecified causes; in November 1892, at Ewa, more than 200 walked to Honolulu to demand the firing of a *luna* who had helped a fellow *luna* fight off 5 attackers; in June 1893, at Kukuihaele, Hawaii, the entire workforce of 250 struck and marched to Honokaa to attend the trial of a *luna* who had shot and wounded a Japanese who had allegedly attacked him with a knife; in July 1893, at Hamakuapoko, Maui, 140 refused to work, claiming a holiday; in December 1893, at Paauhau, Hawaii, 63 struck over a meager water allowance; in January 1894, at Koloa, 150 chased a *luna* who had beaten a laborer and then paraded through the streets; in February 1894, at Mana, Oahu, more than 100 strikers were sentenced to work on the Pali road and at a quarry; in August 1894, at Ewa, a riot erupted over a plantation policeman's fight with a worker; in November 1894, at Kahuku, 150 marched to Honolulu, protesting a brutal *luna* and general mistreatment; in January 1895, at Kahuku, 120 struck over *luna* cruelty and walked to Honolulu; in June 1896, at Olowalu, Maui, workers assembled to protest unreasonable rules; in March 1897, at Waianae, Oahu, 200 struck over the arrest of two men who had refused to work, and at Spreckelsville, Maui, 300 mobbed and killed a Japanese interpreter; in July 1897, at Wailuku, Maui, 52 were discharged for refusing to work; in November 1897, at Ewa, 81 struck over a *luna* who had broken a worker's arm; in October 1899, at Olaa, Hawaii, 89 refused to work.[2]

After the annexation of Hawaii in 1900 and the termination of penal contracts, Japanese workers increasingly saw themselves in class terms and recognized that their strength lay in collective action. That the planters anticipated an upsurge in worker militance is revealed in a warning sent by sugar factor H. Hackfeld and Company to its plantation managers, predicting that the elimination of labor contracts meant "that any contract laborer may refuse to work at any time and you will have no remedy against him" and that laborers would very likely organize massive strikes to "take advantage of their present position and demand higher wages and other concessions."[3] A government report listed twenty strikes by Japanese plantation workers, men and women, during 1900 alone. The largest single work action involved 1,350 strikers, and the total number of strikers in the year was 7,806 field hands, cane cutters and strippers, and mill laborers.[4] Not included in the tally were lockouts, such as the ten-day lockout of 43 Japanese and Portuguese women field hands at Kilauea plantation on Kauai for demanding a wage increase from $8 to $10 a month, an action ultimately won by the women.[5]

Strike Strategies

By 1905, the federal commissioner of labor expressed alarm over the frequency and seriousness of strikes involving Japanese plantation workers, describing those struggles in the workplace as racial, rather than class, conflict and the movement among Japanese workers as "blood unionism." Japanese laborers, alleged the report, "do not feel any hostility toward employers or capitalists as a class, nor do they feel that they have economic rights to be asserted as a principle." Strikes were not usually instigated by a desire for higher wages, claimed the commissioner, but because of "intense race solidarity and the powerful influence over the workers exercised by such organizations as they possess." Thus Japanese strikes were reactions of men, not workingmen, to personal insult or injury inflicted by overseers, and took "no account of economic results, either for the employer or for the strikers."[6] The misrepresentation of Japanese resistance as a race conflict would soon become the standard view of those who ruled and guarded Hawaii.

Although Japanese workers failed to grasp fully the concept of international class struggle, as pointed out in the labor commissioner's report, they certainly understood economic principles of competition and profits, markets and prices, production and labor, and they knew that the most convincing case they could make for improving work and living conditions was to withhold their labor. They also learned, from participating in strikes, that shared ethnicity did not guarantee a common class interest, as was evident during the Waipahu strikes of 1904.

The Waipahu plantation strike lasted for four days in May 1904. Strikers called for the removal of head *luna* Patterson, who, together with his *lunas*, sold lottery tickets for a dollar each to the workers and apparently reaped a handsome profit. Workers claimed they were compelled to participate in Patterson's lottery because refusal invited reprisals. In the settlement, Patterson was dismissed, and mandatory participation in lotteries and gambling was done away with. Two months later, 1,300 Japanese at Waipahu demanded the removal of a Japanese *luna*, Suyehiro, and refused to accede to a compromise arranged by the Central Japanese League that Suyehiro be transferred to oversee Korean workers. "Does it behoove us . . . to shirk this combat [Russo-Japanese War] by forcing the oppression of this Suyehiro on these poor Koreans?" asked a Japanese striker.[7]

Between the two strikes, the League instructed its branches to work to avoid strikes because they damaged "the reputation of the organization in the eyes of the public, particularly of the employers of the Japanese laborers, with whom we earnestly wish to maintain just and cordial relations." The communication was adamant: "Strikes and all other violent acts, especially for trivial causes, are, in their nature, like the doings of unruly children or like the acts of barbarians, rather than of civilized men. We are absolutely opposed to them."[8]

In December 1904, 1,196 Japanese field hands joined in a strike of contract cane cutters at Oahu's Waialua plantation. The strike began when management rejected the cane cutters' demand that their rates be tied to the fluctuating price of Hawaiian sugar on the world market. The logic behind the demand was that wages had been set at 32 cents per ton for cutting and loading cane in 1903 when sugar prices were low, but in 1904, the price of Hawaiian sugar had climbed 4½ cents per pound, justifying a concomitant rise in pay. Besides showing an understanding of economic principles, the workers at Waialua were organized; not only would cane cutters stop working, they threatened, but they would be joined by other laborers on the plantation, shutting down the entire operation. Moreover, the workers timed the strike to begin after a full day of cutting had taken place, inserting an element of economic pressure into the equation because the longer the cut cane lay in the field, the greater the loss of sugar content in each stalk.[9] Although the Waialua strike of 1904 failed to achieve all its objectives, it served as a model for Japanese workers on the benefits of planning and timing strikes according to market and production conditions. To employers, the strike was a portent of things to come.

Repression

Marching ranks of workers, growing ever larger and more confident, were met by Hawaii's planters and the government with increasing force of arms and violence. Six police officers on foot and ten mounted police, all armed with rifles, were dispatched from Honolulu to Waipahu during the May 1904 strike, and forty-six armed policemen protected Waipahu plantation property during the July strike of that year. In May 1905, at Lahaina, Maui, a crowd of 1,400 Japanese workers protesting the blinding of a laborer, Iwamoto, by a *luna* during a brutal beating were fired on by local police, killing one and seriously wounding two or three others. Suppression of the strikers required the Lahaina police force, sixty officers from nearby Wailuku, and forty-five police and thirty National Guardsmen, armed with rifles and field artillery, sent from Honolulu by the sheriff and governor.[10] Although no further violence occurred, the show of firepower in defense of the propertied class clearly underscored the divide between ruler and ruled. Troop and police squads descended on the strikers' quarters in Lahaina and, according to the labor commissioner, "entered without ceremony or shadow of legal right and roused the inmates, using persuasion that came but little short of force to get them out to a conference which the management desired to hold with the men."[11]

The strong hand of authority was long overdue, editorialized the *Pacific Commercial Advertiser* on May 23, 1905, during the Lahaina strike. Under the heading "Japanese Labor Question," the newspaper declared: "The peril is obvious. The more these Japanese get the more they want; and unless they are stiffly curbed they will do great damage to the sugar interests of Hawaii." The labor commissioner reported that what was at stake was a matter both of plantation discipline and the personal safety of whites: "At the time of the Lahaina strike," testified the commissioner, "considerable fear was felt at first by some of the white residents on account of the violence and the collision between the police and the Japanese, and it was felt that in the face of the overwhelmingly Asiatic population the whites were in some danger."[12] To many Japanese resisters, the exercise of their rights as laborers did not pose a "peril" to Hawaii, nor was the dramatic show of force warranted. A Japanese reporter wrote that "it was all a strategy on the part of the planters to cow the workers into submission."[13]

Wildfire

The planters' worst fears were realized in 1909 when 7,000 Japanese workers from all major Oahu plantations joined together in a four-month-long strike for higher wages and full equality in the workplace. Motoyuki

Negoro, a Honolulu attorney who had studied law at the University of California, Berkeley, opened the campaign for higher wages in an article entitled "How about the Higher Wages," published in the July 31, 1908, edition of the *Nippu Jiji*. He linked the value of labor with the gains accrued from that labor: "We regret that the wages in Hawaii are disproportionately low in comparison with the large profits" realized by industry, he wrote. And although the Gentlemen's Agreement tended to cause wages to rise by limiting further labor migration into the territory, its provision cutting off Japanese migration from Hawaii to the U.S. mainland placed the workers "in the position of slaves." Negoro argued that Japan, being "well aware that its subjects are not born to be slaves of the capitalists of Hawaii," should intervene and seek dissolution of the discriminatory restriction on Japanese mobility. "The time is ripe," urged Negoro. "Though the Hawaiian immigrants do not say it in so many words, it is their hope of years and their silent prayer that they recover the lost liberty of choosing and changing their place of abode and become a full-fledged man and to be in a position to earn a just reward for their labor."[14]

Negoro elaborated on his reasons for advocating higher wages and "full-fledged" manhood in subsequent *Nippu Jiji* essays. Conditions for Hawaii's Japanese had changed, he argued, from 1885 when they arrived as migrant laborers to 1908 when they had become "desirous of making their permanent homes here." He offered as testimony of this desire 21,500 married women, 12,500 children between the ages of one and six years, and 4,966 school-age children between seven and fifteen. These settlers, living in communities with thirty-three Japanese shrines and temples and twenty-six Christian churches, required decent wages and living conditions. Instead, the Japanese were given "pigstylike homes" and earned wages of only $18 a month, while Portuguese and Puerto Rican laborers doing the same work lived in "family cottages" and received monthly salaries of $22.50. These conditions continued at a time when the sugar industry was booming, profits were high, and the cost of living was rising. "The prosperity enjoyed by the sugar industry does not extend to the Japanese who are suffering from the steadily rising living costs and weighted down by a practice of a discriminatory wage system."[15]

Sometaro Shiba, editor of the *Hawaii Shimpo*, hotly disputed the contention of Negoro and the *Nippu Jiji*, believing that "it was an inopportune time to stir up agitation on the subject among the laborers." The two papers, joined by other Japanese papers and the English dailies, waged a bitter verbal battle over higher wages throughout the remainder of the year and into 1909.[16] In early November 1908, the *Nippu Jiji* called a meeting at the Asahi Theater in Honolulu, attended by thirteen or fourteen Japanese businessmen, to discuss an organized higher-wage movement that would unite the Japanese community, including the competing newspapers, and would "spread the higher-wage sentiment among Japanese in these islands by and through the efforts and assistance of the newspapers." That object was the agenda of the next two meetings, bringing together Shiba and Yasutaro Soga, editor of the *Nippu Jiji*, in the hope of achieving a reconciliation between the two principals. After about two weeks of little progress, Kinzaburo Makino, a drugstore owner, chaired a meeting at the Japanese Young Men's Christian Association (YMCA) in Honolulu "with the purpose of coming to a definite plan for pushing this question further." The Zokyu Kisei Kai, or Higher Wages Association, resulted from that meeting, along with the election of Makino as chair, Negoro as secretary, and Matsutaro Yamashiro as treasurer, supported by a committee of sixteen to twenty members.[17]

Composed of the urban, educated elite, the committee's first task was to mobilize support for higher wages among plantation workers. The campaign involved publicity through the Japanese press and pamphlets, visits by association members to the plantations, and letters and cards mailed to workers, urging support for the movement and for the formation of local higher-wage associations on each plantation. Soga described plantation police intimidation of the labor organizers: "The night we stumped the Ewa plantation Honouliuli area, the plantation police all carried pistols" and had orders "to shoot the intruder dead" if the visitors "put one foot in the canefields." [18]

On December 12, 1908, 1,700 Japanese attended a mass rally at the Asahi Theater in Honolulu and adopted a resolution calling for an end to the "coolie" wage system and requesting a meeting between representatives of the HSPA and the Higher Wages Association. A formal letter was sent to the planters on December 19. Although the HSPA acknowledged receipt of the request and informed the association that the matter was being referred to the HSPA directors, the HSPA ignored the petition.

Finally, in January 1909, having been rebuffed on their request for a meeting, the Higher Wages Association submitted a carefully argued and documented letter to the HSPA, asking for a raise from $18 to $22.50 per month and appealing to the "reason and justice of the planters." The wage increase, began the document, was based on the principle of equal pay for equal work. Why should the Portuguese or Puerto Rican laborer receive $22.50 for the same amount and quality of work done by a Japanese laborer? "The Japanese here are not coolies. . . . Therefore they deserve the same consideration as any other labor." A 25 percent increase in the cost of daily necessities, the growing number of workers' dependents, and a need to provide for children's education and against sickness and old age were other reasons cited as justifications for higher wages. Subsistence wages would no longer be tolerated by a people who provided 70 percent of the sugar industry's workforce and whose labor "did so much for the upbuilding of Hawaii's only industry"; instead, Japanese workers deserved a "living wage" to "maintain their families and their dependents in a decent, respectable manner." The labor leaders urged: "Our demand is not unreasonable. We are not thinking what we will do if our request be not heard by the planters. We are trusting to the planters' good sense and sense of justice and equity, and trusting that they will listen to the voice of reason and justice."[19]

The Higher Wages Association appended statistical documentation to their letter, showing price increases in basic commodities and the number of women and children, Japanese schools, churches, and temples. A Honomu plantation laborer's monthly balance sheet showed that only $2.10 remained after paying all his bills each month. A worker's wife testified that she had lived on the plantation for fifteen years, that her husband was forty-eight years old, that they had four children, and that her mother-in-law in Japan was seventy-three years old and depended on them for support. Rice alone cost the family $10 a month, and it was becoming impossible to make ends meet: "She related with tears in her eyes how difficult it [was] to get along with only her husband's earnings, especially when the prices of everything [were] high. She wondered what she would do if her husband should be overtaken by sickness or otherwise be disabled, and she said that her only hope was that the children should grow up so that they may help support the family." Another exhibit reported on housing for plantation workers in an area on the island of Hawaii where laborers had to build their own houses with discarded timber and where management seemed indifferent to the workers' health. "The camps need immediate improvement," wrote a reporter. "Nothing is more urgently needed than that. The present camps are utterly unfit for human habitation, both from the moral and sanitary points of view. The privies are especially objectionable." [20]

Instead of negotiating with the Higher Wages Association, the planters spoke through the English dailies and their Japanese allies, letting the press conduct the debate and denying the association the dignity of a response or recognition. Among the "radicals" were the *Nippu Jiji* (Honolulu), *Oahu Jiho* (Waipahu), *Maui Shimbun* (Wailuku), *Shokumin Shimbun* (Hilo), and *Kona Echo* (Holualoa); among the "conservatives" were the *Hawaii Shimpo* and *Hawaii Nichi Nichi* (Honolulu), *Kauai Shimpo* (Lihue), *Maui Hochi* (Waihiken), and *Hilo Shimpo* and *Kainan Shimpo* (Hilo). The conservatives, whose position was articulated by the *Hawaii Shimpo*, essentially agreed with charges made in the English-language press that plantation workers were contented with their situation and the higher-wage proponents were outside "agitators" and "thugs" seeking to use laborers as a platform for their own gain. "We are afraid if the present agitation is kept up," editorialized the *Shimpo*, "real anarchism will prevail among the less thinking classes and the new spirit among us of conciliation and assimilation with the American people will come to an end." As for rumors about collusion between the planters and the *Shimpo*, the editors trivialized the allegation: "The charges of spying for the white people or receiving subsidy from the planters are too ridiculous to be specifically answered." [21]

On February 26, 1909, Soga of the *Nippu Jiji* was arrested on charges of inciting unrest. Although he was released shortly afterward, Higher Wages Association leaders realized that the die had been cast—Japanese workers overwhelmingly supported their cause, and the planters were adamant about their position. Both sides girded themselves for the coming conflict. Japanese plantation workers on Kauai, Maui, and Hawaii pledged their support, and business and social organizations, including prefectural associations (*kenjinkai*), the Honolulu Retail Merchants Association, the Public Bath Operators Association, the Carpenters Association, the Japanese Hotel and Inn Association, and the Barbers Association, publicly endorsed the higher-wage movement. The Honolulu Merchants Association, however, remained neutral.[22] The HSPA trustees signed a compact on May 10, 1909, to distribute the losses from strikes over wages to all member plantations; the HSPA agreed "to bear all losses which may be occasioned by the resistance of strikes on any and all plantations arising out of a conflict over wages, it being understood that the plantations will be guided by the policies laid down by the Association from time to time dealing with strikes for higher wages."[23] Such cooperation among previously competing plantations was compelled by the mounting defiance of masses of workers that cut across the borders of individual plantations.

Laborers at Waipahu plantation submitted a proposal for higher wages to management on May 5; four days later, 1,500 workers at Aiea plantation voted to walk off the job. On May 12, Waipahu workers, led by Masao Haneda, joined the Aiea strikers and defended their action in a letter to manager E. K. Bull signed by eighty-six men and their representatives, Watanabe, Shigeta, Hamada, Miyauchi, Seo, and Takeyama. The signatories expressed their gratitude to Bull for the opportunity to contribute to the development of the plantation and territory, but, because of circumstances, "it has become our painful burden to hereby respectfully present to you our request for [a] reasonable increase of wages." Their request— their "painful burden"—included monthly raises of $8 for field hands, $10.50 for mill workers, and 10 cents per ton for cane cutters and carriers; twice the daily rate for Sunday work; and ten-hour workdays with overtime pay for hours beyond that limit. Wages had not increased for years, explained the strikers, while prices had climbed, the cost of living having risen both in Hawaii and Japan where elderly parents depended on remittances, and former bachelors now faced the added expenses of raising a family in the islands. Democratic impulses of equality and justice also prompted their demand for higher wages: "Is it not a matter of simple justice, and moral duty to give [the] same wages and same treatment to laborers of equal efficiency, irrespective of race, color, creed, nationality, or previous condition of servitude?" the workers asked. "It is respectfully submitted that it is most unjust to discriminate one from the other and pay one laborer $22.50 and give a cottage and land besides, and pay another only $18 and nothing else."[24]

Plantation workers struck Waialua on May 19, Kahuku on May 22, Waianae on May 23, and Ewa on May 24. "Just as if with the force of wildfire," described Soga, "7,000 of the compatriots, from each of Oahu's plantations, launched the great strike in the month of May."[25] Reaction by management was swift and stern. Plantation managers Ross of Aiea and Bull of Waipahu issued eviction notices to the strikers, ordering them to leave plantation property by noon of May 22. Meanwhile, urban strike sympathizers held a mass meeting of support in Honolulu for the Higher Wages Association, whose office served as headquarters for the solicitation of money and goods for the strikers from among the nonstriking Japanese community. Aiea merchants donated their entire treasury of $1,572.50 for strike assistance, monetary and material contributions poured in from Oahu and the outlying islands, and Chinese merchants in Honolulu extended credit with generous terms to the strikers and supplied the displaced with much needed rice throughout the summer. That support constituted a lifeline for the swelling numbers of strikers and their families evicted from their homes and seeking food and shelter in Honolulu, nearly 3,500 of them by May 24.[26]

Stamping Out the Fire

Between May 24 and 27, the planters mapped their counteroffensive. A meeting of over sixty plantation owners and business leaders called for a united front among HSPA members and an adamant refusal to recognize or negotiate with the Higher Wages Association. The statement emanating from the meeting juxtaposed the HSPA ideal of cooperative "partnership" between the plantations and workers with the "Negoro-Makino program" that appealed to "loafers." "The agitator naturally wants large gangs of men earning daily or monthly wages, who have no particular inducement to do a full day's work for their wages, and who, of course, would be amenable to the strike agitators and the loafers in and around the plantation camps," the statement declared. "The plantations, on the other hand, are interested in getting the men in partnership with the plantation, as it were, and the work done along lines where the laborer gets more money for the more work he performs."[27]

Meanwhile, on May 25, Japan's Consul General Senichi Uyeno, as "a representative of the Japanese Emperor," issued a message expressing regret over the strike and urging the strikers to return to work. He asked the strikers to consider the wider ramifications of their action—how it might damage future relations between employers and Japanese in Hawaii—and demanded the obedience of recalcitrants: "Those who do not heed his advice," reported the *Shimpo* and *Nichi Nichi,* are "being disloyal to the Emperor."[28]

On June 7, plantation managers gave twenty-hour eviction notices to Japanese strikers at Ewa, Kahuku, and Waialua; the next day, police at Waipahu rounded up strikers to force them back to work and arrested thirty nonplantation residents for "inciting unrest." The number of displaced strikers seeking shelter in Honolulu by now totaled about 5,000 adults. They were housed in vacant buildings, theaters, and private homes and were fed at four outdoor kitchens that served three meals a day in the Japanese districts of Kakaako, Moiliili, and Palama.[29] "The city of Honolulu was just like a battlefield," wrote Soga, "with everything in extreme confusion. . . . Women volunteers turned out in full force and helped in caring for them [the strikers]."[30]

The planters recruited non-Japanese—Hawaiian, Chinese, Korean, and Portuguese—strikebreakers at $1.50 per day, twice the rates paid to their former Japanese workers. Many of the strikebreakers, realizing that they were being hired "to threaten the Japanese," seized the opportunity to improve their situation by refusing to work under company *lunas* and demanding the appointment of overseers from their own groups. Chinese and Portuguese already employed by the plantations objected to hiring strikebreakers at rates that exceeded their wages, causing some to quit work and others to threaten to leave their employers and become strikebreakers on other plantations.[31] As the strike dragged on and strike resources dwindled, the solidarity of Japanese workers crumbled. The strikers, singly and in small groups, returned to work, scabbing on their fellow Japanese.

The planters employed a network of spies from among the Japanese to monitor the higher-wage movement; despite his earlier denial of collusion, Shiba and his *Hawaii Shimpo* were later found to be beholden to the planters. Shiba had purchased the *Shimpo* in 1908 with a $1,500 loan from an official of the HSPA and had since been receiving a $100 monthly subsidy from the planters. During the higher-wage campaign in February 1909, Shiba recruited the *Hawaii Nichi Nichi* to the planters' side, qualifying it for the same monthly subsidy. Together, the *Shimpo* and *Nichi Nichi* received additional bonuses totaling $11,700 between April 1909 and March 1910. Further, Shiba had planned a hostile takeover of the rival *Nippu Jiji* during the strike when the paper was under constant attack and its reporters and editors imprisoned, leaving Shiba with a virtual monopoly of the Japanese-language press.[32]

Perhaps the single most effective weapon employed by the planters against the higher-wage movement was the harassment, arrest, and imprisonment of strikers and strike sympathizers under the provision of "emergency measures." Strike leaders were arrested on charges of conspiring to harm industry, and their homes and offices were broken into and documents illegally seized in police raids. On June 10, Makino, Negoro, and Yamashiro of the Higher Wages Association, Soga, reporters Yokichi Tasaka and Keitaro Kawamura, and three other *Nippu Jiji* men were arrested and imprisoned on conspiracy charges. Said the arresting officer, High Sheriff William Henry, "I took the position in making these arrests, that the Higher Wages Association, together with its organ, the Nippu Jiji, was a criminal organization, organized in the first instance with the deliberate plan to violate the law in carrying out the purposes of that organization." The following day, Henry ordered a ban on all mass meetings and public speeches for the strike's duration, explaining that the city "practically was in the control of these strikers." [33]

The trial of the strike leaders began on July 26. In the midst of proceedings on August 3, Tomekichi Mori, a higher-wage delegate from Maui, stabbed and seriously wounded Shiba outside the courtroom. The act seemed to affirm the government's contention that Japanese strikers were pawns of their leaders—"all standing together, all suppressing information that was required by the authorities, and all evidently in sympathy with and acting with the Higher Wages Association"—pointing to the guilt of the leaders for having instigated and conspired to commit assault, battery, and murder. As Henry testified, "I was not arresting them for an offense already committed and completed, but I was arresting these men in the very act of perpetuating and keeping in motion the systematic coercion of thousands of Japanese laborers." [34] On August 22, the defendants were found guilty of third-degree conspiracy and sentenced to ten months in prison and a $300 fine.

The "great strike" had already ended, however, unilaterally and without any evidence of success. On August 5, two days after the attempt on Shiba's life, Higher Wages Association representatives met in Honolulu and voted to end the strike. The wildfire had been contained.

Plutocrats and Coolies

Containment neither extinguished nor erased the scars of the fire. The "great strike" was both humbling and exhilarating for Japanese workers, who received a taste of the planters' power and their own strength through collective and organized resistance. The realization must have been underscored three months after the strike's close, on November 29, when the HSPA raised the minimum wage of contractors to $22 per month, adding a bonus system for day laborers, and ostensibly abolished wage discrimination based on race and ethnicity—two objectives of the strike.[35] On the anniversary of America's independence, July 4, 1910, the jailed strike leaders Makino, Negoro, Tasaka, and Soga were pardoned and released from prison to a welcoming crowd of several hundred supporters. "We four were buried in leis and commemorative photographs were taken," recalled Soga. The group passed through Aala Park, a former gathering place for evicted strikers, and arrived at the Yamashiro Hotel, former strike headquarters, where a crowd of nearly 1,000 cheered their leaders with three rousing *"banzais."*[36]

The strikers were denied the satisfaction of having achieved any victory by the planters and their Japanese clients. In what appeared to be a well-timed sequence of events, representatives of the six conservative Japanese newspapers met on October 11, 1909, and adopted a resolution that condemned the Higher Wages Association for having misled "our innocent laborers" and used them "as mere tools for the selfish purpose of agitators." The conservatives claimed to be the true leaders of the community and resolved to "protect our laborers from the lawless demonstrations of these people [agitators] in order to restore the well-earned good reputation of our countrymen already imperiled by the foolish agitation." They urged a "spirit of cooperation" on the part of Japanese laborers—"to wait patiently and continue in the faithful performance of their work"—and petitioned the planters for improvements "as far as practicable." Finally, the newspaper group sent their delegate "to wait upon members of the Hawaiian Sugar Planters' Association to present to them our views." On November 29, the HSPA secretary, W. O. Smith, wrote to Shiba, informing him that the resolution had received "the respectful consideration of the association" and that the trustees had responded by raising wages to $22 and instituting the bonus system.[37]

Despite the planters' facade of business as usual, the great strike of 1909 could not be denied or ignored. For the first time in Hawaiian labor history, plantation workers had joined together in an industrywide strike of all the major plantations on an island and were supported by laborers on other islands. They were organized and had the support of the nonstriking community, raised a strike fund of about $42,000, and inflicted losses to the planters totaling an estimated $2 million.[38] Although most strikers returned to their former plantations, more than a thousand left Oahu for the other islands. The number and percentage of Japanese workers on sugar plantations declined from 28,106 (64 percent) in 1910 to 24,046 (53.5 percent) in 1915 to 19,474 (44 percent) in 1920.[39]

That decrease was accompanied by a steady rise in the number of non-Japanese laborers and migrants recruited for Hawaii's plantations. "The question of immigration has been before your Trustees more or less during the whole of last year," reported the HSPA president at the association's annual meeting in December 1909. "One of the immediate results of the labor disturbance was to cause them to take in hand very vigorously the question of obtaining supplies of fresh labor from every available source." Lucius E. Pinkham and Oswald A. Steven had been sent to the Philippines "to revive native immigration from that point," and the 600 to 700 Filipinos recruited by the pair and already in Hawaii had "taken hold of field work in a very satisfactory manner, being industrious and tractable."[40] The extent of Pinkham and Steven's success can be seen in the rapid rise of Filipinos on Hawaii's plantations: a mere 155 (.3 percent) of the total workforce in 1909, 1,490 (3.4 percent) in 1910, 3,258 (7.3 percent) in 1911, 7,456 (16.2 percent) in 1913, and 8,812 (19.3) percent in 1914.[41]

Besides displacing rebellious workers with "industrious and tractable" migrants, the planters sought to isolate and thereby neutralize the Japanese "threat." The irony for Japanese workers was that in seeking to become Americans through a demand for equality, they were denied national membership and branded as foreigners, undesirables, and seditionists. A Higher Wages Association pamphlet distributed during the strike pointed out that a desire for decent wages and living conditions was not "the outgrowth of a mere selfish, egotistic nationalism" but was an indication of the Americanization of Japanese, marking their evolution from transient to settled laborers who would eventually form "a thriving and contented middle class—the realization of the high ideal of Americanism."

The dissidents did not stop with their vision of what America should be, however; they offered a biting indictment of the planter oligarchy in their plea for a "new Hawaii," describing the territory's social relations as "the present undemocratic, un-American condition of Hawaii, that of plutocrats and coolie."[42] The great strike, therefore, was not an ordinary labor conflict but contained the seeds of a truly revolutionary idea because the democratization of the islands—Hawaii's Americanization—would bring to an end the "plutocratic" rule of the propertied class.[43]

The planters cast the struggle in racial terms, aided in that effort by the fact that the strikers were of a single ethnic and racial group, that the non-striking Japanese community rallied around the rebels, and that leaders of the Higher Wages Association called for solidarity on the basis of *Yamato damashii*, "Japanese spirit." At the same time, the contours of the struggle had been defined by those who held political and economic power, not by the Japanese, through the instruments of racial and ethnic migration, labor segmentation, and discriminatory wages, housing, and living conditions. In the closing days of the strike, the HSPA's labor committee candidly described the underlying reason for recruiting Filipinos: to supplant "the Jap," "to clip his wings," and "to keep the more belligerent element in its proper place."[44]

The 1909 strike was a Japanese strike because the Japanese constituted more than 60 percent of the total plantation workforce and were among the lowest paid of all ethnic and racial groups employed there. Further, the Japanese community was openly divided on the issue of higher wages, and, despite the planters' hiring non-Japanese strikebreakers at twice the wages paid the Japanese, the strikers steadfastly focused on the owners, not their fellow workers, as the root of the conflict—what Soga termed the great struggle against "the power of wealth and the oppression of the government authorities."[45]

In the strike's aftermath, Governor Walter Frear reported to the secretary of interior on "the great Japanese strike of 1909." The "facts," wrote the governor, indicated that the strike arose not among workers but among editors, hotelkeepers, and businessmen; the essential nature of the strike "was racial, and perhaps partly political," although without the support of the Japanese government.[46] Seeing ignorant workers as led by outside agitators and employing racial explanations for class conflict marginalized and vilified the resistant class as a racial group.

What was at stake, according to the planters, was the economic, political, and cultural supremacy of whites/"Americans" over Japanese/"foreigners." They were correct insofar as the working class on the plantations was overwhelmingly Japanese and the aim of that class was equal partnership in a democratic Hawaii where an oligarchy of whites prevailed. Where Americanization meant Europeanization and Anglo conformity, clamor for inclusion by people of color was dissonant, even subversive. Japanese workers were simply behaving in an American way, but their attempt to democratize Hawaii became the "Japanese problem" and, since that "problem" involved the overthrow of the existing order, it eventually became a "military problem." A concerted effort by the planters, territorial government, and military to resolve the multifaceted "Japanese problem" would arise only after the nation's involvement in World War I and the unprecedented Hawaiian sugar plantation strike of 1920.

The Period of Migrant Labor, 1865–1909

Hawaii's anti-Japanese movement began in 1865 with Wyllie's "we are in much need of them," a plea that set off the scramble for Japanese laborers for the kingdom's sugar plantations. "Three fundamental elements essential to our progress," outlined Wyllie, "are cheap land, cheap money and cheap labor."[47] The Great Mahele and the Masters and Servants Act supplied the legal bases for the appropriation of land and subjugation of labor; the concentration of capital in the hands of a few, affiliated through bonds of marriage and interlocking directorates, permitted a ready flow of "cheap money." The third ingredient was more difficult to obtain. Not only recruiting "cheap labor" but also controlling the workers was a recurrent problem for Hawaii's planters. Asian migrants might have been indispensable to the planters for the transformation of Hawaii from a precapitalist to a capitalist mode of production, but they were undesirable to white supremacists as permanent settlers and citizens.

As Asian workers began forming durable communities, members of the white elite expressed alarm over the "peril" posed by an alien, unassimilable, and substantial body within the population. According to its architects, the 1887 Reform constitution was designed to protect life and property "in defense of established order," and consequently barred Asians from the franchise.[48] By 1890, Chinese and Japanese people totaled nearly 33 percent of Hawaii's population, compared with whites at 21 percent and Hawaiians at 45 percent. John Stevens, U.S. minister to the kingdom, wrote in 1892 that Hawaii had "reached the parting of the ways. She must now take the road which leads to Asia, or the other, which outlets her in America, gives her an American civilization and binds her to the care of American destiny."[49] The *Hawaiian Gazette* editorialized: "The asiaticizing of the Hawaiian Islands is proceeding at such a rapid rate that those citizens who know what such a course must lead to, may well stand appalled before such a prospect." Planter William Alexander warned that when the Japanese came to constitute a numerical majority, Hawaii would become a virtual "Japanese colony."[50] American annexation, for partisans of the white oligarchy, was a way of avoiding being swamped by the "yellow wave" or by a coalition of Asians and Hawaiians against whites.

Long before annexation, the planters' system of migrant labor had effectively curbed the rise of the Japanese from the ranks of servitude. Despite their early intention to recruit Japanese men, women, and children for a permanent plantation workforce and despite their perfunctory attempts to Europeanize labor in the islands, the planters imported mainly Asian male workers simply because it was cheaper and was a way of institutionalizing labor controls. The system of migrant labor was first and foremost premised on a mobile, impermanent workforce that included only the most productive members of a marginalized segment of society. These attributes of labor benefited capital, particularly in labor-intensive industries, through reducing labor costs because impermanence (i.e., performing the required work and leaving when no longer needed) and gender- and age-specific migration (i.e., migration of a single gender and age group that fit the needs of a specific task) eliminated the expenses— the social costs—of maintaining unproductive members of the population such as children and the elderly. Additionally, migrant and marginalized members of society were especially vulnerable to exploitation because they had few constitutional rights and were virtually powerless.[51] Racial minorities were even more susceptible to alienation and expropriation because they were easily distinguishable from the rest of the population and were ready targets for racism.

The number of Japanese women in the islands during this period illustrates the gender gap typical of migrant laborers. In 1890, for example, women constituted a mere 19 percent of the Japanese in Hawaii; in 1896, 21 percent; and in 1900, 22 percent. There were numerous reasons, from personal to cultural, that fewer women than men left Japan for Hawaii. Viewed as a social process, however, Japanese migration to Hawaii clearly was stimulated by a desire for laborers on the sugar plantations for the kind of work generally done by men. Furthermore, the status of *issei* as perpetual foreigners made it appropriate to generalize the movement of individuals across the Pacific as a migrant labor stream. The experiences of the *gannenmono, kanyaku imin,* and *jiyu imin* testified to the extent of their lack of power and civil liberties, even their lack of legitimation as human beings with human rights. Labor contracts, plantation rules, *lunas,* registration and passes, evictions, and lynchings reduced plantation labor to "involuntary servitude or semi-slavery." In the words of a *hole hole bushi*, the "poor bastards" who failed to escape the contract ended up "as fertilizer for Hawaii's sugar cane."[52]

Issei workers were ripe for exploitation. Planters saw them as commodities, and leaders of the Central Japanese League dismissed their struggle for dignity as "trivial" and "the doings of unruly children or like the acts of barbarians." Workers were requisitioned like goods. In a letter from Honolulu factor Theophilus H. Davies to C. McLennan, manager of Laupahoehoe plantation on the island of Hawaii, Japanese laborers were ordered along with frying pans, brake blocks, Hennessy brandy, bolts, fertilizers, and lumber: "Another small lot is coming but only enough to give about 75% of the balance due on old orders, and no new orders have the slightest chance of being filled. . . . Only one of your last lot of Japs was rejected, not 2 as we told you last week."[53]

Integral to the Hawaiian system of migrant labor was a multiethnic workforce divided on the basis of race and ethnicity, which repressed class consciousness and class alliances. Nevertheless, the planters never fully achieved that ethnic ideal because of the worldwide market for labor, the costs of importing Europeans, and the interplantation competition for workers. As a result, planters frequently had to take whoever was available.[54] Thus, instead of a diverse workforce, a plantation's racial and ethnic configuration typically revealed a single predominant group. In 1872, Hawaiians constituted 82.8 percent of the plantation workforce; ten years later, their proportion dropped to 25.1 percent, as the Chinese surpassed them as the largest group, totaling 49.2 percent. By 1890, Japanese workers exceeded Chinese; the Japanese constituted 42.2 percent of the plantation workforce, and reached a high of 73.5 percent in 1902. Twenty years later, Filipinos made up 41 percent of plantation laborers, outnumbering the Japanese. In 1932, when the Japanese were a mere 18.8 percent of the plantation workforce, Filipinos supplied 69.9 percent of the laborers.[55]

Such clustering did not prevent planters from hiring and segregating workers by race and ethnicity, promoting the retention of ethnic identity, pitting groups against one another through differential job categories and wages, and seeking a new infusion of workers, generally Asians, from a single ethnic group. The new group would displace earlier workers who had outlived their usefulness—their costs exceeded their benefits as a result of strikes or salary increases.

An additional benefit from migrant labor was its tendency to depress wages that would normally rise as workers gained seniority and specialized skills. On Honokaa plantation, for example, Hawaiian and Chinese workers between 1876 and 1879 received a basic rate of $11 and $12 a month; in 1881, with the arrival of Portuguese laborers, the basic monthly rate decreased to $8. That base rate gradually rose to $15–16 for Portuguese workers, but the newly arrived Japanese were paid $9 in 1885. Japanese workers' wages increased to $15 by 1888, but in 1892, with an infusion of fresh Japanese migrants, the basic rate fell to $12.50.[56] The pattern of successive groups displacing the prevailing group contained an internal logic that maximized profits and acted as a buffer against capitalist economic cycles of expansion and recession. It also retarded labor organizing and siphoned off worker disaffection.

A class basis of the mechanisms of oppression can be seen in the alliance of Hawaiian labor recruiters and capitalists in Japan, including Robert Irwin, Takashi Masuda of Mitsui Bussan Company, and Keihin Bank, and of plantation managers and Japanese in Hawaii, including Joji Nakayama, Consul General Miki Saito, and the Central Japanese League. As owners of capital and the means of production, they were united in squeezing sweat and blood from Japanese workers. Although class interests cut across racial lines, race and class alignments were essentially two tiered, especially after the fall of the Hawaiian kingdom, with whites on top and people of color on the bottom.

Japanese resistance to exploitation and oppression could not be contained indefinitely. Hawaii's annexation and the end of labor contracts saw laborers leave for Honolulu and the U.S. mainland, seeking expanded opportunities. A rash of strikes and protests, begun as individual and small-group attempts at redressing grievances, grew in scope and sophistication to a mass movement for higher wages.

The Gentlemen's Agreement of 1908 and the "great strike" of 1909 were watershed events in Hawaii's anti-Japanese movement. They marked the end of the period of migrant labor and the beginning of the period of dependency. The Gentlemen's Agreement essentially cut off further labor migration from Japan, and the strike, in its demand for full equality, was an attempt by workers to restructure social relations by overthrowing the oligarchy and making Hawaii truly democratic. The system of migrant labor was challenged by workers who defied impermanence by growing their "roots deep and with green leaves" and by insisting on a "living wage" and dignity in the workplace and at home. In setting the arena for the next historical stage, the planters and territorial government recast the workers' democratic impulses as nationalistic and couched the domestic struggle between capital and labor as racial.

As applied to Hawaii's plantations, the migrant labor model requires some modification. The Hawaiian monarchy was attracted to the Japanese as laborers, but also as a "cognate race" to repopulate the kingdom and fortify it against the rising tide of foreign (*haole*) domination. For the planters, stability in the workforce was desirable because cane cultivation was a year-round, not a seasonal, activity. Planter paternalism and the various attempts to prevent laborers from leaving Hawaii for the mainland were efforts directed at reducing impermanence. At the same time, the hospitality extended to Asian laborers was limited to their utility. Migrant labor was thus an immediate, not a long-range, solution to plantation labor needs and the problem of creating a permanent citizenry in postannexation Hawaii. Accordingly, frequent discussion arose among Hawaii's political leaders about ways to Americanize Hawaii's workforce with "citizen labor"—in effect, displacing Asians with whites. The failure of exclusion made necessary the strategy of absorption or control of undesirable by-products of an otherwise profitable labor system, determining the nature of the next historical stage of Hawaii's anti-Japanese movement.

Part II

Years of Dependency,

1910–1940

Chapter 4

Cane Fires

*You have faithfully stood to the last of this long
strike, as inhabitants under the rule of the
United States, respecting and obeying its laws,
as members of this association, and as laborers,
preserving your honor and dignity.*
—Hawaii Laborers' Association

Conflagrations

World War I and America's entry in the war led to rapidly
rising sugar prices and soaring costs of goods and labor.
Bonuses paid to plantation workers, instituted as a result of
the 1909 strike, were pegged to the price of sugar. As an indication of the rapid rate of inflation, in 1914, bonuses paid
to workers amounted to 5 percent of their earnings; a year
later, bonuses rose to 20 percent. In 1917, as the price of
sugar climbed to a new high, the planters, fearing that in-
flated bonuses would permanently raise the earning expectations of workers, arbitrarily reduced the bonus. Instead
of paying workers one-fifth of the bonus every month and
four-fifths every six months, they withheld half the amount
until the end of the year.[1]

Meanwhile, plantation laborers felt the pinch of the rising
cost of living. Prices of staple commodities soared because
of Hawaii's dependence on the mainland and the wartime
shipping shortage along the West Coast. Even after the war
ended, living costs continued upward. The price of a 100-
pound bag of rice rose from $8 to $15, and a gallon of *shoyu*,
which had cost $1.50, rose to $4, then $8, and finally $10.[2]

Also, about 29,000 *issei* and *nisei* (second-generation Japa-

65

nese) registered with the Selective Service System, out of a total of 71,280 registrants in Hawaii. The Japanese had generally been excluded from the National Guard, but the practice was modified during World War I when "friendly aliens" were permitted to volunteer. (Japan had joined Britain and the United States in declaring war on Germany.) In August 1917, 838 Japanese formed Company D of Hawaii's National Guard, leading the *Pacific Commercial Advertiser* to comment: "It is going to be a good company. . . . In fact, with the enthusiasm displayed by the Japanese and their desire to give a practical demonstration of their loyalty to the American flag, it is safe to say that it is going to be one of the largest companies of the Guard in numbers and one of the crack organizations in point of efficiency."[3]

Hawaii's Japanese continued to settle in and make the islands their permanent home. In the years following the 1909 strike, Japanese leaders urged Japanese women to avoid breastfeeding infants in public, exhorted the Japanese to wear Western-style clothing, and advised them to invest in Hawaii. The "reform and enlightenment" campaign was publicized in the Japanese press, through various associations, at lectures, and in night schools.[4] Japanese participation in the National Guard added to their claim to the rights and privileges of citizenship, yet most Japanese veterans of World War I were denied U.S. citizenship, contrary to the federal provision that granted naturalization rights to veterans of the war.[5] These and other events of the post-1909 strike years provided the impetus for the historic strike of 1920.

The sugar plantation strike of 1920 marked a milestone in Hawaiian labor history because of the numbers of workers involved, the length of the strike, the participation of two ethnic groups in a single work action, and the nature of the strikers' demands. Moreover, the strike was historically significant because of the way in which it was interpreted by Hawaii's planters, the territorial government, and the military, leading to far-reaching consequences for Hawaii's Japanese.

The strike was set against a backdrop of growing militancy among both agricultural and urban laborers and rising worker expectations. Roosevelt's interdictory 1907 executive order and the exclusionary 1908 Gentlemen's Agreement led many Japanese to see that their future lay in Hawaii and not on the U.S. mainland. The 1920 strike reiterated the 1909 strike demands, but indicated an Americanized settler community as opposed to an alien migrant one. Significantly, the strike arose amid a program of planter paternalism and social welfare, formed in response to restrictions on Asian migration set by the national government but also in response to worker resistance to the strong hand of authority.

Preparations

Japanese plantation workers reflected on their circumstances throughout the summer and fall of 1917 after the planters had changed the bonus system. As in the 1909 strike, discussions led to the formation of an Association for Higher Wages, and on November 20, 1917, the association submitted a proposal for higher wages and reforms in the bonus system to the HSPA. The petitioners argued that prevailing wages were inadequate to cover the living costs of a single plantation laborer, much less a family with children, and contended that the rules governing bonuses exploited workers. Bonus rules required men to work twenty days a month and women fifteen days; both men and women had to remain on the same plantation for an entire year in order to qualify for the bonus. The association proposed a wage hike, a revision of the bonus system, and the construction of day-care facilities for children of laborers so that both husband and wife could work.[6]

In response, the HSPA adopted a new bonus system on December 8, 1917, that reduced the bonus by about 20 percent. Ten days later, Royal D. Mead, HSPA secretary, wrote to the Association for Higher Wages expressing surprise over the petitioners' complaints about wages and the bonus system and indicating no interest in establishing day-care centers.[7] The association thereupon adopted a declaration condemning the planters' response and calling for a united labor movement. But because of widespread skepticism about Japanese motives in labor conflicts and wartime exhortations to loyalty and patriotism, the association could go no further. It eventually had to retreat and disband.[8]

In January 1918, 132 Japanese cane contractors in Hana, Maui, struck over a two-year lapse in renewing their expired contracts; and in October 1919, nearly a year after the war's end, Japanese plantation laborers throughout the territory prepared for a renewed push for higher wages.[9] The first to organize was the Young Men's Buddhist Association (YMBA) on the island of Hawaii, representing workers from five Hamakua plantations. Meeting on October 19, 1919, in Hilo, the association declared its intention to launch a mass movement of workers and to demand a wage increase, an eight-hour day, and an end to the bonus system.[10]

The sentiment for higher wages, like a wind-whipped cane fire, leaped from plantation to plantation. The Waialua YMBA held a mass rally on October 25; two days later, a committee to support the campaign for higher wages was formed in Honolulu. By mid November, workers at Aiea, Ewa, Waialua, Waimanalo, and Waipahu plantations had organized higher-wage associations, and before the end of November, workers on the outer islands had organized themselves into the Kauai Labor Federation and the Maui Labor Unions Federation.[11]

Unlike the 1909 strike, which had been spearheaded by urban intellectuals, the impetus for the 1919 higher-wage movement came from young people on the plantations. The vehicle for local labor organizations was an arm of the Buddhist church, the YMBA.[12] Ironically, Buddhist churches had been established on the plantations with the active encouragement and financial support of the planters. But the YMBAS served as a training ground for *nisei* youth in developing leadership skills and as a forum for studying and debating wages and working conditions on plantations.[13]

During the week of December 1, 1919, higher-wage representatives from various plantations met in Honolulu to consolidate their efforts in a flexible federated structure that accommodated both central and local control. The delegates proposed a representative assembly, a standing committee, four undersecretaries, a chief secretary, and four district agents. In effect, they created "a model of the American Federation of Labor by locating the power of the organization in the autonomous units of each plantation."[14] At the end of the five-day conference, the fifty-eight delegates announced the formation of the Federation of Japanese Labor and declared:

> We are laborers working on the sugar plantations of Hawaii.
>
> People know Hawaii as the paradise of the Pacific and as a sugar-producing country, but do they know that there are thousands of laborers who are suffering under the heat of the equatorial sun, in field and in factory, and who are weeping under 10 hours of hard labor and with the scanty pay of 77 cents a day?
>
> Hawaii's sugar! When we look at Hawaii as the country possessing 44 mills, with 230,000 acres of cultivated land area, as a region producing 600,000 tons of sugar annually we are impressed with the great importance of the position which sugar occupies among

the industries of Hawaii. We realize also that 50,000 laborers who, together with their families number about 160,000 are a majority of the total population of 250,000 in Hawaii. We consider it a great privilege and pride to live under the Stars and Stripes, which stands for freedom and justice, as a factor of this great industry and as a part of the labor of Hawaii.

"Look at the silent tombstones in every locality," the delegates directed. "Few are the people who visit these graves of our departed friends, but are they not emblems of Hawaii's pioneers in labor? Turn your eyes to the ever diligent laborers. They are not beautiful in appearance, but are they not a great factor of Hawaii's production?" Although "certain capitalists may regard us [as] ignorant creatures," they observed, workers helped to advance civilization and fought "to safe-guard justice and humanity as members of the great human family."[15] Inclusion within the category of humanity was an audacious first step. Once included, workers could expect wages and conditions befitting their status as "members of the great human family."

The federation made eight demands: an increase in the minimum wage for men from 77 cents per day to $1.25, and for women, from 58 to 95 cents a day; bonuses for men who worked for fifteen days or more each month and for women who worked for ten days or more; an eight-hour day for both field and mill laborers; an eight-week paid maternity leave for women workers; twice the regular wages for work on Sundays, legal holidays, and overtime; 60 percent of the profits to sharecroppers instead of the prevailing rate of 40 percent; increases in wages and bonuses for independent cane growers; and expanded and improved health-care and recreational facilities for workers.[16]

A delegation submitted the federation's resolution to the planters at the HSPA annual meeting on December 4, 1919. The labor leaders were apparently optimistic about their prospects for success; after all, it was widely known that most workers favored a wage hike of $3 a day, more than twice the amount being asked for by the federation. The planters nonetheless rejected the federation's demands.[17] Undeterred, the workers put forward a similar proposal three weeks later, with a carefully documented justification for their demands, believing that the planters would be compelled by reason. A survey of forty-five staples showed an increase of 40 to 208 percent compared with prewar prices, accounting for the following rise in the monthly cost of living:

	May 1916	November 1919	Increase
Single person	$24.81	$35.19	41.8%
Married couple	46.81	57.05	21.9
Couple with two children	52.36	75.72	44.6

Because men commonly earned only about $20 a month, even with bonuses, it was clear that the current wage levels had not kept pace with inflation.[18]

Once again, on January 14, 1920, the planters rejected the federation's demands as the work of "agitators." Yet they quietly had approved at a December 6, 1919, meeting of the HSPA trustees, the monthly payment of bonuses at the level demanded by the federation. They also established a Social Welfare Committee to improve plantation living conditions. They hoped that these measures would forestall a strike until the end of 1920 when large bonus packets would smother the spreading fires of discontent.[19] Their hopes were to be dashed.

Strike

On January 20, 1920, 2,600 Filipino sugar plantation workers and 300 Puerto Rican and Spanish workers walked off their jobs at several plantations on Oahu. Pablo Manlapit, leader of the Filipino Labor Union, was apparently unprepared for the walkout and lacked the resources for a sustained strike.[20] Despite the fact that the strike followed several years of labor organizing among Filipino and Japanese plantation workers, the Federation of Japanese Labor was likewise caught by surprise. Both unions had recognized the need for coordinated action, but the Filipinos had set January 19, 1920, as their strike date, while the Japanese planned a strike in the late spring or early summer, to coincide with the peak of the harvest.[21] To confuse matters further, Manlapit, under pressure from the Federation of Japanese Labor, tried to call off the strike, but the order failed to reach the rank and file. Thus, the walkout on January 20 was ill timed and botched.

The Federation of Japanese Labor reluctantly joined the strike on January 23, ordering a general walkout to begin on February 1 at the six Oahu plantations the Filipinos had struck—Aiea, Ewa, Kahuku, Waialua, Waimanalo, and Waipahu.[22] Apparently many Japanese workers had refused to cross Filipino picket lines, and thus the federation was drawn by circumstances into striking.[23] Before the scheduled walkout, the federation tried to head off a confrontation, but the HSPA refused to meet with them. Taking another tack, representatives of individual locals approached their plantation managers with the union's demands; that, too, was rejected.

In July 1920, the federation explained events that led to the strike in a pamphlet titled "Facts about the Strike on Sugar Plantations in Hawaii." "We passed through uneasy days," recalled the writer. "We could no longer keep our patience." The federation dispatched two of its secretaries to the HSPA to arrange for a meeting between planters and union leaders. Instead, HSPA secretary Mead informed them that " 'the Hawaiian Sugar Planters' Association will settle its own industrial troubles.' " Thus, recounted the writer, "the door was closed before our eyes; there was no more room for negotiation. The time had finally come when we were compelled to resort to our last means."

"We had tried every peaceful method we knew of," reminded the writer. "We do not wish to strike. We want peace and order; we love labor and production. But when we think of the group of capitalists who show no sympathy whatever toward the struggling laborers, turn deaf ears to their cries and reject their just and reasonable demands under the pretense that they are formulated by 'agitators,' we cannot remain silent. We must act. And so we went on strike . . . honorably and bravely, as laborers living under the great flag of freedom and justice."[24]

Laborers Living under the Great Flag

The strike involved 8,300 Filipino and Japanese workers, or about 77 percent of the plantation workforce on Oahu.[25] "The camps [at Aiea plantation] appeared deserted," wrote Takashi Tsutsumi, Federation of Japanese Labor secretary. "Everywhere the camps were shrouded in dead silence."[26] The strike brought plantation operations to a virtual halt, despite the announcement by Manlapit on February 8, 1920, that Filipinos would return to work. Apparently, Manlapit called off the strike after accepting a $25,000 bribe from HSPA attorney Frank Thompson, or after becoming distressed over the lack of financial support from the Federation of Japanese Labor.[27] Whatever the cause, Manlapit stated that he no longer believed that the strike was a simple industrial work action designed to secure higher wages but a Japanese scheme "to cripple the industries of the Territory of Hawaii in the hope that they may be taken over by an unscrupulous alien race."[28]

John Waterhouse, president of HSPA, declared that the planters "would fight to a finish, no matter what the cost or how long it took."[29] As in the 1909 strike, the planters hired over 2,000 strikebreakers—including Chinese, Filipinos, Hawaiians, Koreans, Portuguese, and even Japanese—reportedly at two to three times the wages being asked by the strikers.[30] The HSPA announced on February 14 that all strikers would be evicted from their plantation homes; evictions began four days later. According to an eyewitness, "A pitiable and even frightful scene that day [was] presented to us—household utensils and furniture thrown out and heaped up before our houses, doors tightly nailed that none might enter, sickly fathers with trunks and baggage, mothers with weeping babes in arms, the crying of children, and the rough voices of the plantation police officers."[31] Federation of Japanese Labor figures showed 12,020 persons displaced: 5,087 men, 2,796 women, and 4,137 children. Of the total, 1,472 were Filipinos who had cast their lot with their fellow workers.[32]

One account claimed that the HSPA timed the evictions to coincide with the peak of an influenza epidemic that was raging, and that the evictions took place over the protest of Acting Governor Curtis P. Iaukea.[33] Almost 6,000 expelled workers had to find temporary shelter in Honolulu, despite the unhealthy conditions there. The flu spread quickly in the crowded, makeshift tent cities, churches, and rented buildings, resulting in numerous deaths. By April 20, a Federation of Japanese Labor estimate showed ninety-five Filipinos and fifty-five Japanese dead because of the flu.[34] One federation report described the epidemic at Waialua:

> There were in Waialua on one occasion 800 patients; there were deaths every day; 43 died in 10 days. With one plantation hospital and one Japanese physician, these poor laborers struggled and suffered. Matters became worse and worse each day. The school building was changed into a temporary hospital. Wives weeping with their sick babies over the loss of their husbands, children made orphans overnight, husbands burying sons and wives on the same day—these could not be looked upon without tears. Lives went out like candle flames in a gust of wind.[35]

Meanwhile, Japanese businessmen, including the manager of Sumitomo Bank and presidents of the Japanese Chamber of Commerce and

Japanese Association of Hawaii, joined prominent whites in a committee headed by the Reverend Albert W. Palmer of Central Union Church.[36] They drafted a proposal called the Palmer Plan, which asked the Japanese federation to "recognize the unwisdom and peril of any such organization along national lines and that it therefore call off the present strike, abandon the field of plantation labor, and thus leave that field clear for an organization of the employees within the sugar industry itself." The proposal asked the HSPA to "announce that it will arrange for an election by secret ballot on each plantation of an employee's committee to confer with the plantation manager in securing the utmost cooperation between the management and the men."[37] Submitted on February 14, the Palmer Plan was essentially antiunion and in line with the American Plan that was gaining ground on the mainland. The American Plan advocated an open shop, implying that opposition to it was anti-American and associated with aliens and Bolsheviks.[38]

Initially, the Federation of Japanese Labor repudiated the Palmer Plan; on reflection, however, and after a meeting with the Palmer committee on February 27, the federation accepted the proposal. The following day, it announced: "The directors and secretaries of the Federation of Japanese Labor accept the general principles laid down in Mr. Palmer's plan and stand ready to take the steps to put it in operation just as soon as it shall appear that the Hawaiian Sugar Planters' Association has accepted the general principles of the said plan and also stand ready to put it in operation."[39] But the HSPA refused to reveal its position on the Palmer Plan until after the Japanese federation had signed the document, and so the proposal failed.

As the strike dragged on, morale and money ran low. Cracks began to appear within the Japanese strike community. The *Nippu Jiji* of March 24, 1920, reported a quarrel over tactics between Japanese federation leaders and Kinzaburo Makino, editor and publisher of the militant and supportive *Hawaii Hochi*, and federation members were accused of beating and kidnapping Japanese who opposed the strike. In early March, a Japanese laborer who had returned to work at Waimanalo was reportedly abducted by federation supporters, and a federation member was indicted on charges that he had kidnapped a conservative *nisei* at Waialua.[40]

Strike leaders sponsored theatrical performances to lift the sagging spirits of the workers, and on April 3 they organized a parade through the streets of Honolulu. The "77 cents parade"—77 cents was the daily wage of male workers—was scheduled to coincide with Hawaii's centennial celebration of the arrival of Christian missionaries. Makino, who organized the parade, believed it would put the planters on the defensive because of the adverse publicity it would generate outside Hawaii: "A 77¢ parade would be the best way to hit the planters in their weakest spot. A 77¢ parade will be sure to be taken up by the news wires and will expose the underhanded attitude of the capitalists to the world."[41]

Some 3,000 Japanese and Filipino men, women, and children paraded around Aala Park, then up King Street toward Alapai Street in downtown Honolulu. The marchers were divided into four groups: Unit A consisted of a band from Ewa plantation; unit B carried miniature American flags and banners; unit C carried portraits of President Abraham Lincoln; unit D was made up of women and children. Parade banners bore the strikers' messages: *77 Cents—This Is Our Pay for Ten Hours of Hard Labor; We Want to Live Like Americans; How Can We Live Like Americans on 77 Cents? All We Want Is $1.25; We Pledge to God That We Are Not Radicals; We Deeply Desire Prosperity for Hawaii; God Has Created Us Equal.* Children waved banners that read: *My Papa 77 Cents a Day* and *My Mama 58 Cents a Day.* Inscribed on Lincoln's picture was, *We Believe In Lincoln's Ideas.*[42] Commented the *Honolulu Star-Bulletin*: "Americans do not take kindly to the spectacle of several thousand alien Asiatics parading through the streets with banners flaunting their hatred of Americanism and American institutions and insulting the memory of the greatest American president since Washington."[43]

Because of the vicious anti-Japanese propaganda, the Federation of Japanese Labor called a meeting on April 20 and changed its name to the Hawaii Laborers' Association, dropping the ethnic label. Leaders urged all racial groups to join the association; resolved to expel any member "tainted with Communism, radicalism, or anarchism"; and applied for membership in the American Federation of Labor.[44] These changes were directed at the most damaging charge of the planters and the territorial government, that the strike was not a labor conflict but an expression of Japanese nationalism.

Finally, federation representatives defiantly resolved by unanimous vote: "We hereby pledge ourselves and declare that we will continue this strike until the Hawaiian Sugar Planters' Association express their sincerity and show their willingness to increase our wages, make changes in the bonus system, and take necessary steps for the improvement of our living quarters as well as the social life on the plantations."[45] Nonetheless, the vitality of the movement had been drained through nearly six months of intense struggle and suffering. The good fight would soon be over.

On July 1, at the bidding of Bishop Hosen Isobe of the Soto Mission, representatives of the strikers met with the HSPA's Waterhouse at the Alexander Young Hotel in Honolulu. The half-hour meeting was tense; the minutes of it recorded the encounter:

> Mr. Waterhouse stated that, as he had told Mr. Isobe, he would be perfectly willing at this time to meet with the Japanese laborers, provided they were in no way representing the Japanese Federation of Labor.
>
> He then stated that he understood that some of the men present were members of the Federation but that they were not present as representatives of the Federation.
>
> To this statement all of the laborers answered that Mr. Waterhouse was correct.
>
> Mr. Waterhouse then said that his simple statement was this: That the Hawaiian Sugar Planters Association would not at the present time consider any change whatsoever in the wage or bonus schedule. He also stated that he could not talk much with the people present at this meeting because they were not at present employees of the sugar plantations. He stated that the thing for them to do was to go back to work and resume the relationship of employee and employer; after they did that he was sure that the Managers would meet them and discuss their problems with them in the future, the same as they had done in the past. Mr. Waterhouse stated that he thought this was all he had to say.
>
> Mr. Waterhouse then shook hands with Mr. Isobe and all of the laborers present.
>
> Mr. Waterhouse then added that he wished to state that the Hawaiian Sugar Planters Association bore absolutely no ill-will against the laborers or the Japanese.
>
> Mr. E. Yokoo, formerly employed by Ewa Plantation Co., then made a few remarks, promising to work hard and peacefully.
>
> He was followed by Mr. Wakabayashi of Wahiawa (pineapple laborer) and Mr. Miyamasa, formerly employed by the Oahu Sugar Co. Their remarks were of the same tenor as those of Mr. Yokoo.[46]

On the same day, representatives of the Hawaii Laborers' Association held a special meeting and declared "that the great controversy between capital and labor on the sugar plantations of Hawaii, which has lasted for the past six months, has been completely settled by the mutual and confidential understanding between the magnanimous capitalists and the sincere laborers." The declaration appealed for "the maintenance of the spirit of Aloha which leads to mutual understanding and close coopera- tion" because "laborers have always known that industry could never exist without capital, and we believe that the capitalists are not slow to recognize that industry can not advance without labor."

Acknowledging the heavy costs borne by the strikers, the declaration addressed them in valediction: "You have faithfully stood to the last of this long strike, as inhabitants under the rule of the United States, respect- ing and obeying its laws, as members of this association, and as laborers, preserving your honor and dignity."[47] The strike was over.

The Reaping

When the stalks were ripe with sugar, cane fires were set to clear out the underbrush and burn off the razor-sharp leaves, facilitating the har- vest. Frequently, fires were started at sunset, and the sky would fill with smoke and boil like an angry volcano. But fires were also set as a form of resistance, before the young cane had ripened, destroying the season's bounty. The strike of 1920 was a cane fire that scorched earth and sky. The consequences of that act of resistance extended beyond the more than $600,000 spent by workers and the estimated $11.5 million lost by the six struck plantations in breaking the strike.[48] Like the morning after a cane fire, ashes could be seen everywhere.

The workers hoped for a new beginning. In their declaration announc- ing the end of the strike, the leaders of the Hawaii Laborers' Association recalled the extended hand of Waterhouse: "We hope that this joining of the hands of the capitalists and of the laborers will bring forth the flower of peace that will continue to bloom forever."[49] Waterhouse saw it another way: "No concessions whatsoever, either direct or implied, were made." He regretted that "we still have with us . . . the Japanese newspapers and Japanese and Filipino agitators whose main excuse for existence seems to be to create trouble." He added, "I doubt, however, that they care for a repetition of the lessons taught them this year."[50]

In November and December 1919, while the Association for Higher Wages was articulating a new dispensation for workers, military intel- ligence was busily following the activities of the officers and men of a

visiting Japanese cruiser, the *Yakumo*. Naval intelligence intercepted com-
munications between ship and shore, and army intelligence officers spied
on the sightseeing visitors and welcome parties hosted by local Japanese
residents.

Lieutenant Colonel George M. Brooke, an army intelligence officer,
lamented the limitations placed on the military by democracy and the
Constitution: "It is unfortunate that the United States has not stricter laws
in this territory for dealing with espionage, considering the strategic value
of Oahu in particular. A great need of this territory from the strategic point
of view is a commission form of government, stricter laws preventive of
espionage and more extensive prohibited areas in fortified zones." [51] Sentiment for "a commission form of government" was strengthened by the
strike of 1920 and became irresistible as the likelihood of war with Japan
increased.

During the strike, using the military to suppress the workers was considered, but Acting Governor Iaukea, mindful of the role of American
imperialism in the demise of the Hawaiian monarchy, declined to exercise
that option: "It is a matter of history that armed forces of the United States
were used to over-awe the Hawaiians at the time of the overthrow of the
monarchy," he reminded his detractors, "and there seems to be a desire
to repeat this measure of intimidation." [52]

The army was unimpressed with Iaukea's history lesson. Army officers bypassed the territorial government by contacting plantation managers directly and asking them to keep army intelligence informed of any
"emergency arising from the Strike." [53] The army's circumvention of the
territorial government reflected its belief that containment of the "Japanese problem" would require that democracy take a back seat to national
defense.

The workers saw oppression as their problem. Tsutsumi, the Federation of Japanese Labor's secretary, wrote that the strike was brought on
not by various "isms" such as nationalism or Bolshevism but from "the
heart of men oppressed for ages by the capitalists." He saw the strike as
a struggle of the working class "to safeguard their livelihood against the
tyranny and encroachments of capitalists." [54] About a year after the strike,
Tsutsumi wrote:

> If destruction of present condition is dangerous, I am a man of
> dangerous thoughts.

If all defiance of power and dignity is disquieting, I am decidedly a disquieting person.

But without progress in present condition, there would be no freedom in obedience to power and dignity.

In unprogressive community, corruption and stagnation prevail.

. . . If humanity is equal, if freedom of individual is approved, I shall not hesitate to defy the long established power and dignity, in order to safeguard a more equal and free livelihood.[55]

The planters, the territorial government, and the army persisted in portraying a movement that sought a minimum daily wage of 95 cents and $1.25, maternity rights and child care, and an eight-hour workday as a race war. The cane fires, sparked by the democratic impulses of plantation workers, would have an effect for years to come.

Hand across the Sea

Early in the strike, the planters dismissed the movement for decent wages and better living conditions as an anti-American plot aimed at the takeover of Hawaii's sugar industry. On February 6, 1920, Waterhouse declared: "The action taken by the Japanese Federation of Labor is, as we see it, an anti-American movement designed to obtain control of the sugar business of the Hawaiian Islands."[56] That message was amplified by the *Honolulu Star-Bulletin* and *Pacific Commercial Advertiser*. The January 27, 1920, *Advertiser* reduced the strike to a single question: "Is Hawaii to be an American territory or is it to be an Oriental province?" The paper denounced Buddhist priests, Japanese newspaper editors, and other "subjects of the Mikado" as "agitators" who had stirred up the placid waters of planter–worker relations. "What we face now," warned the *Advertiser*, "is an attempt on the part of an alien race to cripple our principal industry and to gain dominance of the American territory of Hawaii."

The campaign to discredit the strike and point an accusing finger at the Japanese in Hawaii also alleged a link between that domestic community and a foreign power—Japan. Despite the fact that the Japanese consul in Honolulu, Yeiichi Furuya, and his successor, Chonosuke Yada, publicly disavowed any connection with the Federation of Japanese Labor and chastised the union, Hawaii's rulers saw the sinister hand of Imperial Japan reaching across the Pacific. In a January 30, 1920, editorial entitled "The Hand across the Sea," the *Advertiser* charged: "The inference is plain and unmistakable: The Japanese government . . . is back of the strike, it is back of the organization of Japanese labor in the American Territory of Hawaii; it reaches out its arm and directs the energies and activities of its nationals here in these American islands, just as it directs those at home." Three days later, the *Advertiser* elaborated on that theme by citing Japan's exploits in Asia:

> The strike is an attempt on the part of the Japanese to obtain control of the sugar industry. It is in line with Japanese policy wherever they colonize. It is a part of the Japanization of Korea, Manchuria, Eastern Inner Mongolia, Shantung, and Formosa. In those countries Japan's methods have met with striking success and the Japanese evidently think they can use them with equal success in Hawaii. They evidently fail to realize that it is one thing to bluff, bulldoze and bamboozle weak oriental peoples and another thing to try to coerce Americans.[57]

On February 13, in the midst of the strike, the *Honolulu Star-Bulletin* editorialized:

> What the alien Japanese priests, editors and educators are aiming at, in our opinion, is general recognition of their claim that they can absolutely control the 25,000 Japanese plantation laborers of this territory. If they could gain that point they would be as completely the masters of Hawaii's destiny as if they held title to the land and the growing cane. They would be the autocratic dictators of Hawaii's industrialism. Hawaii's industries would prosper or languish at their whim. If the alien agitators could establish their pretensions to control of labor, Hawaii would be as thoroughly Japanized, so far as its industrial life is concerned, as if the Mikado had the power to name our governor and direct our political destiny.
>
> Had the agitators been successful in this attempt, had the planters yielded and consented to deal with them, Japanism would have become triumphant in Hawaii. . . . And this is what the *Star-Bulletin* had in mind, when at the very outset of the present strike, it declared that the issue involved was this and nothing else: Is control of the industrialism of Hawaii to remain in the hands of Anglo-Saxons or is it to pass into those of alien Japanese agitators? This is what we meant in declaring that back of the strike is a dark conspiracy to Japanize this American territory.

. . . Never lose sight of the real issue: Is Hawaii to remain American or become Japanese? A compromise of any nature or any degree
with the alien agitators would be a victory for them and an indirect
but nonetheless deadly invasion of American sovereignty in Hawaii.
The American citizen who advocates anything less than resistance
to the bitter end against [the] arrogant ambition of the Japanese
agitators is a traitor to his own people.[58]

The imagery of the yellow peril was not confined to a press eager for
sensationalism; it was accorded legitimacy by respected leaders in the
territory. Even Acting Governor Iaukea, who had written that he was
"convinced that the racial issue has been deliberately emphasized to cloud
the economic issue,"[59] cautioned H. H. Miyazawa, secretary of the Federation of Japanese Labor, in a letter dated February 26: "First of all let me
impress upon you the delicate situation the entire Japanese community
is thrown in by the suspicion that has been spread throughout the community that there is a racial or nationalistic conspiracy behind the present
strike. It is therefore of the utmost importance to all the Japanese people
in this Territory that this suspicion be allayed."[60]

The idiom suited the purposes of white supremacy by fragmenting
the working class on the basis of race. In attempting to break the strike,
planters manipulated race and ethnicity by allegedly bribing Manlapit, by
inciting discontent among the Filipino union leadership with the Federation of Japanese Labor, and by hiring Filipinos and other Asian groups as
scabs. No friend of the Filipinos, the planters depicted them as "ignorant"
and "mere catspaws": "As regards the Filipinos, there is good reason to
think they are mere catspaws, used by wily agitators to further the interests of the subjects of the Mikado. . . . If there shall be violence and
lawlessness in connection with the strike, it is a safe prediction that the
ignorant Filipinos . . . will be the goats?"[61]

The impact of the strike cannot be completely appreciated by a summation of its financial costs or the degree to which the objectives of planters
and workers had been achieved. The strikers resumed their role under
planter hegemony and without any concessions or even a recognition of
their right to organize and bargain collectively. Yet, three months later
and without fanfare, the HSPA abolished the racial differential wage scale
(at least theoretically), raised wages by 50 percent, and allowed monthly
bonuses.[62] Further, the planters expanded worker recreation and social
welfare programs and made extensive improvements in housing and sani-

tation. The HSPA's Social Welfare Committee formed an Industrial Service Bureau in 1922 to promote and coordinate these efforts and, from 1922 to 1925, spent more than $3 million on housing repair and new construction.[63] Despite these gains for workers, the instruments of oppression grew in scope and sophistication.

The planters and the territorial government both employed racism to isolate and weaken the Japanese, identifying white supremacy with the national interest. They launched a national campaign to reintroduce Chinese migrant labor, hoping to rid themselves of the Japanese.

Chapter 5

In the National Defense

*Hawaii may have its labor problems . . . but we
believe that the question of National Defense and
the necessity to curtail the domination of the
alien Japanese in every phase of the Hawaiian life
is more important than all the other problems
combined.*
　　　　　　　—Hawaiian Labor Commission

Feigned Necessity

Racism gained a national hearing in the U.S. Congress,
in the executive branch, and among the American public
through an orchestrated campaign by Hawaii's planters and
the territorial government. They merged race with national
security for the purpose of displacing Japanese plantation
laborers with Chinese migrants.

On April 20, 1921, at the suggestion of a new HSPA
president, E. Faxon Bishop, a special message was sent to
the territorial legislature. After several days of meetings
with Hawaii's delegate to Congress, Jonah Kalanianaole; the
president of the territorial Senate, Charles F. Chillingworth;
House Speaker H. L. Holstein; Attorney General Harry
Irwin; editors George F. Nellist and Sam Trissel of the *Star-
Bulletin* and *Advertiser*; George P. Denison, president of the
Chamber of Commerce; Albert Horner, president of the
Pineapple Association; E. Faxon Bishop of the HSPA; W. H.
McInerny, representing the retail merchants; and Walter F.
Dillingham, representing the railway interests, Governor
Charles J. McCarthy's message called "attention to the grave
labor shortage existing through the Islands of the Territory

and pointing out that a serious loss to the Territory would result from that shortage unless it be relieved through Governmental agencies."[1] Six days later, the territorial legislature passed a joint resolution,

> requesting that the Congress of the United States of America provide, by appropriate legislation, for the introduction or immigration into the Territory of Hawaii of such a number of persons, including orientals, as may be required to meet the situation; limiting such immigration, however, to such numbers as will not operate to increase the number of persons of any alien nationality in the Territory at any one time beyond twenty-five per cent of the total population of the Territory; and providing further that such persons be admitted for limited periods of time, be obliged to confine their efforts to agricultural labor and domestic service, and be guaranteed and secured their return to their respective countries upon the expiration of such limited periods of time.[2]

Despite the vague reference to aliens "including orientals," Hawaii's planters and legislators clearly had the Chinese in mind. As baldly put by one planter, the Chinese "are efficient, mind their own business, will never strike or meddle with matters that do not concern them. They remain by preference socially isolated, and would never know enough about American questions to try to dictate to us how to run the government under which they draw their pay." With Chinese migrants filling the need for manual labor and with American citizens ("whites, Hawaiians, Portuguese and possibly Filipinos") occupying skilled positions, declared the planter, "slowly this would eliminate the class [Japanese] that is now holding places as tradesmen, storekeepers, mechanics, fishermen, coffee planters, and give them to citizens who have the interests of our country at heart. Such a move would be the best method to Americanize Hawaii."[3]

As authorized by the territorial resolution, the governor appointed a Hawaii Emergency Labor Commission on April 29, 1921, and directed the commission and its chair, Walter F. Dillingham, to proceed to Washington, D.C., to assist Kalanianaole in guiding the resolution through Congress. The commission's activities have been thoroughly documented by the late scholar and social activist John Reinecke, in a book whose title, *Feigned Necessity*, aptly captures the work of the commission—fabricating the need for labor.

But feigning necessity was only the beginning of an ambitious effort to mobilize political support to abrogate or sidestep the Chinese Exclusion Act of 1882. The feat called for some adroit moves to get around anti-Asianists—especially West Coast politicians and organized white labor—and the military. The "Japanese menace" provided a splendid rationale for reintroducing Chinese migrant labor because it was an argument on which all segments of the opposition could agree. It proved so appealing that it quickly became the singular focus of attention, overshadowing the planters' original appeal for labor relief.

Yellow Perilism

The commissioners sailed for the mainland on May 8, 1921, with data supplied by the HSPA for their lobbying effort.[4] They arrived in the nation's capital May 18. Three days later, they met with President Warren G. Harding, who, according to Dillingham, "received us most cordially and showed a real interest both in our situation and in a desire to help solve the problem."[5] Hearings on the Hawaii petition were held before the House Committee on Immigration and Naturalization from June 21 to 30 and on July 7. In his opening statement, Dillingham cited Japanese laborers, who "have ceased to appreciate the opportunities given them," as a cause of Hawaii's labor shortage. Instead, claimed Dillingham, they "now aim collectively to revolutionize the control of agricultural industries to the end that Japanese capital acquire substantial planting interests for itself, instead of merely contributing the labor for those interests under American control."[6]

Dillingham went further, applying the lesson learned from the West Coast to the situation in Hawaii. "The experience they are having in California is repeated in Hawaii," he observed. The Japanese had even offered to buy a sugar plantation, but "we would not entertain it. We did not care to go into it further at all, believing that if the start was made, the entering wedge driven home, it would be only a question of time until the control of our industry would pass into alien hands, just as surely as the potato business of California and the strawberry business of California . . . have passed over into the control of these people."[7]

The 1920 strike, testified Dillingham, demonstrated that Japanese nationalism and racial solidarity prevailed over Americanism, even among the educated *nisei*, thus shattering any illusion about "the intermingling of the two nations" or "the bringing of them [Japanese] into the full American spirit."[8]

The commission hired E. P. Irwin, editor of the *Pacific Commercial Advertiser* during the 1920 strike, to prepare a report "on the Japanese phase of the situation in the Territory with respect to labor supply and the contemporary political and economic situations."[9] Irwin's work became the basis for the commission's confidential brief, "Hawaii and the Japanese," which was distributed to the House and Senate committees considering the Hawaiian labor petition and was "widely circulated among influential persons in Washington and elsewhere." Although not formally submitted as evidence for the record, the brief was, in effect, an offical statement of the territorial government's position.[10]

"No intelligent consideration of the present acute labor problem in the Territory of Hawaii, particularly as it affects the agricultural interests of the Territory, is possible without some knowledge of the history of the Japanese in the Islands and of the situation as it especially concerns them today," the opening statement in the government brief declared.[11] In recent years, Irwin noted, the Japanese have not been content to remain agricultural laborers and "now aim collectively at the control of the agricultural industries of the Territory." The goal of Japanese workers was "to secure control of established industries, or to make continued American control difficult and expensive" by striking or withholding their labor, an effective strategy because they constituted such a large segment of the island's total workforce.

The Japanese, including the American-educated *nisei*, the document alleged, had no desire to assimilate. Whenever a conflict arose, "the great majority of these young American citizens of Japanese birth have stood firmly on the side of their parents and their parents' country, against Americans and America." The number of Japanese in Hawaii, Irwin wrote, was "cause for apprehension" and their high birthrate and low death rates were "further cause for alarm." The rapid increase in Japanese attending public schools drove white children to private schools "where their language cannot be contaminated by the 'pigin [*sic*] English' of . . . Japanese children." Nearly all Japanese schoolteachers were aliens with little understanding or respect for American institutions, and the tendency of the language schools was "un-American and to a large extent even anti-American."

A section devoted to the general attitude of the Japanese recalled how when Japanese workers first arrived in Hawaii, they achieved the reputation of being industrious, obedient, and reliable. "Of late years," however, "and particularly during the past two years, they have shown an increasing tendency to become arrogant, insolent, domineering and truculent." That change was dramatically illustrated in the strike of 1920, which was "planned and fomented by the Japanese language press, the principals and heads of Japanese language schools, and the Buddhist priests" and was organized "to obtain economic domination of the sugar industry of Hawaii." Although there was no evidence to show that Tokyo directed the strike, "it is certain that some of the strike leaders led their followers to believe that such was the case."[12] Moreover, the strikers attacked America: "American culture was derided, American principles and ideals ridiculed, the Christian religion was denounced as savagery, and the American people were branded as a race of barbarians and beasts."

The question of Japanese landownership in Hawaii did not pose the same problem that it did on the West Coast because of the oligarchy's virtual monopoly of land. The privileges of U.S. citizenship, including the right to vote, ultimately presented a greater threat to white Hawaii, the report predicted; it was "inevitable" that the Japanese would "dominate the political situation" and "elect [the] legislature and other governing bodies, thereby controlling the destinies of the Territory."[13] By introducing economic competition in the form of Chinese migrants, the brief argued, many Japanese would be driven back to Japan, "thus removing to a considerable extent the danger of Hawaii's becoming a community dominated, both industrially and politically, by an electorate of alien blood."

The document concluded: "The Japanese problem is one of the gravest that today confronts Hawaii." Although working hard to solve the problem, the territory was severely handicapped by restrictive laws that were suited to the mainland but not to the islands. "Hawaii believes that her political and industrial salvation lies in securing labor from some other source than Japan, provided this labor is inherently able to work in her fields and neutralize the effect of the large alien race that now predominates in the Territory." Cheap labor, it was argued, would turn the wheels of industry, displace Japanese workers, and save the territory from alien domination. The "Japanese menace" thus brokered the wedding of capitalism to the national security.

That marriage struck a responsive chord with California's congressmen. During the House committee hearings, the following exchange took place between Royal D. Mead, former HSPA secretary, and committee member John E. Raker, representing northeastern California.

Declared Mead: "I have had to do with the two different strikes we have had out there of the Japanese, and I have never had any delusions in regard to Americanizing them. . . . Without doubt, as a race, the absolute coherence and solidarity of the Japanese is marvelous."

"Irrespective of whether they were born in Hawaii or not?" questioned Raker.

"Absolutely, sir," Mead responded.

Raker followed up: "And this is one of the things you have to contend with?"

A somber Mead replied: "That is the big thing we have to contend with. Not only do we have to contend with it from an industrial standpoint, but it is a thing the United States Government has to contend with from a military standpoint." [14]

Predictably, members of Congress from California were among the most vocal anti-Asians and were adamantly opposed to the commissioners' proposal to import Chinese migrant laborers. John I. Nolan, head of the California delegation, testified at the committee hearings on behalf of the California State Federation of Labor, the Asiatic Exclusion League, and other organizations opposed to Asian migration: "Those of us who were raised in California know how much of a menace the Chinaman is," offered Nolan. A Chinese was acceptable only "because many years ago he ceased to be an economic menace." The Chinese exclusion law was passed to rid America of the "Chinese menace" and "we do not want Chinese to enter into any of our possessions any more than the Japs." [15]

Nolan argued that exclusion was the answer to the "Japanese menace," including restrictions on the mobility of those already in the United States, such as limiting them to unskilled labor and preventing them from owning or leasing land. "I do know something about the Japanese and their methods," declared Nolan. "Whether it is in California or Hawaii, there is nobody that has a closer feeling of kin than the Japanese." Ethnic solidarity, opined Nolan, governed Japanese behavior whether in business or in "trying to capture some fertile valley in the State of California or some place else." [16] Despite disagreeing with Hawaii's commissioners over the means by which the "Japanese threat" could be overcome, Nolan and his fellow mainland anti-Asians agreed with the Hawaiian delegation's end— to nullify the menace posed by the alien race.

After a second round of hearings, held from July 22 to August 21, Secretary of State Charles Evans Hughes asked that action on the Hawaiian resolution be delayed until after the Washington Disarmament Conference. Hughes feared that anti-Japanese oratory resounding in the halls of Congress might be embarrassing to the United States and might impede the work of the conference. The commissioners considered the secretary of state's request at its September 29 meeting and unanimously agreed to postpone all public action on the resolution until after the adjournment of the disarmament conference.[17] Nonetheless, the commissioners decided to continue the work of lobbying individual members of Congress and the American public through a public relations campaign intended to create "a friendly public sentiment toward the resolution."[18]

Taking It to the People

Creating that "friendly public sentiment" required tapping the deep wells of anti-Japanese sentiment without muddying the waters of anti-Asianism generally. The commissioners hoped to capitalize on anti-Japanese, not anti-Chinese, racism to achieve their end: Chinese labor migration. Edgar Henriques was appointed on July 28, 1921, by Hawaii's governor to lead the public education task. Henriques recruited the editors of Hawaii's two leading newspapers "to active publicity and advisory duty," employed three stenographers, and organized a letter-writing campaign directed at members of Congress. He ordered the Department of Public Instruction to furnish pictures of "school children where the Japanese predominate" that would bear the caption children "who will . . . be allowed to vote and make it possible to control the political situation," and he asked members of the oligarchy to appeal to fellow alumni of Harvard, Yale, and Stanford who had gone into government service.[19]

In a "Personal and Confidential" letter dated August 23, Dillingham mapped the basic strategy of the propaganda campaign to the new governor, Wallace Rider Farrington. The object was "to place the real seriousness of our problem before the American people in order to overcome the opposition that is certain to be inspired by the deliberate misrepresentations of Gompers [American Federation of Labor president] and others." The commissioners, he reported, were in agreement that the economic argument of the need for labor would not sway Congress, and "the only ground on which we will be able to secure the relief we seek is the one of the danger of losing control of the Territory." Nevertheless, for "home consumption," wrote Dillingham, "I agree with what I presume is the opinion there, that discussion of nationalistic features should be avoided." On the mainland, "looking to influence with Congressmen and others . . . the nationalistic and political features of the problem must be emphasized to accomplish results."[20]

Dillingham's approach hit the mark. Individuals and groups on the mainland rallied to the cause when they were awakened to the realization that Hawaii's "Japanese menace" was not a distant tremor but one that sent shock waves to California and, indeed, to the nation as a whole. As San Franciscan W. D. Caldwell put it in a letter to a friend in Honolulu, Californians should "support you in this fight that you are making in the interests of the white race in America."[21] The Los Angeles and San Francisco Chambers of Commerce, California Manufacturers' Association, Foreign Trade Club, and San Francisco Electrical Development League all sent endorsements to the commission. The San Francisco Chamber of Commerce sent a delegation to Hawaii that included an ardent anti-Asian and influential newspaper publisher, V. S. McClatchy.

McClatchy had in 1919 proposed a plan for Chinese bonded labor similar to the Hawaiian government's 1921 resolution, so Dillingham actively pursued his endorsement. Like Hawaii's proposal, McClatchy's scheme sought to solve the "Japanese problem" in California and ensure a supply of cheap labor. His solution included canceling the Gentlemen's Agreement but enacting a Japanese exclusion law, as well as a law that specifically excluded picture brides, barred Asians—including those born in America—from citizenship, and allowed the entrance of Chinese workers for fixed periods and specific jobs.[22] Despite McClatchy's repudiation of his 1919 plan, Dillingham lobbied him "in a distinctly Californian tone, emphasizing the entrance of Japanese into small business as a danger to American control of Hawaii." In the end, McClatchy admitted to Dillingham: "I do not recommend the legislation but concede something should be done immediately and know of no other or better plan."[23]

Dillingham also courted McClatchy's confederate in the Asiatic Exclusion League, former California Senator James D. Phelan. In correspondence, Phelan revealed to Dillingham his opposition to reintroducing Chinese migrants to Hawaii, despite acknowledging that the Chinese were "far less objectionable than the Japanese." Might not Hawaii's displaced Japanese, he asked, become California's problem? "The planters ought to arrange to deport the Japanese to Japan if they are given an opportunity to introduce labor capable of supplanting them," he suggested.

In the fall of 1921, Phelan wrote "The Hawaiian Situation," which was later entered into the *Congressional Record.* California and Hawaii, he charged, were the "two alarming breeding grounds endangering the whole country." The situation in Hawaii, especially, posed a danger to the national security because "it is inconsistent with our national interests to harbor in the islands a people, now composing one-half their entire population, who owe loyalty and military service to Japan and can not be Americanized." The strike of 1920, wrote Phelan, demonstrated the reality of that threat in the near-takeover of the territory's plantations.

His solution, similar to McClatchy's repudiated scheme, involved canceling the Gentlemen's Agreement, passing a Japanese exclusion law, and denying citizenship to American-born Asians. It also proposed a land settlement program for whites to induce their immigration to Hawaii. Meanwhile, as a temporary expedient, Phelan endorsed the commission's resolution, "to gain time . . . and give our Government a chance to turn around, like the strategic move of a general confronted with stubborn facts and an agile enemy." [24]

Next to the West Coast anti-Chinese forces, organized labor posed the most formidable obstacle to the passage of the Hawaii Emergency Labor Commission's petition. Dillingham anticipated labor's opposition. Thus, one of the commission's first acts was to meet with the president of the Central Labor Council of Honolulu, George W. Wright. Generally, labor leaders in Hawaii were unconvinced by Dillingham's contention that Chinese migrants would displace the Japanese, force their outmigration, and reduce their competition with white tradesmen. Observed Wright of discussions with the commissioners: "Considerable time was wasted trying to develop a nationalistic and racial sentiment to cloud the issue." [25]

In congressional testimony, both Wright and Gompers of the AFL rejected the commission's racebaiting and instead offered a class interpretation of Hawaii's plantation struggles. Wright pointed to planter mismanagement and argued that the strike of 1920 was an industrial action, not a nationalistic movement. Gompers added that the right of collective bargaining was "a natural and inherent right which I would support." He charged that the idea that the strike was based on Japanese nationalism or ethnic solidarity "is purely an invention of the sugar planters and their adherents and associates in the United States." [26]

But organized labor's opposition to the reintroduction of Chinese workers was not prompted by a desire to prevent planter abuses of "coolie" labor. Similarly, its class analysis of the 1920 strike and its defense of collective bargaining can hardly be perceived as pro-Japanese.[27] The history of white organized labor, and particularly of Gompers and the AFL, belies any hint of a class alliance between white and Asian workers. Instead, the consistent position of white organized labor, both on the mainland and in Hawaii, was that Asian workers lowered wages and threatened white labor. As declared in a resolution of the Iron Moulders Union No. 350 in Honolulu: "To-day we are competing with the Jap, which is bad enough, and if the planters are allowed to flood this Territory with cheap foreign labor we Americans will be compelled to leave here."[28]

In testimony before the House committee, Wright outlined the strategy of white labor for combating the "Japanese menace": "[Our] efforts have been directed with this point of view, of keeping the Japanese on the plantations as far as possible. Our fear, our menace, has been the upward crowding of the Japanese, and we have believed that any means that could be devised to keep the Japanese on the plantation where he was originally brought to do his work, would be the solution of the problem."[29] The efforts of white labor—to keep the Japanese on the plantations and restrict their "upward crowding"—clearly supported white supremacy and its social reproduction.

When the Senate hearings on the Hawaiian resolution finally resumed on June 7, 1922, most of the arguments for and against the proposal had been heard. But the work of the commission—"feigned necessity"—had dramatically changed from establishing the need for labor in the territory to magnifying the threat of the "Japanese menace." "If it were not for the Japanese menace," asked the committee chair, LeBaron B. Colt, of Hawaii delegate Frank F. Baldwin, "would you be here asking for this extraordinary legislation?" Responded Baldwin: "I hardly think so, Senator. A great many of the Japanese who are born in the Islands go back to Japan to be educated. After they get their education, they come back to Hawaii, which they can do, being American citizens. Their feeling is Japanese. There are a few who are making every effort to become Americanized, but as a race they do not assimilate with the Americans."

Baldwin's answer prompted California's Senator Hiram Johnson to exclaim: "Once Japanese, always Japanese; and you can make all the four-power agreements and all the alliances you want to, and they will remain

Japanese to the end." Two decades later, an army general in charge of the defense of the West Coast during World War II, John L. De Witt, echoed Johnson's sentiments when he justified the mass removal and confinement of Japanese Americans by saying, "A Jap's a Jap. It makes no difference whether he is an American citizen or not. . . . Theoretically, he is still a Japanese and you can't change him. You can't change him by giving him a piece of paper."[30]

The White Light of Publicity

Even before the congressional committee resumed its hearings in June, Dillingham had proposed to Secretary of Labor James J. Davis the appointment of a federal investigating commission. On May 18, 1922, during a planning meeting of the Hawaiian commission, Dillingham reported on preliminary arrangements for the appointment of "a disinterested commission" to investigate conditions in the territory and recommend some form of labor relief. In fact, Dillingham tried to secure a federal commission that would simultaneously favor Hawai's plan and have influence within the AFL. He thus recommended that the five commission members consist of two from the Labor Department, a member of the American Legion, and two "conservative and friendly men" who were prominent in the AFL.[31]

In a wire to Governor Farrington, Dillingham reported on a June 19, 1922, meeting with President Harding, who "was extremely cordial and showed every disposition to help our proposition along." After Dillingham had explained to him "the effort we had made to sidetrack Gompers and his opposition" and had outlined the advantages of a federal commission, Harding asked Dillingham to have the governor send him a formal request for a commission, "outlining the necessity for early investigation looking to the relief of the situation which confronts us in Hawaii."[32] Dillingham advised Farrington on what the general thrust of his letter should be, underscoring its public relations function: "Your letter will be basis for both executive action and *then publicity* and it can not place too much stress on danger of losing American control through preponderance in numbers of Japanese."[33]

In his response two days later, Farrington stated that the labor relief resolution being considered in Congress was simply a stopgap measure "to tide over a field labor crisis" in the territory. Referring to the Japanese, the governor wrote: "Seventy-five per cent of the common labor of our agricultural industries is performed by a single alien element, and a very determined section of that alien element has shown a disposition to assume a position that threatens the American control of Hawaii's agricultural industries." The 1920 strike, declared the governor, "if successfully carried through would have meant complete domination of the sugar and pineapple industries by Japanese labor leaders, alien by birth, and, so far as I know, having no sympathy with or interest in American industry or American principles, except as a means to further their own aims." The Japanese, he wrote, "used every art they could command of threat, and appeal to racial and national solidarity, to establish, consolidate and perpetuate their control of industry, which would mean eventual economic and political control."

Despite his demurrer that "there is no ill will against the Japanese," Farrington conceded that Hawaii's "racial elements are out of balance and are seriously in need of adjustment," and he predicted that a restored balance would guarantee "permanent American strength in the future." The governor assured the president that "a sincere spirit of loyalty to our country and steadfast belief in the destiny of Hawaii as a friendly and prosperous American outpost" prompted the territory's appeal for labor relief and request for a special investigating commission. "We do not fear the white light of accurate publicity," wrote Farrington in his public letter, "or doubt the conclusion of intelligent discussion."[34]

After some delay, on November 9, 1922, President Harding announced the formation of the Hawaiian Labor Commission and its members: Hywel Davies, commissioner of conciliation for the Labor Department; John Donlin, president of the Building Trades Department of the AFL; O. W. Hartwig, president of the Oregon Federation of Labor; Fred Keightly, secretary of the Amalgamated Association of Iron, Steel, and Tin Workers, AFL; and L. E. Sheppard, president of the Brotherhood of Railway Conductors. Anticipating the president's announcement,[35] Farrington wired Secretary of Labor Davis on October 23 to advise the secretary on the areas of the commission's investigation:

> First: agricultural industries, treatment of labor, and labor requirements, including character of labor best suited to meet emergency;
> Second: extent to which Japanese have invaded all lines of business, their preponderance in numbers, and resulting danger of Japanese economic and political control;

Third: permament plan for establishing balance of races in order to guarantee continued American control.[36]

The governor's proposed plan for a balance of races was no doubt a concession to critics of the original petition, which did not address the Americanization of Hawaii. In its latest form, Hawaii's request for Chinese labor migration was presented as a temporary expedient until a way could be devised to attract sufficient whites to the territory to achieve a racial "balance." The scenario now involved Chinese migrants displacing the Japanese, the return migration of unemployed Japanese to Japan, and white immigrants gradually replacing the Chinese.[37]

The 1920 strike figured prominently in Secretary Davis's November 3 instructions to the new commissioners: "In 1920 a strike occurred among the sugar plantation workers in the Hawaiian Islands. . . . It is alleged that as a result of this strike many [Japanese] left the plantations and went into other lines of endeavor, thereby creating a serious labor shortage in the sugar industry." To meet that shortage, the territorial government requested special legislation to permit the importation of "considerable numbers of Chinese Coolies to work on the plantations."

"The object of the investigation," explained Davis, "would be to determine the advisability of the legislation from the standpoint of the welfare of the Islands and American workers and interests there. Investigation should, therefore, cover every phase of the labor situation with definite recommendations to the Secretary of Labor as to what recommendations for legislation should be made to Congress."[38]

The commissioners arrived in Honolulu at the end of November and met with the governor, members of the Hawaii Emergency Labor Commission, HSPA directors, army and navy commanders, and "the heads of the various organized interests in Hawaii." Ostensibly giving the federal commissioners free rein, these men made certain that the commissioners heard "the right contacts" and "carried away a suitably unfavorable impression of the Japanese and of local labor agitators."[39] Apparently the ruse worked, perhaps all too well with regard to the commissioners' perception of the "Japanese menace." When the commissioners departed for the West Coast on December 16, they carried with them a quantity of material furnished by the HSPA together with a confidential statement by the army commander of the Hawaiian Department called the Summerall report.

The Specter of Alien Domination

On January 5, 1923, the federal commission issued its findings in a report submitted to Labor Secretary Davis. The secretary had a preview of the commission's conclusions as early as December 27 when the commissioners wired him from Hawaii: "Commission did not find any serious shortage at present. . . . Therefore do not recommend adoption of pending resolution. Commission fully appreciates danger of menace of alien domination by one race and strongly recommends question of national defense should receive prompt remedial legislation."[40]

In its formal report, the commission identified two areas of concern: the need for an adequate supply of labor and the danger of alien domination through a labor monopoly. The commission attributed the current crisis to the territory's past practice of meeting its plantation labor requirements through "alien labor," Chinese, Japanese, and Filipino. Its composition heavily weighted on the side of white labor, the commission urged that labor recruitment "be handled in the future with greater regard to the well being of the Territory as part of the United States, and in a way that will prevent the possible domination of the Industrial, Commercial, Social or Political life in the Territory by an alien race."[41]

Instead of boosting the territorial petitioners' cause, the federal commission rejected the claim of a labor shortage and recommended against Hawaii's proposal to import Chinese migrant workers. (The report did favor the migrant labor solution, but only in the event of a documented labor emergency.) In fact, concerns over labor were seen as trivial because of the obvious falsity of the claim, in marked contrast to the immediacy and reality of the "menace of alien domination," a concern that superseded all others. "The question of National Defense," stressed the commission, "submerges all others into insignificance. If these Islands are to remain American, the assured control of the Political, Industrial, Commercial, Social and Educational life of the Islands must also be American."[42]

The commission concluded, "Hawaii may have its labor problems and the Commission believes these problems can be solved from time to time as the emergency arises, but *we believe that the question of National Defense and the necessity to curtail the domination of the alien Japanese in every phase of the Hawaiian life is more important than all the other problems combined.*"[43]

The commission reported a general climate of fear among Hawaii's white population. So widespread was this fear that "no one on the Island cared to discuss the Japanese menace publicly because so much of the life of the Island is now dependent upon Japanese labor." Accordingly, in order to encourage candor, the commission closed the proceedings to the public, generally heard only one witness at a time, and had no steno- graphic notes taken. White and Hawaiian women, the report noted, were "very much more outspoken than the men and one has to hear their analysis of the danger and menace of this alien race to fully *appreciate the atmosphere of fear in which the average white American forming only 10% of the population is already living in.*" The particular sensitivity of women to the "Japanese menace" was in part attributed to the "infiltration" of Japa- nese into the homes of white people. "We have only to note that the domestic service of the Islands is in hands of Japanese men and women. This robs the family of much of its privacy and freedom of frank discussion of this phase of Hawaii's real problem." [44]

According to the commission, the Japanese constituted nearly 50 per- cent of the territory's population, and their numbers were increasing, despite the Gentlemen's Agreement, through the picture bride system, which provided "a method of genetal reproduction . . . that will soon overwhelm the Territory numerically, politically and commercially." [45] In fact, the Japanese were "so confident of the ultimate control of the Islands that they put on an air of confidence that is apparent to the large majority of the Americans and native Hawaiians in the Islands." [46]

The commission found it "very interesting from a military defense point of view when we note that the Japanese residential districts are adja- cent to the various forts." A map showing their locations—the Palama settlement and River Street district, Japanese temple district (Punchbowl area), Pawaa district, and Moiliili settlement—revealed that the Japanese congregated near what the commission considered strategic sites, includ- ing forts and the high ground overlooking the harbor. The report asked, "Does not this map . . . indicate some method on the part of the Japanese to segregate themselves in the neighborhood of these forts?" [47]

Besides their penetration into virtually all sectors of the Hawaiian econ- omy, concluded the report, the Japanese controlled essential services such as taxis, telephone exchanges, and water pumping stations, and Japanese fishing "sampans" could transport thousands of men and had a sailing radius of 500 miles. The only way to curb the economic power of Hawaii's Japanese, the report proposed, was "with a working force that will as- similate our American ideals and living conditions." [48]

The commission sought to impress on its readers the extreme gravity of the situation, castigating "idealists" who were "largely blinded to the menace" and who "hypnotize themselves in the belief that the splendid American school system is going to Americanize the 20,000 plus Japanese children now forming 50% of the school attendance." The commission warned:

> It may be difficult for the home staying American citizen to visualize the spectre of alien domination which like a thunder cloud in the distance grows larger almost day by day, with the belief that when the infinite patience of this Asiatic Race has reached the point for action the cloud will break and America will wake up to the fact that it has developed within its Territory a race through whose solidarity and maintenance of Asiatic ideals will sweep everything American from the Islands.[49]

Appended to the commission's report, as Exhibit A, was an assessment of "the Japanese situation in relation to our military problem" submitted by the commander of the army's Hawaiian Department, Major General Charles P. Summerall.

Feigned Necessity Undone

Secretary of Labor Davis praised the commission's report and distributed it, in executive session, to congressional committee members considering the Hawaiian petition with the following instruction: "Strictly confidential. Not for publication in any form."[50] Davis had apparently intended to release the report, but Secretary of State Hughes, fearful of its possible international repercussions, urged that the report be classified confidential. Hughes explained that the report contained "statements which might be construed as offensive and which in some respects are difficult of proof. It assumes, and this is really the basis of the report, that the Hawaiian-born Japanese are Japanese at heart, and not American at all, and intend to seize the Islands for the purpose of furthering the cause of Imperial Japan."[51]

Hawaii's governor, in contrast, had no reservations about the report's findings and wrote to commission member Hywell Davies on February 14, 1923: "I am enclosing herewith a memorandum of my statement to the press regarding the excellent report of the Labor Commission. I do not think I could say more. I have read the full report which shows that you and your associates got at the heart of things in a very short time." [52]

Despite the fact that the federal commission had found no labor shortage on the plantations, Hawaii's rulers were encouraged by its recommendation that the migrant labor option should be made available to the territory in the event of a proven emergency. But that glimmer of hope vanished in a Congress bent on adjournment: "Imagine the case in Congress facing final adjournment on March 4 and with 500 men trying their best to get favorable action on their own bills," explained Dillingham. "With 10 days to go there were some 10,000 measures looking for 'a place in the sun.'" [53] The Hawaiian resolution reached the floor of the House and Senate only to be passed over without consideration. As was customary, the day before adjournment, members of the House were given four minutes to place on record anything they chose to say. Representative William K. Lankford from Georgia closed his remarks with "white supremacy is not oppressive tyrannical supremacy, but is compassionate, God-like supremacy exercised for the good of our Nation, the happiness of the human race, and the civilization of the world." [54]

In the Saddle Again

Although the HSPA-sponsored plan to import Chinese migrant workers failed, the effort demonstrated the determination of the planters to rid themselves of "unreliable labor." There were too many Japanese workers; they were unionizing and were becoming unruly. The strike of 1920 served notice to the planters that a serious challenge was being mounted against their hegemony. Worker resistance, however, was not of the variety depicted by Hawaii's rulers—for the economic and political control of the territory. As noted by Japanese Consul General Yada, the idea that the Japanese in Hawaii were poised to take over the economy was preposterous: "For the Japanese in Hawaii to conceive, much less accomplish such purpose, they would have to be 'super-men' of enormous wealth, whereas the great majority of them are of the laboring class, with but elementary education, slight business experience and only such money as they have been able to save from their wages, which can, in their normal standard, just amount to enough to meet the dire necessity of daily life." [55]

Still, worker resistance posed a problem for the planters, especially as it grew in size, frequency, and sophistication. Centralization of the sugar industry was a *sine qua non* for the efficient control of workers. Before 1920, managers usually competed for workers, even raiding neighboring plantations; they ignored HSPA rules on holding wages at industrywide levels. After the 1920 strike, the HSPA resolved to maintain a uniform wage policy that evolved into a rigid system of controls and negated the benefits of planter paternalism.[56]

In 1919, the legislature had enacted a law that defined criminal syndicalism as "the doctrine which advocates crime, sabotage, violence or other unlawful methods of terrorism as a means of accomplishing industrial or political ends." Conviction of criminal syndicalism carried penalties of imprisonment for up to ten years or a maximum fine of $5,000.[57] The broad sweep of the law certainly encompassed Japanese "alien agitators" and their "co-conspirators," who sought "to cripple our principal industry and to gain dominance of the American territory of Hawaii."

An anarchistic publications act was passed in 1921, aimed at the Japanese-language press. The law prohibited the publication of material that advocated or incited, directly or indirectly, violence, breach of the peace, intimidation "for the purpose of restraining or coercing or intimidating any person from freely engaging in lawful business or employment or the enjoyment of rights of liberty or property." Further, the act enjoined the printing of materials "designed and intended to create or have the effect of creating distrust or dissension between peoples of different races or between citizens and aliens." Conviction under the anarchistic publications law carried a penalty of $1,000 to $5,000 in fines or imprisonment for up to a year or both.[58]

Then, in 1923, the legislature passed a picketing and protection-of-labor statute prohibiting "unlawful interference with the right to work." Persons and groups were forbidden to use "profane, insulting, indecent, offensive, annoying, abusive or threatening language" toward any person trying to work, or to attempt to influence a person to quit employment. Also, the legislation defined as unlawful, picketing "in any manner" persons or businesses legally engaged in work, and it proscribed any activity that sought "to induce or influence others not to trade with, buy from, sell to, work for or have business dealings with such person, so that thereby the lawful business or occupation of such person will be obstructed, interfered with, injured, or damaged." The penalty imposed under this law was a maximum fine of $1,000, a year's imprisonment, or both.[59]

The 1925 trespassing law "was invoked repeatedly as a means of preventing labor meetings or organizers from entering plantations or business premises"; it was even used to regulate plantation visitors.[60] The statute declared that whoever entered the buildings or lands of another, "after having been forbidden to do so by the person who has lawful control of such premises . . . shall be guilty of a misdemeanor," punishable by a maximum fine of $250, imprisonment for up to three months, or both.[61]

The labor laws passed following the 1920 strike were not for the "protection of labor"; instead, they punished those who interfered with "the right to work," while placing no similar penalties on employers who intimidated their laborers to work and impeded their right to organize. Commenting on the criminal syndicalism, anarchistic publications, and picketing laws, a student of Hawaiian labor wrote: "The similarities between these three anti-labor laws are evident. Each one is a potential weapon in restricting the right of labor to organize for security; none places any responsibility upon employers for coercive acts committed during an industrial dispute."[62]

The failure of the campaign for "labor relief" underscored the political reality that the system of migrant labor—with the exception of Filipino migration—would no longer be possible and that there would not be an endless stream of cheap Asian labor to supplant the previous generation of aging or restive workers. Stifled by mainland exclusionists, the planters sought to recruit Asians from a U.S. colony, the Philippines, and to reinstitute their control over the existing workforce in the islands through paternalism and restrictive labor laws. The planters were back in the saddle again.

A Menace to the Nation

The strike of 1920, begun as a reluctant walkout by sugar plantation workers on the island of Oahu, achieved national and international significance largely because of the reaction of Hawaii's planters, the territorial government, and the military. Despite protestations by strike leaders that the conflict was a domestic American issue between capital and labor, Hawaii's oligarchy and the military insisted that underlying the strike was the struggle for dominance in the territory between Japan and the United States. In reality, according to Federation of Japanese Labor secretary Tsutsumi, the organizing principles of the strike were the progressive American ideals of freedom and equality and not a reactionary Japanese nationalism. Pointing to the planters, he asked: "Although [the] Hawaiian Sugar Planters' Association brands this strike as a racial movement, why is it that white men control the industry of Hawaii and refuse to give a single opening to other races?"[63]

Nevertheless, the planters' racial line of attack, although hypocritical, was obviously not irrational. As attested to by the commotion it created and the objectives it achieved, the campaign was superbly conceived and directed. In fact, Hawaii's rulers had succeeded in maneuvering the metropole by camouflaging their self-interest with allegations of a Japanese menace. Admittedly, the effort launched to reinstate Chinese migrant labor fizzled in Congress, yet the case made by the planters—that the well-being of capitalism in Hawaii and the repression of the Japanese were in the national interest—was adjudged sound. In endorsing the Hawaiian emergency labor resolution, the House Committee on Immigration and Naturalization reported: "This entire problem is a national and not a local one. . . . If they [the Hawaiian islands] be held economically and politically by one alien race, they can constitute only a grave menace to the American Nation."[64] Accordingly, the "Japanese problem" was no longer simply a labor problem; it was fast becoming a military problem.

Chapter 6

Race War

*It is the determined purpose of Japan to
amalgamate the entire colored races of the world
against the Nordic or white race, with Japan at
the head of the coalition, for the purpose of
wrestling away the supremacy of the white race
and placing such supremacy in the colored
peoples under the dominion of Japan.*
                              —Bureau of Investigation

Military Intelligence before 1920

Situated in the Pacific Basin, Hawaii was a conduit for
America's Pacific trade and a military outpost designed to
protect and advance U.S. interests. The territory's position
determined the roles of the navy and army in the islands:
the navy kept open the Pacific sea lanes, while the army
defended Hawaiian soil—especially the island of Oahu and
its naval base at Pearl Harbor—against both foreign and
domestic enemies.

Around the time of World War I, military intelligence in
Hawaii, like its mainland counterpart, was concerned about
the activities of aliens, radicals, and communists. In fact, it
seemed that mainland interests, specifically those of army
headquarters in the nation's capital, dictated the concerns
of the military in Hawaii. From 1917 to 1918, the army's
General Staff directed the Hawaiian Department to initiate
investigations of island German residents; a major portion
of the work of army intelligence in the territory was devoted
to investigations of German "enemy aliens" and to drawing
up a suspect list for possible internment.[1]

By war's end, the mainland suspicion of Germans and the nation's underlying nativism and obsessive fear of aliens had generally taken on a local perspective, focusing on the "Japanese problem." That the "Japanese problem" was seen as a military problem in the territory is not difficult to understand given the size of the Japanese population in Hawaii, Japanese significance in the economy, and the location of the islands midway to Asia. Moreover, Japanese workers on Hawaii's sugar plantations were becoming increasingly restless, seeking to throw off the yoke of planter hegemony.

Beginning in 1917, the main duty of army field clerk Nelson W. Raymond, a member of the Hawaiian Department's Corps of Intelligence Police, was to collect information on patriotic organizations such as the American Legion and the Boy Scouts and to maintain surveillance on the most important labor leaders of all racial groups in the territory.[2] The army was concerned about labor because it underpinned the economy and thereby determined political stability. Race could be used not only to divide workers but also to unite them, as the 1909 sugar plantation strike had shown. The army was accordingly interested in race relations insofar as it eroded or bolstered white supremacy. Patriotism and nativism, represented by the American Legion, helped counter the threat of "alien domination"; assimilation and Americanization, embodied in the Boy Scouts, aided in dissolving racial and ethnic solidarity.

From its initial scrutiny of all labor leaders, Army intelligence narrowed its scope to concentrate on the Japanese. Unlike the planters, whose main concern was a rebellious workforce, the military saw the problem as one of national security. Competitors for political influence, the planters and the military were nonetheless united in seeking control over the Japanese because they threatened the interests of both.

The Merriam Report

The first notable indication of the army's stress on the "Japanese problem" was a report entitled "The Increase of Japanese Population in the Hawaiian Islands and What It Means." It was forwarded by Major H. C. Merriam, intelligence officer in the Hawaiian Department, to the chief of the Military Intelligence Branch in Washington, D.C., on May 6, 1918.[3] The report viewed with alarm the disparity between Japanese and white population growth rates and discussed its military implications. The Japanese had increased by 22,805, while whites had increased by 4,626 over a seven-year period. "The main *cause of increase in Japanese population* is the importation of Japanese women from Japan as wives (picture brides), a preference being shown for women direct from Japan, rather than island born Japanese. These Japanese women are prolific," charged Merriam.

According to the 1910 census, continued the report, 50 percent of Hawaii's Japanese were eighteen to forty-four years old, meaning that at least 35,000 Japanese males were available for service. Would these men remain loyal to America? Merriam's answer was unequivocal: "Practically all the Japanese would side with Japan." Even with the most optimistic scenario—the *nisei* favoring the United States—the situation in terms of sheer numbers was grave: "We would have a Caucasian-American population of about 15,000 living in a community of some 65,000 hostile foreigners or outnumbered four to one." Further, by peaceful means, the Japanese could eventually determine the political life of the territory through the ballot box with an estimated 19,000 eligible Japanese voters in the islands.

The report identified three sources of anti-Americanism. First, the Japanese government, through its consul, monitored the activities of all Japanese in the territory and actively promoted Japanese nationalism: "It is apparently the desire (perhaps natural) of the Japanese Government to keep the Japanese on these islands, Japanese instead of *American*." Second, Japanese schools, scattered throughout the islands, taught language but also "Japanese national history, customs, religion and literature." Merriam cited 1916 statistics compiled by the Japanese consulate that showed 13 schools with 2,758 pupils in Honolulu, 15 schools with 1,339 pupils in the rest of Oahu, 23 schools with 1,739 pupils on the island of Maui, 44 schools with 3,718 pupils on the island of Hawaii, and 21 schools with 1,662 pupils on Kauai. A third source of anti-Americanism was Buddhism. The forty-eight Buddhist churches throughout the islands negated the influences of Christianity and Americanism: "The Hongwanji [a Buddhist sect] run their schools to counter-act any advance of the Christian religion among their Japanese, and to infuse any exclusive Japanese national spirit which will neutralize the Americanizing influence of the public schools."

The Merriam report marked a departure from the earlier military intelligence in its focus on the Japanese community. Also, the report was apparently the first to identify the sources of anti-Americanism that were to gain prominence in subsequent investigations by military and civilian intelligence agencies. An increase in population was not the sole source of concern; equally threatening was the fact that the Japanese were becoming a settled community, a permanent feature in the territory. Their presence, pregnant with political and social ramifications, according to the Merriam report, was alien and antagonistic to the American way of life, posing a danger to national security.

Naval Intelligence

Naval intelligence in Honolulu underscored points made by the Merriam report. In a communication sent to the Director of Naval Intelligence in Washington, D.C., August 20, 1918, Robert Shingle, head of the Thrift Stamp Drive, alleged that Japanese Consul General Rokuro Moroi had "over one hundred agents" in Hawaii, which formed a tightly disciplined network appointed by and answerable to Moroi alone. Later conversation uncovered that the agents reported "on general conditions throughout the islands" and that their service as agents was "an honorary position without remuneration." According to Shingle, the agents "were positively under his [Moroi's] orders and will do as he says." That "admission," the report concluded, was highly significant and revealed the true intent of the Japanese government: economic and political control of the territory. "It is not apparent why a Consul if engaged only in commercial matters," reasoned naval intelligence, "should request over 100 agents to report to him. It would appear from this that the Japanese Consulate system is political as well as commercial."[4]

Naval intelligence also confirmed Merriam's characterization of Buddhist priests as subverters of Americanism. On August 14, 1918, the Office of Naval Intelligence (ONI) in Washington, D.C., forwarded a report from a Japanese informant in Hawaii to the Military Intelligence Division (MID) of the army, charging that "Buddhist priests in Hawaii, while ostensibly loyal to the United States, are in reality doing everything in their power to undermine any American allegiance entertained by the Japanese in Hawaii."[5] Toward that end, the report noted, Buddhist priests sought to dissuade Japanese from buying Liberty Bonds or War Saving Stamps, or from contributing to the Red Cross.

A September 4, 1918, memorandum from ONI in Hawaii, citing a planter's proposal to petition Congress for permission to resume importing Asian migrant labor, framed the plan as a threat to the national defense: "It is suggested that the introduction of twenty or thirty thousand additional Japanese laborers (presumably most of them males) might be a matter of vital importance in the possible defense of these Islands, and is a matter in which the military authorities at Washington may be interested."[6] The proposal stirred much consternation among concerned agencies in the nation's capital, and a Mr. Taylor, head of the Criminal Department of the Immigration Service, was dispatched to Honolulu to ascertain if the planters envisioned importing Chinese or Japanese workers. Presumably, the Immigration people were interested because the plan infringed on existing restrictions on the importation of Chinese and Japanese laborers. But ONI saw the influx of Asian workers as potentially threatening militarily.

By 1918, the number of Japanese laborers and men in Hawaii were apparently matters of vital importance to the military. The intertwining of migration, labor, and race was assuredly not new. What was new, and original to Hawaii, was that the "Japanese problem," which comprised a convergence of migration, labor, and race, was perceived as a military problem in the defense of American soil. At stake was the preservation of America's military and commercial outpost in the Pacific. Accordingly, the problem assumed significance beyond West Coast concerns, which were primarily over economic competition, cultural contamination, and miscegenation.

Postal Censors

As early as January 1919, both MID and ONI maintained a Honolulu Postal Censorship Station headed by military censors and assisted by a staff of Japanese translators. After reading intercepted mail, Captain Philip E. Spalding, assistant military censor at the Honolulu station, submitted a report entitled "Japanese in Hawaii" to MID in Hawaii. The report was forwarded to the director of MID in Washington, D.C., on January 29, 1919.[7] Spalding claimed intimate acquaintance with "the character and ideals of the Oriental population" and proceeded to divide the Japanese into two groups, Christians and non-Christians, that cut across generations and citizenship. Christians showed "an independence of thought" and were imbued with "more of the ideals of American democracy";

non-Christians, who constituted "a very large majority," worshipped the emperor. Buddhist priests taught most of the *nisei* in Japanese-language schools. "The question has been raised," wrote Spalding, "of the propriety of young Americans being inculcated with the doctrines of Japanese Imperialism and expansion."

To support his claim, Spalding quoted from two intercepted letters written by Buddhist priests. The first priest spoke glowingly of a Mr. Konna, manager of the Kona Development Company on the island of Hawaii, who had borrowed $270,000 from Tokyo capitalists to build a sugar plantation on the Kona coast. The priest praised Konna as a model for the territory's Japanese in seeking "control" of the sugar industry and in standing up to white people: "My cherished hope is that men like Mr. Konna, a great businessman and a man of remarkable ability, may appear here in great numbers and control the sugar industry of Hawaii. Japanese children are too submissive to white men. They are taught to look upon white men as supermen." Instead, the priest admonished parents, "Don't, for mercy's sake, produce any worshipper of the white man." The second letter, written by Reverend R. Nishiyama of Kohala Mill, Hawaii, described pending legislation that sought to close Japanese-language schools in the territory as a conflict between Christianity and Buddhism and called Japanese Christian ministers "unworthy countrymen" and "traitors" who deserved to die.

Spalding warned that unless something was done to stem the tide of "Japanization," Hawaii would be swamped. "This situation, if allowed to continue, will create a condition in the not distant future where local politics will be controlled by Japanese-Americans who have been carefully schooled in ideas of patriotism to Japan and not to the United States." The army was interested in Americanization because it was a matter of national defense, explained Spalding, and Christianity and public education were essential to the fulfillment of the military's mission in Hawaii.

Besides revealing the concerns of the military, letters intercepted by ONI postal censors show that the Japanese understood the bases of the anti-Japanese movement and the stakes involved.[8] In a March 7, 1919, letter, a Jodo Buddhist priest in Hawi, Hawaii, commented on the anticipated passage of the Japanese-language school bill by the legislature: "The reason American people are afraid of Japanese in Hawaii is because Japanese embrace more than half of the whole population, and their children, over half of the total number of school children. Some day these children who have been granted by the Constitution of the United States the rights and privileges of a citizen, will usurp, the voting power." On March 12, another Jodo priest in Honolulu wrote again on the Japanese-language school issue: "The real root of the problem is the racial prejudice and hatred—the desire of wiping off the Japanese from these islands. Because of this, the problem is unsolvable. But it is a question of life and death to us."

The "Japanese Problem"

By 1919, the "Japanese problem," in the eyes of military intelligence, had taken on epic proportions: a battle for the control of Hawaii. The problem was rooted in the growing and permanent Japanese population of the territory: their birthrate, the number of men of military age, the number of eligible voters, and the loyalties of aliens and citizens. The conflict engaged the forces of Americanization, including the Christian churches and public schools, and the forces of Japanization, including the consul and his network of agents, Japanese-language schools, and Buddhist priests. The national paranoia about aliens and radicals expressed itself in Hawaii in a perception that the Japanese presence, culture, and institutions were subversive and constituted a military problem.

The army was not idle in dealing with its fears. According to Governor Charles McCarthy, army intelligence instigated the 1919 bill for the regulation of Japanese-language schools: "At the request of the Intelligence Bureau of the Hawaiian Department, there was introduced at the regular Session of the Legislature in 1919 an act providing for the regulation of foreign language schools."[9] The bill required that all language teachers be able to read, write, and speak English and that they have "a working knowledge of the American Government and its institutions." Although the bill failed in the territorial Senate, after passing in the House, the military clearly took its reports seriously and sought to legislate support of its role as guardian of the national security.

Military Intelligence during the 1920s

On October 11, 1920, George Brooke, head of the Hawaiian Department's G-2 (military intelligence) section and a proponent of a "commission form of government," submitted a report entitled "Estimate of the Japanese Situation as it Affects the Territory of Hawaii, From the Military Point of View." Brooke had been a military attaché in Tokyo, and he spoke and read Japanese. According to A. A. Hopkins, an agent for the Bureau of Investigation (predecessor of the FBI), Brooke was "a profound student of the Japanese and Oriental Question." [10]

In fact, Hopkins credited Brooke with having laid the foundation for the army's surveillance of Hawaii's Japanese: "I find that the Military Intelligence had gathered very little information relative to the Japanese situation in Hawaii prior to the incumbency of Colonel Brooks [*sic*] as Assistant Chief of Staff G-2, and practically everything contained in their files had been gathered by him during the past 18 months." [11] Brooke's influence was apparently strong; more important, his ideas on the military nature of the "Japanese problem" reached beyond the territory's army command and triggered a consideration of the problem by army headquarters in Washington, D.C.

Military intelligence in Hawaii in 1920 was amateurish. There was very little information on the Japanese, prompting the army commander to declare: "Our ignorance of the machinations, intrigues, and activities of the Japanese population in Hawaii, is abysmal. The Japanese would endeavor to take the Islands tomorrow if they dared. We have been severely handicapped in our efforts to gather information, and need help." [12] Reported Hopkins of Brooke: "He has practically no secret service fund; works no confidential or under cover informants in the sense that the Bureau [of Investigation] uses such informants: has a Volunteer Intelligence system of 'Volunteer Aids for Information' consisting chiefly of prominent Americans throughout the islands, principally planters, but apparently is getting very little from them." Further, observed Hopkins, Brooke was inexperienced in undercover operations and was unable to get "real inside information." [13] In contrast, the HSPA's secret service, formed by Royal Mead during the 1920 strike, employed one Filipino and three Japanese agents and maintained the most comprehensive surveillance of labor in the territory.[14]

Despite his limitations, Brooke compiled an impressive amount of information on Japanese activities in the islands, from Japanese prestrike planning at Waialua and Kahuku plantations in November 1919 to a Waimanalo teacher's comment that "the Japanese school children showed a marked lack of interest in anything regarding the United States and American ideals, but seemed very much interested in everything concerning Japan." Brooke cited this comment as showing how anti-American sentiment had percolated down from parents to their children.[15] Writing during the height of the strike, Brooke reported: "There is convincing proof that this strike has behind it strong forces connected with the Japanese government." He also wrote of the danger posed by Japanese fishing vessels, sampans, operating in Hawaiian waters because their crews knew every reef and harbor, and they ranged as far as 1,200 miles. "It would seem," he suggested, "that there should be a law prohibiting the employment of alien crews on fishing vessels and the exclusion of all aliens from fishing rights in the waters of the United States or its possessions."[16] The anxiety over Japanese fishermen would continue to nag those responsible for America's security until World War II, when they would be among the first casualties of the war.

Brooke's comprehensive assessment of the "Japanese problem," "Estimate of the Japanese Situation," was written after the bitter 1920 strike. He placed the problem in a national and international arena. To him, signs pointed to a "new crisis" in relations between Japan and the United States, "brought about by the attitude of California and in general of the Pacific Coast States toward the Japanese as expressed by legislation pending in California [1920 ballot proposition tightening the alien land law]. In addition to this the language school agitation in this territory is also a point of friction." Japan's response to anti-Japanese sentiment in Hawaii and California was a "notoriously immoral" campaign of "wide-spread propaganda and intrigue as well as . . . bluff" that fomented labor conflicts and tried to lure the industrial states of the Northeast into siding with international capitalism (i.e., trade with Japan) over national interests, pitting that region against California and Hawaii. Despite Japan's divisive tactic to frame the problem as a class issue, the real conflict, declared Brooke, aligned whites against Asians in a race war, with the ultimate goal dominance in the Pacific and Asia:

> Japan knows that if with the aid of hosts of aliens, of radicals, of pacifists and of renegades of every sort and description now rampant in the United States, as well as fermenting under cover, that she may be able to aid in tying up the United States with strikes, and that she may be able to make the aliens, the radicals and the discontented working classes buck war even when war is necessary to preserve the vigor of our nationality. At the same time her propaganda tends to put the eastern states of the United States against

California and Hawaii. If she can gain her points [through] these aids she may continue her peaceful expansion and penetration and her active procreation, which may make even of polygamy a virtue. And she will carry her absorption and consolidation schemes to a point in the dim future, when with the assistance derived from the pressure of other Asiatic races having a foothold in the Americas, she will make it vastly harder for America to finally resist her aims.[17]

Brooke described the "very complete system of espionage" maintained by the Japanese consul in Hawaii, beneath whom were Buddhist and Shinto priests, Japanese-language schoolteachers, owners and editors of Japanese newspapers, and "radical" labor leaders. Japanese workers, wrote Brooke, were not organized to promote their class interests, but were organized to advance Japan's nationalistic ambitions. The Federation of Japanese Labor, accordingly, was "a powerful and purely Japanese interest, for Japanese national ends alone. These ends may safely be interpreted as first, to create an economic weapon for the use of the Japanese economic machine; second, as an instrument for the control of a large part of the Japanese civil population in case of emergency." Japanese ethnic solidarity was boosted by civic and self-help groups such as *kenjinkais*, which, while ostensibly social in purpose, were "suspected of having affiliation and as affording cover for military espionage . . . to promote colonization in various parts of the world."[18]

Thus, concluded Brooke, the Japanese were inscrutable and their method of operating was two-faced, creating a false sense of security among white Americans. While America slept, Japan prepared for total war. Japanese churches, schools, cultural and social organizations, and economic and political activities all functioned within the law, were protected by the Constitution, and appeared to be innocent and familiar institutions in American life, but beneath that veneer of normalcy, those organizations promoted Japan's imperial design. "No one without thorough study of and contact with the Japanese problem here can form a true estimate of its seriousness," cautioned Brooke. "The Japanese community here, which is half the population, is a practically impervious and self-sustaining body. Its tentacles, in the form of economic agencies such as workers, servants, contractors etc. penetrate every phase of American life in this territory, from government bureaus to the homes of very poor people."[19]

Brooke's successor, Captain S. A. Wood, Jr., expanded on these foundations in "The Japanese Situation in Hawaii," a report focusing on second-generation Japanese. The report was prompted by ongoing lobbying efforts on the part of the Hawaii Emergency Labor Commission for Chinese migrant workers and was sent to the MID director in Washington, D.C.[20] The concern in Hawaii, explained Wood, was not over Japanese ownership of land, as in California; instead, it was over the number of Japanese in the territory, their rapid growth, and the coming of age of the *nisei*. The situation was "already getting serious," and, according to the governor, by 1927 *nisei* would constitute 11,000 of an estimated 28,000 registered voters in Hawaii. "What will happen when all these votes are cast as directed by the leaders of the Japanese community?" Parenthetically, Wood added, "It must be remembered that they feel that they are as much subject to Japan's laws and regulations as if they were actually living in Japan." The crucial question was "Will these voters who are American citizens of Japanese ancestry vote according to the principles of American citizens in the United States or will they vote according to the best interests of the Japanese community, and this means as directed by the Japanese government?"[21]

Thus, for Wood, the extent of *nisei* Americanization was the key question. The Japanese community in Hawaii, he wrote, was divided into two major segments: workers on plantations and workers and shopkeepers in towns. Both segments lived and operated in segregated, tightly knit communities. "There is no evidence of the Japanese having become Americanized. They do not associate with white people to any extent and the white people show no disposition to associate with them." Further, Japanese-language schools, churches, and the press all exercised a strong influence over the thoughts and actions of the people, teaching "that loyalty to Japan and reverance [sic] to her institutions and culture must always be first in their lives." Japanese culture made it "impossible" for the *nisei* to become "American" because of its insistence on collectivity: "One of their natural tendencies is the suppression of individualism so they have been brought up in a life where they have always acted with other Japanese."[22] Americanization had failed to shake the bonds of Japanese ethnicity and nationalism.

The problem was compounded by Japanese dominance in industry, continued Wood, especially as displayed in the plantation strike of 1920 and in commercial fishing. The former was a vivid demonstration of anti-Americanism on the part of Japanese leaders, who "criticized everything

American, and condemned the American leaders of the community and American ideals and institutions." It also exemplified Japanese disregard of fair play: "One of the most important features about this strike as far as the American community is concerned was the methods used by the Japanese in carrying on the strike. These methods brought home to the Americans the fact that when the Japanese have decided upon a course of action they allow nothing in the world to stop them from gaining their objective." Japanese "control" of Hawaii's fishing industry also held a sinister meaning for Wood. With the average age of sampan crew members between twenty-five and thirty, and with several having served in the Japanese navy and merchant marine, it was not difficult for Wood to imagine "the assistance that these men could be to a foreign power if there should ever be an attempt made to capture these islands." [23]

While Brooke's investigations pointed to an international dimension to the "Japanese question," Wood's study assessed the extent and likelihood of internal subversion. Both, nonetheless, were impressed by the alleged unconventional strategies pursued by Hawaii's Japanese, and both saw American democracy as ill equipped to cope with that alien menace. Further, both defined the question primarily in terms of race, rather than class, conflict. "Such is therefore the lesson of Hawaii," concluded Wood. "A democratic form of government is being destroyed by the infiltration of an alien and unassimilable race." The Japanese were "incapable of blending by intermarriage and therefore of helping to make a homogenous population without which there can be no real equality and true democracy." [24]

Creating an Intelligence Network

The 1920 strike and the flurry of military intelligence reports emanating from Hawaii caught the attention of the Bureau of Investigation's J. Edgar Hoover, then a special assistant to the U.S. attorney general. On October 19, 1920, Hoover proposed the following to Brigadier General C. E. Nolan, MID director in the War Department: "Our offices on the coast have recently called to our attention the situation existing in Hawaii and it has been suggested that in view of the fact that representatives of the Military Intelligence Division are stationed in Hawaii that if this office could be afforded the opportunity of examining the reports of the officers of your division who are stationed in Hawaii that much valuable information could be obtained which would be of great use to our offices on the coast."[25]

Later that year, the bureau's Los Angeles office dispatched special agent A. A. Hopkins to undertake a survey of the situation in Hawaii "for the purpose of making an under cover investigation of Japanese Activities in the Territory of Hawaii, and to develop trustworthy confidential sources of information relative to same, and for the further purpose of establishing a more perfect co-operation and liasion between the Intelligence investigations of the 8th Division, the Department of Justice, the Military Intelligence of the 9th Corps Area, and the Department of Hawaii."[26] Hopkins conferred with army headquarters of the Ninth Corps Area in San Francisco, then sailed for Hawaii, arriving there on December 21, 1920. He assessed intelligence gathering in the territory and contrasted the sophistication and size of the intelligence units of the army and the HSPA. Despite being comparatively well funded, the HSPA's secret service, Hopkins discovered, "dealt almost exclusively with Japanese Activities in connection with the strike and labor difficulties, and that general information as to Japanese activities in Hawaii such as Military, Naval Espionage, Political, Economic, etc., had only been reported when same had a direct bearing on the Labor situation."[27] The situation was not encouraging in terms of a comprehensive surveillance of Japanese activities in Hawaii.

As a result, Hawaii's army commander and G-2 head asked the bureau to establish an office in the territory and to coordinate the intelligence effort. Wrote Hopkins: "Major General Morton and Colonel Brooks [*sic*] are both exceedingly anxious that this Bureau establish an office or detail an Agent in Hawaii." In the meantime, Mead's successor, J. K. Butler, promised Hopkins that the HSPA's secret service would collect information on Japanese activities in areas other than labor and would forward copies of all reports from its agents and informants to the bureau's office in Los Angeles.[28] Before the end of 1921, apparently, the bureau sent special agent Ralph H. Colvin to Honolulu to head the newly created Hawaii District under the bureau's Eighth Division office in Los Angeles. Starting in August of that year, Colvin's weekly reports on the "Japanese situation" in Hawaii had been filed with the bureau's Eighth Division office, MID Hawaiian Department, MID Ninth Corps Area, and MID Washington, D.C. In addition, since at least November 1920, MID Ninth Corps

Area had been receiving reports on Japanese activities from the ONI.[29] By September 1921, the bureau's Los Angeles office, under special agent Frank M. Sturgis, added its data on Japanese activities in California to Colvin's "Japanese situation" reports, although the bulk of the information still consisted of intelligence from Hawaii.[30] By the end of 1921, an intelligence network had been created, linking Hawaii, California, and Washington, D.C., involving the bureau, MID, ONI, and HSPA.

The weekly situation reports offer insights on that intelligence community. Included were commentaries on the activities of the Pan-Pacific movement. Formed in 1917 by Hawaii's business and political elite, the Pan-Pacific Union sought mutual understanding, cooperation, and commercial relationships among all Pacific nations. Also included in the reports were peace and disarmament groups, labor organizations, the American Legion, and Japanese "propagandists." Regarding the latter, Colvin noted that according to a newspaper account, the Hawaii Laborers' Association had received numerous requests, especially from mainland libraries, for Japanese leader Tsutsumi's account of the 1920 strike. Commented the bureau agent, "If true [it] is undoubtedly an effort to place the Japanese side of the strike of the Japanese laborers, before the American public thru the public libraries, in line with the well known method used by Japanese propagandists in getting their stuff before the public." Seeking to root out collaborators in that effort, Colvin mused: "It would be interesting to ascertain from some of the California libraries which will no doubt receive copies of the book, just what agencies were responsible for the acquisition of same by the library."[31] One such center for Japanese propaganda was Stanford University, and the news that the university had established an endowed chair in Japanese history and civilization drew the following comment from Colvin and Sturgis: "The announcement if true, is significant, in view of the well known proclivities of this University to harbor pro-Japanese professors and propagandists."[32]

A familiar theme in the weekly situation reports was the alleged network of agents maintained and directed by Japan's consul general. In the October 8 report, for example, Colvin and Sturgis described how the Japanese delighted in providing information to the consul, and, in fact, "take pride" in being selected for that honor. Japanese banks and other businesses regularly reported on American political, economic, and social conditions to their home office. Buddhist missions filed similar reports with their home temples, which in turn made monthly reports to the Bureau of Religion of Japan's Interior Department. Visiting Japanese naval vessels provided opportunities for direct contact between local Japanese and Japan's military: "It is quite possible that some of these [sailors] may have been left here for espionage work, and that some of those listed as 'Enlisted Men' may really be commissioned officers," speculated the report. "It would be quite feasible to leave them here and substitute others in their places when time comes for them to go back to Japan, as they were not checked in or otherwise identified by Immigration or other officials. Their identity would soon be lost among the 109,000 Japanese residents."[33]

Racism was clearly evident in the bureau's reports, matching the most lurid yellow peril fantasies being churned out by journalists, writers, and filmmakers.[34] The Bureau's Eighth Division summary report for August 1, 1920 to January 31, 1921, devoted considerable attention to "the Japanese Problem in the United States."[35] "The ramifications of this problem are almost unbelievable in their scope to any one who has not made a study of the matter and does not understand the ultimate program of Japan concerning territorial expansion; . . . Japan's program for world supremacy is similar to that entertained by Germany prior to 1914." Japanese expansion, it was argued, arose from the need for Japan to find some outlet for its "constantly increasing surplus population." California was an early target because the Japanese as a race were unfit for tropical or frigid climes and were best suited to temperate zones. "Thus California became the first state in the nation to feel the weight of Japan's hand in her program of 'peaceful penetration,' and is considered by the Japanese as superior to Hawaii and the Philippine Islands."

According to the summary report, the battle was a race war; the prize, world domination. If the tide of Japanese immigration was not stemmed, "the white race, in no long space of time, would be driven from the state, and California eventually become a province of Japan . . . , further, that it would be only a question of time until the entire Pacific coast region would be controlled by the Japanese." In this race war, America's Japanese allied themselves with blacks: "The Japanese Associations subscribe to radical negro literature. In California a negro organization, formed in September, 1920, issued resolutions declaring that negros would not, in case of the exclusion of Japanese, take their place; a prominent negro was liberally paid to spread propaganda for the Japanese; and various negro religious and social bodies were approached in many ways."[36] Japan's ultimate aim was global domination by turning the world's people of color against the white race: "It is the determined purpose of Japan to amalgamate the entire colored races of the world against the Nordic or white race, with Japan at the head of the coalition, for the purpose of wrestling away the supremacy of the white race and placing such supremacy in the colored peoples under the dominion of Japan." That scenario, admitted the report, might appear "fantastic," but it was the blueprint of Japan's government and must be taken seriously by Americans.

Signs of eventual control of Hawaii and the West Coast by Japan could already be seen, argued the report. The Japanese population was concentrated in Hawaii and along the West Coast, and in California Japanese congregated in just seven of the state's fifty-eight counties, magnifying their presence despite their overall inferior numbers compared with whites. In Hawaii, the demographic picture clearly favored the Japanese and would inevitably result in their political control of the territory through the ballot box: "It is authoritively [sic] stated," claimed the report, "that by 1933 the native-born Japanese in the Hawaiian Islands will be of sufficient number to control the election; and at the present time it is a fact that in the Hawaiian Islands the Japanese control legislative matters, and their papers published in the Islands frequently proudly announce that not later than 1933 the Japanese vote in Hawaii will decide whether Republicans or Democrats shall win."

According to intelligence agents, the Japanese, through a concentration of effort in select industries, had achieved a virtual stranglehold on several key sectors of the economy in Hawaii and California, practically controlling California's fishing industry and much of its agriculture, supplying more than 80 percent of orchard labor and producing in excess of 90 percent of the strawberry and cantaloupe crops. Hawaii's 1920 plantation strike confirmed the reality and magnitude of the "Japanese menace" and demonstrated that Japan sought economic and political supremacy. In sum, the Japanese displaced white workers, were undesirable citizens, and remained Japanese to the core.

> The Japanese, as a rule, will work longer hours for less money (until he has a foothold): is thrifty, industrious and ambitious. He is a competent farmer—truck-gardener and orchardist. He can and does underbid American labor whenever necessary until he has driven it out; this done, his standards of living are so far below those of the Caucasian that it is utterly impossible to live in competition with

him and maintain American standards. In addition, the Japanese is an undesirable citizen because he does not assimilate. He does not intermarry, nor is it desirable that he should. He does not become an American, save in very rare instances, always remaining a Japanese. Even when born in this country, and educated in our common schools, he is still compelled to attend Japanese schools before and after the public school hours. He is taught by Japanese teachers, who usually speak no English, and who have neither knowledge nor sympathy with the principles of American government and citizenship. He absorbs Japanese ideals and patriotism and that contempt for all other nations which is the spirit of every Japanese school textbook.

A. A. Hopkins usually wrote the bureau's reports in 1922, chronicling the activities of California's Japanese Association, the Japanese in Mexico and the Philippines, Japanese laborers in Hawaii, and Japanese travelers in Los Angeles.[37] The most extraordinary report was filed on March 18. Entitled "Japanese Espionage—Hawaii," Hopkins called attention to the "force of so-called 'Commercial Agents' placed in strategic places and positions" by the Japanese consul for carrying out political, commercial, and military espionage. He proceeded to list 157 Japanese by name, town of residence, and occupation, information derived from a "confidential correspondent in Hawaii." The list included 40 merchants and storekeepers, 31 Buddhist priests, 24 Japanese-language school principals and teachers, 19 laborers, 10 Christian ministers, and 4 professionals.[38] This apparently was the first list of Japanese deemed subversive or potentially dangerous by either civilian or military intelligence.

The Summerall Report

By 1922, the Hawaiian Department's G-2, headed by Colonel Stephen O. Fuqua, was well organized. Its most important duty was "keeping track of the Japanese population."[39] Fuqua was assisted by field clerk Nelson Raymond of the pre-Brooke era and military police from the Corps of Intelligence. Their duties included gathering general information on the Japanese; compiling statistical information on Japanese organizations; keeping track of the activities of certain individuals; meeting all steamships and checking passenger lists; collecting data from Japanese, Chinese, and Korean informants; and investigating the backgrounds of those seeking commissions in the Hawaii National Guard.[40] During the first six months of 1922, Fuqua compiled statistical data, held a conference with "prominent American citizens," and undertook a comprehensive survey of the "Japanese problem" that most likely provided the basis for the Summerall report, which supported the findings of the federal Hawaiian Labor Commission in the fall of that year.[41]

The Summerall report considered in detail those factors that made Hawaii's Japanese a "military problem." These included familiar concerns: the Japanese population and its growth, their concentration and areas of settlement, Japan's consul and his agents, Japanese-language schools and the education of *nisei* in Japan (*kibei*), Buddhism and Shintoism, economic penetration and takeover, the ethnic press, and *nisei* voters and bloc voting. Of particular concern was the loyalty of the second generation because the *nisei* were coming of age and were seen as a testing ground for Americanization.

On the other side of the ledger were ameliorating influences, such as the "Christianization and Americanization campaign" of a Christian minister, Reverend Takie Okumura; the Boy Scout movement; and the Americanization campaign begun by the Japanese consul in 1921, which urged the use of American dress, abolition of the common bath, and improved sanitation around the home. "Under the efficient guidance of some of the best members of the American community," praised the report, "the scout leaders are instilling into these boys the thought that they are Americans and that they must always conduct themselves as American boys are taught to do in the United States."[42]

The Summerall report was largely an update of the Merriam report, albeit with the benefit of some hindsight. Like the earlier report, Summerall's version highlighted the number of Japanese, their rate of increase, and men of military age. The Japanese, noted Summerall, "formed a higher per cent of the population in 1920 than they had ever done in the past" (more than 42 percent) and their birthrate "has been much higher than that of the other racial groups" (238 births per 1,000 Japanese women as compared to 97 births per 1,000 white women).[43]

The Summerall report viewed with dismay Japanese children who attended schools with "American" children but at heart were "almost as much Japanese as their parents were when they left Japan"[44] because of the Japanese-language school, which "had for its principal purpose the inculcating into the young Hawaiian born Japanese child the knowledge that he was a Japanese citizen and that the Yamato race was the greatest race on earth."[45] Such instruction, cautioned the Summerall report, resulted in a whole generation of military-age youth taught "that they must be loyal to Japan."[46] Even more unassimilable were *nisei* educated in Japan—the *kibei*—who were "at heart Japanese and can never be changed into material for American citizenship."[47]

Relying primarily on census figures and estimating the number of births, deaths, and naturalizations, Summerall predicted that, by 1930, the Japanese would constitute 23.2 percent of all potential voters in Hawaii; by 1940, that percentage would climb to 37.6, and by 1950 to 45.6 percent.[48] The report noted the impact of the *nisei* vote. During the general election of November 7, 1922, over 95 percent of the *nisei* voted for the Democratic candidate in the delegate to Congress race because his opponent openly favored the Hawaii Emergency Labor Commission's resolution involving Chinese migrant laborers. This allegedly showed "the complete solidarity of the voters of Japanese ancestry and further that they will cast their votes in the interest of the Japanese community . . . rather than the hopes of the American community."[49] The 1922 election, argued Summerall, also showed how a relatively small group like the *nisei* could swing the election in a tight race[50] and could virtually control Hawaii's elections within ten years when they would constitute about 25 percent of the electorate.[51]

The Summerall report added new areas of concern. Having witnessed the 1920 strike, Summerall expressed apprehension over the extent of Japanese involvement in the economy and the rising militancy of Japanese workers and their unionization. Their upward mobility and employment diversification were termed an "invasion" and their acquisition of skills was considered potentially dangerous to the national security because "their expert and detailed knowledge if directed against the United States could do irreparable damage in a remarkably short time."[52] Japanese "controlled" the fishing industry, rice cultivation, and the operation of taxi cabs. They also far exceeded whites as barbers, blacksmiths, builders and contractors, plumbers, watchmakers, and confectioners, and as operators of drugstores, drygoods stores, fish markets, florist shops, restaurants, and theaters.[53]

Summerall observed a steady decrease in the number of Japanese on sugar plantations over the past fourteen years, but pointed to the rise of Japanese labor unions and the significant role they played in the 1920 strike. According to the report, the strike was a racial conflict in the eyes of both whites and Japanese. Strike leaders appealed to ethnic solidarity and "criticized everything American, condemned the American leaders of the community, American ideals and institutions."[54] Further, the strike and the Japanese community's support of the strikers impressed upon the *nisei* "the ideas of allegiance to the Japanese race, principles of racial solidarity and the necessity of all persons of Japanese descent working together for the support of the Japanese in the Hawaiian Islands."[55] In fact, the consensus among plantation managers was that "the most radical element among the strikers were the Hawaiian born Japanese." The *nisei* had failed their "first real test." Predicted the report: "It is believed that in similar tests that occur during the next ten years they will also fail."[56]

Japanese culture preserved the "solidarity of the Japanese race," but more basic was the relationship between *nisei* and their parents: "One of the most serious drawbacks towards the Americanization of the Hawaiian born Japanese," stated Summerall, was "their attitude towards their parents." Filial affection and respect tied the *nisei* to Japan "as the homeland of their parents, as the land which their parents love, to which they owe their allegiance."[57]

Japanese naval vessels anchored in Hawaiian waters to display Japan's strength and to remind those in the territory that they were Japanese.[58] For the Japanese government, according to Summerall, naval visits served the dual purpose of advancing Japanese nationalism and collecting intelligence information. The report alleged several instances of spying by Japanese naval officers and crew members while on shore leave; some of them disappeared into the local Japanese community and later found employment in various federal and territorial offices such as the court system, immigration service, tax office, school system, and city police. This infiltration, the report warned, placed Japan "in a position to learn many of the important details of the government of the Territory."[59]

The forty-seven-page Summerall report, having weighed the evidence, concluded that the *nisei* were "a military liability to the United States." It predicted that in an emergency, a majority of the *nisei* would remain neutral, depending on local conditions, while only a small number would be loyal to the United States. The report stated categorically that the *nisei* "can never be assimilated" but could be "Americanized," especially after "the present generation of alien parents has passed away" and "the strong Japanistic centers of influence in the Territory have been eliminated."[60]

Surveying the Japanese Situation

The next stage in the development of how military intelligence perceived the Japanese is revealed in the June 1, 1926, MID study, "A Survey of the Hawaiian-born Japanese in the Territory of Hawaii," which discussed eight factors bearing on the "problem" and concluded with an estimate of *nisei* loyalty.[61] This survey again described the Japanese population, its distribution, and factors such as education, religion, politics, culture, the economy, and the Japanese-language press. The survey's findings were familiar: the Japanese lived in segregated, self-contained districts that were "typically Japanese"; they attended Japanese-language schools and Buddhist and Shinto temples, retarding Americanization; they showed ethnic solidarity in their voting pattern during the 1922 election; they were involved in virtually all areas of the economy and were organized into ethnic unions; and the uneducated masses were led by Japanese-language newspapers that were pro-Japanese and anti-American.

Unlike the Summerall report, however, the 1926 survey measured the effects of the Americanization movement, which arose, according to the survey's author, after the white community discovered "growing up in its midst an entirely foreign element, an element that was really as much Japanese as were their parents when they left Japan and further that this element was Japanese because absolutely nothing had been done to make it anything but Japanese." Pivotal in that awakening was the 1920 strike, which showed the "almost perfect solidarity" of the Japanese in trying to dispossess whites of plantation ownership. In spite of Americanization's moderating influence, concluded the survey, the *nisei* would be "a military liability" should there be a war with Japan.

The 1926 survey was revised by the Hawaiian Department's MID in October 1929. "A Survey of the Japanese in the Territory of Hawaii" focused, once again, on the *nisei* and their loyalty.[62] This report, too, examined demographic factors, the 1920 strike, Japanese-language newspapers, education and Japanese-language schools, economic and political "penetration," religion, cultural organizations and festivals, and relations with other racial and ethnic groups. The survey gave special mention to the Okumuras's Americanization efforts, which had "the financial backing of the missionary and Christian business elements in the Territory of Hawaii."[63]

A new category, "combat factors," estimated the military strength of Hawaii's Japanese. It involved 4,500 *issei* who had military training in

Japan, and 175 *issei* and 400 *nisei* who received military training in the United States. The MID failed to uncover any Japanese military organization in the territory, but cautioned: "It should be remembered, however, that the Japanese local industrial and social organization is such as to permit ready creation and putting into effect an organization sufficiently military in character to constitute an important force." As an example, the report cited the Japanese sampan fleet, 500 boats that could easily be transformed into landing vessels.

A second new category listed leaders in the Japanese community, including Japan's consul and vice-consul, but also Japanese residents in the territory: a University of Hawaii professor, a Buddhist, and a Shinto priest, a Japanese-language school principal, two editors of Japanese-language newspapers, business and professional men, and Takie and Umetaro Okumura. Unlike the earlier Bureau of Investigation list, this enumeration made no claim that these people were spies, but candidly declared that they were enumerated solely because they were leaders in the Japanese community. The distinction was an important one; as we later see, the search for spies was abandoned in 1933 for a more pragmatic and wanton approach to internal security.

The 1929 survey concluded that it was apparent "beyond any question that the Japanese race in the Hawaiian Islands, whether alien or native born, is a very definite military liability to the United States, and any failure to estimate the race as such will in the final analysis, result adversely for the army." It was true, continued the report, that whites had tried to suppress Japanism by regulating language schools and the ethnic press and by educating and Americanizing, but those efforts were of little value to *nisei* who were already of military age, and white racism had produced deep resentment among the Japanese, alienating them even more from assimilating into the dominant race. *Issei* and *nisei* alike should be classed as enemy aliens: "In the event of a war with Japan all Japanese, alien and Hawaiian-born, of all ranks, should be considered as enemy aliens ab initio [from the beginning]."

Planning the Defense of Oahu

While intelligence studied the Japanese danger, the army's War Plans Division (WPD) contemplated the defense of Hawaii, or more precisely, of Oahu and Pearl Harbor. Preparations, called "Project for the Defense of

Oahu," formed part of a comprehensive Orange War Plan that anticipated war with Japan (designated "Orange") in combination with a number of potential allies. The Orange War Plan was begun by the WPD during the early 1900s when war with Japan over Pacific dominance seemed inevitable.[64]

Apparently, the secretary of war had approved a plan for the defense of Oahu on January 15, 1921. This plan, revised in 1923 and approved by Army Chief of Staff General John J. Pershing, evidently envisioned the internment of enemy aliens: "The Department Commander will plan to provide for interned aliens and the civilian population, including plans for rationing, conservation, and prevention of waste," directed the order.[65] Other documents shed further light on the nature of the army's thinking on internment. Most helpful was a letter to the army's judge advocate general dated May 21, 1923, from a colonel who was the WPD acting assistant chief of staff. Colonel John L. De Witt would become commander in charge of the Western Defense Command during World War II and would play a pivotal role in the mass removal and confinement of Japanese on the West Coast. De Witt's work on the "Defense of Oahu" project might have influenced his perception of the "Japanese problem" within the Western Defense Command nearly nineteen years later.

In his letter, De Witt detailed the WPD's plans for dealing with Oahu's civilian population, including a proclamation of martial law, registration of all enemy aliens, internment of those deemed a security risk, and restrictions on labor, movement, and public information. De Witt argued for martial law on the grounds of military necessity and asked the chief judiciary officer to rule on the legality of a proclamation and general order that would establish military control over Hawaii. "From a military standpoint and as a measure for adequate defense of the Hawaiian Islands in the event of war with an Asiatic Power or a combination of Powers including an Asiatic Power," wrote De Witt, "the establishment of complete military control over the Hawaiian Islands, including its people, supplies, material, etc., is highly desirable."[66]

De Witt's plan included a draft proclamation that, by reason of a state of war and by virtue of a presidential decree, would impose martial law throughout the territory and would install the department commander as military governor of Hawaii. The writ of *habeas corpus* would be suspended, and civil and judicial officials would function at the pleasure of the military. All enemy aliens would be required to register with the provost marshal, to be classed as those considered dangerous to the community, who would "be interned by district commanders until further orders"; those willing to work on military projects, who would "be permitted to work under guard" and "be interned by district commanders when not at work"; and plantation laborers, domestic servants, and small merchants who wanted to remain employed and who would "be allowed to continue work under constant supervision."

The key features of De Witt's plan included martial law, selective detention rather than mass confinement, and the twin purposes of ensuring internal security and maximizing labor productivity. Whether or not WPD considered all Japanese to be enemy aliens, as MID would define them six years later, was unclear from the proclamation, but WPD certainly believed martial law to be indispensable to Hawaii's defense because of the large and, in their view, undifferentiated population of Japanese in the islands. De Witt's general order showed the efficiency of governing by decree. It proscribed aiding the enemy or hindering the war effort; it mandated immediate military duty for all unemployed men between the ages of fifteen and sixty; it established a curfew and prohibited assemblies and the operation of automobiles, except by military permission; it stripped "enemy aliens" of their telephones; it closed down foreign-language newspapers, theaters, and pool halls; and it regulated radios, firearms, cameras, and liquor. With one stroke of the pen, martial law allowed extensive controls over the lives of civilians.

W. A. Bethel, the judge advocate general, responded to De Witt's inquiry on June 28, 1923, by reviewing the rare occasions when martial law had been instituted in American history and citing the Supreme Court ruling in *ex parte Milligan* (1866) that civilians could not be tried in military courts, even in wartime, when civil courts were operating. He pointed out that martial law was not authorized under the Constitution or existing statutes, but was an extralegal measure "adopted only when necessity demands—the necessity of national self-preservation" and permitted only when there was "a compelling necessity." The situation in Hawaii, wrote Bethel, held all the elements of such necessity. He explained that if the United States were at war with "a strong Asiatic naval power many of whose nationals reside in Hawaii and such persons should be liable to obstruct the measures adopted by our military forces in Hawaii for its prosecution, the civil courts not being able to restrain them, the exercise of military authority over them to whatever extent might be necessary to thwart their acts or intentions would be justified."[67] Bethel thus ruled that martial law in Hawaii was both possible and justifiable—on the grounds of military necessity—and commented that the proclamation and general order were well designed to accomplish the purpose of national security. He noted, however, that under martial law, the writ of *habeas corpus* could not be suspended for the general population but only for those actually held by military authorities. The plan submitted by De Witt, with minor corrections and revisions, was distributed and appropriately filed.[68]

Throughout the 1920s, the 1921 plan for the defense of Oahu, as revised in 1923, remained essentially the same because, as indicated by the Hawaiian commander, Major General E. M. Lewis, there were no changes of importance in the local strategic situation.[69] In 1925, Governor Farrington asked Summerall for a rescinding of the ban on *nisei* serving in the National Guard. Farrington argued that "such a policy will secure the loyalty of these citizens and will remove the resentment which they now feel at the discrimination that is made against them." The WPD in Washington held a contrary opinion: "The Hawaiian Islands may be considered as an outpost of the Pacific Coast. As such their occupation by an enemy would be a serious blow to our security. They are, therefore, of great strategic value and no effort should be spared to insure their proper defense. For this reason the troops which in time of emergency may be called upon to defend the islands should be composed of individuals whose loyalty to America is beyond question."[70] The *nisei*, the WPD held, were surrounded by Japanese influences and were imbued with Japanese culture; thus their enlistment in the National Guard would "seriously prejudice the proper defense of the islands." The WPD recommended against a change in the policy.

A Military Liability

From its beginnings as a labor problem, the "Japanese problem" became one that Hawaii's planters, the territorial and national governments, and the military found most disquieting. At first, the perceived danger posed by the Japanese was a part of a prevailing distrust of aliens, radicals, labor leaders, and blacks. Brooke, writing in Hawaii, depicted Japan's "notoriously immoral" campaign, which allied "hosts of aliens, of radicals, of pacifists and of renegades of every sort and description now rampant in the United States"; the bureau's Eighth Division, headquartered in Los Angeles, envisioned Japan fomenting a black rebellion in America and leading a worldwide revolt of colored people against whites.

By 1922, both military and civilian intelligence in Hawaii and California considered the "Japanese problem" their leading concern. "The most important general intelligence work being done in the Eighth Division," wrote its superintendent, bureau agent H. B. Pierce, in early 1921, "which is not only of local character but national and international in its scope and on a question that is of vital moment to the Government (and by many authorities believed to be of a decided and immediate menace), is the Japanese question or problem, which is often designated and most frequently referred to as the Japanese–California Question." [71]

Clearly, however, the "immediate menace" posed by the "Japanese problem" derived less from its imagined international dimensions than from its domestic manifestations. The earliest indication of its elevation to preeminence, the 1918 Merriam report, had been prompted by the permanence and growth of the Japanese population in Hawaii. Those men, women, and children were said to constitute the combatants in Japan's "peaceful invasion." The military concerns, henceforth, were the sources of Japanism and ways of eliminating them, the Americanization of the second generation and the degree of their loyalty, and the best means to ensure national security while maintaining full productivity.

The military rejected the idea that *nisei* could be assimilated by programs such as the Okumuras' Educational Campaign and thereby made safe for democracy. The Americanization of the second generation was an impossibility, argued Wood in 1921, because Japanese racial and cultural features prevented complete assimilation. Even if they became Americanized in dress and mannerisms, according to the Summerall report, the Japanese could never be fully absorbed into American life and hence would always constitute an alien and troublesome presence. According to a 1921 Bureau of Investigation report: "He [the Japanese] does not become an American, save in very rare instances, always remaining a Japanese."

Insofar as the military preserved the status quo—by guarding against industrial sabotage, suppressing political dissent, and maximizing Japanese labor productivity—it served the purposes of capitalism and Hawaii's oligarchy. The interests of the planters, the territorial government, and the military converged on the "Japanese problem." By the end of 1921, an intelligence network had been created, linking the planters' (HSPA) secret service with the military's MID and ONI and the federal government's Bureau of Investigation. The partnership amassed information and drew up plans to counter the perceived Japanese menace.

In 1922, the Bureau of Investigation listed persons it considered to be dangerous to internal security. Those so-called espionage agents constituted a special group because, according to an earlier bureau report, "it is said, and no doubt with considerable truth, that every Japanese in the United States who can read and write is a member of the Japanese intelligence system."[72] By 1923, the army's WPD planned the internment of selected enemy aliens, registration of all enemy aliens, and imposition of martial law, thereby restricting labor, movement, and information. The extraordinary measure of martial law, argued De Witt, was justified on the grounds of military necessity due to the large numbers of Japanese in the territory.

Before the end of the decade, in 1929, MID proposed to classify all Japanese, aliens and citizens alike, as enemy aliens. Unlike the bureau's 1922 list of spies, the report named Japanese simply because they were leaders in the community. That astonishing development meant that the Japanese interned during World War II were not deprived of their civil liberties because they were subversive, but because they occupied positions of leadership. Further, MID's indiscriminate grouping of all Japanese as "enemy aliens" reflected its judgment rendered on the *nisei*—that they were a military liability—despite the efforts of the planters and the territorial government to Americanize them.

Chapter 7

Extinguishing the Dawn

Do not count on education to do too much for
you, do not take it too seriously. Do not expect a
college degree, an A.B. or a Ph.D., to get you
ahead unduly in this world.
                              —David L. Crawford

Eradicating Japanism

Some called it the "spectre of alien domination"; others, "peaceful penetration"; still others, the "second generation problem." Whatever the designation, the problem in Hawaii during the 1920s and 1930s was the durable Japanese presence and determination to share in the promise of America.

The problem was particularly pressing because the Japanese constituted a significant proportion of the population, 42.7 percent in 1920 and 37.9 percent in 1930.[1] In addition, the generation born with the rights of U.S. citizenship posed a greater problem than their alien parents did because they could, through constitutional means, eventually control the political life of the territory. That possibility accounted for the focus on the *nisei* by military and civilian intelligence and for the Americanization movement launched by the oligarchy during the interwar decades.

The Americanization movement had two basic goals: the elimination of "Japanese" tendencies and the promotion of "American" values. The movement was based on the need for Japanese labor and a recognition of Japanese permanence in America, as opposed to the exclusionist sentiment that sought to displace the Japanese. The movement was also predicated on the notion that the loyalty of the Japanese could be assured through assimilating them.

Becoming American required the elimination of "Japanism." As early as 1918, the Merriam report had identified agents that negated Americanizing influences: the Japanese consul, Japanese-language schools, and Buddhist churches. Accordingly, key features of the Americanization movement involved the education and Christianization of the *nisei*. Besides language schools and Buddhist churches, another obvious target was the Japanese-language press. All these sources of Japanism were subject to surveillance and restrictions.

The *Pacific Commercial Advertiser* on March 17, 1919, offered an editorial opinion on how constitutional guarantees might not apply to the Japanese: "The Constitution, it is true, grants to every man the right to worship according to the dictates of his own conscience, but that does not mean that a religion hostile to our principles shall be taught the children of residents of America, children who are some day to exercise the right of franchise and perhaps help make our laws."

The "Repaganization" of Hawaii

Buddhist priests maintained a comfortable relationship with planters until about 1920. Buddhist missions were encouraged, indeed subsidized, because plantation managers used ethnicity to divide the workers. In return, Buddhist priests frequently intervened on the side of the planters, advising against strikes. The collaboration disintegrated when ethnic solidarity became a powerful instrument of resistance, whereupon Buddhism increasingly became a liability on the plantations.

Buddhist churches played a prominent role in the strike of 1920 with branches of the YMBA serving as nuclei for labor organizing on plantations. During the 1919 movement for higher wages and on the eve of the strike, heads of major Buddhist sects in Hawaii—Bishop Yemyo Imamura of Honpa Hongwanji, Bishop Hosen Isobe of Soto-shu, Acting Bishop Ryozen Yamada of Jodo-shu, and Bishop Chosei Nunome of Nichiren-shu—along with other Buddhist and Shinto priests signed a letter urging the HSPA to accede to the demands of the Federation of Japanese Labor. Buddhist churches also opened their doors to evicted strikers, providing shelter and food. In contrast, "Takie Okumura and other Japanese Christian clerics advised their congregations to oppose the strike because, as Shiro Sokabe put it, the planters had always been 'so good to the church.' " Umetaro Okumura, son of Takie, was hired as a translator for the HSPA on January 19, 1920.[2]

The *Pacific Commercial Advertiser* on October 31, 1919, pointed out that three Buddhist teachers and three YMBA officials sat on the twenty-member executive committee of the Association for Higher Wages. And according to the February 19, 1920, issue of the *Advertiser*, HSPA secretary Royal D. Mead declared that the strike was not prompted by low wages or poor working conditions but was instigated "by the Japanese newspapers and agitators, aided and abetted by the Japanese school teachers and priests." The newspapers amplified that theme with headlines announcing "Buddhist Priests Interfere to Aid Strikers." The papers charged that "pagan priests" were abusing the constitutional guarantee of religious freedom by meddling with "our affairs of government" and stirring up "social and industrial disturbances."[3]

Although out of favor with Hawaii's planters, Buddhism flourished among the Japanese. A 1920 federal commission study reported that the Nishi Hongwanji sect alone had a membership of about 75,000, maintained 60 churches, 30 YMBAS and 40 YWBAS, and operated 42 Japanese-language schools.[4] Christian ministers deplored the "repaganization" of Hawaii (the original "paganism" of Hawaiians having been eradicated by early missionaries) and saw the "Japanese problem" as a question of faith. They viewed with alarm the persistence and growth of Buddhist influence among the Japanese and agreed with an *Advertiser* editorial that "paganism is increasing and heretics are infesting the community."

The hostility that Christians exhibited toward "pagan temples" was not a simple matter of doctrinal purity or revulsion against idolatry. Christian ministers stigmatized Buddhist priests with the stamp of political disloyalty and condemned the "alien priests" for promoting Japanism and luring the *nisei* away from American (Christian) influences. According to a historian of Buddhism in Hawaii, "the Christian clergy continued to label Buddhist educational practices a Japanizing force responsible for Hawaii's social and religious problems. The schools run by the 'priests of paganism' thus continued to be condemned ipso facto as 'un-American in principle [and] subversive to patriotism.' "[5]

Planters' Gospel

Near the strike's end, in June 1920, Christian leaders began an "American-ize and Christianize the plantations" movement, which strove to estab-lish a Sunday school on every plantation. Takie and Umetaro Okumura opened an "Educational Campaign among Japanese labor on various plan-tations" in January of the following year, drawing endorsements from prominent members of the Japanese government and business commu-nity, led by Viscount Eiichi Shibusawa, and from the inner circle of Hawaii's oligarchy, including the Atherton, Castle, and Cooke families.[6]

Shibusawa was chairman of the Nichi-Bei Kankei-Iin-Kai (Japan–America Relation Committee), the main objective of which was trade. In endorsing the Educational Campaign, the committee asked the visit-ing Takie Okumura: "On your return to Hawaii, will you not inform our countrymen in Hawaii of our aims, and enable them to cooperate with us in the promotion of everlasting, cordial relations between America and Japan, and the two peoples?"[7]

In his autobiography, Takie Okumura explained his motives for starting the Educational Campaign, which lasted for about ten years, from January 1921 to December 1929. The strike of 1920, he wrote, had stirred up anti-Japanese hostility among white people, and "thoughtful leaders feared that even Hawaii would be engulfed in ugly racial disturbances like those of California." Thus, "while there was still time, we felt that we must strive to dispel the thickening clouds, enabling the Japanese to see their mistakes and urging them to go more than half way in settling their differ-ences with American people."[8] According to Okumura, the root cause of anti-Japanese sentiment was Japanese culture. He thus advised: "Forget the idea 'Japanese' and always think and act from the point of view of the American people, as long as you live under their protection and enjoy many privileges and blessings."[9]

Takie and Umetaro Okumura visited forty-seven plantations on the islands of Kauai, Oahu, Maui, and Hawaii during the first seven months of the campaign and, in consultation with each plantation manager, se-lected a group of ten to twenty workers. "With these men," they wrote, "we hold a face to face conference, present our ideas very frankly, and try to convince them. When the men are convinced, and decide to cooperate with us, or act as volunteers in the community while we are gone, we ask their pledges."[10]

The Okumuras reported that all but one of the plantation managers cooperated with them; the lone exception believed that the *nisei* were unsuitable as workers. "Americanization work is no use," he was quoted as saying, "no good; a Jap should always be a Jap. Hawaiian-born Japs are no good. They're too weak. All they want is a soft-snap job. We don't want them." [11] Most plantation managers were receptive to the idea of the campaign's brand of *nisei* education, for which the Okumuras were grateful: "We were impressed greatly by the frankness and readiness of plantation managers to do all that they can for the laborers. We believe in some cases too much has been done and no efforts were made to have the laborers realize that they must work in order to secure any reform or improvement." [12]

During the remaining months of that first year, the Okumuras visited twenty-eight additional plantations. Having surveyed workers on seventy-five plantations in all, they concluded that on some plantations, "Japanese laborers are looked upon as very unreliable laborers. They become easily provoked over little things, pack their belongings and shift from place to place." As a result, observed the Okumuras, the reputation of Japanese workers had suffered and, more important, the Japanese as a group were "gradually losing the confidence of [the] American people." Consequently, "we urged them [Japanese workers] that their pressing duty today is to build up their character and efficiency, and be recognized by the plantations as really reliable and indispensable laborers." [13]

Umetaro Okumura acknowledged his debt to the planters in a letter of March 19, 1927, to plantation manager B. D. Baldwin. The annual Educational Campaigns, he wrote, had been fashioned "to make the Japanese laborers see the value of labor on the sugar plantation and [to] encourage the young element to follow the footsteps of their parents." Okumura asked Baldwin not to reveal the true purpose of the campaign (its stated goal was to promote goodwill between whites and Japanese) and, above all, that it was financed by the HSPA (the Japanese were under the impression that the campaign was financed by Japanese dignitaries like Viscount Shibusawa).[14] Still, Japanese workers remained skeptical of the Okumuras: "Just as I expected," wrote Takie Okumura, "the Japanese misunderstood me. They thought that I was out to break up the labor unions or spread Christianity under cover of Americanization or educational campaign." [15]

The merging of religious belief with political allegiance by the Christian clergy was in accord with the Americanization movement's claim that Buddhism and other alien ideologies encouraged rebelliousness, while Christianity promoted patriotism. According to Takie Okumura, the Japanese could never consider themselves to be "true Americans" until they could say to white people, "Your country is my country; your God is my God." [16] Superintendent of Public Instruction Vaughan MacCaughey agreed with that sentiment when he wrote: "The variety of Buddhism dominant in Hawaii is medieval, ultra-superstitious and intensely Japanese." In Buddhist homes, "true Americanization" could never take root and flourish; thus, concluded the public servant charged with the education of the territory's youth: "Hawaii can not be American until she truly Christianizes her population, and makes dominant *the Christian home.*" [17]

The newspapers likewise cautioned against the perils posed by Buddhism to American democracy. During the 1920 strike, the *Star-Bulletin*, in its May 24 edition, pointed to the involvement of Buddhist priests on the side of the strikers and saw it as a challenge "flung out by a growing paganism that is un-American, undemocratic, [and] destructive . . . in its influences on American institutions and standards in the territory." In offering that challenge, the *Star-Bulletin* of July 12, 1920, declared, Buddhism had overstepped the bounds of religious freedom and had shown its true self, as a sinister force that "must always by its very nature, be arrayed against sound Americanism."

The Educational Problem

Japanese-language schools, like the Buddhist churches, were nurtured and funded by the planters, but when ethnicity solidified worker resistance, the language schools, too, were condemned and curtailed. The language-school bill of 1919 showed that fall from grace. Although the bill failed to pass the Senate, the territorial legislature authorized the governor to request that the federal Bureau of Education undertake a survey of education in Hawaii and allocated funds for the study. Commissioners gathered testimony in Hawaii during the fall of 1919 as the movement for higher wages on plantations was gaining momentum and released their recommendations two weeks after the end of the 1920 strike. The results of the survey, transmitted to the secretary of interior in July 1920, formed the basis of the first law regulating Japanese-language schools in the islands.

Education, the commissioners stated, served the nation by molding "dependable, patriotic, and worthy citizens." It served the local community by providing "competent leaders and efficient workers in all its occupations." And it served the individual by developing personal abilities. Nevertheless, conditions unique to Hawaii militated against the successful implementation of American ideals of education. Foremost was a "racial situation" in the islands brought about by the territory's efforts "to secure cheap laborers in sufficient numbers to care for the crops of sugar cane."[18] The net result was a racial situation that existed nowhere else in the United States, consisting of white people in a numerical minority and a rapidly growing Japanese population no longer satisfied with filling the need for cheap plantation labor, but holding ambitions of economic and political dominance in the islands. That racial situation constituted the "educational problem" in Hawaii's public schools.

The problem was compounded by Japanese-language schools, which existed "outside the law" and independent of the territorial educational authorities.[19] The report traced the origins and purposes of the language schools, their connections with Buddhist churches, and their early support by the planters "in order that their employees may be better satisfied with plantation conditions."[20] It examined in detail the curriculum and textbooks used in the language schools, translating choice selections to show how the readings promoted race pride.[21]

The commission was convinced that the language schools were "centers of an influence which, if not distinctly anti-American, is certainly un-American. Because of these schools, children born here of foreign parents, soon to become the voters of this Commonwealth, soon to play a prominent part in the affairs of the Territory, are being retarded in accepting American customs, manners, ideals, principles, and standards."[22] Before drawing up recommendations on the issue, the commission invited the opinions of civic and business organizations in the territory.

The Daughters of the American Revolution (Aloha chapter) urged the abolition of the language schools, declaring itself to be "unequivocally opposed" to all practices "subversive to the peace and order of our Nation and the undivided allegiance of our people." "We take a firm stand for Americanism in it [*sic*] truest and loftiest form, and for one language— that of our heroic Revolutionary ancestors who gave their fortunes and their lives that the United States might live and prosper, and one flag— 'Old Glory.' "

The Honolulu Chamber of Commerce recommended that public supervision of language schools make it "impossible for any person to serve as a teacher of youth who does not possess ideals of democracy and a knowledge of American history and methods of government and of the English language." The Ad Club proposed the gradual elimination of language schools and the absorption of foreign-language study into the public school curriculum.[23]

Taking these responses as reflective of public opinion, the commission proposed to "abolish all foreign language schools at the next session of the legislature." Excluded were schools for Asian migrant children not supported by public funds but by the parents of those children. The proposal was designed to reduce public expenditures on migrant laborers and eliminate a principal source of "Japanization" among those who would remain and eventually form part of the electorate. The commission recommended that foreign-language classes be offered in the public schools where there was a demand for such courses, after the regular school session, and taught by certified public school teachers.

The commission proposed other restrictions as well. Only students making satisfactory progress in the regular curriculum would be allowed to take foreign-language classes, and parents would be required to pay a surcharge to support the cost of language courses. A newly created division of foreign languages in the Department of Public Instruction would supervise the operation of language classes and examine, appoint, and dismiss teachers to "bring together a corps of persons who combine a mastery of the oral and written language, teaching skill and unquestioned loyalty to American ideals." The commission also voted to extend the school day for children whose parents worked in the fields so that education would not interfere with agricultural production.[24]

Abolition of the language schools was, in fact, the goal of the Americanization movement. "God pity us," lamented Judge Horace W. Vaughan, "if, in a few years, when the Japanese . . . have the voting majority, they chose to vote for race rather than principle." Instead of leaving that choice to chance, Vaughan urged the education of the *nisei:* "It is a matter calling for preparation, and the immediate consideration in that preparation is for us to do our full duty in Americanizing those who . . . are citizens of Hawaii or are soon to be citizens of Hawaii; and that means the elimination of the Japanese language schools."[25] Albert Palmer seconded Vaughan's sentiment in calling attention to the "evils" of the language schools: "I summon you today to a renewed faith in American ideals and American education," he admonished. "These Islands must be 100 percent American . . . [and] the first and most obvious step is the elimination of the foreign language schools." [26]

Toward the end of 1920, the attorney general and the Honolulu Chamber of Commerce drafted bills for the regulation of foreign-language schools. A special session of the legislature was called in November to consider a bill drawn up on the lines of the federal commission's recommendations. Faced with the inevitable, leaders of the Japanese community sought to salvage some measure of dignity and accordingly formed a committee to draft a counterproposal. They submitted it to the Honolulu Chamber of Commerce, which endorsed the measure over its own version after having received the promise of Japanese business, professional, and religious leaders that they would support the enactment and enforcement of the compromise bill. After a unanimous vote in the Senate and a five-to-one margin in the House, Act 30, as it was designated, became law on November 24, 1920, with the governor's signature.[27]

Act 30 steered a middle ground on the question of foreign-language schools. Its intention was not to abolish the schools but to regulate them under the jurisdiction of the Department of Public Instruction. The law authorized the department to issue and revoke permits to language schools for their operation and to test and certify teachers, requiring them to have a knowledge of the "ideals of democracy, American history and institutions and the English language." It also empowered the department to regulate the curriculum, textbooks, and hours of operation.[28] Finally, the act required that all teacher applicants sign a pledge to "direct the minds and studies of pupils . . . as will tend to make them good and loyal American citizens." [29]

The act did not go far enough for the Americanizers, who found ways to impose additional restrictive controls. Under the act, the Department of Public Instruction appointed a joint textbook revision committee consisting of whites appointed by the department and Japanese appointed by Consul General Yada. Instead of working together, white committee members met separately and made proposals that exceeded their original charge of revising textbooks. Most notable was their plan to eliminate kindergarten and the first two grades of Japanese-language schools and to limit language-school admission to those who had completed the second grade of public school. Despite the protests of the Japanese community and mass parent meetings, the Department of Public Instruction adopted the new regulations on August 26, 1922.[30]

Commenting on the "snap judgment" of the department, Lorrin A.

Thurston, *Advertiser* editor, wrote on September 13, 1922: "I venture no opinion as to the technical correctness of this ruling; but morally and practically it is a partial abolishment, for if the Board can eliminate three out of nine years it can eliminate six; and if it can eliminate six it can eliminate any other number, until the course is frittered away indirectly, although the law specifically states that its object is to 'regulate and not abolish.' " The future of the Japanese-language schools appeared bleak.

Promoting "Americanism"

While eradicating Japanism, the Americanization movement sought to promote Americanism. Some, like Takie Okumura, formed their own organizations and became itinerant preachers taking the gospel of Americanization to the plantations; others directed their work of education through existing bodies, such as the public schools, churches, Young Men's and Women's Christian Associations, and other civic and business groups. The goal, whatever the means, was assimilation or Anglo conformity.[31]

Still others advocated breaking up Asian communities and relocating their members throughout the nation. Wallace M. Alexander, president of Alexander and Baldwin, discussed the problem in the March 8, 1928, edition of the *Star-Bulletin*: "One of the greatest problems we will have to meet within the next five or six years, is that of what to do with the second generation of Orientals here. It is also going to be one of California's problems, although upon a smaller scale." Asians, Japanese and Chinese, born "to all the rights of citizenship" posed an insoluble problem except by "in some way spreading the American citizens of foreign ancestry throughout the United States." Alexander's opinion on the matter was apparently shared by "a considerable number of the sugar men."[32]

Competent Leaders, Efficient Workers

The campaign to win the hearts and minds of the *nisei* was broadly conceived as an educational effort, to inculcate American values but also to direct the second generation into useful labor. American schools, the 1920 federal survey on education in Hawaii stated, ought to produce "competent leaders and efficient workers" to serve the particular needs of the local community. The school "can never be charged, rightly, with influencing its children to turn away from legitimate labor of any kind."[33] Hawaii's schools should provide academic training for literacy and the opportunity to pursue professional work, argued the commissioners, because "outside of teaching, the islands offer comparatively few opportunities in the professions." The schools must educate the "great mass" of children to "find their opportunities either in agriculture itself or in occupations directly related to agricultural enterprises."[34]

"The elementary school in this connection, for example, should be devoting much attention to training in the various forms of handwork, manual work, cooking, simple sewing, the making of beds, and the care of the house, the making of school and home gardens, the organizing of pig clubs and poultry clubs," directed the study. "Every junior and senior high school in the Territory should have near by a well-stocked farm in charge of a practical, progressive, scientific farmer and his wife who herself should be an expert in all those matters properly falling within the field of the duties of a housewife on a farm."[35]

Agricultural training in the schools was not aimed at independent farming but at work on the sugar and pineapple plantations. "It must be clear," explained the survey authors, "that the vocational needs as well as the vocational opportunities of the islands are in large part connected directly or indirectly with the sugar industry, and in a less degree with pineapple growing. Obviously, the educational system of Hawaii must take into account the specific opportunities for employment which the sugar industry affords in all its phases."[36]

The same educational philosophy that advocated vocational training for Hawaii's masses—mainly Asians—defended segregated public schools that produced, in one track, "efficient workers," and in the other, "competent leaders." The institutionalization of segregated schools was thinly masked as a movement to preserve the English (American) language from the corrupting influence of pidgin English spoken mainly by the non-white majority. During the summer of 1920, at the height of the strike, 400 concerned parents petitioned Superintendent MacCaughey for a school for English-speaking children. Writing to Governor McCarthy on July 1, 1920, the school superintendent outlined his reasons for supporting the petitioners: "The children of those parents who have known no other allegiance than to America have as much right to an education at public expense as have children of parents of other origins. Such children *have a right to such an education* under conditions which will insure them and their parents that it can be had without endangering those standards and character quality which are distinctly *American* and which must be preserved and kept inviolate and are a part of them because of their parentage."[37] MacCaughey's logic prevailed. Central Grammar School became the first "English standard school" in the fall of 1920.

Despite MacCaughey's assurance that race or nationality would not be considered in selecting students, Central Grammar School, later renamed Lincoln School, had a student body in 1925 of 546 white children, 135 Hawaiians, 78 Portuguese, and only 27 Chinese and 16 Japanese—at a time when the Chinese and Japanese constituted about 60 percent of the total number of students enrolled in public schools.[38] The standard schools had, in effect, become segregated institutions. Three other elementary schools in Honolulu were designated standard schools: Thomas Jefferson, Kapalama, and Aliiolani. Later, Robert Louis Stevenson Junior High School and Roosevelt High School completed the segregated twelve-year system. They were joined by Lihue Grammar School on the island of Kauai, Kaunoa Grammar School on Maui, and Riverside School in Hilo on the island of Hawaii.[39]

The dual school system was shown to be inherently unequal as late as 1941 in tests comparing children in standard schools with those in nonstandard schools. The survey showed that sixth graders in standard schools achieved a 6.2 grade level, while their counterparts in nonstandard schools scored at a 5.4 level. The gap widened as students continued their schooling. Ninth graders in standard schools achieved a 9.4 grade level, while their peers in nonstandard schools fell to a 7.6 level, and twelfth graders in standard schools scored two full grade levels above nonstandard students.[40] The segregated public schools, functioning until 1947, not only protected the "pure Americanism" of white children but nudged some children toward becoming "competent leaders" and steered the masses of children toward becoming "efficient workers."

The planters, nonetheless, were not uniformly in support of education for Asian workers, especially during the period of migration, when most of them believed that an ignorant workforce was a docile workforce. As Pahala, Hawaii, plantation manager James C. Campsie declared: "Public education beyond the fourth grade is not only a waste, it is a menace. We spend to educate them and they will destroy us."[41] School chief Mac-Caughey described the sentiment prevailing in 1919: "Education for the working people was generally opposed as unfitting the serfs for menial field labor"; in contrast, whites built academies for their children. "These finishing schools have been largely cultural, academic and esthetic, with little vocational emphasis." [42] That idea and practice prompted the 1920 federal commission on education to lecture the planters: "Men who work in occupations deemed unworthy, and who do so only because driven to it by the biting lash of necessity, are in reality not free men. They work only in the spirit of the slave. There is no place in America for such, and it is as much the business of education to teach men this as it is to make them literate." [43]

Hawaii's version of progressive education can be traced to nineteenth-century missionaries whose schools were essential to their "civilizing" mission of teaching good citizenship and comity. The Baldwin House and American Citizenship Schools on Maui exemplified missionary ideals by providing, free of charge to plantation workers, a kindergarten, night classes, and a library. Fourteen citizenship schools existed on the island by 1920, sponsored in large part by the Baldwins, masters of Maui, and with a predominantly Japanese student body. [44]

But progressive education held that schools should direct Hawaii's masses toward manual labor in the basic industries. Among the foremost proponents of vocational education during the 1920s was Governor Farrington, who directed that "the Superintendent [MacCaughey] and his department should be friendly to industry and should instruct the children in the dignity of manual labor." Farrington advised the department to increase its spending on promoting agriculture and to create a domestic-service component in the public schools "to encourage more Filipinos to become domestic servants." As publisher of the *Honolulu Star-Bulletin*, he sponsored contests rewarding children for their horticultural achievements. [45] As a result, concluded a study of educational practices in Hawaii, "the schools made a concerted effort to counter the flow of young men off the plantations so that planters would not have further reason to continue to import foreign labor." [46]

Their Own Worst Enemy

The Americanizers targeted the *nisei* not only because of their citizenship but also because they increasingly replaced aging *issei* in the workforce. According to an Educational Campaign participant, "during the campaign, Mr. Okumura came into contact with many American citizens of Japanese ancestry and realized that the major problem . . . was not that of educating the alien Japanese, but that of 'Americanizing' the new citizens, because these New Americans were gradually replacing their parents as workers on the plantations."[47] Thus was inaugurated the Conference of New Americans, under Okumura's tutelage, in August 1927.

The Conference of New Americans blamed the "Japanese problem" on the Japanese, rather than on those who defined the Japanese as a problem. "Japanese on all plantations had peculiar prejudices and misunderstandings against the American people," wrote Okumura. "Americans, they imagined, were all 'big shots,' so to speak, and had no interest in Japanese laborers. . . . They were always laboring under the misunderstanding that these Americans were forever trying to take advantage of them."[48] Prejudice against whites, Okumura thought, could be overcome by introducing *nisei* to prominent whites as peers. Thus he invited promising *nisei* throughout the territory to attend an annual conference in Honolulu, away from the rural plantations.

In all, 640 delegates, representing seventy-five communities, attended the fifteen annual conferences held from 1927 to 1941. All the delegates, with three exceptions, were American citizens; women constituted one-fourth of the total; and about half came from Honolulu.[49] Each conference lasted several days and usually followed a format of guest presentations and group discussions on selected topics that fell into three broad areas of work, culture, and politics. "The agricultural industries and their occupational opportunities were discussed most frequently," reported an observer. "The sugar industry was discussed at every session as were the employment opportunities in this basic Hawaiian industry." *Nisei* identity was the theme at eight of the twelve conferences: "The discussion generally centered about the question of what customs and manners of the Japanese the New Americans should retain and what they should discard." Political topics included the importance of registering and voting, party affiliation, and the danger of bloc voting.[50]

The Burden of Race

Governor Farrington headed the list of speakers at the first conference in 1927. In his talk, Farrington reminded the *nisei* that they were the topic of discussions both in Hawaii and throughout the nation and were "one of the very serious problems of this part of the world." The problem, however, was neither unique nor unsolvable, and it remained for the *nisei* to decide the future of the Japanese in America. "As to the immediate problem," advised Farrington, "you have a real worthwhile piece of work to do. You are new Americans. . . . One of the problems is whether or not boys and girls are going to mould into our American life. . . . In doing this, in proving that it can be done . . . you are doing a double service— service to the United States where you were born, and also to the people of the ancestry of which you come."[51] The governor's opening remarks set the framework for the fifteen conferences, placing the burden of the problem squarely on the shoulders of *nisei* "boys" and "girls."

The burden of race and the continued association of *nisei* with Japan in the mind set of Hawaii's rulers loomed ever larger as war clouds gathered. When Admiral Yates Stirling, Jr., commandant of the Fourteenth Naval District, spoke to the delegates at the sixth conference in 1932, he did not mince words; at the outset, he declared that he doubted the loyalty of the *nisei* because of race: "I had in mind the ancient civilization of the Japanese people, their art, literature, their achievements in peace and war, their code of Bushido, their veneration for their emperor, and their obsession of filial duty to their parents, and those from whom they have received the sacred blood of kinship." How could a people with such a proud heritage "truly efface their allegiance to Japan and adopt full loyalty to a nation so different in historical background?" Stirling challenged the *nisei* to prove their undivided loyalty, but cautioned: "Gentlemen [twelve of the forty-seven delegates were women], your task of convincing all America of your unquestioned loyalty is not an easy one."[52]

In Their Parents' Footsteps

The goal of the Educational Campaign—"to make the Japanese laborers see the value of labor on the sugar plantation and [to] encourage the young element to follow the footsteps of their parents"—also undergirded the "new Americans" enterprise. David L. Crawford, University of Hawaii president, told delegates at the first annual conference that the "Japanese problem" was one of absorption into the mainstream and that assimilation depended on fit, or "congeniality," between the immigrant and the indigenous population, on how well the "new Americans" met the needs of the employers. "Looking concretely at our problem here, it is obvious that a great number of our young people must go into the agricultural industry—sugar, pineapples, coffee and general farming." *Nisei* should not scorn "rough work," "menial and drudgery work," the university president advised. "Too many of the young people of Japanese and Chinese ancestry consider agriculture as beneath them—they want white-collar jobs. This is due largely to the teaching of their parents, either consciously or unconsciously, to avoid drudgery which they themselves have had to endure." Instead, Crawford declared, young people "must be satisfied with what they can get at first and hope to work up." He concluded by offering the *nisei* two blunt alternatives: develop a "proper attitude" toward farming or emigrate to Japan or the mainland, "for there are not enough positions in other lines here." [53]

Superintendent of Public Instruction Will C. Crawford underscored the university president's counsel. "The majority of the Japanese parents today," he decried, "are trying to push their children through all of the schools—elementary, high school and university. There is a danger in this." Rather than push "a child of inferior ability" through the university, parents should "enlist the interest of children in vocational education, especially in agriculture," he advised.[54] That admonition was repeated three years later when David Crawford addressed the fourth conference:

> Do not count on education to do too much for you, do not take it too seriously. Do not expect a college degree, an A.B. or a Ph.D., to get you ahead unduly in this world. There may have been a time when a college degree was pretty effective in doing that but that time, if it ever existed, has gone long ago. Education is important today, more important than ever before, but it must be education in the proper sense. Education is a process which goes on through life, in which degrees are merely incidents along the way. If your life affairs should take you along a road where these degrees are not handed out, just remember they are only incidents and will not be missed.[55]

The contradiction between the American ideal of equal opportunity and the "back-to-the-soil" admonition was strikingly apparent to the delegates. During the second conference, in 1928, the *nisei* discussed the question why young people were leaving the plantations: "We are willing to start to work from the very bottom, but plantations keep us there, that's the trouble," explained a delegate. "When we find a more profitable work, and as long as the plantations import cheap labor, why should we choose to go back to the life of our fathers?" A *nisei* commentator summed up the discussion: "The general consensus of opinion seemed to be that wages on [the] plantation are entirely incompatible with American standard of living, that the 'Back-to-the-soil' movement as suggested by the territorial agriculturists is wrong in principle. The young people's tastes for Occidental things are increased while the means of securing them is not. Until this situation is remedied, the exodus to the congested centers will continue."[56]

During the 1931 conference, a *nisei* recalled how the sweat of the *issei* generation legitimized the *nisei*'s claim to better work opportunities: "When our parents came to Hawaii thirty to forty years ago, they worked on the plantations and were treated as coolies. It was a struggle between capital and labor. Being treated in this manner, they always reminded their children not to seek work on the plantation. It is natural for our parents to try to better the conditions of their children." Still another spoke from personal experience: "No one denies the fact that we have to go back to the soil. But I have known many young people who are still in the same position, after they have struggled hard for many years. This brings added discouragement to the laborers. As long as they are classed as coolies, there will be no encouragement for young people."

The group leader, seemingly oblivious to what had been said, exhorted the *nisei*:

> The Department of Public Instruction has modified its curriculum to encourage field work. The inferiority complex in the plantation should be entirely discouraged. You must get in step with the new educational policy and the new era. The doors are open to the people who are willing to get into the industries of Hawaii. You must always remember that men like Lincoln, Edison, and Ford have sprung from the lowest type of work. They gave to the world instead of just taking from the world. In proportion to what you give to the world, you will get any value from it.[57]

Nisei disenchantment with plantation work was widespread. Frank C. Atherton, president of Castle and Cooke, sought to address questions posed by the "new Americans" at their sixth conference in 1932. Calling

Hawaii's employment situation one of the "grave problems" of the day, Atherton reminded his audience that most of them would have to find employment in agriculture or face unemployment: "As you go back to your homes remember that 7 out of 10 of those in the schools today, if they earn an honest living will have to work in one of these [sugar or pineapple] industries, otherwise they are liable to become paupers, or turn to criminal pursuits." He asked: "Isn't it better to make an effort to get work and prove yourself capable and then try and secure improvements in conditions, as an employee, rather than to remain unemployed and simply criticize the way things are conducted?" Atherton closed by citing improvements made on plantations during the past twenty years and urged: "Please remember we are not a set of hard-boiled people trying to get all we can as cheaply as possible. We want to be fair and to build up in a fair way." [58]

"Simon-pure" Americans

At the end of the first conference, Clifton H. Yamamoto, a delegate from Honolulu, summed up his views of the discussions: "As I see it, the young people are charged with improving themselves, socially and economically through more individual effort. They are advised to pick out the best qualities in both the Japanese and American cultures; to acquire more frankness, aggressiveness, thrift and other beautiful qualities." [59] Several speakers admonished the *nisei* to remember their Japanese heritage and, in the words of Rokuro Nakaseko, "Americanize" it. "You must become true Americans," he declared. *"But as the descendants of the Puritan remember the blood that flows in their veins,* you must not forget your Japanese blood. Remember the true characteristics of the Japanese race—indomitable spirit, loyalty and obedience to those in authority, love of peace and humility. Americanize these characteristics and be good Americans!" [60]

In reality, the Americanizers advocated conformity to the ways of the dominant group. Victor S. K. Houston, territorial delegate to Congress, praised certain aspects of Japanese culture but also advised that Americanism demanded the ability to speak standard English and not pidgin: "In order that we may be recognized as a thoroughly sound American community . . . we must realize the importance of speaking correctly the English language. . . . Don't allow it to be said that you speak poor English. We are Americans, let us speak as Americans do, and I am sure by doing so you will reap greater dividends."[61]

Takie Okumura praised the *nisei* at the 1932 conference for being "thoroughly American in thought and feeling," for speaking better English than Japanese, and for identifying with America to such an extent that American citizenship was to them "a badge of honor and distinction." They were "truly 100 per cent American." Still, whites doubted the assimilability and loyalty of the *nisei*—not because of the "new Americans" but because their parents continued to hold on to the customs and language of Japan. "In short," concluded Okumura, "all the criticisms and misunderstandings under which the Hawaiian-born are laboring are the results of evidences manufactured not by the young people but by the adult Japanese." Consequently, "what the Hawaiian-born ought to do is to ignore the parents and adult Japanese and lead the young people in removing all forces which retard their development as American citizens, and prove that they are good and loyal American citizens."[62]

Okumura's way demanded a heavy sacrifice. Not only were the *nisei* told to ignore their parents; they were advised to submerge their own desires for the wishes of whites. "In everything," declared Okumura to the assembled delegates at the eighth conference, "we must cooperate with the American people, and in every issue we must always think and act from the point of view of the American people. At times you may be misunderstood by the older Japanese, or you may differ with them. You must not forget your respect for them, but you must not be dictated by them." He exhorted the *nisei*: "In all things you must not forget that you are American citizens, and you must do your duties as loyal citizens. Don't be a fence-straddler, but be strong, simon-pure Americans!"[63]

Regular Channels

Frank Atherton spoke on political responsibility at the second conference: "Perhaps there is going to come the temptation to form a clique and work for one of your friends of your own nationality," surmised the chief of Castle and Cooke. "Personally I feel more progress will be made if we forget our race when it comes to elections and work through the regular channels, work with inter-racial groups, not with racial groups for the best men put up by the party, or independently. I do think it would be a mistake for groups of Hawaiians, Anglo-Saxons, Japanese, Chinese or Portuguese to vote as a race in a solid block, rather than voting for the best candidate irrespective of his nationality."[64]

Nisei delegates at the 1930 conference dissected the idea of a color-blind electorate during a discussion on youth, politics, and bloc voting. "If the other nationalities do bloc voting," commented one delegate, "the Japanese have the right to bloc [vote] also." Another demurred: "But we must not try to form bloc just because others do. We should refrain from bloc voting. On account of the alarming statements made by many people regarding future control of politics in Hawaii, the attention of the mainland people is on Hawaii and we Japanese must be very careful in our conduct or else commission form of government may be introduced here." Delegates, in rejoinder, questioned the merits of a democracy that threatened repression for exercising freedom of choice and pointed out that the Japanese had no representatives in the legislature. "How can we get a representative without being criticized?" they asked. "We should have somebody to represent the Japanese because there are many Japanese who pay taxes. The Japanese have similar problems as any other nationality." Another delegate added that the Japanese were defeated at the polls "because the plantations controlled most of the votes. The big people bought the votes."[65]

Speaking at the seventh conference, the army's Hawaiian commander, General Briant H. Wells, addressed Japanese loyalty, Japan's interest in Hawaii, and the potential for "peaceful penetration" through the ballot box. He warned the *nisei*, "I can only emphasize the fact that these Hawaiian Islands are American Territory; that they will always remain so; and that if foolish individuals or groups, through conspiracy, intrigue, or ambition should aspire to change or modify that status, even though the coast seems clear to do so, and the procedure be patterned in the 'American Way'; they would inevitably realize nothing but disappointment in the hour of anticipated triumph."[66]

The question of *nisei* loyalty became increasingly a central subject of the conference, which from its inception in 1927 had invited mainly business and political leaders from the white and Japanese communities. There was no military presence until 1931 when an American Legion representative addressed the delegates and in 1932 when Hawaii's army commander and the Fourteenth Naval District commandant spoke to the *nisei*. Henceforth, from 1932 to the last conference in 1941, military leaders were regular conference features. Also, beginning in 1932, the delegates visited, on alternate years, Pearl Harbor and Schofield Barracks.

The military called for a demonstration of undivided loyalty from the *nisei* to the country of their birth. In 1939, Major General Charles D. Herron, commander of the Hawaiian Department, challenged the delegates to "nail your colors to the yardarm," while Commander John H. Buchanan, representing the Fourteenth Naval District, admonished the *nisei* to "be proud of your government."[67] Herron spoke to the delegates the next year on the menace of "Fifth Columnists" who used "bribery, treason and treachery" to advance their cause. He described the malevolent influence of Japanese-language-school teachers and directed the *nisei* to "purge language schools of alien teachers." "I believe the time has come to put our house in order," advised the general. "In regard to matters I have today discussed you young Americans have not only a very special interest, but a very special power. You cannot ignore them except at your peril."[68]

About five months before Pearl Harbor, Captain Irving H. Mayfield, speaking on behalf of the commandant of the Fourteenth Naval District, declared, "We count on you." He counseled the *nisei* to reject the influence of their parents and grandparents if that led them away from loyalty to America. "The American people as a whole welcome you with your fine traits of loyalty, perseverance, industry and thrift; they ask only that you adapt your virtues to your citizenship and that you cast aside the customs and loyalties of your forebears when such customs and loyalties are not consistent with true American citizenship."

Lieutenant Colonel Walter C. Phillips, representing the army commander, followed Mayfield and warned against the "alien germ." He itemized the responsibilities of the *nisei* in the national defense effort: to "support all counter-propaganda objectives by emphasizing the unreliability of alien promises"; to "affirm our loyalty on all occasions; if necessary creating an opportunity to do so"; to "join in whole-heartedly in all defense efforts; half-way measures cannot be permitted and will be misinterpreted"; to "report to the responsible authorities all disloyal persons or subversive plans of which we know or which may come to our knowledge"; and to remain calm.[69]

Despite lectures on democracy, responsible citizenship, and voter participation, the *nisei* were not free to elect a candidate on the basis of qualifications, run for office, or seek proportional ethnic representation. They were warned against forming political cliques and reminded that their voting record was being carefully monitored, both locally and nationally. Delegates at the 1930 conference reported on their observations of what actually happened during elections. "The voters are being watched by the plantations as to what people they vote for," they testified. "The plantations hire people to go around campaigning for the candidates they want elected and they see to it that the laborers vote for these candidates." When asked what their response was to the situation, one delegate replied: "If you are earning your bread and butter from the plantation and can not get any other job it is better for you to do what the plantation wants you to do. In fact, there is no other way out of it." Responded another, "On Kauai any person who runs against the Haole is in danger of losing his job."[70]

Similarly, appeals to patriotic duty made *nisei* feel they had to demonstrate loyalty in an unequivocal and tangible way. "Actions are demanded, not words," stated Commander W. H. Hartt, Jr., speaking for the commander of the Fourteenth Naval District. "In years past a great deal has been said to you about loyalty, Americanism, and the necessity for unambiguous alignment on one side or the other of the citizenship issue. You have been asked to get off the fence when most of you probably did not realize you were on one. If this advice was sound five years ago, it is clear that it is still sounder today."[71]

That inexorable demand formed the backdrop of a "pledge of allegiance" resolved by delegates at the eighth conference in 1934. The pledge acknowledged that *nisei* loyalty had been "on numerous occasions . . . questioned and impugned"; that the source of that suspicion were the *nisei*, who might have "by inadvertence and our seeming indifference to certain obligations and privileges caused these persons to deny our loyalty"; that those allegations in general were "unjustified and unfair"; and that "this misapprehension of our truly profound sense of loyalty" was "detrimental to the interest of the Territory of Hawaii" and was "equally subversive of American-Japanese amity and goodwill." Therefore,

> we American citizens of Japanese ancestry do hereby solemnly profess and reiterate our undivided allegiance and loyalty to our country; that we as individuals and as a group exercise unremitting effort in the endeavor to dispel doubts of our loyalty; that we manifest our profound sense of loyalty to our country and our pride in her government and institutions by active participation therein, by the

studious and intelligent exercise of our privilege of franchise; that we consider expatriation from Japan and the eradication of dual national status a duty of the individual and of the group, and urge and exhort all Americans of Japanese extraction to rouse themselves from their inertia and apathy which are often mistaken for lack of allegiance and indifference.[72]

The following year, the delegates resolved "to associate ourselves actively in the whole scheme of national defense in Hawaii and request the army and navy officials to recognize us and with sympathetic understanding accept our voluntary offer and encouragement of our fellow associates to join the national armed forces."[73]

Resisting "Americanism"

Even as the Americanization movement sought to assimilate them, Hawaii's Japanese struggled to determine their own identity and destiny. Despite efforts to stem the tide of repaganization in the islands, Buddhism continued its surge, and Buddhist priests remained respected members of the community. The Department of Public Instruction's broad interpretation of Act 30 failed to eliminate Japanese-language schools; their enrollments grew, and the restrictions imposed on their functioning were challenged in the courts. Although education was designed to steer them back to plantations and stunt their political participation, *nisei* seized the promise of equal opportunity and pursued learning as a way of moving beyond the curtain of cane.

"Repaganization" Resurgent

Conversion to Christianity, with its attendant social privileges, and the corresponding association of Buddhism with an archaic and undesirable style prompted Buddhists to adapt their forms of worship to an American context. As explained by a *nisei* reformer, Katsumi Yamasaki, Buddhism had lost its appeal because it adhered to outworn rituals: "In most of the Buddhist temples of Hawaii, Buddhism in its ritual and formula is an exact replica of the system in vogue in Japan. Few of our Japanese priests have made any real effort to keep up with the times or to adapt themselves to this country or try to understand the young people of their own blood, born here. They conduct their ceremonies for the youth in a manner highly uninteresting and utterly unsuitable to local conditions." Yamasaki urged priests to "study the needs of the younger generation and attempt to fill those needs" and make Buddhism a "living spiritual force" in the daily lives of the people. He proposed that teachers and priests should be competent in the English language.[74]

Buddhism in Hawaii did in fact adapt to changing conditions. As early as 1918, Bishop Imamura saw the need for a local, English-speaking clergy, and by the 1920s, Buddhist temples, songs, and services were patterned after their Christian counterparts. A Congregational minister, writing in 1928, described a Hongwanji temple and service: "I went into a Buddhist temple, which ministers to a Congregation of English-speaking young Oriental Americans. It is most tastefully appointed. Except for the altar equipment, which is, of course, pronouncedly Buddhistic in its symbolisms, you would almost have to be told you were in the courts of the 'heathen.' It looks much like a church." The minister purchased a hymnal and declared, "Much of the ritual is excellent, and with substitution of the name of Christ for that of Buddha could be heartily recommended to many of our churches."[75] Buddhist adaptations provoked the Right Reverend Samuel Harrington Littell, Episcopal bishop, to charge that the Young Men's and Women's Buddhist Associations, Sunday schools, women's associations, and social work were not "essentially Buddhistic," but were false imitations.[76] The ideas generated by Hawaii's Buddhist reformers were not mere imitations, however, but were rooted in Asian tradition and were genuinely innovative.

The first Pan-Pacific YMBA Conference, held in the summer of 1930, illustrated that robustness. The conference was conceived as an international forum for the eventual creation of a unitary belief system that would break down the sectarian divisions within Asian Buddhism. Young Hawaiian Buddhists such as Katsumi Yamasaki had urged an end to sectarian jealousies and the strengthening of the Buddhist ideal of "Unity, Compassion, and Brotherhood." The conference designated Hawaii as the "nucleus from which nonsectarian Buddhism, adapted to Western countries, may be spread to Pacific countries."[77] About 170 delegates from Hawaii, the U.S. mainland, Burma, Canada, China, India, Japan, Korea, and Thailand attended the six-day conference, adding momentum to the propagation of Buddhism among Hawaii's *nisei*. No doubt the idea of Hawaii's serving as the base for the spread of Buddhism throughout the

Pacific fueled the fears of Hawaii's political and military leaders over the repaganization of the islands and the future of the territory.

During the 1930s, Buddhism and Shintoism experienced a resurgence, with Buddhist churches claiming a membership totaling one-third of Hawaii's entire population. Imposing temples were erected by the Jodo-shu Buddhists in Honolulu, the Ken-Hokkekyo, a subsect of Nichiren-shu, in Nuuanu valley, and the Honpa Hongwanji in Kapaa, Kauai. On the island of Hawaii, Buddhist temples outnumbered Christian churches by two or three to one. Shinto adherents celebrated the emperor's birthday in elaborate services that drew crowds of more than 50,000, and *obon* became a large tourist attraction.[78] Besides formal displays of religiosity, many more Japanese observed Buddhist and Shinto practices as expressions of ethnicity rather than theological understanding and belief. As observed by a commissioned history of the Japanese in Hawaii, "Buddhism and Shintoism for the immigrants were . . . more of a traditional custom in carrying out the rites of birth, marriage and death rather than an understanding of their difficult theology."[79] Although its secularization distressed many, Buddhism created for the bulk of the Japanese a sense of ethnic identity that resisted assimilation and Americanization.

Standing Up for One's Rights

Hawaii's Japanese sought to reinstate another community institution that helped maintain their ethnic identity: the Japanese-language school. On January 1, 1923, Governor Farrington approved the Department of Public Instruction restrictions on foreign-language schools under Act 30. In promulgating the restrictions, he made clear his expectation of the Japanese response: "This regulation represents the conclusions of the best educational leaders of Hawaii, whose ideas and ideals are sincerely American and whose friendly attitude toward our alien people cannot be questioned. I anticipate no opposition from loyal Americans or those resident aliens who are friendly toward our country." Although there was "no more friendly spot for alien races" than Hawaii, declared the governor, "we have no thought of allowing our friendship and tolerance to be abused, so that there shall be established here alien principalities that foster a spirit of opposition to American institutions and defiance of those who support them."[80]

On December 28, 1922, in anticipation of the governor's action, the

Palama Japanese-language school filed a petition in territorial circuit court testing the constitutionality of Act 30. Other Japanese-language schools joined the petition as co-litigants, and by the end of 1923, 87 of the 143 Japanese-language schools in the islands had become a part of the test case. Circuit Judge James J. Banks rendered a decision on February 6, 1923, in which he held that "Act 30 and the portion of the regulations relating to text books were valid, but that the portion of the regulations relating to qualifications for attendance was without the authority of the Department under the terms of the Act."[81] Both sides appealed Banks's decision to the U.S. District Court, Ninth Court of Appeals in San Francisco, and finally to the U.S. Supreme Court. Meanwhile the territorial legislature, on April 27, 1923, passed Act 171, which not only incorporated the regulations imposed by the governor but also empowered the Department of Public Instruction to exercise tighter controls over the language schools and assess a one-dollar fee on each student per year. Those restrictions were carried even further by the legislature in 1925 with the passage of Act 152, which, among other things, provided for penal remedies for the collection of the fee.[82]

But the U.S. Supreme Court, on February 21, 1927, rendered a unanimous decision in favor of the Japanese-language-school petitioners. The justices acknowledged the "Japanese problem" in Hawaii, but ruled that the Constitution had to be affirmed: "We of course appreciate the grave problems incidental to the large alien population in the Hawaiian Islands. These should be given due weight whenever the validity of any governmental regulation of private schools is under consideration; but the limitations of the Constitution must not be transcended."[83]

At a mass meeting on March 29, about 5,000 supporters of the successful constitutional challenge celebrated their victory and declared their "Americanness" in a series of resolutions. The dissident patriots declared: "We re-affirm our confidence in the friendship and good-will of the American people, and reassert our pride in the fact that our children are American citizens"; "we assure the people of the Territory of Hawaii that we harbor no resentment or ill-will toward the officials of the Territory who sought to enforce the language school laws, and credit them with acting from sincere motives"; and "we emphatically reaffirm our continued loyalty to America and our desire to rear our children as loyal, patriotic and useful citizens of the United States."[84]

Kinzaburo Makino, a test case leader, in his speech to the gathering, called the protest movement "the right of a people living in a free democracy to seek legal clarification regarding constitutionality of their laws," and urged the Japanese to cooperate with Hawaii's rulers by rearing children who were "good Americans capable of understanding both the English and Japanese languages." But, cautioned Makino, "we must never forget that we have to stand up for our rights as guaranteed under the Constitution."[85]

To the governor, the constitutional challenge must have seemed more an abuse of white friendship and tolerance than a heroic stand for civil liberty. In 1929, Takie Okumura formed, with the "financial and moral support" of influential members of the white community, including Frank Atherton and Will Crawford, the Japanese Language Education Association, whose object was to provide all Japanese children with the opportunity to learn the Japanese language.[86] Instruction, however, was to be carried out in public school buildings, rather than independent schools, because "we believe it is proper to educate them [*nisei* children] in the public school building and according to the ideals and customs of public school education."[87] Superintendent of Public Instruction Crawford opened the public schools to the association, and in September 1930 language classes began in six Honolulu schools. By 1933, "chain schools" had been introduced in nine schools throughout the city; in 1934, ten such schools had an enrollment of 1,009 pupils.[88]

Chain schools met for an hour in the afternoon, after the close of public school. In addition to language instruction, they stressed "moral education" for the Americanization of the youth. "Spokesmen for the chain schools," wrote a historian, "promised DPI [Department of Public Instruction] officials to disbar all subjects which tended to teach Japanism and to make every effort, in accordance with the policy of the public schools, to Americanize the local-born Japanese."[89]

Buddhist leaders saw chain schools as another attempt to eliminate foreign-language schools and erode the Supreme Court guarantees, drawing students from the independent schools and thereby closing them down. They thus discouraged parents from enrolling their children in chain schools and petitioned Superintendent Crawford to terminate the program, arguing that the use of public school buildings for Japanese-language classes was an unfair expenditure of taxes. Crawford was unmoved, and chain schools continued to operate. Still, the independent schools did not suffer as a consequence; in fact, they flourished. In 1900, there were 11 independent Japanese-language schools with an enrollment of 1,552; in 1907, 120 schools and 4,966 students; in 1920, 143 schools with 17,541 students; in 1933, 190 schools with 43,606 students; in 1940, 200 schools with over 40,000 students. On the eve of World War II, the independent schools enrolled more than 80 percent of all *nisei*.[90]

Fighting for One's People

Despite public education's stress on vocational training to produce "efficient workers" for the plantations, many people dreamed of leaving manual labor for the professions. Their aspirations were recorded in educational surveys undertaken by the sociologist Romanzo Adams during the 1920s. A 1922 survey of youth, about 60 percent of whom were Chinese or Japanese, attending Honolulu's McKinley High School revealed that 15 percent wanted to become professionals, 50 percent skilled workers, and only 5.5 percent agriculturalists and laborers. In 1928, Adams surveyed seventh and eighth graders at seventeen plantation schools and found that 12 percent hoped to become businessmen, 11 percent physicians, lawyers, or teachers, 8 percent engineers, and only about 2 percent wanted to be laborers. These results were repeated at high schools attended predominantly by Japanese students on the outer islands of Kauai, Maui, and Hawaii. Although less than half of all plantation elementary school students actually went on to high school, 88 percent said they expected to reach the higher grades.[91]

Writing in 1924, Adams noted a general movement of Japanese men away from plantation labor and toward skilled employment: "The men are leaving plantation labor for more desirable occupations. They are increasing in skilled employments; 2537 in 1910 and 4199 in 1920. They are getting out of occupations of little dignity and the blind alley occupations. They are entering the professions; 221 in 1910, and 651 in 1920. Some are becoming independent business men; 273 merchants in 1910 and 1150 in 1920. There are numerous Japanese small contractors and a few are managing enterprises of considerable magnitude."[92]

For many, education was a democratizing institution and an animator of the American dream. As one of Adams's respondents said, "When my father came from Japan, he was handicapped in his work. I intend to go to school to get an education to lead a better life and live up to the ideals of an American." Another, having seen plantation life and labor firsthand, stated as his reason for continuing his education: "I went back to school with the determination that I would fight for my people."[93]

Perhaps one of the most influential educators of the *nisei* was the principal of McKinley High School, Miles Cary. During his long tenure as principal, from 1924 to 1948, Cary worked to instill self-reliance and independent thinking in his students. He rejected vocational education and introduced academic majors such as art, journalism, languages, mathematics, social sciences, and science. By 1929, there was only one vocational course, cafeteria management, at McKinley, and it enrolled only eight students that year.[94] Cary saw racism as the motivating factor behind the English standard schools. When Roosevelt High School opened as a standard school in 1929, most of the white students who formerly attended McKinley transferred to Roosevelt, which was built on a hill overlooking "Tokyo High," as McKinley was dubbed.[95] Cary interrupted his duties as McKinley's principal during World War II to work among the Japanese in one of America's concentration camps in the Arizona desert.

Jim Crowism

In 1930, a decade after the federal education commission report, Governor Lawrence Judd appointed an advisory committee to reexamine Hawaii's schools. George M. Collins, trustee of the Bishop Estate, chaired the committee. Members included Frank Atherton of Castle and Cooke; Richard Cooke, president of C. Brewer and later president of the HSPA; Walter Dillingham, president of Oahu Railroad and Land Company; James Dole, president of Hawaiian Pineapple Company; and E. W. Greene, manager of Oahu Sugar Company. The committee's report advocated an education for the "real demands" of life in Hawaii. "To function usefully as a member of a community," counseled the report, "a young man must perform such duties as fall to [his] lot." Public schools, in the words of a committee member, should be "directing thousands of our Hawaiian-born children into happy service in connection with our basic industries."[96]

Members of the Japanese community were openly critical of the report. The *Hawaii Hochi* of February 9, 1931, contemptuously referred to the governor's committee as the "Jim Crow Commission" and castigated it for seeking to establish "the ultimate division of the people of Hawaii on a

Jim Crow basis and the confining of higher education to a small group of favored members of the white race." Its recommendations, if implemented, predicted the *Hochi*, would result in a dual school system, one for "darker skinned peasants" and the other for "fair skinned aristocrats." The report drew mixed reviews from Hawaii's whites, some of whom applauded vocational education and reduced expenditures for public schools, but expressed discomfort with the explicitness of proposals that clearly contradicted the rhetoric of American democracy. The report's recommendations were set aside; in its place, a plan proposed by Department of Public Instruction Superintendent Oren E. Long was adopted, to build public high schools in rural areas near plantations as "the best strategy for feeding trained laborers back into the plantation system." [97]

Frank E. Midkiff, principal of Kamehameha Schools and Bishop Estate trustee, described how "progressive" education met, rather than spurned, industry's need for "efficient workers" in his 1935 doctoral dissertation at Yale University. In the study, Midkiff pointed to the alienation of the plantation worker as a cause of labor conflicts, low morale, high turnover rates, and inefficiency. "On the whole," wrote Midkiff, "it must be admitted that in the past, plantation labor being imported 'coolie' class immigrants, there was an established feeling that these plantation persons were not a part of Hawaiian society and culture—that rural persons, particularly plantation personnel, were not incorporated into the social life of the Islands but were mere units of labor, belonging to the plantations." [98]

Progressive education, explained Midkiff, would teach "the necessity and the values of rural or rural village life," making that life more attractive and satisfying.[99] Those reforms would result in greater productivity and reduced labor costs: "It may be possible, over a period of years, to measure the results of Education in increased agricultural productivity, greater independence in the matter of subsistence foods, and decreased direct and indirect costs connected with importing labor." [100]

The numbers of schools and students, particularly in rural areas, in accord with Oren Long's strategy, rose sharply during the 1930s. New high schools were proposed for the isolated islands of Molokai and Lanai, and in Hana, Maui. In 1936, eleven junior high schools were opened in rural districts, making a total of twenty-six such schools. By 1938, 39 percent of all school-age children attended secondary school, compared to a mere 11 percent in 1920. High school attendance for Japanese youth jumped from 35 percent of all high school-age Japanese in 1920 to 54 percent in 1930.[101] According to advocates of progressive education, these students would constitute a new breed of plantation workers—literate, contented, and well trained in the advancing requirements of industrialized agriculture. Further, they would maintain a higher level of morale, a lower rate of turnover, and experience "no costly disturbances due to agitation."[102]

The contradiction was that the tools provided by education and sharpened by dedicated teachers within classrooms infused with the ideals of democracy would eventually unyoke the bonds of planter rule and transform the political order.

Forestalling the Dawn

Through the long plantation night, the *issei* hoped for a new dawning with the *nisei* generation. To Hawaii's political and military leaders, the *nisei* were the "second generation problem" primarily because of their U.S. citizenship. In the frank words of California's Senator Phelan, who had introduced a constitutional amendment—a plan favored by Hawaii's Governor McCarthy—to deny citizenship to those born to "aliens ineligible to citizenship," the crux of the problem was how "to discourage their coming here and to render them innocuous when they do come."[103]

The Americanization movement was neither benign nor conceived for the uplifting of a subordinate group. Americanization involved the economic, political, and cultural domination of the Japanese in the interest of maintaining white supremacy. Americanization subdued not only a race but also a class—Japanese workers—for the furtherance of capitalism in Hawaii and the Pacific. This helps explain the apparently odd endorsement by leaders of Japan's government and industry of the Okumuras' Educational Campaign and their urging of Hawaii's Japanese to eschew Buddhism and other "Japanese" traits and adopt "American" ways.

Viscount Shibusawa's Nichi-Bei Kankei-Iin-Kai likewise blamed the Japanese in Hawaii for the "severe criticism" they received from whites over the issue of assimilation. "If Japanese are truly obedient and loyal to the laws and customs of America," the trade group stated, "and if they share the joys and sorrows of American people, Americans, not only in Hawaii but on the mainland, would come to recognize the sincerity and earnestness of Japanese in their endeavors to become Americanized and cordial relations between two peoples would become everlasting." [104] Those "cordial relations," in turn, would grease the wheels of commerce and trade, producing profits for capitalists in Japan and the United States.

The gains accumulated by Hawaii's planters from the Americanization movement were less obvious; consequently, their participation was diffident and halting. Some continued to cling to the antiquated ideal of master and servant; others recognized the need for more sophisticated instruments of control. Education played a significant role in maintaining white supremacy under the new liberal dispensation, much of which was contrived to channel the *nisei* in the footsteps of their parents. Vocational education and segregated standard schools lay the foundation for the institutionalization of inequality, and the Okumuras' Educational Campaign sought to suppress worker unrest, urge greater productivity in labor, and direct the *nisei* back to the plantations. The Conference of New Americans was more explicit in promoting planter interests by extolling the dignity of agricultural labor and exhorting the *nisei* to "congenial" work (i.e., plantation labor) as a near-patriotic duty, while dampening hopes for college or even a secondary education.

At the 1936 conference, a *nisei* offered a poignant summation of his life: "I am a true son of the plantation. My father came here from Japan about forty years ago and worked on the plantation the entire period and is still on the plantation pay roll in spite of his old age. I was forced to quit school early in life and for the past fifteen years have been employed by Papaikou plantation. It is my intention now to work for the plantation for the rest of my life." [105] Although conference organizers probably heard that testimony as a ringing endorsement of their back-to-the-soil message, the experience spoke more eloquently of restricted opportunities, not because plantation labor was inherently odious, but because both father and son were constrained by a range of devices designed to keep them on the plantation and to preserve the paternal ideal of "competent leaders" and "efficient workers."

The educational efforts of the Americanization movement, together with the new paternalism, apparently reaped a harvest of new workers for the sugar plantations. After the 1920 strike, the number of Japanese plantation laborers decreased, reaching a low of 9,395 (18.8 percent) of the total plantation workforce in 1932, but ten years later, Japanese employment on the plantations had increased to 10,397 (30.6 percent) of the workforce.[106] However slowly, the Japanese were turning back to the

Japanese homes, Wainaku plantation village, island of Hawaii, ca. 1890. With the arrival of women, the establishment of families, and the birth of children, workers sought permanence, decent homes, and "a just reward for their labors." *Photo C. Furneaux, Bishop Museum, Honolulu*

Plantation workers, Koloa, Kauai, ca. 1916. Women and men labored side by side in the fields. Pictured here is a *ho hana* (hoe cultivation) team. *Bishop Museum*

Wedding picture of Mr. and Mrs. Kimura, Parker ranch employees on the island of Hawaii. Men usually dressed in Western suits, while women wore the traditional kimono. *Photo Baron Goto, Bishop Museum*

Sand Island concentration camp, January 13, 1942. The camp commander had directed the internees to pitch the tents that sheltered them. *U.S. Army photograph*

The Honouliuli camp opened after March 1, 1943. It was built in a gulch surrounded by fields of sugarcane. R. Harry Lodge, former superintendent of an
installation of Oahu Sugar Co., Ltd. where the camp was located, took this
picture. *University of Hawaii photo collection*

Internees at Honouliuli camp, where nine men shared a barracks. The men busied themselves about the camp to keep their sanity. *Photo R. Harry Lodge, University of Hawaii photo collection*

plantations, while the number of *nisei* plantation laborers steadily grew as they found employment in skilled positions. According to a 1937 HSPA survey, the thirty-eight sugar companies in Hawaii employed 5,895 *nisei*, compared to 5,566 *issei*, on their plantations. The majority of the second generation had at least a junior high school education, and the *nisei* were the mainstay of plantation skilled laborers, employed as clerks, technicians in sugar mills, machine shop operators, carpenters, painters, and surveyors.[107]

The ambiguities of the Americanization movement, in terms of gains for the planters, vanished during the 1930s with an end to Asian migration. The advantage plainly lay in educating the *nisei*. The Tydings–McDuffie Act of 1934 cut off Filipino labor migration, and the nation, in the grips of the Great Depression, was in no mood to contemplate an infusion of foreign workers. In fact, in 1932, like the Filipino repatriation movement on the mainland, 7,200 "excess" Filipino plantation laborers in Hawaii were sent back to the Philippines, at industry's expense, to reduce the costs of unemployment.[108]

Conditions compelled the planters to turn to the existing pools of labor in the territory, including the *nisei* and women and children, who constituted cheaper sources of labor than men.[109] At the same time that the planters were wooing and molding a new Japanese worker—educated and contented—the *nisei* found only limited employment opportunities in urban industries, largely because of racism, hastening their return to the plantations.[110]

The education of the *nisei* served the planters' labor needs, but was also essential for the national defence. Thus the 1920 federal survey of education framed Hawaii's "educational problem" as the contest for economic and political dominance. According to the federal commissioners, the "problem of the schools" involved "the possibilities of the domination of the Territorial electorate by representatives of a single racial group, such as the Japanese," based on population projections estimating that the Japanese would constitute 47 percent of the electorate by 1940.[111]

In the winter of 1932, Connecticut Senator Hiram Bingham introduced a bill in Congress aimed at placing Hawaii under the Navy Department and a governing commission. As argued by Admiral Stirling in that same year, American democracy was ill equipped to deal with the Japanese menace. Stirling's argument was unabashedly racist: "If these Islands were populated . . . by American citizens, comprised in large measure of the Caucasian race, their allegiance and loyalty to the welfare of the whole Nation might not be questioned." Instead, "several claimed unassimilable" races predominated in Hawaii, giving to the situation "a decided element of doubt, if not of actual alarm." The threat must not be underestimated: "The safety of the United States is far too important for us to close our eyes and refuse to appreciate the importance of this fact in the military problem in these islands." It was inevitable, Stirling contended, given the demographic trend and system of one man, one vote, that those of "doubtful reliance" would take over the reins of government and although "ours is a democratic government under a constitution, and . . . that one of our basic principles of government is against legislation without representation . . . , do we apply this axiom of government to our ships of war and to our military reservations?" [112]

The proposal for a commission form of government was vehemently opposed by Hawaii's oligarchy because military control would undermine their hegemony. Bingham's bill failed. The following year, the Rankin bill, which authorized the president to appoint a nonresident governor of Hawaii, also failed, despite President Franklin D. Roosevelt's endorsement. These ripples in the federal government nonetheless revealed deeper currents running through the respective strategies of Hawaii's oligarchy and the military. For the planters and the territorial government, the Americanization of the Japanese or, at the least, an appearance of *nisei* assimilation was critical to the continued hold over workers and voters and to countering the demands of the military for a commission form of government. The army and navy thought federal rule necessary because of their skepticism of the effectiveness of Americanization to render the Japanese "innocuous," especially when the prospect of war loomed on the horizon.

Chapter 8

Dark Designs

One obvious thought occurs to me—that every
Japanese citizen or non-citizen on the island of
Oahu who meets these Japanese ships . . . should
be secretly but definitely identified and his or her
name placed on a special list of those who would
be the first to be placed in a concentration camp
in the event of trouble.
                                    —Franklin D. Roosevelt

Sabotage and Martial Law

During the 1930s, military and civilian intelligence and the
army's War Plans Division intensified activities to counter
the "Japanese menace." Much of the work involved refining
plans laid in the 1920s, especially regarding martial law and
what was to be done during the period immediately preceding a formal declaration of hostilities. Hawaii became more
closely integrated into a global defensive scheme that began
with the U.S. mainland and extended to its outlying territories and possessions, and army headquarters in Washington played an increasingly active role in the Hawaiian
Department's local defense plans.

On April 14, 1931, WPD requested a second ruling from
the judge advocate general on a key aspect of the plan for
the defense of Oahu: the imposition of martial law.[1] Colonel
A. W. Brown, acting judge advocate, sent his opinion in a
memorandum to WPD on July 6, 1931.[2] The Constitution,
ruled Brown, forbade martial law except in a "theater of
active military operations in time of actual war and when
the civil administration has been deposed and the civil

courts have been closed." The Hawaiian Organic Act (1900) permitted martial law in the case of a demonstrable "imminent danger." The governor, as commander of the territorial militia, could call on the militia to restore order, but could neither command the regular U.S. armed forces nor interfere with the actions of the army commander in the performance of his mission to defend Hawaii. The president, ruled Brown, had no power to abolish the civil government by proclamation or to substitute a military government in its place.

Unlike Bethel's ruling eight years earlier, Brown's opinion was directed at the precise way in which martial law would be instituted, rather than at what conditions would justify the imposition of martial law. WPD's concern was with the Constitution and the respective executive powers of the president, the army commander, and the governor. Brown wrote that in the event of "an attack in force," the commanding general of the Hawaiian Department would have "full authority to impose such restrictions upon, and to take such measures, with reference to, the civil population as the actual necessities of the case might require to enable him to perform successfully his military mission." Nevertheless, warned Brown, the commander would "be personally accountable for any restrictions or other normally illegal measures beyond those demanded by actual necessity."

The WPD concurred with Brown's ruling, stressing the primacy of the department commander over the governor in the defense of Oahu and preferring that conditions and terms of martial law be kept vague. "It is not believed advisable," wrote the head of WPD, "to ask the President at this time to define in any way the conditions under which he would declare martial law for the Island of Oahu, nor to ask him to state categorically that he would designate the Commanding General, Hawaiian Department, the Military Governor for the time of emergency."[3] Despite the deliberate indefiniteness over how martial law would be declared, WPD was certain of the supremacy of the department commander under martial law: "Whatever be the means by which it [martial law] is brought about, the military commander becomes the supreme authority in the locality, responsible only to the Commander-in-Chief." The delineation of line of command, in "Responsibility for the Defense of Oahu," was approved by the secretary of war on August 12, 1931.

As the winds of war in Asia gathered momentum with Japan's 1931 invasion of Manchuria and its bombing of Shanghai the following year, the army's WPD initiated a major reassessment of its plan for Hawaii's defense. On April 5, 1933, Brigadier General C. E. Kilbourne, head of WPD, asked military intelligence to "prepare a brief estimate of the situation with respect to the menace of the Japanese population in the Hawaiian Islands to our defense of that outpost in the event of war."[4] Kilbourne listed some of the critical areas: the Japanese population and its growth; an estimate of loyalty; the number of Japanese army and navy officers and reservists residing in the islands; the possibility of planned sabotage and the likelihood that a secret arms cache was being collected; the extent to which naturalized Japanese had infiltrated the government and military; Japan's knowledge of the local defense system; Japanese fishermen with their control of the industry and knowledge of the islands' beaches and coastline; and Japanese social organizations and their influence. A week later, the secretary of war asked that the commander of the Hawaiian Department, General B. H. Wells, submit a similar estimate of "the menace of the Japanese population in the Hawaiian Islands to our defense of that outpost."[5]

In May 1933, the Hawaiian Department forwarded a fifteen-part report, "Estimate of the Situation—Japanese Population in Hawaii," addressing the concerns posed by Kilbourne. History, the estimate argued, revealed that Japan long desired control of Hawaii and planned an eventual takeover through the implantation of its citizens and their infiltration into key areas of the economy. The study gave a detailed description, on a county-by-county basis on each of the major islands, of Japanese involvement in local politics. It noted that in 1930, for the first time, two *nisei* had been elected to the territorial House and that two more had been elected in 1932.

A major portion of the estimate dealt with Japanese "racial traits," such as their fecundity, mental inferiority to whites, fatalism and fanaticism, double-dealing and lack of integrity, arrogance and officiousness, natural clannishness, thrift and frugality, and superior industry. Parents, Buddhist and Shinto priests, and language-school teachers instilled in children a "pride of race" and a resistance to Americanization. Japan's highly developed consular agent system, meanwhile, enforced its hold over the second generation, leading the report to conclude that the *nisei* were "wholly under the sway of their militarists."

On the critical question of loyalty, the estimate reported that whites believed "the local Japanese population will be disloyal to the United States," and army intelligence estimated that "there will be, in any war, an appreciable group loyal to the enemy." Regardless of its size, that group will know "where all power plants are located; where all wires and cables (including the fire control cables) are placed; what the sources of water supply are; where dams, reservoirs, and pumping plants are built; and where all military, naval and civilian owned gasolines and oils are stored." Accordingly, individuals were capable of inflicting "considerable damage by the employment of sabotage" and could "seriously interfere" with the defense of Oahu.

That situation made it impossible for the army to defend against sabotage and increased the probability that the Japanese might succeed in delivering a serious blow to the islands' defensive system. "There is no way by which such action can be prevented," stated the report, "other than by placing guards over the entire length of this cable system. This would disperse the available military strength, and withdraw such guards from other very necessary duties." Also, considerable havoc could be wreaked by even a small number of extremists: "It is entirely possible and thoroughly feasible for a small number of carefully selected Japanese who are definitely loyal to Japan to plan for effective sabotage, simultaneously executed over practically the entire Island of Oahu."

At this juncture, a crucial new element was introduced into the scenario for the defense of Oahu. The 1921 plan, revised in 1923 by De Witt, envisioned the internment of "enemy aliens" deemed dangerous to the community, but failed to define the criteria by which Japanese would be placed in that category. In addition, the plan, in the opinion of the local commander, was deficient in defending against the possibility of sabotage before actual armed conflict had broken out between Japan and the United States. In this document, the Hawaiian Department laid out its concerns in carrying out its mission of defending Oahu: "It is believed that the most practicable plan for controlling sabotage or other Japanese activities cooperative with Japanese armed forces is to control the individuals who are leaders among them. This control must of course be exercised during that critical period of 'strained relations' and before the damage is done. It is during this particular period that the military Commander lacks authority over civilians. The question is one that has always been of deep concern to the Department Commander." [6]

The study summed up the case for "peaceful penetration" and predicted a gloomy outlook for continued American (white) control of Hawaii: "There are definite indications that the resident Japanese, by peaceful conquest, and by the use of American methods, are creating under the American flag, a situation, which, in the course of time, unless halted will, in fact, produce a Territory Japanese and not American controlled." Indications of that prospect included Japanese high birthrates and low death rates, their steady and aggressive "infiltration" into the economic fabric of the islands, their recent inroads into elected officeholding and their voting potential, their manifold "Japanistic" loyalties and tendencies, their lack of progress toward Americanization, their racial solidarity and amenability to control by Japanese leaders, and their aloofness from other racial and ethnic groups in the territory.

Those trends, the study proposed, would eventually lead to the eclipse of white supremacy and the demise of recognizable American traits in the islands: "Thus, it seems probable, that the Japanese may within the present century, by peaceful means, complete their conquest of Hawaii, and develop a Territory which if not actually Japanese will not be reliably American." As to the question of loyalty, the estimate anticipated four kinds of Japanese: those who would side with the United States, a small percentage of the total; those who would side with Japan, also a small number, but a serious threat in terms of espionage and sabotage; those who would remain neutral; and those who would side with whichever country won the war, the largest segment of all.

That restatement of the "Japanese problem" by the Hawaiian Department in 1933 undeniably bore the imprint of Brooke, Wood, and the author of the Summerall report, helping to create a line of thinking whose guiding principles were internal security and economic stability and whose primary methods for achieving those goals were martial law and selective detention. Simultaneously, however, the army studies revealed an evolving solution to the "problem" that throughout the 1920s and 1930s was refined and made more explicit in its mode of implementation.

Armed with the Hawaiian commander's latest study, Kilbourne penned a detailed memorandum to the chief of staff, dated July 19, 1933, that recommended amending the army's "Defense of Oahu."[7] "From a defense point of view," Kilbourne asked, "do the present conditions in the Hawaiian Islands, and especially on Oahu, call for especial precautions, and does the present form of civil government in Hawaii insure that necessary measures can be taken, during a period of strained relations with Japan, by the military authorities charged with responsibility for the defense of Oahu?" The Hawaiian Department's discussion of sabotage and the need to preempt that danger before war had been declared had convinced Kilbourne, who reported "that there is an organization with the intention of carrying on sabotage in event of war is accepted as a fact by the Department Commander."

In the light of that "fact," and without a clear delineation of authority, Kilbourne argued, the department commander would be unable to prevent sabotage in the critical period immediately preceding a formal declaration of war. "The situation would not be so serious if the alien and clannish Japanese minority were balanced by an homogeneous and patriotic majority. Such is not the case." Under the existing plan, the governor could refuse to cooperate with the military and thereby increase the chances for chaos during an extreme emergency. Intent on eliminating that ambiguity, the WPD head recommended that the president be asked "to issue secret instructions to the Governor of Hawaii to cooperate with the Commanding General, Hawaiian Department, in planning for a transfer of control to the military authorities in emergency and directed to effect such transfer upon request of the Commanding General."

Kilbourne's suggestion refocused attention on how martial law would be declared, an issue deliberately left vague since 1931 but now perceived to be crucial. Consideration was given to drafting a presidential executive order mandating military rule, but that plan was scuttled by the judge advocate, Major General Allen W. Gullion.[8] Instead, he argued, an act of Congress could accomplish that same object and avoid potential conflict over an unconstitutional delegation of authority by giving to the president powers already possessed by the governor.[9] As a result of Gullion's ruling, Secretary of War Henry L. Stimson introduced legislation titled "A Bill to Strengthen the Defenses of the Territories of Hawaii and Puerto Rico" to Congress in the fall of 1941.

The bill authorized the president to "suspend the privilege of the writ of *habeas corpus,* or place either or both of the said Territories, or any part or parts thereof, under martial law" in the event of "rebellion or invasion, or imminent danger thereof, when the public safety requires it." In explaining the necessity for the bill to the chair of the Committee on Military Affairs, Senator Robert R. Reynolds, Stimson wrote: "Due to the fact that approximately one-tenth of the population of Hawaii are aliens, the danger of sabotage or other subversive activities could be a major problem in the event of war."[10]

In the end, neither federal approach—secret presidential instructions or an act of Congress—would resolve the sticky question of how to institute military rule. Martial law would be finally achieved through the insistence of a determined army commander and the acquiescence of a reluctant governor.

Washington versus Hawaii

Meanwhile, Hawaii's Joint Defense Plan ("joint" because it integrated the defensive schemes of both the army and navy in Hawaii) was deemed inadequate to cope with the "Japanese problem" by the Washington military establishment. Accordingly, Lieutenant Colonel Sherman Miles of the General Staff directed WPD to revise the local planning document with an eye toward anticipating and preventing sabotage. Very significantly, WPD was instructed to give close attention to the control of *nisei*, in addition to *issei* "enemy aliens." In a memorandum to WPD dated October 22, 1934, Miles explained the deficiencies of the existing strategy: the Joint Defense Plan was based on a system of registration and identification that "could not be effective during the critical period of the war (the first six weeks)"; it maintained "a very loose control under reserve officers of doubtful efficiency"; it lacked "positive measures to prevent sabotage, or anything else until overt acts have been committed"; it neither provided for surveillance of "the large Japanese population on the other islands" nor prevented their movement to Oahu; above all, it emphasized "enemy aliens almost to the total exclusion of American citizens of Japanese ancestry, although the latter may be equally dangerous to us." [11]

A directive to override the prerogative of the Hawaii Department by army headquarters was highly unusual; normally, matters of local defense were left to the commander in the field. "Nevertheless it is believed that the potential danger of sabotage or even armed resistance on the part of the Japanese population in the Hawaiian Department, including at least some of those who are legally American citizens as well as those who are aliens, is so great that the plans to meet this danger should have the approval of the Chief of Staff," concurred Kilbourne. [12]

Miles's criticism had been prompted by an aspect of Hawaii's Joint Defense Plan that called for a system of "indirect rule" through selected "competent enemy alien chiefs." [13] The system divided Oahu into ten military districts, placing them under reserve officers who would administer them in the following way: Each officer would undertake a registration of his district's civilian population, install a system of identification, and consult with "prominent, intelligent and adaptable of the enemy aliens" in his district and inform them that their status was essentially that of "prisoners of war," that they were subject to obligations, restrictions, and penalties, and that they were required "to administer their own affairs to the maximum degree permitted by the situation." Only "aliens, sympathizers and leaders of disturbing elements who commit overt acts" would be held in detention in prisons administered by civilian authorities, and those suspected of disloyalty would be free but kept under "strict surveillance." The system of "indirect rule," Hawaii's military reasoned, would make efficient use of Japanese labor, free the military from some of the burden of administering martial law, and enable the army to concentrate on the external threat.

Washington found Hawaii's Joint Defense Plan was based on a system of "very loose control," prompting Kilbourne's critique.[14] The WPD, he wrote to the Hawaiian commanding general, had studied the recommendation "for the utilization of Japanese man-power in Hawaii" and concluded that the task of registering the entire population was too cumbersome and that the internment of only those who committed overt acts was too restrictive of military control. Additionally, *nisei* were as great a danger as *issei* to internal security, and Japanese living on the outer islands "should at least be prevented from reaching Oahu." Despite his criticisms of the Joint Plan, Kilbourne conceded that the Hawaiian Department faced an extremely difficult situation. The most effective way to prevent sabotage would be to confine all the Japanese, but that would present enormous practical and legal problems for the army. "Indirect rule" was permissive and inadequate to protect against sabotage. In reality, observed Kilbourne, "the Department Commander must decide not only what he would like to do but what he can do." The WPD head closed by asking the Hawaiian commander to reassess the probability of internal subversion, the steps that should be taken to control "aliens and alien sympathizers," and the method for preventing sabotage.

In response, Major General Halstead Dorey sent a detailed memorandum to WPD on January 30, 1935.[15] "An adverse reaction of Orange [Japanese] aliens and sympathizers to United States authority is considered certain," was his categorical reply. "Such reaction will take the course of organized individual and group sabotage primarily directed against military installations and to a lesser extent against facilities for the support of the local civilian population. It is unlikely that mass action, either armed or unarmed, on Oahu or from other islands directed at Oahu, will develop." Mass internment of Japanese, Dorey argued, was neither practical nor desirable "because of the size of the bloc and the psychological, legal and logistical factors involved, and . . . because of insufficient military strength." Instead, he proposed guarding vital targets with a minimal troop contingent and reinforcements when required, keeping a list of "suspicious characters" who would be immediately interned at the outbreak of war, and designating Japanese community leaders who would be "secretly selected" in advance and who, during the war, would be held "strictly accountable for action of Orange population."

As far as can be determined, Hawaii's Joint Defense Plan remained as described by Dorey until 1937 when a refined strategy for controlling the Japanese was introduced into the comprehensive plan.

Surveillance Network Resumed

Apparently, in May 1934 the Bureau of Investigation closed its Honolulu office, despite an appeal by Major General Briant H. Wells, army commander, for the bureau to remain: "There is a real need here at all times for a loyal, intelligent experienced operative of the Bureau of Investigation, who will work through the local United States Attorney in co-operation with the Army authorities. Because of its location at the junction of world passenger routes, because of its strategic military value, and because of the many alien races strongly represented here and the cosmopolitan character of its society, Honolulu is and has long been a focus of intrigue." [16]

About a year before the bureau closed, agent J. P. Mac Farland filed an investigative report, "A Survey of the Japanese Situation in Hawaii," based primarily on information supplied by an unnamed Japanese source. Mac Farland described how Japanese social and religious organizations negated Americanization and spun a web of espionage. [17] The bureau agent claimed that army intelligence maintained "a complete list of all Japanese organizations in this Territory" and proceeded to name fifteen Japanese community leaders and "Japanese sympathizers" with brief biographical sketches of each. The list was expanded in an addendum report dated October 31, 1933. Copies of Mac Farland's report were sent to MID and ONI.[18]

Reports by army intelligence in Hawaii concurred with Mac Farland's survey of the situation. Major James I. Muir, head of G-2 in 1934, studied the United Japanese Society and listed all its member organizations.[19] His analysis revealed the "efficient organization of the local Japanese"; the "domination of that organization by the alien-born"; the "lack of active opposition by the native-born to the alien-born"; and the positive "feelings of the local Japanese towards the ruling family of the Japanese Empire." In July, Muir detected a marked shift in Japanese public opinion, away from America and toward Japan, which he attributed to "Japanese propaganda."[20]

During the mid 1930s, ONI and MID were enlarging counterintelligence operations on Japanese activities in Central and South America, and the Bureau of Investigation was intensifying its surveillance of the Japanese community in the United States. On August 24, 1934, a State Department report illustrated that heightened concern: "The Imperial Japanese Government has agents in every large city in this country and on the West Coast. These people, who pass as civilians and laborers, are being drilled in military maneuvers . . . when war breaks out, the entire Japanese population on the West Coast will rise and commit sabotage. They will endeavor by every means to neutralize the West Coast and render her defenseless."[21] T. T. Craven, Thirteenth Naval District commandant, reported that a Japanese espionage ring in Seattle and Portland was secretly gathering information on West Coast defenses, and the 1936 annual naval intelligence report reached the disquieting conclusion that "Japanese espionage continues to increase . . . the work of investigating is now beyond the capacity of present personnel."[22]

The concerns of the wider intelligence community and the Washington military establishment formed the context for the local Hawaiian Joint Planning Committee's decision to review the plans for Oahu's defense with an eye toward the suppression of internal subversion.

Roosevelt, Suspect Lists, and Concentration Camps

In an "Estimate of the Situation Orange [Japan/Japanese]" dated October 1935, the MID in Washington discussed the formidable logistical problems facing Japan in an attack on Hawaii and how those impediments could be overcome by a program of internal subversion: "If Hawaii could be taken internally by Orange adherents in the territory Orange could without great risk dispatch an expedition to make its capture secure."[23] Colonel F. H. Lincoln, head of G-2 at army headquarters, repeated that point in a December 24 memorandum: "Current Estimate of the Situation—Orange Plan." "The weakness of Hawaii," he wrote, "is the possibility of a surprise attack by Orange using commercial vessels plus naval forces combined with the joint effort of Orange nationals legally resident there."[24] Washington's concerns were transmitted to Hawaii's Joint Planning Committee.

As Hawaii reconsidered its plans, Admiral W. H. Standley of the military's Joint Board in Washington sent a letter to the secretary of war on May 19, 1936, in which he argued that conditions had changed sufficiently to warrant a revision of the original "Project for the Defense of Oahu" approved by the Joint Board in December 1919 and subsequently endorsed by the secretary of war.[25] America's defensive forces, observed the admiral, must now guard against two possible scenarios: a surprise attack from the sea and air, including a small landing force aided by "the great potential power of hostile sympathizers on those Islands"; and a major overseas expeditionary force invasion, which was highly unlikely. "Against the first form of attack," wrote Standley, "the existing peacetime forces of the Army and Navy in the Hawaiian Islands, including their necessary munitions and supplies, are believed to be adequate. The success of our defense against this form of attack will depend almost entirely upon our not being totally surprised by the enemy and will require an efficient intelligence service, not only in the Hawaiian Islands but elsewhere." The danger posed by "hostile sympathizers," according to the admiral, was "sabotage or armed insurrection."

The secretary of war agreed with Standley's assessment and made it part of Hawaii's Joint Defense Plan on May 21, 1936. Nevertheless, the president did not rest easy and anxiously awaited recommendations from Hawaii's Joint Planning Committee. On August 10, 1936, Roosevelt wrote to Standley,[26] "Has the local Joint Planning Committee (Hawaii) any recommendation to make? One obvious thought occurs to me—that every Japanese citizen or non-citizen on the Island of Oahu who meets these Japanese ships or has any connection with their officers or men should be secretly but definitely identified and his or her name placed on a special list of those who would be the first to be placed in a concentration camp in the event of trouble." The president had another thought, that the plan for Hawaii's defense give comprehensive consideration to the entire island chain, not only Oahu, and the Japanese population of the outlying islands. He maintained a personal interest in the situation: "Please let me have further recommendations after studies have been made."

Standley, writing to the army's chief of staff on August 24, 1936, elaborated on the circumstances that had prompted the president's memorandum.[27] Roosevelt, explained Standley, had been shown a May 25, 1936, report of Hawaii's Joint Planning Committee that apparently discussed Japanese espionage in the territory, the visits of Japanese naval vessels in Hawaiian ports, and the entertainment of officers and men of those ships by local Japanese residents. After reading that report, the president inquired of Standley and the acting navy secretary, "what arrangements and plans have been made relative to concentration camps in the Hawaiian Islands for dangerous or undesirable aliens or citizens in the event of national emergency." Standley closed by noting that the Joint Board was in the process of reviewing the report on espionage in Hawaii from the Joint Planning Committee.

Acting Secretary of War Harry H. Woodring responded to the president on August 29, 1936: "The espionage report from Hawaii to which your memorandum referred is now being studied by The Joint Board. Two other matters not covered in that report, but which were mentioned in your memorandum, are within the cognizance of the War Department. The Navy Department has therefore requested the War Department to give you the information you desire thereon."[28] The matters referred to involved the suppression of "aliens and alien sympathizers" and the garrisoning of outlying islands, both of which were being addressed by a "service command" in Hawaii. The war secretary explained:

> This control [of "aliens and alien sympathizers in all the Islands"] will be exercised by the Army through an organization known as the "Service Command," recently established by the Commanding General, Hawaiian Department. The Service Command is organized in time of peace in skeleton form under a senior officer on the staff of the Department Commander. In war that Command would be the link between the military and the civil control forces in the Territory. It will be charged with the control of the civil population and the prevention of sabotage, of civil disturbances, or of local uprisings. It will function on all the islands utilizing certain National Guard

units, police, other civilian organizations, and units of "limited service men" when mobilized. It should be greatly aided in its control of potentially hostile Japanese by the local knowledge of its agents. It will, when necessary, receive the backing of Regular Army units.

In October 1936, the Joint Board completed its evaluation of the Hawaii report on Japanese espionage.[29] Standley, writing for the Board, addressed the president's concerns regarding a list of suspects: "It is a routine matter for those responsible for military intelligence to maintain lists of suspects, who will normally be the first to be interned under the operation of the Joint Defense Plan, Hawaiian Theater, in the event of war"; and regarding his request for further recommendations, the Joint Board proposed that Japanese workers on defense projects be gradually replaced and Japanese fishing vessels in Hawaiian and southern California waters be regulated to prevent espionage.[30] The reply concluded that the Joint Board had "for years suspected espionage activities on the part of the indicated nation in the Pacific" and considered "the curbing of espionage activities in the Hawaiian area to be of the highest importance to the interests of national defense."

The Board recommended that priority be given to the problem and that the resources of governmental agencies besides those of the army and navy be joined in a common effort. By June 1937, the president had designated the secretary of war as chair of an interagency committee, consisting of the attorney general and the secretaries of labor, navy, state, treasury, and war, "to work out some practical solution to the problem" of curbing Japanese espionage.[31]

Hawaii's Hostage Plan

Under Washington's prodding, Hawaii's Joint Planning Committee reexamined its plans for the defense of Oahu, giving special consideration to the problem of internal subversion. One of the likely outcomes of that review was a document written by the head of the army's G-2 from 1935 to 1937, Lieutenant Colonel George S. Patton, Jr.: "Plan: Initial Seizure of Orange Nationals."[32] If not a direct outcome of the committee's reconsideration, the plan was at least conceived in the midst of Washington's discussions on Japanese espionage in Hawaii, Roosevelt's thoughts on suspect lists and concentration camps, and the Joint Planning Committee's review. In fact, Patton's plan was written at the behest of Hawaii's army commander, Major General Hugh Drum, and probably was the department's response to Washington's concern over espionage and sabotage. (It represented the department's thinking until May 9, 1940, when it was relegated to the repository.) "Initial Seizure of Orange Nationals" built on the department's earlier plans, and although shelved before Pearl Harbor, was implemented in its principal aspects when war with Japan finally came.[33]

The plan, wrote Patton, was designed to achieve "internal security and censorship" through arresting and interning "certain persons of the Orange race" who were "most inimical to American interests" or who, because of "their position and influence in the Orange community," would be desirable "to retain as hostages"; confiscating all amateur radio sending and receiving sets from the Japanese; closing all harbors to Japanese vessels, regardless of registry and size; seizing all Japanese banks, trust companies, and travel agencies, and placing Japanese-owned hotels under military custody; removing all Japanese, including servants, from military bases; closing all Japanese-language schools; establishing press, mail, cable, and radio censorship; proclaiming martial law; establishing a military commission to try persons accused of "military offenses"; and confiscating all Japanese automobiles and taxicabs.

Patton's plan was well organized, complete with lists of Japanese suspects, radio operators, and businesses on Oahu and the outer islands and their addresses and telephone numbers. These were grouped into geographical sectors and placed under the custody of teams of "arresting squads." On the designated day, the telephone company would cut the phones of named persons and businesses with a busy signal; the old hospital building at Schofield Barracks would be prepared as an internment center for designated Honolulu Japanese; and "arresting squads" would be dispatched to impound automobiles and taxis, apprehend suspects, and send them under guard to Schofield Barracks. The teams were told: "In case it is difficult to identify your man among several take all of them. Use no more force than is necessary. Reassure the relatives that no immediate harm will befall those whom you take." Each command district would oversee the tasks of arresting and interning suspects, collecting radios, closing language schools, and preventing Japanese vessels from leaving ports within its sector.

Patton's hostage list resembled earlier lists compiled by military and civilian intelligence agencies in that aliens and citizens were lumped together indiscriminately, and leadership in the Japanese community was the primary criterion for inclusion. Patton's hostages totaled 128; 95 were aliens and 33 were American citizens. By occupation, and a few individuals were named in more than one category, the list included 39 businessmen, 25 health-care professionals, 25 religious leaders, 10 politicians, 9 publishers, 8 educators, 8 Japanese diplomats, and 7 attorneys. Two of the hostages were white Americans—a Buddhist priest and a Shinto priestess. Both Takie and Umetaro Okumura were marked for confinement.

In compiling his hostages, Patton, like his predecessors in Hawaii's military intelligence since 1933, was not so much concerned about identifying individual subversives as depriving the Japanese community of leadership. Americanization, Christianity, and even whiteness failed to shield those marked by intelligence for internment; influence within Hawaii's Japanese community was sufficient cause for confinement. Thus, Patton's use of the term *hostage* was neither unique nor suggestive of a prisoner-of-war swap or mass execution.[34] A more economic reading suggests that the interned leadership would constitute "hostages" in that they would be held to guarantee the docility of the masses.

Intelligence Invigorated

Despite the interagency intelligence committee established by Roosevelt in mid 1937, questions of overlapping jurisdiction persisted. Accordingly, on June 26 and September 6, 1939, the president sent memoranda to relevant departments, mandating that the Justice Department and Federal Bureau of Investigation (FBI) be responsible for domestic surveillance and investigations of espionage, sabotage, and subversive activities. As a result, a joint conference of representatives from the State Department, FBI, MID, and ONI agreed on May 31, 1940, that the FBI should maintain its field office in Honolulu (reopened in August 1939) and should "assume responsibility for all investigations of subversive activities of civilians" in the islands.[35]

Following up on that agreement, on June 5, 1940 the FBI, MID, and ONI signed a "Proposal for Coordination of FBI, ONI and MID," in recognition of the necessity for close cooperation and for delimiting their respective spheres of responsibility.[36] The FBI was responsible for all intelligence gathering by civilian agencies on subversive movements in the continental United States and all territories except American Samoa, Guam, Panama Canal Zone, and the Philippines, and was directed to transmit information on "Fifth Column" activities to MID, ONI, and the State Department. The MID would secure all army establishments and their civilian workers, including the Canal Zone and Philippines; ONI was similarly charged with securing all navy bases and civilians employed thereon and American Samoa and Guam.

Despite its leadership role, the FBI was woefully ignorant of the "Japanese situation," both on the mainland and in Hawaii. The ONI maintained perhaps the best intelligence on mainland Japanese; the MID, exclusive of the HSPA, held preeminence in Hawaii. At a joint meeting of FBI, MID, and ONI representatives on June 18, 1940, Hoover was able to estimate the number of German, Italian, and "communist" leaders scheduled for internment during a "national emergency" but could not even speculate on the number of Japanese because, surprisingly, "it was pointed out by Mr. Hoover that no provision has been made in the Bureau's estimate for a war involving the Japanese."[37] At a subsequent meeting of the joint intelligence group, Hoover acknowledged that ONI had done "far more in this field [surveying America's Japanese] than has any other agency heretofore" and thus asked ONI to continue its surveillance of Japanese and share its findings with the FBI.[38]

Hawaii's military intelligence, wrote Hoover on July 5, 1940, suffered from a staff shortage and the absence of a reliable system of intelligence gathering.[39] ONI had a section officer, two reserve officers, one enlisted man, two clerical assistants, one translator, and one undercover operative; MID consisted of the head of G-2 at Fort Shafter and several clerks, and a contact officer in Honolulu with three enlisted men and one translator. Military intelligence continued to depend for information on members of the Big Five firms—John Waterhouse of Alexander & Baldwin, Alexander Walker of American Factors, Frank Atherton and Alexander Budge of Castle and Cooke, John Russell of Theo. H. Davies—as well as Walter Dillingham of Oahu Railway, Stanley Kennedy of Inter-Island Steamship, and Atherton Richards of Dole Pineapple, and other prominent citizens such as Frank Thompson, the HSPA attorney, and Wendell Carl Smith, an attorney for sugar interests in Hilo.

When agent Robert L. Shivers reestablished the FBI office in Honolulu in August 1939, he found a group of understaffed and overworked military intelligence officers assigned to survey Hawaii's Japanese. Before 1935, the army's contact office in Honolulu had apparently consisted of a single room in the downtown Federal Building; after 1935, the office was expanded, and by 1939, the section occupied four rooms in the Federal Building and became formally known as the "contact office." As the likelihood of war with Japan increased, the volume of work handled by G-2 grew, and in October 1941, the contact office moved to the Dillingham Building, sharing the second floor with the FBI.[40]

That close physical proximity, although realized only a few months before Pearl Harbor, indicated the long-standing harmonious working relationship among different segments of Hawaii's intelligence community. In 1939, the FBI, MID, and ONI divided their work in Hawaii as agreed by their chiefs in Washington on a global scale: the FBI was held accountable for the civilian population; the MID, for army installations; and ONI, for navy bases. Weekly meetings of the heads of the agencies helped coordinate their activities. "At these meetings," wrote army contact officer Lieutenant Colonel George W. Bicknell, "all matters of action and policy pertaining to internal security, subversive activities or possible sabotage were openly discussed and appropriate lines of action for each case decided upon."[41] Thus, it seems that Hawaii's intelligence community was closely linked and made all the more efficient in its scrutiny of the "Japanese problem."

On March 4, 1940, FBI agent J. H. Polkinhorn penned "Japanese Activities in the United States," one of the earliest reports from the bureau's newly reopened Honolulu office.[42] Based on a report written by two customs inspectors who had conducted investigations on the visits of Japanese naval vessels in Hawaiian waters, the survey simply restated the familiar theme of Japanese nationalism—local Japanese "lionized" officers of visiting ships, the community leaders were "rabid Japanese patriots," and priests and language-school teachers promoted "Japanistic" tendencies. But unlike military intelligence, which largely drew from members of the white community, FBI agents such as Polkinhorn cultivated and relied heavily on a network of confidential informants, especially from within Hawaii's Japanese community. In that way, FBI agents were able to progress beyond the well-established caricatures and offer a more complex view of the "Japanese situation."

A remarkable example of that breakthrough was the September 27, 1940, report of agent N. J. Alaga, "Japanese Activities in the Territory of Hawaii."[43] Alaga's findings, based on informants designated HO-18, HO-19, HO-20, and HO-21, stood in marked contrast to the accepted view:

> Confidential Informants state local alien Japanese, although strongly sympathetic towards Japan, not organized for purposes of sabotage or subversive activity; believe second generation Japanese predominantly loyal to United States; state fact that many have failed to expatriate not an indication disloyalty to the United States; opine need not fear first generation Japanese in event hostilities, due to their age and due to loyalty of second generation Japanese to United States. Friction between first and second generation Japanese indicated. Influence Japanese language school teachers and Buddhist Priests discounted.

HO-18, a Honolulu resident for many years, stated that "he never observed in the Japanese community any evidence of espionage activity or of subversive or anti-American activities." While *issei* held a natural sympathy for their native land, they believed that America had provided them with new opportunities, and their donations of money and "comfort kits" to Japan were not expressions of anti-Americanism but of obligations to their land of birth. Further, *issei* differentiated between the American government and white people. Racism in employment and naturalization, for example, was deeply resented by *issei*, but they attributed it to whites, not to the government. "As a result, their resentment is directed more toward the Caucasian Race than the American government as such," contended HO-18. These *issei* attitudes, together with their advanced age and spirit of resignation, "will result in their being little problem in the event of hostilities."

HO-18 saw the *nisei* as having a "natural sympathy" for Japan and for their parents that they could not express out of fear that whites would misinterpret it as anti-American. Reported Alaga: "He stated that they [*nisei*] are so intent on not giving the haole population any grounds for such a belief [i.e., of *nisei* disloyalty], that they had been avoiding actual participation in the activities of the alien Japanese which had as their purpose the aid of Japan in its trouble with China." That avoidance led to "considerable friction" between the *issei* and *nisei*, the *issei* seeing *nisei* behavior as disrespectful of parental authority.

Nisei reluctance to give up Japanese citizenship (dual citizenship, continued HO-18, was not an indication of anti-Americanism) was a practical matter of owning property in Japan or seeing Japanese citizenship as a safety net in the event that they were forced to leave Hawaii for Japan. Many, "although they much prefer the United States to Japan and would like to continue living here, feel that in view of the racial discrimination in the United States and the recent influx of haoles into Hawaii, life may eventually become much more difficult for the second generation Japanese than it presently is." Language schools and Buddhist churches were not all that influential in swaying *nisei* political allegiance and were mere expressions of culture.

HO-19 reinforced HO-18's assessment of *issei* and *nisei* attitudes and loyalties, distinguishing between attachments to Japan and anti-American sentiments, confirming the split between *issei* and *nisei*, and sensing no subversive intent among Japanese cultural and economic associations. *Issei* saw themselves as guests in the islands and, accordingly, sought to avoid giving offense to their hosts; *nisei* were, almost without exception, genuinely patriotic. Thus *nisei* "resent deeply the suspicion of the haole element in the Hawaiian Islands that they are all potential Fifth Columnists. They feel they are American citizens, just as loyal to this country as any of the haoles." In fact, concluded the source, "the second generation Japanese know nothing whatsoever of Japan and care little about it. Their main interest is in making a comfortable living in the United States and he does not believe their loyalty to the United States need be questioned."

The FBI undertook further comprehensive and detailed studies of Hawaii's "Japanese problem," which were submitted to Hoover in December 1940 and January 1941.[44] An agent was assigned to each of the major islands: Alaga covered Oahu's Japanese; D. M. Douglas, the Japanese of Hawaii; F. G. Tillman, Maui's Japanese; and R. L. Moore, the Japanese of Kauai. Although each described conditions unique to his particular island, all focused on the sources of "pro-Japanese influence and propaganda," which included Japan's consul general, consular agents, Buddhist and Shinto priests, language-school teachers, and business and professional men.

Securing Subservience

Unlike military intelligence, the FBI attached scant significance to allegations of Japanese espionage. Although bureau agents believed that the

Japanese government received intelligence information through spies, they discounted its importance because strategic data, except for the military's actual plan of operations, could be easily obtained through legal and obvious means. "It would appear that there is little information of espionage value in the Hawaiian Islands which could not be secured by the Japanese," declared an unsigned FBI memorandum of November 15, 1940.[45] The Japanese were in virtually all lines of work; local newspapers regularly reported the movement of ships; and the location of military bases, ammunition dumps, aviation fields, radio stations, power lines, and other strategic targets were readily visible and known to any island resident.

Nevertheless, the question of Japanese loyalty during a war with Japan deserved some attention, noted a November 15, 1940, FBI memorandum. Although an estimated 90 to 100 percent of the *issei* would be loyal to Japan, they "would not be a particularly dangerous element in the event of hostilities at the present time," except for "their leaders; that is, the Buddhist and Shintoist priests, the Japanese language school teachers, the consular agents and a small percentage of prominent alien Japanese businessmen." In fact, "these alien Japanese are overly polite, subservient and outwardly strive to please the White American populace," claimed the report.

The memorandum described a pro-Japan "propagandization" campaign led by the Japanese government through its network of consular agents, priests, and language-school teachers "to develop within [the Japanese population] a strong feeling of loyalty to Japan and to undermine any feeling of loyalty to the United States which is presently alive." That "persistent propaganda campaign" was "a far greater danger to the internal stability of the Hawaiian Islands and its defense in the event of hostilities than would be the efforts of a group of espionage agents."[46]

The bureau's strategy for counteracting the "far greater danger" was a counterpropaganda campaign and a program of selective detention. At the outbreak of war, proposed the memorandum, the "inner circle" of Buddhist and Shinto priests, language-school teachers, consular agents, and selected professionals and businessmen would be interned. Predicted the memorandum: "Upon the interning of the Japanese leaders in the community, there need be no fear of the reaction of the local Japanese population in the event of war with Japan."

Meanwhile, in preparation for the approaching conflict, the FBI recommended that the government wage a secret war against the forces of Japanism by launching a propaganda campaign among *nisei* youth: "The only effective solution to this problem would be the institution, by some governmental agency of the United States of a propaganda campaign of its own—a counter-propaganda system as it were." The agency "would contact and develop the confidence of a representative group of second generation Japanese and would organize them for the purpose of banding together the second generation Japanese of the Hawaiian Islands into an association which would definitely establish itself as being pro-American and anti-Japanese," and "would go a long way toward minimizing the effect of the Japanese propaganda presently being disseminated in the Hawaiian Islands."

The FBI plan directed a broadside at ethnic identity and culture, not Japanese nationalism, prescribing that the *nisei* counterpropaganda system express antagonism toward cultural and economic organizations such as the United Japanese Society and Japanese Chamber of Commerce, advocate renunciation of Japanese citizenship for dual citizens, seek the elimination of all Japanese-language schools, and end *nisei* group travel to Japan. If twenty-five or more "prominent and responsible" *nisei* endorsed the propaganda campaign, the memorandum predicted, "its policies would cause such a violent reaction within the Territory of Hawaii and would receive such support from the White American population that the second generation Japanese would feel called upon to either join the society and support its policies or to brand himself as being pro-Japanese and anti-American." It would also cause intergenerational conflict, encouraging "the vast majority" of *nisei* "to revolt against the influence which the first generation Japanese now have over them."

Hawaii's military arrived at the same solution as the FBI. Army intelligence officer Bicknell traced the immediate origins and purposes of the *nisei* counterpropaganda system of 1940–1941. The army's problem was "to guarantee security to the islands and still maintain economic stability as well as adherence to the democratic principles of American government."[47] The military discussed several options for achieving those goals: "mass deportation of Japanese to the mainland, segregation of all Japanese on one of the smaller islands of the Hawaiian group, or establishment of large-scale detention camps in the valleys of Oahu. These plans had been discussed with prominent civilians, and many local Japanese residents were well aware of them."[48] All, however, had serious drawbacks.

Mass deportation was clearly impractical and destructive of the territorial economy. Mass internment on an outer island was faulty for the same reasons, and mass internment on Oahu posed huge tactical and internal security problems.

Faced with these limitations, continued Bicknell, MID sought to develop an alternative plan: "In 1939 and 1940 steps were taken to make a logical survey of solutions for this admittedly bad situation in order to alleviate it before war came and it was too late to do anything about it."[49] But MID and ONI were understaffed and found infiltrating the "clannish" Japanese and penetrating the "mystifying" Asiatic mind virtually impossible. The intelligence community found the task overwhelming and, by 1940, decided that they could never determine the loyalty of 160,000 individual Japanese. They thus simply *assumed issei* disloyalty; what remained in doubt was the loyalty of the second generation.[50]

Accordingly, wrote Bicknell, intelligence launched an Americanization campaign among the *nisei* to counteract Japanese propaganda emanating from Japanese newspapers, radio, language schools, and religious institutions. The operation was to begin with a select group of *nisei*, carefully screened and directed, forming an "advisory committee" to spearhead the Americanization program. At mass rallies organized by the committee, *nisei* would be assured that they had nothing to fear if they remained loyal; if, however, they acted against American interests, swift and sure punishment would follow.[51]

The campaign described by Bicknell began when Charles E. Hemenway, president of the Hawaiian Trust Company, met with a group of *nisei* at the University of Hawaii, probably between April and June 1940.[52] Present at the inaugural meeting were university professor Shunzo Sakamaki, businessmen Clifton Yamamoto, Masatochi Katagiri, and Jack Wakayama, school administrator Shigeo Yoshida, and city employee Tommy Kurihara. The advisory group met weekly and discussed the question of Japanese loyalty and the likelihood of espionage and sabotage. The *issei*, Japanese-language schools, Buddhist and Shinto priests, and Japanese economic and cultural associations were among the subjects under consideration. The group concluded that there was very little espionage being carried out by the Japanese, but if anyone should be viewed with suspicion, it would be the *issei* leaders of the community because "if anti-American activity should be attempted by Japan, it would be through them."[53] The Americanization program was seen as a way of neutralizing *issei* influence and other elements of Japanism. Yoshida and Sakamaki especially stressed the need for a public campaign of education to exact *nisei* loyalty.[54] Members of the advisory group organized citizens' committees and launched the Americanization program in early 1941.

The Period of Dependency, 1910–1940

Although the contours of dependency were drawn by Hawaii's planters and territorial government, the requirement for a new hegemonic matrix testified, in large measure, to the persistence and efficacy of Japanese resistance. The "second-generation problem" arose because women in significant numbers migrated to the islands, worked and bore the *nisei*, or citizen generation, and established families that sent roots deep into Hawaii's volcanic soil. The transition from migrant to settler provided the impetus for the 1909 strike that, in the words of Motoyuki Negoro, sought higher wages and "full-fledged" manhood. The Japanese were no longer exiles but were "desirous of making their permanent homes here." The unanticipated infusion of picture brides, despite the restrictive Gentlemen's Agreement of 1908, resulted in a more stable community as women achieved greater numerical parity with men, constituting 31 percent of all Japanese in Hawaii in 1910, 42 percent in 1920, and 46 percent in 1930. Insofar as women frustrated the aims of migrant labor, their presence, labor, and reproductive powers resisted a system instituted for their subjugation.

Similarly, Japanese resistance in the workplace stimulated the HSPA recruitment drive for Filipino workers that followed on the heels of the 1909 strike and redoubled after the 1920 strike, with the explicit goal of supplanting "the Jap," clipping "his wings," and keeping "the more belligerent element in its proper place." The number of Filipino plantation workers surged from a total of 155 (.3 percent) in 1909 to 8,695 (19.4 percent) in 1915, 18,189 (41 percent) in 1922, and 34,915 (69.9 percent) in 1932; the number and percentage of Japanese ebbed from a high of 28,106 (64 percent) in 1910 to 16,992 (38.3 percent) in 1922, and a mere 9,395 (18.8 percent) in 1932.[55] That restructuring of the workforce and its correlate, planter paternalism, like the various strategies to cope with the "second-generation problem," affirmed the consequential character of Japanese resistance in altering the forms and conditions of hegemony.

Japanese reproduction and the coming of age of the *nisei* in the inter-war period constituted a major source of anxiety for Hawaii's planters, the territorial government, and the military because of the implications for political control of the islands. An internal State Department memorandum, commenting on the Labor Department's Hawaiian Labor Commission report, pinpointed the Japanese challenge: "The situation which it is desired to remedy is that created by the permanently resident Japanese population. They constitute over forty per cent of the inhabitants of the territory of Hawaii. Their children are growing up with all the rights and privileges of birth in the United States." [56] The threat posed to white supremacy by that demographic reality was first recognized by the military in the 1918 Merriam report, which warned of Japanese permanence; their increase in numbers, especially because of picture brides; and their eventual control of the vote. Hawaii's Japanese, those residues of migrant labor, could no longer be ignored as sojourners who would return to Japan after their usefulness had expired or as perpetual aliens devoid of constitutional rights. They had to be dealt with as permanent residents and youthful citizens—"new Americans"—who had the legal ability and demographic potential to revolutionize the pattern of hegemony through the ballot box.

The structures of dependency, during this phase of Hawaii's anti-Japanese movement, upheld the white oligarchy through economic, political, and cultural dominance. On the plantations, economic dependency was implemented in a system of paternalism that sought to pacify dissidence while extracting profitable labor. The HSPA trustees, during the 1909 strike, advised planters "to get our house in order before a storm breaks" by instituting paternalism. "Once the great majority of the laboring classes are busy under conditions which breed contentment and eliminate grievances, then can we expect a gradual and effectual diminution in the power of the agitating element." [57] Economic dependency involved the concentration of Japanese labor in an extractive industry that required large numbers of cheap, unskilled workers. In 1890, when nearly all of the 12,610 Japanese in the islands were workers, 7,560 were employed on sugar plantations. The concentration of Japanese in the sugar industry continued through World War II, constituting the largest clustering of Japanese labor, especially when combined with the pineapple industry. In 1930, when a total of 44,758 Japanese were employed, 10,321 worked in the sugar and pineapple industries.[58]

Another way of enforcing Japanese economic dependency involved task segregation, or a racial division of labor that reserved positions of unskilled labor to Asians and skilled labor to whites. A discriminatory wage scale also paid Asians lower wages than whites for the same job. In 1910, when the Japanese constituted 64 percent of all plantation employees, they made up only 22 percent of the overseers, while white overseers constituted 63 percent of the total, although they were a mere 13 percent of the plantation workforce. Japanese *lunas* received an average monthly salary of $31.95; whites, excluding Portuguese, averaged $96.03. The cost of replacing Asians with Hawaiians and whites in skilled positions alone, estimated the 1910 federal report, would be about $210,000 per year, the amount planters saved through economic dependency.[59] Despite the formal abolition of the racial wage scale after the 1920 strike, in 1939 non-Portuguese whites on plantations earned a monthly average salary of $112.96, Portuguese received $65.74, Japanese, $53.97, and Filipinos, $47.27.[60]

But largely as a result of the labor shortage and the higher cost of white labor, plus the mechanization of plantations, the Japanese increasingly learned skills as carpenters, electricians, mechanics, and plumbers, allowing them to leave the plantations for urban trades and professions. That rise of the Japanese from unskilled to skilled labor prompted a California congressman, John Nolan, to complain that the planters had "turned everything on the plantations over to the Jap—not along [only] the laborious work in the fields, but the building of pipe lines, contracting for the building of ditches, and work like that. They turned over to them practically everything of a mechanical nature on the plantations."[61] Predicted Wilmot R. Chilton, treasurer of the Honolulu Central Labor Council, in commenting on the Japanese "invasion" in "all lines of business" before the House Committee on Immigration: "They [Japanese] work like a ratchet. . . . Every time you shove the ratchet, the pin stays put, and when a Japanese gets a raise from the plantation, he will not go back any more."[62] In the words of the Hawaii Emergency Labor Commission, the Japanese had "ceased to appreciate the opportunities given them."

To counter that upward mobility, the Americanization movement and the Okumuras' Educational Campaign and Conference of New Americans of the 1920s and 1930s, in their promotion of "efficient workers" and the back-to-the-soil message, bolstered a sagging economic dependency that had been weakened by worker resistance. The 1920 strike of Japanese and Filipino laborers had brought to an end, at least on paper, the racial wage scale, and the coalition of workers across ethnic lines served notice of a multiracial union that would strive to dissolve the barriers imposed by the cultural division of labor. Additionally, it was unlikely that the planters would be able to reinstate migrant labor, as shown by the failure of the Hawaii Emergency Labor Commission and passage of the Japanese Exclusion Act of 1924 and Tydings–McDuffie Act of 1934. Those federal obstructions to a century-old reliance on cheap, migrant Asian labor steered "progressive" elements of planters and the territorial government toward "educating" the younger generation to follow in their parents' footsteps back to the plantations and to find contentment in paternalism.

Japanese leaders of the Americanization campaign knew that their work served the planters. A Christian minister, Shiro Sokabe, described the purpose of his Honomu Gijuku (boarding school) on the island of Hawaii: "I wish to have a Christian home for them [Japanese workers]. . . . I can soon include 30 or 40 laborers of whom no need for strike or any troubles because they are always instructed in Christian home. Servants be obedient unto them that according to the flesh are your masters with fear and trembling in singleness of your heart as unto Christ." Sokabe was well aware that the planters benefited from his boarding school: "These are of course the evangelical work but at the same time this is profitable to plantation so I asked Mr. Pullar, Honomu manager, to support some lot and building. It is surely profitable to the plantation to keep always 40 or 50 or some more number of labourers of whom need no fear of strike, nor need anxious if their work well or lazy." [63] Enjoined in the Okumuras' educational effort were Japan's government and business leaders with Hawaii's planter oligarchy, revealing a convergence of class interests across racial and national lines in securing the economic dependency of Japanese workers.

De jure and *de facto* subordination characterized Japanese political dependency. *Issei*, as "aliens ineligible to citizenship," were placed in a separate, inferior category, permanently disenfranchised and excluded from the political process. The full extent of their powerlessness was revealed during World War II when the arrest, removal, and detention of *issei* failed to stir even a ripple of concern among the jailers over the legality of these arbitrary measures, whereas twisted justifications had to be invented for *nisei* "subversives." The second generation, although accorded legal status as citizens, were pushed to the brink in having to prove that they were worthy of the rights accorded others simply because of birth or skin color. The dream of full equality, *nisei* learned, had to be deferred because of the burden of race—the "sacred blood of kinship"—and the race guilt that infected all Japanese. Patriotism, membership in the company of 100 percent Americans, demanded quiet acquiescence to racial discrimination and "appropriate" political participation, which essentially meant voting for white candidates and, during World War II, resigning from elected office. Perhaps most important, *nisei* were bullied into forfeiting their civil liberties for the sake of "democracy" in Hawaii.

Cultural oppression—supplanting Japanese with white American culture—was the third pedestal upholding dependency. Ethnic culture was a double-edged sword; throughout the period of migrant labor, the planters used culture to exploit workers by dividing them along ethnic lines, but during the 1909 and 1920 strikes, Japanese workers showed that ethnic solidarity was a powerful instrument for mobilizing the laboring class to resist oppression. Likewise, white American culture and institutions possessed the potential for both oppression and resistance. English was simultaneously the "language of command" on the plantation and a means for workers to understand the rulers and to articulate grievances. Hawaii's schools ironically trained the Japanese for servitude but also supplied them with the tools with which to dismantle white hegemony. These complexities applied equally to the historical actors who might have pursued objectives against the interest of their ethnic group, wittingly or unwittingly, for admirable and principled motives. "We are not looking for any recompense or reputation," wrote the Okumuras. "We simply want to better the relationship between American and Japanese peoples, in appreciation for all that has been done for us in the past." [64]

Whatever their motives, individuals like the Okumuras moved within a wider social context, either affirming or denying the status quo. The Japanese could only become "true Americans," preached the Okumuras, by emptying themselves of Japanese thoughts and acts, and by putting the interests of white people ahead of their own desires and needs, to avoid offending whites or appearing impudent and ungrateful. The core of Japanese culture—language and religious belief—was not exempt from that housecleaning. Japanese-language schools and "paganism" not only undermined Americanism but also internal security; that idea, during World War II, justified the detention of Buddhist and Shinto priests and language-school principals and teachers and the liquidation of Japanese school property. Japanese apparel and hairstyles, community observances and festivals, Buddhism, and the Japanese language were relegated to obsolescence through coercive public drives such as the "Speak American Campaign." But the Japanese cultural identity, along with youthful innocence and ambition, was buried in backyard gardens years before the wartime destruction of family records, photographs, flags, and mementos.

Cultural modification, assimilation, or Anglo conformity promoted self-debasement and a dependency on the dominant group, whose members counseled the Japanese to resign themselves to inferiority. "Do not expect a college degree, an A.B. or a Ph.D.," University of Hawaii president David Crawford had lectured *nisei*, "to get you ahead unduly in this world." Instead of moving ahead "unduly," *nisei* were directed into vocational education that extolled the dignity of manual labor and into nonstandard and plantation schools that slowed their educational advance and developed in them a "proper attitude" toward agricultural labor. Indeed, that education resembled the "civilizing" of reluctant Hawaiian workers by missionaries intent on pursuing God and mammon a century earlier.

Despite institutionalized racism and public campaigns designed to relegate *nisei* to the level of "efficient workers," significant numbers of the second generation continued to aspire to higher education and professional employment. Those aspirations were frequently motivated by a desire for self-improvement, but also by a profound sense of community and justice, as expressed by one *nisei*: "I went back to school with the determination that I would fight for my people." Perhaps the greatest achievement of Hawaii's Japanese in resisting cultural hegemony during the interwar period was the communitywide effort that led to the U.S. Supreme Court victory in overturning Act 30 and governmental regulation of the language schools. In "standing up for their rights," the litigants not only secured their civil liberties but also helped to affirm the Constitution and the rights of all citizens.

The military, as a branch of the federal government in Hawaii, stood apart from the planters and territorial government, but as a defender of national sovereignty joined the economic and political elite in surveying and seeking to contain the "Japanese menace." In 1919, the army attempted to institute controls over Japanese-language schools through the territorial legislature, and during the 1920 strike, the military bypassed the territory's acting governor and contacted plantation managers directly about intervening in the emergency. The army saw itself as constrained by the nation's Constitution and political system, which accounts for its desire for a commission form of government and later its insistence on martial law. Democracy could not cope with the uncommon, devious enemy who operated openly and clandestinely, prompting skepticism within the military over the ability of the planters' and territorial government's program of Americanization to render Hawaii's Japanese innocuous. The army accordingly devised a military strategy for ensuring hegemony, positioning itself as the oligarchy's loyal opposition but also as its accomplice in white supremacy.

The comprehensive strategy, designed during the 1930s to combat Japan's total war, contained elements of Washington's concern over curbing the *nisei*, Franklin Roosevelt's desire for concentration camps for secretly identified citizens and aliens, and Patton's hostage plan. As explained in a 1933 estimate of the situation, "the most practicable plan for controlling sabotage or other Japanese activities" was "to control the individuals who are leaders among them." They would be held hostage for the good behavior of their people; the search for spies was abandoned for that "most practicable plan."

By 1940, the army had determined to declare martial law by whatever means necessary; to intern leaders of the Japanese community even before an actual declaration of war to preempt the possibility of subversion and hold hostage the rest of Hawaii's Japanese; and to direct Japanese activities, mainly their labor, to sustain the flow of goods and services.

Meanwhile, army intelligence and the FBI planted a *nisei* counterpropaganda system within the Japanese community to negate Japanism, exacerbate the tensions between *issei* and *nisei*, and stir up white racism to coerce the second generation into public demonstrations of unsullied patriotism, even if that meant repudiating their parents and their ethnic identity. The price ultimately exacted from the second generation was paid in blood on desolate battlefields far from home.

Part III

World War II, 1941–1945

Chapter 9

Into the Cold Night Rain

I bid farewell
To the faces of my sleeping children
As I am taken prisoner
Into the cold night rain
       —Muin Otokichi Ozaki

Total War

Years before bombs fell on Pearl Harbor, Hawaii geared for war. The "Gibraltar of the Pacific" had to be made impregnable against enemies both within and without. The Army Service Command, established in 1935, tied "civil control forces" to the military in a close partnership to prevent sabotage and local uprisings, arguing the need for a total effort because of Hawaii's isolated location in mid Pacific but also because over one-third of its people were Japanese.

The cooperation of the sugar planters was critical to the success of the army's defense plans. Representatives of the Service Command spoke at the 1935 annual meeting of HSPA to explain how crop diversification was a matter of national defense. In response, HSPA formed a diversified crops committee to explore the economics of moving away from an exclusive reliance on sugar. Going a step further, the army presented its own food plan to plantation managers in the fall of 1940, which proposed a comprehensive program of close control over the production and distribution of food during wartime and identification of sugar lands on which cane would be plowed under for less profitable table crops.[1] Predictably, the prospect of reduced revenues vexed some planters; nevertheless, the relationship between the military and the planters during the war was generally mutually beneficial.

Despite the army's assurances that it was prepared to meet all emergencies, anxious business and community leaders met in the Honolulu mayor's office in July 1940 to consider Hawaii's war readiness. They agreed that although the territory's fall was unlikely, it was still possible, and they advised that plans be made to remove the dangers of "sabotage during the period of strained relations" and of war involving "partial blockade; bombardment; bombing; landing of parachute troops; landing of major boats or troops."[2] Civilian concern over sabotage and military preparedness was almost certainly influenced by the fortunes of war in Europe. The widespread fear of a Fifth Column—a term coined during the Spanish civil war of 1936–1939 in which Madrid was betrayed from within—seemed to have held particular relevance to many members of Hawaii's elite. Their anxiety increased when France's Vichy regime surrendered and the German Luftwaffe launched the Battle of Britain in the summer of 1940.

The army's plan for total warfare in Hawaii led to the creation of a paramilitary organization called the Provisional Police in July 1940. The Provisional Police was apparently established through the efforts of the Honolulu mayor, the chief of police, and managers of plantations on Oahu; it consisted of plantation employees, members of the American Legion, and utility workers trained in guard duty. The Provisionals were led by a plantation manager, T. G. S. Walker, and their mission was to prevent and suppress any emergency such as "sudden and unpredicted overt acts by disloyal inhabitants."[3]

The all-civilian Provisionals were headed by an officer corps under a field commander who directed large numbers of men in the field. Rural Oahu was divided into five districts, which were subdivided into local beats. Although the districts encompassed strategic installations, they were essentially demarcated by plantations, rather than by bridges, power stations, and the like. The idea was to free the regular militia from guard duty by utilizing plantation laborers familiar with local faces, terrain, and conditions, who could be easily mobilized, efficiently managed through the existing plantation hierarchy, and were eyes and ears for detecting sabotage and infiltration by outsiders.[4]

The plantations thus relieved the military of a potential manpower drain and the expenses of housing, food, and transportation; the army provided weapons, mainly riot guns, and training. By April 1941, over 1,500 Provisionals were ready for action. Soon after, Provisionals were organized on the outlying islands, making the system territorywide in scope.[5] The planters were not moved by patriotism alone, although partnership with the military was certainly appreciated by the army commander, who commended the HSPA for its "splendid co-operation." What was important to the planters was the fact that the Provisional Police not only secured the territory but protected their private property as well.

The Honolulu Police Department provided another likely source of recruits for the army's paramilitary forces. The FBI, the agency in charge of domestic surveillance since May 1940, asked that the city police form an espionage bureau. This was established in December 1940, following approval by Police Chief William A. Gabrielson, the mayor, and the board of supervisors. According to Police Captain John A. Burns, "This unit [espionage bureau] had been formed at the request of the FBI who said they had neither money nor personnel to do the job that was required to be done here, and they specifically asked for my services as the head of the organization."[6] The police bureau employed a Japanese, a Korean, and a *hapa haole* (Japanese–white); all of them spoke Japanese, investigated matters for the FBI, and engaged in undercover operations. Burns also served as a liaison with certain Japanese, called the "contact group," who advised military and civilian intelligence on matters euphemistically referred to as "morale."

War Games

The army conducted military maneuvers and war games that not only prepared the armed forces for combat but also involved the entire civilian population in the army's plan for total war. A twenty-minute blackout of Oahu climaxed the 1939 army maneuvers; for the first time, civilians participated in the annual military exercises. Residents turned off their lights and sat in the dark, while searchlights raked the sky for airplanes.[7] The effects of the demonstration—pitch darkness, columns of light shooting into the night sky, and the droning of airplanes—on local residents must have been profound.

The 1940 military maneuvers, sketched in an April 13, 1940, document, fabricated a general war situation and gave a day-by-day account of the local progress of the war. It indicated the kind of war expected by those responsible for the territory's defense. Apart from the blackout, military exercises were kept secret from the public and were carried out, according to War Department instructions, "to greatest extent possible without creating public hysteria or provoking undue curiosity of newspapers or alien agents."[8] As part of the war game, army personnel relied on intelligence reports in trying to anticipate and respond to the shifting imaginary situations as they arose.[9]

According to the script, the 1940 maneuvers actually began in November 1939 in preparation for war with RED, an Asiatic nation, unspecified but manifestly Japan.[10] According to the scenario, large numbers of RED nationals resided in the territory, and many RED social, religious, and athletic organizations were scattered throughout the islands. As tensions increased between RED and the United States, the department commander was instructed to be "especially vigilant against sabotage," but to avoid any appearance of hostile actions toward RED nationals. Although no act of sabotage was yet committed, "prowlers" were observed in the vicinity of military and strategic installations.

According to the scenario, RED newspapers and community organizations redoubled their propagandizing efforts to discourage loyalty to America and lay the groundwork for the Fifth Column campaign that would follow and become an integral part of RED's invasion plans. "RED expects to be materially aided by RED citizens and sympathizers in the Hawaiian Islands, organized for sabotage, acts of violence and rebellion," predicted the situation report. The objectives of local RED sympathizers were defined as the overthrow of the civil government, disruption of the army's defensive plans during a RED attack, and harassment of the military on the island of Oahu.

The navies of RED and the United States moved into positions for confrontation in the Pacific, and diplomatic relations became critically strained. War was eventually declared, and the Hawaiian Department commander was appointed military governor under martial law. RED citizens and sympathizers soon began a strategy of "passive resistance," refusing to work. Limited acts of sabotage were committed, but these were confined to a few disgruntled individuals, rather than a systematic campaign of terrorism. Gradually, however, the RED element grew increasingly bold, causing riots and street fights, and small bands roamed the countryside, destroying installations and preventing or delaying troop movements.

As the RED fleet approached Hawaiian waters, RED nationals attempted to take control of Kahuku, Waialua, Kaneohe, Waipahu, and Waianae. Meanwhile, chaos in Honolulu continued. Timed with a dawn attack by RED airplanes, an assault by RED nationals on key civil and military installations disrupted the military supply system and destroyed several military emplacements, but failed to capture those objectives. The 1940 exercise ended here. By 8:00 o'clock in the morning, it seems, the air raiders had been repulsed, the uprising quelled, and the troops returned to their home posts.

The 1940 military maneuvers probably contained both a best- and worst-case scenario. The best case involved the optimistic assessment that Hawaii's military was prepared to handle an air attack and, simultaneously, a determined Fifth Column effort by local Japanese. The RED air attack and ground operations, beginning sometime at dawn, ended incredibly within a few hours. The worst-case scenario envisioned widespread sabotage and outright insurrection on the part of RED nationals. But that situation, especially armed rebellion, was never seriously considered to be even a remote possibility by either military or civilian intelligence.

Nevertheless, several elements of the 1940 maneuvers were based on the current thinking. The Hawaiian Department did not expect to be surprised by a Japanese naval attack, nor did it expect a Japanese expeditionary landing because of the distances involved. Thus the logical thrust would be limited to an attack by air and Fifth Column subversion on the ground. In that war, the army anticipated martial law in Hawaii, with the department commander functioning as military governor, and expected that martial rule and military preparedness would be sufficient to curb civil unrest.

Military Necessity

In the fall of 1941, while Washington contemplated the best way to impose martial law, including a presidential executive order and an act of Congress, the "men in the trenches" were not idle. According to the official history of Hawaii's Office of Military Governor, throughout 1940, the Hawaiian Department commander, Lieutenant General Walter C. Short, and Lieutenant Colonel Thomas H. Green, his judge advocate, "had been analyzing the situation and constructively thinking in an effort to determine the problems and prepare possible solutions." Joining them in deliberations were Major William R. C. Morrison, who had arrived in January 1941, and Major James F. Hanley, who arrived two months later. "Throughout the ensuing period to December 7, 1941," continued the official history, "Green, Morrison, and Hanley devoted their combined efforts to preparing a workable plan for effectuating Martial Law in the Territory."[11]

Introduced in February 1941, the Hawaii Defense Act, or M-Day Act, gave extraordinary powers to the governor in the event of an emergency. Consideration of the bill was postponed under the rush of other legislation before the legislature's adjournment; however, backers of the bill continued to press for its passage. The "Bill to Strengthen the Defenses of . . . Hawaii" forced the hand of Governor Joseph B. Poindexter, who called a special session of the territorial legislature on September 15, 1941, to preserve "home rule," wherein Hawaii, not Congress, would determine the territory's fate.[12] The M-Day bill, although attacked for being "totalitarian" and employing "Gestapo methods," was defended by Short, who ostensibly welcomed "civilian martial law" as a way of freeing the army from the onerous task of governing.[13] The bill assigned legislative powers to the governor, including the power to "regulate, control, or prohibit employment and utilization of workers in any establishment or industry." It authorized the training of guards and air-raid wardens, registration and fingerprinting of the population, and evacuation of any designated area. The bill stopped short of martial law by exempting the judiciary from executive control and retaining *habeas corpus*.

The Hawaii Defense Act passed both territorial houses and became law on October 3, 1941; with its passage, the bill in Congress became a moot point. Despite Short's public support of the M-Day Act, the army had long held that military rule was essential for internal security. As early as 1923, WPD's John De Witt had argued the case for martial law; a decade later, C. E. Kilbourne had proposed military rule through a presidential directive to Hawaii's governor. In the territory, the army's Hawaiian Department's 1940 maneuvers involved military control of the government, and the army's own accounts reveal that a workable plan for implementing martial law was being drafted in Hawaii in January 1941.[14]

The army, thus, anticipated and secretly planned for martial law, even as its Hawaiian Department publicly supported "civilian martial law" and disavowed a militarily imposed solution. During testimony before the territorial legislature, Short spoke in favor of the M-Day bill, stating flatly,

"The essential legislation to provide this protection is entirely a function of the government and legislature. The military authorities have no place in such action."[15] Yet on the morning of December 7, Short pressed Poindexter to ignore the M-Day Act and relinquish civilian rule, suspend the writ of *habeas corpus*, and place Hawaii under martial law.[16] The army commander's justification to the obliging governor was "military necessity."

Necessary Patriotism

While the territorial government and the military mobilized for total war, Hawaii's Japanese increasingly found themselves isolated from the general preparations. At the same time, they must have been painfully aware of the fact that they were central figures in the war plans. Not included in the territory's arrangements for its citizens, they were being asked to prove themselves worthy of inclusion in the category "citizen." As Hawaii's governor had declared to the "new Americans" at their 1933 conference, "The eyes of the Nation are directed toward Hawaii and upon you." Unlike the citizenship of white Americans, that of the *nisei* was perceived as neither a birthright nor permanent; it had to be earned.

The *nisei* plight was an essential part of the military's strategy for maintaining economic and political stability. *Nisei* were to be driven to patriotism, with virtually no other choice. Furthermore, the definition of patriotism, as determined by Hawaii's political and military leaders, meant subordination to their will whether that meant quiet acceptance of inequality or complicity in the destruction of things Japanese. Both *issei* and *nisei* thus were provoked to extraordinary demonstrations of loyalty; anything less would have been interpreted as anti-American and pro-Japanese. In addition, the army made it clear that any deviation by individual Japanese from official expressions of patriotism would be blamed on the entire race. Acquiescence as a people was a precondition for the privileges of individual citizenship.

Mass meetings were organized by *nisei* groups such as the Oahu Citizens' Committee for Home Defense, formed in early 1941, to promulgate uniform codes of patriotism among the Japanese. The committee pledged "to work with the constituted authorities in the continuing task of evaluating what went on in the Japanese community"; to cultivate and make manifest "the inherent loyalty of the Americans of Japanese ancestry toward the United States"; and "to prepare the Japanese community psychologically to their responsibilities toward this country in the event of war and for the difficult position in which the war would place them in their relationship with the rest of the general community."[17]

Toward that end, the committee sponsored a flag-waving rally of 2,000 *nisei* at McKinley High School on June 13, 1941. *Issei* publisher Tetsuo Toyama organized another mass assembly the following month. At the June patriotic rally, the *nisei* resolved to "reaffirm our unreserved loyalty," "pledge ourselves to do all within our power, individually and collectively, to serve our country even at the sacrifice of our lives," and "urge all fellow Americans to place implicit faith in our constituted authorities and work together to protect those democratic traditions which have made our country great."[18]

The entire Japanese community in Hawaii, not just those in attendance, was instructed on the meaning of patriotism at these youth rallies. Civilian and military leaders exhorted their listeners to eschew Japanism, embrace Americanism, and labor for the common good, holding out the prospect of inclusion as full-fledged members of the island community and promising "drastic action" against disloyal persons and groups. Speaking for the Hawaiian Department commander on July 18, 1941, Lieutenant Colonel Eugene M. Foster expressed confidence in "the people of the Japanese race," members of Hawaii's "team for defense." Team membership, however, carried with it duties, including informing against fellow Japanese whose words and deeds damaged American interests, because if any act of sabotage were committed by any member of a particular group, "all members of that group will be under suspicion until the guilty party is apprehended, and proof is given that his acts were not supported or conducted by others of the group." The army spokesman reminded the resident Japanese elite: "You men of business have much to lose . . . for an accusation against you of disloyalty might cause loyal citizens to boycott you and ruin you."[19]

Military and civilian intelligence penetrated and helped reshape citizen groups to advance their purpose. The Committee for Inter-Racial Unity in Hawaii was formed by Hung Wai Ching in December 1940 at the height of the Sino-Japanese War to promote racial and ethnic harmony among the territory's diverse population.[20] Chinese, Japanese, Hawaiians, Filipinos, and whites met to discuss ways to counter the anti-Japanese sentiment in the islands that had accompanied Japan's military aggression in Asia and the Pacific. The committee later sought the advice and inclusion of business leaders, politicians, and military men in its work. Robert Shivers, head of the local FBI office, was named chair of the committee's steering group, which included key Asians, whites, and the heads of army and navy intelligence. Interracial unity, the committee's founding purpose, was no longer an end in itself but became a means toward another goal: a strong national defense. "The people of Japanese ancestry, both citizens and aliens, compose about one-third of our population," declared the committee. "Accepted and united in purpose and action, they are an asset to the community. Rejected and treated as potential enemies, they are a burden, even a danger, to our security."[21]

Nisei, some of whom belonged to Hemenway's advisory group, sought to educate *nisei* youth by launching the "expatriation campaign" in the fall of 1940. Named the Hawaiian–Japanese Civic Association, it set out to obtain 25,000 signatures of *nisei* high school students on a petition to Secretary of State Cordell Hull, asking him to obtain from Japan a simple procedure whereby dual citizens could renounce their Japanese citizenship. The HSPA supported the campaign by distributing the petition to plantation managers and facilitating visits of association agents to the plantations.[22]

In a November 7, 1940, speech, Shunzo Sakamaki, executive secretary of the campaign committee, explained the reasoning behind the expatriation campaign. *Nisei,* he stated, considered themselves to be as American as any other native-born citizen, yet they faced discrimination and suspicion. They were not fully equal. Nonetheless, *nisei* had to be patient ("we cannot expect any sudden change of feeling, for that would be too much to ask of human nature") and should realize that they shared the blame for their situation. Equality, predicted Sakamaki, would eventually be realized "when our modes of behavior, our ways of thinking, our manners of expression have become so much alike that we shall be as natural and comfortable in sustained social association with people of other racial origins as we unquestionably are today when congregating among our own racial groups." For the moment, *nisei* could lay to rest suspicions of disloyalty by joining in the expatriation campaign: "By signing this petition, we publicly record our stand as loyal American citizens who believe in the principles of American democracy and in the magnificent idealism for which the Stars and Stripes stand."[23]

The campaign succeeded in gathering 30,115 signatures during the month of November alone, exceeding its original goal, and the association mailed a copy to Territorial Delegate Samuel Wilder King for presentation to Hull. The *Honolulu Advertiser* hailed the *nisei* campaigners as the "new spokesmen" and "true voice" of Hawaii's Japanese, praised their "strictly American" viewpoint, and lauded them for their determination to separate themselves from certain *issei* and for "fanning patriotism by rallies which are calling for the defense of America."[24] The army commander congratulated the committee for refuting suspicions of loyalty and breaking "a long and disturbing silence." "To my mind," he wrote, "more has been done in the last three months to clear the local atmosphere than in many years, and in this you have had a large part."[25] The association's petition, meanwhile, made the bureaucratic rounds in the nation's capital, passing from the State Department to the Interior Department and back to Congress without achieving its objective.

Precautions

Although he praised the Oahu Citizens' Committee for Home Defense for its loyalty resolution and expatriation campaign, army commander Short informed the army's adjutant general about the need for man-proof fences and floodlights around public utilities in the islands, including reservoirs, water tanks, wells, pumping stations, transformer stations, gasoline and oil storage tanks, and telephone exchanges. Those precautions were necessary, wrote the general, because "the large percentage of aliens and citizens of doubtful loyalty resident on Oahu seriously complicate the problem of anti-sabotage protection in this department."[26]

The military's appreciation of *nisei* patriots was tempered by its assumptions of race. The "Japanese race" was unassimilable, homogeneous, and disciplined through a whole array of individuals, institutions, and cultural forms. *Nisei* Americanizers, to the army, were the entering wedge for penetrating and dividing an impervious community. Winning the *nisei* over to the "American" camp was seen as a "counter propaganda" coup. "We are at present engaged in a counter propaganda campaign whose object is to encourage loyalty of the Japanese population of Hawaii on promise of fair treatment," cabled Short to his superiors in Washington. "The present outlook of results of this campaign on entire population is very favorable. Success of the campaign would promote unity and greatly reduce proportions of our defense problem." The driving force behind the campaign, however, was not "fair play." As the army commander succinctly and frankly put it, "it is impracticable to place total Japanese population of one hundred sixty thousand in concentration camps."[27]

Besides being "impracticable," that ultimate state of security was not feasible economically. Japanese labor would be lost, while white labor would be needlessly expended to guard and manage the concentration camps. Further, scarce resources, especially food, would be consumed by a nonproductive one-third of Hawaii's population. Nevertheless, ruling out mass internment did not preclude the idea of confining selected individuals from among the suspect race, a vital part of the military's overall strategy since the early 1920s. Plans were further refined during the months preceding Pearl Harbor, largely as a result of a nationwide discussion among the army, navy, and Justice Department on the need for detention facilities for crews of enemy merchant vessels and other enemy aliens in the event of war.

The War and Justice Departments, in a document dated March 26, 1941, agreed to intern "dangerous" persons and those whose detention was in "the public interest" in order to avoid legal or political "difficulties" that might arise from "over-internment," the confinement of aliens with dependents or infirm persons, the "reckless internment of labor leaders," or the detention of individuals who might have made "disloyal statements" before the outbreak of war.[28] According to the agreement, the Justice Department would prepare presidential proclamations to control the conduct of enemy aliens and crews of enemy ships and would delegate authority to the attorney general's representative in Hawaii to restrict and confine enemy aliens there. Furthermore, agents of the attorney general, under the direction of the FBI, would arrest enemy aliens under presidential warrants. The War Department was responsible for receiving and caring for persons selected for internment.

In the islands, the army's Hawaiian Department commander responded to the joint agreement and plan in a memorandum dated April 18, 1941.[29] Short reported that the army had surveyed potential internment camp sites on the island of Oahu and had concluded that the immigration station in Honolulu and the quarantine station on Sand Island were best suited for the purpose. His recommendation led to a bureaucratic struggle to wrest control of the stations from the Justice Department and the Public Health Service, which ran the installations. Justice ultimately turned the immigration station over to the army, but the health service continued to hold on to the quarantine station.

The correspondence accompanying that administrative tussle showed that the army was caught by surprise. Its war plan had assumed martial law, which would have permitted it to take over public and private property without much fuss. That, in fact, was ultimately what happened to the quarantine station; the army commandeered it for use as a concentration camp after Pearl Harbor. In estimating the space required for detention facilities, Short revealed that military intelligence, in July 1941, maintained a list of about 500 resident aliens considered prime candidates for internment at the outbreak of war and approximately 1,000 others classed as "suspects to be watched and apprehended upon the first indication of disloyal acts." The army commander's estimate of the number to be interned was therefore 1,500.[30] As it turned out, Short's assessment was fairly accurate.

In addition to such secret precautions, the military prepared the civilian population for war by creating and training the Provisional Police, erecting fences and floodlights around public utilities, and recruiting women volunteers to knit, sew, and roll surgical dressings. Selective Service was initiated, reserve officers were called to duty, and the Hawaii National Guard was activated. Military expenditures rapidly increased, resulting in a defense industry boom and a sudden expansion of Oahu's economy. Wages soared, businesses grew, and laborers left the plantations for better-paying jobs. The mayor of Honolulu set up a Major Disaster Council composed largely of city and county department heads and chaired by the chief of the Provisional Police. The army organized the four major outer islands into military districts designed to counter internal, rather than external, dangers. Accordingly, "the commander of each district was told to further cordial relations with the Japanese residents and to strengthen defenses against sabotage."[31]

Preparations took place from the fall of 1940 through the summer of the following year. Thus, although there was confusion amid the debris and rubble of Pearl Harbor, there was a clear sense of direction in the response to the Japanese attack.

Custodial Detention

Even as *nisei* "spokesmen" worked to prove their loyalty, the FBI was expanding its investigation of the Japanese. In June 1940, the FBI began a national effort to compile a comprehensive list of persons on the mainland and in U.S. territories "whose continuance at liberty during a period of national emergency might be dangerous to the security of the United States."[32] The FBI office in Hawaii simultaneously inaugurated "an extensive informant program" to ferret out any possible nests of subversion or sabotage among the local Japanese. By November 1941, 73 confidential informants and 135 "loyal and reliable" Japanese were cooperating with the FBI and serving as "listening posts" in their communities throughout Oahu.[33]

The growth in the staffing of the bureau's Honolulu Field Division office reflected the seriousness of its commitment to containing the perceived danger. During the 1930s, the office had a solitary agent in charge and a stenographer; after the May 1940 agreement making the FBI the primary investigative agency, six additional agents and two more stenographers were assigned to the Honolulu office. One of those agents was sent to Hilo to open an office there. A Japanese translator, Saburo Chiwa, joined the bureau in April 1941, and between June 1940 and June 1941, the staff steadily increased to thirteen investigative personnel. That number grew to a total of sixteen special agents by December 7 and reached twenty-one special agents by December 21, 1941.[34]

Agents investigated numerous charges of espionage allegedly being carried out by Japanese fishing vessels (sampans); all were found to be groundless. Similarly, the investigation of consular agents uncovered no evidence that could lead to a conviction of espionage. Nonetheless, the FBI persisted in its determination to have Japanese consular agents arrested under the Foreign Agents Registration Act of 1940. The proposal ultimately failed, largely because of opposition from the army commander.[35] The FBI's "custodial detention" program, devised in June 1940 to identify "dangerous" persons for internment during an emergency, met with greater success.

A comprehensive list of "subversives," classed I-A (for internment) or I-B (for surveillance), and a dossier on each individual on the list were kept in the bureau's Washington headquarters, compiled from regional lists supplied by its field offices and from lists provided by ONI and MID.

Lists were kept current and turned over to the Special Defense Unit (later superseded by the Alien Enemy Control Unit) of the Justice Department. In Hawaii, the FBI supplied copies of its file on "subversives" to MID, in anticipation of martial law for the territory and the army's taking responsibility for the emergency detention program. Shivers, the agent in charge of the Honolulu office, submitted an outline of the internment program on March 11, 1941. Expanded versions of his proposal were submitted by Shivers and Bicknell of the army's G-2 on November 17, 1941, for German and Italian aliens, and five days later for Japanese aliens and citizens. The plans were subsequently approved by Short.[36]

The Japanese plan contained three options, depending on whether the war with Japan did not present an immediate threat to Hawaii, or if there was a likelihood of surprise raids against the islands, or imminent danger of a large-scale invasion. Under the first scenario, the FBI, military, and local police would arrest and detain an estimated 217 consular agents, 13 Buddhist and Shinto priests, and 4 unspecified individuals, who would remain in custody pending an examination by a review board to determine whether or not they should be interned permanently. Under the second plan, everyone named for "custodial detention" would be interned plus an additional 54 persons not included among those considered dangerous under the first plan. Furthermore, the remaining Japanese population would be put under surveillance and would be subject to state propaganda to ensure loyalty. The third option mandated "absolute martial law" for Hawaii, resulting in the permanent detention, without benefit of review, of all suspected Japanese. Additional punishment, "prompt and severe," would be meted out as normally prescribed for subversive acts in a wartime theater of operations.[37] As it turned out, a combination of plans 2 and 3 was the strategy employed by the military on "M-Day."

Despite the fact that Bicknell, Shivers, and Burns (of the Honolulu Police Department) agreed that there was scant danger of sabotage, the military's defensive posture changed from "attack alert" to "sabotage alert" a few weeks before Pearl Harbor. Apparently the change came from Washington where the Roosevelt administration seemed more concerned with internal subversion than an attack by Japan. According to Poindexter, Secretary of Interior Harold Ickes "told the governor that Washington felt there would never be an attack by Japan but had instructed the army and navy locally to be on guard against sabotage." Army sentries were stationed at harbor facilities, public utilities, and pumping stations, leading to Poindexter's concern that this action was "a sort of undeclared form of martial law."[38]

The FBI verified the addresses of those on the internment list on November 1, 1941; a month later, detailed plans for the arrest and detention of the "subversives" were complete. Those arrangements resembled Patton's earlier hostage plan in its implementation, including geographical sectors and teams of arresting squads. FBI special agents, the Honolulu police, and the army's Corps of Intelligence police were divided into thirteen arresting squads. Each squad was given index cards with the names, addresses, and citizenship status of all those to be apprehended in that squad's district, and MID telephoned the marked names to MID operatives on Kauai, Molokai, Lanai, and Maui.[39]

On the Friday night before the Pearl Harbor attack, G-2 and FBI in Hawaii sent a revised list of suspects to the War and Justice Departments with a request that the attorney general prepare warrants of arrest for those on the list.[40] As it turned out, the latest update became the operational inventory of names used by the arresting squads, but since the U.S. attorney general had not yet responded by the time Pearl Harbor was bombed, those on that list were apprehended without warrants.[41] Burns, one of the principals who drew up the list, said it was a decision arrived at by a majority vote of Bicknell of G-2, Shivers of the FBI, and himself. If two of the three agreed, explained Burns, "the guy was interned." He recalled that the group did not even bother to investigate consular agents, language-school principals and teachers, and other community leaders because "they were aliens and they were prime and with very few exceptions they were picked up as a unit." Whether these individuals were subversives was not the issue; they were interned because they were leaders. "So there were some things operating very much against the Japanese, to tell you the truth," acknowledged Burns.[42]

Security Blanket

The declaration of martial law on December 7, 1941, was fundamentally an anti-Japanese act. Despite the fact that martial law applied to everyone living under its dominion, military rule had been planned and was subsequently executed specifically to contain the "Japanese problem." Two decades of preparing the ground by the planters, the territorial government, and the military accounted for the easy surrender of civil liberties by Hawaii's governor and the U.S. president before the setting of the sun on that "day of infamy."

In an 11:15 A.M. radio broadcast, Poindexter promulgated the M-Day Act, passed barely two months earlier to avoid the need for military rule. "Civilian martial law" was short-lived. At 12:10 P.M., Short called on the governor to request that he declare martial law. According to Poindexter's testimony, Short defended martial law as "absolutely necessary" because of the imminence of a Japanese invasion aided by local Japanese saboteurs.

Acting on the commander's request, Poindexter consulted with President Roosevelt by telephone at 12:40 P.M. and affirmed the necessity of martial law because of the threat of internal subversion. The telephone conversation, according to Charles M. Hite, territorial secretary and Poindexter confidant, proceeded as follows: "Gov. said Short had asked for martial law and he thought he should invoke it. President replied he approved. Gov. said main danger from local Japs."[43]

At 3:30 P.M., Poindexter proclaimed martial law, suspended *habeas corpus*, and authorized Short to serve as governor and exercise judicial powers.[44] In assuming his position as military governor, Short announced that all Hawaiian residents, "no matter what race or nationality," were enjoined "to refrain from giving, by word or deed, any aid or comfort to the enemies of the United States." Any breach of that directive would be considered treason, and traitors were guaranteed the "severest penalties."

Within minutes of his pronouncement, Short was on the telephone to his G-2 contact office ordering the pickup of targeted persons. The thirteen arresting squads fanned out throughout Honolulu and Oahu's rural districts, and within a three-hour period forcibly removed the "prime" suspects from their homes. By December 8, 391 Japanese aliens and citizens had been apprehended; by the following day, 93 German and 13 Italian aliens also had been picked up.[45] According to Bicknell's assistant, "there was a constant stream of Japanese going through the MID office in those first days, and many were cleared upon first questioning." In other instances, entire groups of Japanese were rounded up and detained for no particular reason; "nobody even knew who they were, where they came from, or under whose authority they were apprehended. They even went without food for a while."[46]

While the bombs were still falling, five Japanese informants reported to the FBI office in Honolulu to offer their services. They were instructed to contact their network of approximately a hundred fellow Japanese "loyal-ists" and "to deploy themselves among the Japanese populace to report any information of subversive acts and statements, sabotage, or espio-nage." FBI agents rushed from one scene to the next, investigating vari-ous explosions in Honolulu, checking out reports of Japanese seen in the vicinity of the water reservoir in Pacific Heights, and responding to calls of Japanese parachute troops landing in Manoa Valley.[47] None of the rumors of landings or sabotage was true, but they provided justification for martial law in Hawaii and mass internment on the West Coast.

About the time that the five informants reported to the FBI, Bicknell merged his contact office with the FBI offices in the downtown Dilling-ham Building. Henceforth, G-2's nineteen operatives collaborated with the FBI's sixteen agents in counterespionage operations. The ONI, MID, and FBI worked in close cooperation, their offices linked by telephonic and teletype communication through a loop with army and navy head-quarters at Fort Shafter and Pearl Harbor. That security blanket also en-compassed the Honolulu police, which participated in the identification and roundup of suspects and, under orders from the FBI, sealed off the Japanese consulate about noon.[48]

Cold Night Rain

Among Hawaii's Japanese, with the dawning of December 7, "an extreme degree of fear was present," according to a contemporary observer. The Japanese were afraid of being questioned, afraid of being suspected of disloyalty, and afraid of being accused of simply being Japanese. They feared that they would be held accountable for the devastation wreaked by Japan. "Their state of mind was comparable to that of a criminal ex-pecting a severe punishment for a major offense."[49] That fear, rooted in Hawaii's anti-Japanese movement, was also grounded in the more im-mediate context of martial law and the summary arrest and detention of community leaders.

"Fear of severe punishment," observed an army document, "is the greatest deterrent to commission of crime." The account credited the mili-tary's no-nonsense program of stringent reprisal and forceful detention for the absence of espionage or sabotage among Hawaii's Japanese. "It is certain," alleged the document, "that many persons who might have been

tempted to give aid, support or comfort to our enemy were deterred from
so doing by the severity and the promptness with which punishment
was meted out by the Provost Courts operating under the martial-law
regime."[50] In the April 27, 1946, *Honolulu Advertiser*, Poindexter said, "Internment of all suspected enemy aliens was the only safe course to put
the 'fear of god' in the hearts of those who would assist the enemy."

The poet Risuke Yasui wrote on December 7:

> Intense anxiety,
> With rumors and false information,
> A day is now toward the end.[51]

The events of that Sunday morning also filled the esteemed Yasutaro
Soga with uneasiness.[52] Instead of his usual kimono, Soga dressed in a
suit and put on shoes. "My family looked at me with [a] queer expression
on their faces, but I read books as if nothing would happen," he recalled.
The anticipated knock at the door came later that evening. Shigeo, his
eldest son, answered it. Soga continued: "There were three, taller than
six feet and young, military policemen. . . . They told me to come to the
immigration office. Without hesitation, I replied, 'surely' and went to my
bedroom to wear my vest. They followed me around the house. My wife
helped me wear my vest and coat." As he was escorted past the gate,
his wife, who had come out with him, whispered, " 'Don't catch a cold.'
I wanted to say something," he remembered, "but the voice couldn't
come out."

Soga was taken by car through the deserted streets of Honolulu, stopping at designated homes to pick up other "subversives." In the blackout,
he lost his sense of direction and had no idea of who his fellow prisoners
were. From time to time, the car was stopped and searched at roadblocks
by armed sentries with bayonets. Finally, they arrived at the immigration
station where the men were led into a room on the first floor. Military
police conducted body searches under a dim light and confiscated many
of the men's personal belongings. They were then marched upstairs in the
dark, Soga's arm grasped by a military policeman. "Suddenly he threw
me in one of the rooms," wrote Soga. "What astounded me was that
first I felt the stuffiness in the dark room and then I didn't know how
many people were kept in the room, but I couldn't find an inch [of] space
for myself to sit down." Soga stumbled about in the dark until someone
helped him to the top of a bunk bed near a window. The muted voices of

men filled the heavy air, their murmurings punctuated by exclamations of recognition on hearing a familiar voice.

At daybreak, Soga discovered that the room was packed with sixty-four "brothers." Rows of triple-decked beds and bed mats spread over the floor provided the furnishings, and there was a single bathroom next door. The crowded and unsanitary conditions created a revolting stench in the bathroom area. Soga knew most of the men, including the venerable and feeble Iga Mori, Bishop Gikyo Kuchiba, Tokue Takahashi, and Tetsuo Toyama. They swapped stories of their arrest, Kuchiba having been the first interned at 3:00 P.M. Takahashi, who lived on Alewa Heights, overlooking Pearl Harbor, was arrested while watching the Japanese attack with binoculars and recording his observations.

Although internee treatment varied from guard to guard, the general atmosphere in the immigration station, wrote Soga, "was bloodthirsty. The M.P.'s attitudes were rough. Things could have burst into bloodshed once a false step was taken." Under these trying conditions, internees had to restrain themselves to avoid physical violence. Soga remembered his first morning at the immigration station when a young military policeman ordered the men around with pointed bayonet. "I was so furious," he wrote, "as if my blood started flowing backward. I almost threw my mess kit at him." Soga noticed an internee who was staring, with "a pale face due to his anger," at the abusive guard. "If we had expressed our feelings," he reflected, "we would have died . . . a dog's death from the thrust of his bayonet."

Suikei Furuya described how when the elderly and sickly Miyozuchi Komeya, proprietor of Komeya Ryokan, entered the room at the immigration station, the men piled up several mats to make him comfortable on the floor. A guard burst into the room and proceeded to pull Komeya off the mats while cursing him, "God damn you!" The men protested to no avail, and the soldier finally succeeded in dragging Komeya completely off the mat and onto the hard floor. Testified Furuya: "I couldn't resist my anger, but I had to consider the situation that all of us were placed. I restrained myself. I couldn't help my body stop shaking from anger."[53]

The internees lined up for meals under the watchful eyes of soldiers with pointed bayonets. Despite the availability of a large room adjacent to the courtyard, recalled Soga, "we had to eat in the yard no matter how wet the ground was, or even when the rain started pouring during our meal." The men were allowed to walk and stretch in the courtyard for only ten to twenty minutes after their meal before being led back to their "filthy small room." Besides poor-quality and sloppily served food, the mess kits on which it was dished out were sometimes too dirty to eat from. Non-Japanese internees always ate before the Japanese, and the latter had to wash their mess kits in the same bucket of water that had been used by the former. "I couldn't stand that because even these prisoners looked down on us," remembered Soga.[54]

On the third day, about half of the 200 internees held at the immigration station were taken to Pier 5. They were surrounded by guards with bayonets and machine guns and put on a barge typically used to haul pineapples. "I thought we were to be sent to Lanai or Molokai," recalled Soga, but the vessel simply transported them across Honolulu harbor to Sand Island. Looking back, the internees could see Honolulu, the verdant Nuuanu Valley leading up to the Pali, and the cloud-covered Koolau mountain range. Ahead of them was the flat and barren Sand Island, and beyond that, the Pacific. Life in an American concentration camp was about to begin.

Sand Island

Sand Island concentration camp was hastily set up on December 8, using the existing facilities of the quarantine station operated by the Public Health Service. The army had planned to use Sand Island as a concentration camp since April 1941 because the island could be easily guarded to prevent escapes, it was adjacent to Honolulu but separated from it by water, and it was near the Office of Military Governor yet isolated from strategic targets. The facilities at the quarantine station—houses, kitchens, and administrative buildings—were excellent and could readily be converted to a concentration camp. Once martial law was declared, the army simply took it over.

According to J. H. Linson, medical director at the station, G-2's Bicknell informed him on the afternoon of December 7 of a probable army takeover of the quarantine station. A company of the Thirty-fifth Infantry moved in the following day, but quarantine station employees remained to operate the boats and the station. On December 11, Captain Carl F. Eifler arrived to head the army camp and promptly announced that he intended to rid Sand Island of the Public Health Service. Three days later,

Eifler ordered all station employees off the island and threatened to build a fence around the entire station, enclosing the recalcitrant Linson and his family in the camp. Wrote Linson: "In view of these facts and because I could see no particular reason for remaining on the station, I decided to leave which I did December 17, 1941."[55]

Others soon joined the Japanese internees transferred from the immigration station, for a total of about 300 internees by the end of the first week of the war.[56] The physical plant was divided into four compounds: two compounds each capable of holding 250 Japanese men; a compound designed for 40 women of any race; and a compound set aside for white men, 25 Germans and Italians. Each compound constituted a distinct unit, operating its own mess and recreational activities and having its own spokesperson. Compounds were then subdivided into companies of 25 internees housed in a single barracks. For the first six months, however, the internees lived in tents.

Soga and his fellow internees were greeted by the camp's first commander, Captain John G. Coughlin, who said, "You are not criminals but you are Prisoners of War. Therefore, everyone will be treated equally under the International War Regulations." The classification of internees as prisoners of war drew Soga's comment, "His speech was agreeable to me, but I felt a doubt about the word 'POW.'"[57] After the speech, the Japanese were directed into a room where they were stripped naked and subjected to body searches. They were then led outside in the rain and gathering darkness and were ordered to erect twenty tents. Because many of the internees were priests, editors, businessmen, and physicians, "most of us never did this type of work," explained Soga. They found the task exhausting and difficult. "We were soaking wet from rain and perspiration, and finally we finished building tents about 9 o'clock at night." Another group from the immigration station arrived about that time with the sickly Komeya, who had fainted and had to be carried by the "brothers." The day ended as fitfully as it had begun: "We all lay ourselves in makeshift beds in wet clothes that night," wrote Soga.

Life on Sand Island was monotonous and stressful. Each day was regimented around rollcalls in the morning and at night. But the orderly flow of activities failed to calm the rage within. Women and men worried about the families they left behind, searched for reasons for their internment, and yearned for their release. "In the beginning we were restless because we were incarcerated without any investigations," wrote Furuya. "But, as the days went by, our nervousness was gone . . . and we began to desire to have investigations as soon as possible, for we were certain that we could go home as soon as the authority [sic] investigate our records. We had never done anything wrong in our lives." In particular, Furuya referred to internees—long-time residents of Hawaii—who had obeyed the law, worked diligently, and educated their children to become "100 percent Americans." For them, he wrote, confinement was especially hard to deal with, and "some of them became neurotic and others became insane."[58]

"I suspected that unless we were mentally strong," wrote Soga, "some of us would begin to have nervous breakdown[s] and act in unusual behaviors. We were insecure and impatient." Soga told of an internee who attempted suicide by slashing his wrist with a razor blade after repeated questionings by the FBI. He survived, but was held in isolation, and his tent mates were subjected to strip searches. Another internee, a priest, insisted that he was pregnant, went insane, and had to be watched and restrained for three days by his fellow internees. "We grew desolated more and more," Soga testified. "Our joyless days continued day after day. In order to divert our feelings, smutty stories (sexual and obscene) were popular in every tent."[59]

The use of their labor was problemmatic because, as prisoners of war, under the Geneva Convention they could not be compelled to work other than to complete tasks required for the maintenance of the camp. Convention provisions were subject to interpretation, however, and these were liberally construed by the keepers of the camp. Soga reported that in addition to the usual chores, internees were assigned busywork. "In those days we were forced to work constantly such as weeding, picking up rubbish, and swatting flies. . . . They didn't want us to rest. So the guards always patrolled around our tents. We were not allowed to stay in our tents except when we were sick."[60]

"One day I saw the construction workers [civilians] building double wire fences around our camp," reported Furuya. The soldier supervising the work crew scolded the men for working too slowly, whereupon they stopped altogether in protest. "Then the commander pulled rather elderly internees," testified Furuya, "and forced them to continue the hard labor to build the fences . . . despite available young internees like me." Two days later, the civilian workers returned to lodge a complaint about the use of Japanese internees as "strikebreakers."[61] The army claimed that the internee camp leaders volunteered "young, healthy, strong Japanese" to erect the fence simply "for the exercise."[62]

The army then corrected its original announcement that the internees were prisoners of war and, according to Soga, told them they were
"merely detainees," and the camp would not be governed by military
regulations. Whatever rules governed the island, terror was clearly what
buttressed authority. When an internee headed for the restroom, a guard
would shout, "Halt!" If the internee did not respond with, "Prisoner," the
guard was instructed to shoot. "They ruled it our mistake to be shot if we
didn't say it," Soga explained.[63] Another internee described how guards
with rifles lined them up against the wall and threatened to shoot them
if they refused to do as they were told. "With that threat," he remarked,
"there was no need to say anything more."[64]

Soga cited the "Okano incident" on December 14, 1941. He and a group
of internees were assigned to work outside the camp. Inspectors stopped
and searched the work gang on their way back and found a knife on
Ryoshin Okano, a priest. The alarm was raised. Several guards quickly
surrounded Okano with pointed pistols, stripped him naked, and then
turned to his work mates. Despite nightfall, recounted Soga, "we were
gathered in the open space and we took off our clothes. We had to remain
standing for a long time until they finished searching our clothes. Other
guards searched our tents and took away our fountainpens and pencils.
We were frozen to death in the cold, windy, and barren field."[65]

Besides having to endure physical and mental anguish, the Japanese
were made to feel completely vulnerable, exposed, and stripped of their
dignity. Recalling such strip searches with indignation, a former internee
exclaimed, "They stripped us down and even checked the anus. We were
completely naked. Not even undershorts. They even checked our ass-
holes."[66]

The whistle, which signaled rollcalls and inspections, blew on the
slightest whim, reported Soga, and sometimes pierced the air seven to
eight times a day, creating a tension that kept the internees on edge. "We
were restless and irritated all the time." The day before New Year's Eve,
wrote Soga, Eifler called all the Japanese internees together to make an
example of George Genji Otani, internee-elected camp leader, who, Eifler
claimed, had "insulted" one of the soldiers. Eifler informed Otani, with
"a threatening look," that he should have been promptly shot to death.
Instead, he ordered guards to take Otani to an isolation cell at army headquarters in Fort Shafter, where he was confined for a week and given only
water and hard crackers.[67]

The physical environment of the desolate coral island made life even more difficult, particularly for the sick and infirm. "A dust wind kept blowing almost every day in December," recorded Soga, "and the night air was shivering cold." When the rains came, the area became flooded, the canvas fabric leaked, and the tents, which were neither raised above the ground nor built with a floor covering, afforded little shelter. Consequently, internee cots frequently stood in pools of water when it rained; even when it was dry, the bed covers were soaked by the rising humidity from the saturated ground.[68]

Kaetsu Furuya described how conditions on Sand Island seemed to have contributed to the death of Kokubo Takara, a fellow *issei* from Kauai. A Japanese-language-school principal, Furuya was apprehended on the evening of December 7 and taken to a military prison in Wailua. The facility had iron bars and an iron slab for a bed. Each internee was given two blankets, one of which was placed on the metal surface while the other was used as a covering. There were no toilets, only a one-gallon can that had to be called for, and the place was so infested with mosquitoes that "we all got swollen faces from mosquito bites," remembered Furuya. Breakfast consisted of black coffee and a cracker so hard that "it wouldn't break even if you bit it."

In February, twenty-seven internees, including Furuya and Takara, were sent from Wailua prison to the Honolulu immigration station where they stayed for a few days before being transferred to Sand Island. "The boss [Eifler] there made us, us men, really cry. It was February and it was rainy—the rain would come down from the mountains and this boss would make us stand in the rain, practically naked, in our undershirt and underpants," declared Furuya. Takara caught a cold and became constipated for a week, receiving no medication. "We had no medicine or means of helping him, so he died," lamented Furuya. His body was shipped back to Kauai, but there were no Buddhist priests to conduct the funeral because all of them had been interned. A priest had to be sent from Sand Island to Kauai to conduct the funeral service, after which he returned to Oahu.[69]

Jukichi Inouye, another Japanese-language-school principal on Kauai, described how his path led to Sand Island. Inouye was arrested in the early morning of December 8 and taken to Waimea jail where he found several of his friends. The quarters were cramped, the toilet was a bucket, and "there was no place to hide." After three days, without explanation, Inouye and nine others were placed in a "dump truck" and driven away.

"We were wondering where they were going to execute us. Some thought the graveyard that we were nearing was going to be the place. But then we went by it without stopping." Instead, the men were taken to Wailua jail where they joined Furuya and about seventy to eighty priests, language-school teachers, and community leaders.

During his confinement in Wailua jail, Inouye was brought before an examination board that included a military officer and three managers from Lihue plantation. In February, Inouye accompanied Furuya to the port at Nawiliwili for transportation to Honolulu. Haruko Inouye, his wife, described the scene: "You should have seen when they were taken to Nawiliwili. They were put in a truck and we couldn't . . . they put all the internees on one side and the families on the other side." Besides being cut off from their loved ones, the families of the internees were shunned by their neighbors and friends, who feared being connected with them. "You should have seen all my neighbors," said Haruko Inouye. "When all the friends, when they see me, they coming this way, they just step aside. They were afraid to talk to me. Later on it got better. They thought anything could happen to them, so they tried to avoid me."[70]

Quarantined on Sand Island was Myoshu Sasai, a Jodo Buddhist priest from the island of Hawaii. The day after Pearl Harbor, a Hilo police officer and two soldiers took Sasai from his home. Sasai knew the policeman very well; in fact, Sasai had helped the man and his family on many occasions through marriage counseling. "They would have an argument, the husband and wife," explained Sasai, "and I would call them over and have a meal with them and make them shake hands." That man took Sasai away from his wife and young child. He was placed on a "sampan bus" that made about a dozen stops, picking up other "suspects" and finally depositing them at Kilauea Military Camp. The men were led to their sleeping quarters, a large hall lined with beds and lockers. Throughout the night, a constant stream of buses emptied their load; by morning, there were more than a hundred internees.

To get to the mess hall, internees had to walk between two columns of soldiers with bayonets, and as he walked that gauntlet, Sasai recalled being shocked by the starkness of the camp. Inside, however, food was plentiful and nutritious. "They really fed us well," reported Sasai, "but outside, around the mess hall, soldiers were surrounding us." Even when going to the bathroom, the internee was accompanied by a soldier, who stood at his side if he sat on the toilet seat.[71] The armed guards were not posted simply to harass, but had explicit orders to restrain their keep. Hishashi Fukuhara told of how an internee tried to escape from Kilauea Military Camp by climbing the fence. "They killed him; they shot him dead," testified Fukuhara.[72]

In February, soldiers, attorneys, and a local "haole big shot" conducted hearings at the Hilo post office. In groups of four or five, internees were taken to the hearings as family members strained to get a glimpse of their loved ones. "While at the hearings, friends and family would crowd the corridors to peer through the windows to get a view," described Sasai, whose "greatest enjoyment" was to see his wife and child during the two or three times he appeared before the panel. After the hearings, two FBI agents told Sasai that he was going to be transferred to a mainland concentration camp. Family members were permitted to enter the barracks to bid their final farewells but, recalled Sasai with sadness, "we really didn't have too much to say besides take care of yourselves and stay well. The talks were long, but that's what it boiled down to."

The men were loaded onto army trucks and driven to Hilo harbor where they boarded the *Waialeale*. Internees were confined to the upper deck, bound for Sand Island; below them, their sons—*nisei* volunteers for the U.S. military—set sail to ransom their people. Sasai reflected on that unhappy circumstance: "Boys born in Hawaii, young boys from Hawaii are going. Even though their citizenship may be different, they are on their way. We are going someplace too. I thought that we were all being forced to go." Sasai spoke truthfully; both decks of the *Waialeale* carried an impounded people, victims of Hawaii's anti-Japanese movement. "It was a scary trip," recalled Sasai. "Normally the ocean is pleasant, but in wartime, the ocean is scary. You don't know what is in it."

The internees were taken to the immigration station where every morning the bugle sounded a new day. Instead of carrying rifles, the omnipresent guards carried machine guns. "Even the food was bad," reported Sasai. "Pork and beans and sausage was the mainstay." At Sand Island, the internees were stripped naked and ordered to carry their clothing from one place to another. They were given only spoons with which to eat, presumably for security reasons, even though a metal spoon could as readily be transformed into a weapon as a knife. The indiscriminate use of spoons tended to reduce adults to infantile dimensions. Even on the rare occasions when they were fed steak, the men had to use spoons.[73]

Women internees were kept separate from the men but, unlike their male counterparts, were racially integrated. At least eighteen Japanese women and about ten German and Italian women were interned at Sand Island. Commandant Eifler's wife served as matron. Unlike her husband, she was kind toward the internees, permitting internee husbands and wives to eat dinner together on Wednesdays.[74] Women internees arrived at Sand Island in the same way as male internees, via jails, military camps, and Honolulu's immigration station; like the men, women internees were generally professionals and often connected with Shintoism or Buddhism. Umeno Harada, wife of Yoshio Harada of the "Niihau Incident," was an exception. She was accused of disloyalty in assisting her husband in the brief escape of the Japanese pilot Shigenori Nishikaichi, downed on the island of Niihau after the Japanese attack on Pearl Harbor.[75] Both Nishi-kaichi and Harada were killed during the escape attempt.

The army arrested Umeno Harada and took her from Niihau to the neighboring island of Kauai on December 15, 1941, for internment at Waimea and later, Wailua jail. She was separated from her three young children, placed in solitary confinement, and watched constantly by armed guards. Soldiers handcuffed her whenever they ushered her from her cell to the interrogation room. In protest, she refused to eat for five days; her keepers summoned a minister to coax within her a desire to live. Harada was among the first group of internees shipped from Kauai to Sand Island in February 1942. "At the time of departure," recalled Kaetsu Furuya, "it was impossible to leave without pain and tears, especially in the case of Mrs. Harada, who had two or three young children, about five years old or younger." She would not have been able to see or bid farewell to her children had it not been for a Korean American soldier who took compassion on her and brought her waiting children to her. That act of kindness held special meaning to the internees because of Japan's aggression against Korea and Japanese discrimination against Koreans. "All of us who witnessed the incident cried," remembered Furuya.[76]

Fragmented portraits of women internees emerge in the accounts of internee men. Soga, for example, described Shizuyo Yoshioka as "formerly with the Nippu Jiji and a Nichiren devotee, who was paroled because she was pregnant," and wrote of Teruchiyo, "a Japanese lyric singer," and of "an alleged street walker, and a nun whose build and beauty was the talk of the men's camp."[77] Furuya wrote about Yoshiye Miyao and Yuki Miyao, mother and daughter-in-law, who both signed their names "Y. Miyao." They were both interned because the authorities could not decide which "Y. Miyao" was a threat to the national security. Furuya also mentioned Tsuta Yamane, who was interned apparently because she defended her husband as he was being arrested.[78]

Men and women, leaders of the community, were reduced to shells of their former selves on Sand Island. Men scrounged for cigarette butts discarded by guards, rolled the tobacco in toilet paper, and passed the precious narcotic from man to man around the tent.[79] When Masaji Marumoto, a young attorney at the time, visited the camp on Christmas Eve, 1941, "he was appalled at the unshaven faces, dishevelled hair, and grimy appearance of the detainees, many of whom were his former friends," reported Soga.[80]

Sand Island also exemplified the courage and strength of a people. Staying alive, much less keeping one's dignity, was a challenge. Soga wrote about the internees' belief in their imminent death and their determined claim to humanity: "Almost all of us slept in the clothes that we wore in the daytime, for we didn't know when a sudden disturbance might occur, and also we didn't want to die disgracefully."[81]

Internees resisted dying "like dogs" while in "protective custody." According to Soga, Shin Yoshida and Zensuke Kurozawa were searched in the immigration station at bayonet point and were told that they would be shot in the morning. Unaware that the officers were "joking," the pair prepared to commit suicide to deny their keepers control over their lives or deaths. Before hanging themselves, however, the men decided to strike back at their oppressors by killing the soldier who carried their meals to them. To their surprise, instead of a soldier, an old woman brought their dinner that evening; relieved, the men dropped their deadly plan.

Soga also reported on the absurdities of life on Sand Island. Josen Deme, a priest, was ordered to leave the camp. Thinking that he was being released, anxious internees gave him messages to take to their families on the outside. After some time, the internees learned that Deme was still in camp but on the German side. Deme had been taken to the immigration station where his name was recorded as "Joseph Deme"; believing "Deme" to be a Germanic name, the authorities sent him back to Sand Island as a German alien. Other Japanese suffered a similar fate. "Maeda" was considered German and "Ipponsugi" Russian. The Japanese internees had an especially difficult time on the European side of the camp because they could not communicate with anyone.

Camp food catered to European tastes, and Japanese internees sorely missed their style of cooking. "We cultivated [a] vegetable field outside the camp," wrote Soga. "Several tens of us volunteered to work in the vegetable field under the eyes of the guards. We were not allowed to take back the grown vegetable." Despite that injunction, laborers occasionally managed to smuggle a few *daikon* (radish) and green vegetables past the guards and into the camp.[82]

Sand Island's purpose, it seems, was to break the spirit of the Japanese. The process began with the swift, forcible removal of individuals from their families and homes. They were given no reason for their arrest or explanation of where they were being taken or for how long. That arbitrary action, though expected, was jarring to many Japanese because of the stern, vindictive way in which they were arrested and confined. Although reminiscent of preannexation plantation power relations between master and servant, this display was more dramatic because these people were not "mere" laborers but the most influential members of the Japanese community. The display of white supremacy and Japanese subordination was pervasive in the immigration station and concentration camp, through the ever-present visibility of arms, the omnipresent guards, the frequent and unexpected rollcalls, and punishment generously meted out for "insolence" and a host of other offenses. Internees had little control over their future, and their lives were inconsequential.

Perhaps most telling was the inhuman treatment accorded internees; it was systematic and not limited to individual guards. Eating in the rain, using dirty utensils and wash water, sleeping in flooded tents, and being forced to relieve themselves in cans and buckets were unnecessary shows of contempt for the flower of the *issei* generation. Solitary confinement, insistent interrogations, make-busy labor such as fly swatting, and cruel punishment such as digging unexploded shells sapped the body as well as the mind. Strip searches were common, and there were no closets in which to hide personal weaknesses. That breaching of the outer defenses was the final conquest of the person. Having wrestled through the night, internees despaired of seeing the dawn. "None of us could see a light in our future," penned Soga.[83]

Breaking the spirit of the internees held wider meaning and significance, exceeding the numbers confined in the concentration camp and extending beyond Sand Island. These men and women were the best that the Japanese community had to offer. Publishers and priests, poets and language-school teachers, they were the voice, the heart, and the soul of a people and culture. From Kona, Hawaii, to Koloa, Kauai, from Waianae to Honolulu they came, these stewards of the community. Breaking them meant, in effect, the subservience of the entire group. Sand Island, nonetheless, was more than a symbol; for Hawaii's Japanese, it served as a conspicuous warning of the consequences of defiance and as an emphatic demonstration of who governed and who served. In that sense, Sand Island held hostage not only the internees but the entire race.

On February 17, 1942, two days before Roosevelt issued the executive order that legalized the exclusion of Japanese from the West Coast, 172 Sand Island internees classified as "troublemakers" were instructed to collect their belongings and were taken to the immigration station. There they were told that they would be shipped to internment camps on the mainland. On hearing this, reported Soga, most "no longer cared about their future because they were in despair." Even the strongest among them broke down and cried when they learned of their fate. During the night before departure, Soga wrote, the immigration building echoed with the singing and weeping of depressed people.[84] On the morning of February 20, military trucks, escorted by jeeps mounted with machine guns, sped the men out through the back gate of the immigration station past the family members who had come to catch a last glimpse of their men. Once on board the *Ulysses Grant*, the internees were confined below deck until the ship arrived a week later at Angel Island in San Francisco Bay.

Chapter 10

Bivouac Song

Steaming with blood and salt,
the 100th Battalion;
Bursting with pride,
the 100th Battalion;
Spirits soaring,
the 100th Battalion;
We never give up,
the 100th Battalion.
— Yukio Takaki

Controlling the Japanese

The Office of Military Governor ruled from Iolani Palace, the last seat of an independent Hawaiian monarchy, where former Judge Advocate Green acted as executive officer for Short, the military governor. Martial law enabled strict "control of the civilian population" through sweeping general orders emanating from the palace that were interpreted by military tribunals and imposed by the military police and civil enforcement agencies. Civilian control was punitive in that every general order carried criminal sanctions, and the structure of the military government resembled an army of occupation.[1] Because its purpose was to contain a specific segment of Hawaii's people, civilian control discriminated against the Japanese.

General civilian controls applied to the entire population: restrictions on labor and wages; controls on rents, prices, food, and liquor; the rationing of gasoline and other commodities; the temporary closing of schools; and the collection of firearms and ammunition. Everyone over six years of age on Oahu was required to register with the Division of Registration, and the entire population lived under blackouts that varied according to the times of sunset, from 6:00 to 8:00 P.M., and curfews that began anywhere from 6:00 to 10:00 P.M. and extended to 5:30 or 6:00 A.M. All civilians were excluded from restricted areas; interisland and trans-Pacific travel were regulated by priority ratings; and the mail, newspapers, magazines, and radio stations fell under military censorship.[2]

In addition, there were controls specific to enemy aliens and citizens of enemy ancestry. The Japanese were the primary target of these extraordinary restrictions because they constituted the largest group embraced by the controls. Only the thinnest line separated Japanese enemy aliens (*issei*) from citizens (*nisei*) in the eyes of the military because of the influence of the *issei* and the *kibei*, who had been educated in Japan.[3] The military justified discriminatory regulations, despite their promise of equal treatment under martial law, as necessary "for their [the Japanese] own protection and for the safety of the United States."[4] The military established the Alien Registration Bureau to administer many of the provisions of enemy alien controls.

Besides having to register with the Bureau of Immigration and Naturalization, enemy aliens were required to carry their alien registration card at all times. They not only had to report changes in residence or occupation but had first to obtain approval for them from the Alien Registration Bureau. Special curfew provisions were applied to enemy aliens, and certain areas and occupations—the West Loch area of Pearl Harbor, Honolulu harbor and waterfront, and work on defense projects—were restricted to the Japanese. Alien Japanese had to obtain permission to travel beyond their home island from the Alien Registration Bureau, which notified G-2 for clearance and requested travel space on the usual waiting list maintained by the Travel Control Bureau. Only then could they purchase tickets, under the watchful eye of a bureau steward who also escorted travelers to the place of departure. Permission to travel by air was granted only in extreme emergencies.

Enemy aliens were specifically forbidden to write or publish any "attack or threats" against the government or against anyone in the military. The provision was broadened by General Order No. 5: "No Japanese shall commit, aid, or abet any hostile act against the United States, or give information, aid, or comfort to its enemies." Although freedom of assembly was permitted, people were encouraged to report to the provost marshal any meeting attended by enemy aliens, and in the case of Buddhist meetings, to report to the army's G-2. Finally, Japanese who received permits to work in restricted areas such as at Pearl Harbor and on the Honolulu waterfront were given special badges to wear, with black borders, that clearly marked them as Japanese.[5]

The special treatment of the Japanese, both alien and citizen, was manifested in other ways. In the military's consideration of the possibility of another Japanese attack, Hawaii's Japanese figured prominently in the army's defense and evacuation plans. The Office of Civilian Defense directed that in rural Oahu during a general evacuation, all Japanese women and children (except boys over sixteen years of age) were to be removed from the danger zone and placed in approved shelters; Japanese men over sixteen years of age were to be placed under guard and used as a "labor battalion" for work on roads and similar projects.[6] On Kauai, the defensive scheme listed as priority 7, of fifteen priorities: "To seize and detail all males of Japanese extraction (and Orientals who resemble Japanese), between the ages of 15 and 65."[7]

Controlling Hawaii's "Japanese race," in fact, was part of an old and ongoing national discussion, involving the larger questions of Japan's intentions vis-à-vis Hawaii and the Pacific and of the balance between internal security and Japanese labor. On December 17, 1941, Brigadier General Sherman Miles, head of G-2, addressed the question of Japan's strategy in "Japanese Potentialities with Respect to Hawaii," a document sent to the president, secretary of war, chief of staff, and heads of the concerned air, naval, and army departments.[8] Miles's well-argued memorandum weakens the contention that "military necessity" compelled martial law in Hawaii and supports the historical interpretation that "military necessity" was not the driving force behind the mass removal and confinement of Japanese on the West Coast.

Miles analyzed Japan's strategy in the Pacific and its military capabilities. The attack on Pearl Harbor, he advanced, was designed to immobilize America's Pacific Fleet, enabling Japanese offensives in Southeast Asia and the western Pacific. An attempt to capture Oahu or any outlying island in the Hawaiian chain was unlikely and was not in the strategic interest of Japan because it would overextend Japan's already thin forces and risk involvement in a protracted war. Instead, argued Miles, the most logical and probable option would be air attacks, such as the Pearl Harbor raid, launched from carriers against the U.S. fleet in Hawaii, to provide security for Japan's operations in Asia and the Pacific. As for the "X" factor in the defense of Oahu, "whatever might have been the possibilities of the Fifth Column," Miles concluded, "they no longer exist."

Miles agreed with pre-Pearl Harbor military intelligence estimates of Japan's intentions and capabilities and with the most recent FBI findings about the degree of danger posed by Hawaii's Japanese. What made his study significant was that it was written after Japan had shown its hand at Pearl Harbor. The "military necessity" argument breaks down, therefore, for both Hawaii and the West Coast, to the extent that Miles was believed. If a Japanese landing in Hawaii was improbable and a landing on the West Coast was even less likely, martial law and mass internment were less compelling. The Pearl Harbor attack, the latest intelligence reports on Japanese troop and hardware strength and their deployment, and the absence of any act of sabotage on the part of local Japanese clearly supported Miles's reading. Further, Japan no longer had the element of surprise, diminishing the likelihood of success and any thoughts of conquest.[9]

Still, the navy pressed for what can only be characterized as further retaliation against the territory's Japanese, despite the fact that all boards of inquiry into the Pearl Harbor disaster failed to produce any evidence of subversion by local Japanese. The army's board of inquiry, for example, found that "no single instance of sabotage occurred while Short was in command up to December 7," and "in no case was there any instance of misbehavior, despite a very exhaustive investigation being made constantly by the FBI, and by G-2, as well as by Naval Intelligence."[10] In January 1942, Secretary of the Navy Frank Knox, who had told a press conference that Pearl Harbor was a result of "the most effective fifth column work that's come out of this war, except in Norway," asked the secretary of war to provide "information as to [the] practicability of concentration of local Japanese nationals . . . on some island other than Oahu."[11] The following month, during a cabinet meeting, Knox suggested the internment of all Oahu's Japanese on the island of Molokai.[12]

Civilian control also involved the question of internal security weighed against the need for Japanese labor. Like the question of Japan's intentions for Hawaii, this equation and its wartime solution were neither new nor at variance with pre–Pearl Harbor assessments and plans. The position, held since the 1920s, arose from two basic realities: the permanence of the territory's Japanese, largely because of the *nisei;* and the reliance of the economy, essentially sugar production, on Japanese labor.

Internal security, accordingly, went beyond concerns over subversion; it included Americanizing the *nisei* and advancing the economic welfare of the planters.

As in the campaigns of the 1920s and 1930s, the Japanese led in the wartime Americanization effort, and, as shown in Shigeo Yoshida's "A Plan to Meet the Japanese Problem in Hawaii," the blame for the "Japanese problem" fell on the Japanese. "Place the greater part of the responsibility on the Japanese themselves," Yoshida advised Hawaii's rulers. "Let the loyal ones help to take care of the few who might be 'on the fence' or potentially disloyal." [13]

Housecleaning

Civilian control inflicted serious and lasting wounds on Hawaii's Japanese community. Besides promoting insecurity, the forced removal and detention of community leaders contributed to social disruption, which was, in fact, a goal of the strategy for defense because it weakened the will and ability to resist. Social inversion, or a reversal of roles and meanings, was a way of achieving that end. The caretakers of the people's identity were stigmatized and held up as persons to be shunned. The people's culture—patterned behavior that ordered their lives—was negated and denied; ultimately, a person's identity as a Japanese was to be hated and despised. Taking that path to its final destination, the supreme proof of loyalty for Hawaii's Japanese was to be anti-Japanese.

Budding social scientists attending the University of Hawaii documented the cultural decline. "Immediately after the outbreak of war," wrote two students, "rumors circulated that any objects which were 'Japanesy' were incriminating and that many Issei were being interned because of possession of them. During the days that followed, almost every Japanese family had a thorough housecleaning, and all objects which were kept for sentimental reasons were pulled out of trunks and destroyed." [14] Family shrines connected with Buddhism, photographs and letters that linked individuals with Japan, Japanese books, magazines, and records, and flags and emblems were all burned or buried. Japanese discarded kimono and *geta* (raised, wooden tongs) for Western dress, shoes, and stockings; women trimmed and curled their long black hair. So pervasive was the need to conform that Japanese who persisted in wearing kimonos were seen by fellow Japanese as defiant of Hawaii's military rulers and a threat to the community's well-being.[15]

Japanese culture, including the *issei* leadership structure and a previously well-ordered community, was a casualty of the war.[16] Japanese-language schools and newspapers were closed by military order; Shintoism was banned; and although Buddhism was officially permitted, nearly all its priests were interned in concentration camps and its adherents threatened with similar treatment. According to a Hongwanji priest, Ernest H. Hunt, certain Christians put "pressure upon the Buddhist youths with implied threats of the concentration camps unless the children attend [Christian] church." The military desecrated Buddhist temples, such as the Jodo-shu temple on Makiki Street in Honolulu, which was converted into an infantry battalion headquarters, and the Hilo temple, whose great brass lamps and ceremonial vestments were apparently plundered by soldiers.[17]

As late as April 1944, the policy of the Office of Military Governor was "to discourage the resumption of Japanese religious activities other than Christian." It delayed, investigated, and frequently rejected petitioners who requested permission to hold Buddhist services. Buddhism, the Office of Military Governor believed, provided the Japanese with an opportunity for "subversive gatherings," whereas Christianity was "less likely to promulgate pro-Japanese matters." [18] As a result, Buddhism was practiced clandestinely, and public and community observances such as *obon*, cemetery lantern lightings, and the Hanamatsuri festival held in Kapiolani Park were discontinued.[19] Attendance at Buddhist churches declined precipitously, and most temples closed their doors.

Other Japanese practices, many religiously based, also stopped during the war. Japanese traditions such as *mochi-tsuki* (rice pounding) were dropped from New Year's Day festivities, and Girl's Day on March 3 and Boy's Day on May 5, during which dolls were displayed and colorful carp flags hoisted, went unobserved. Those activities were not mere expressions of membership in a cultural community but also solidified bonds within the family. As observed by one student, who regretted the wartime demise of *mochi-tsuki:* "This was a special occasion in itself. The whole family turned out for this event. Mother steamed the *mochi* rice, while father pounded the steamed rice into [a] glutinous mass. Then young and old together formed the pounded rice into round *mochi* of varying sizes." [20] Rituals connected with courtship and weddings—the go-between, dowry, elaborate hairdo, dress, and ceremony—gave way to "five dollars and a judge" for some, and the role of the father in marriage arrangements declined. Although these changes reflected a general process of acculturation, they were also prompted by a "fear of being identified with anything Japanese and a strong desire to become like non-Japanese."[21]

The roles of parent and child were reversed. The status of *issei* fell as the standing of *nisei* rose with the differential treatment given the generations by the military. *Issei* bore the stigma of enemy alien; *nisei* were tainted, but nevertheless wooed and cajoled toward Anglo conformity. *Issei* spoke the language of the enemy; *nisei* translated government orders, radio and print news, and social cues, intonations, and sanctions for parents who did not know English well. *Issei* represented an obsolete mentality, an Old World flavor that had become distasteful. *Nisei* symbolized the future, a new direction and style, in full pursuit of the American dream. The transition was liberating for some: "Like a symbol of medieval restraint," wrote a *nisei*, "the kimono has been almost forsaken, and women have been freed of the stiff obi bindings and wrappings."[22] For others, "Speak American" became the new bindings and wrappings.

The "banning" of the Japanese language struck at the heart of the people, beyond an infringement of a fundamental human right. Unlike the major dailies, the *Star-Bulletin*, *Advertiser*, and *Hilo Herald-Tribune*, which were ostensibly shut down by military order but never stopped publishing, the *Nippu Jiji* (renamed *Hawaii Times* during the war) and *Hawaii Hochi* were silenced by military dictate from December 11, 1941, to January 8, 1942. In addition, many Japanese publishers and reporters were interned by the military. The running again of strictly censored presses in January did not signal greater freedoms but was stimulated by the army's need to rule by reaching the Japanese-speaking population.[23] Japanese radio broadcasts were prohibited for the war's duration.

The closing of Japanese-language schools and the Speak American Campaign were complementary processes spearheaded by the Japanese primarily through the Emergency Service Committee, a group constituted in February 1942 with the approval of military intelligence and placed under the Morale Section in the Office of Military Governor. Founding members of the Service Committee were Masaji Marumoto, Shigeo Yoshida, Masatoshi Katagiri, Ernest Murai, Y. Baron Goto, Katsumi Kometani, and Jack K. Wakayama. The committee's work, like that of other "morale" committees for Chinese, Filipinos, Koreans, and Puerto Ricans, was to act "as liaison between the military authorities and the racial and national groups on matters relating to the general adjustment to war."[24] The morale and adjustment of Hawaii's Japanese, however, held special meaning for the army, which saw them as indices of Japanese loyalty and subject to military control.

On the Spot

The Service Committee maintained that bitterness against the Japanese in the islands was understandable because of Japan's treachery at Pearl Harbor and because America's war was with "the country of our ancestors" and with "our parents," Japanese culture provoked suspicion and invited scrutiny, and Japan's treatment of American prisoners of war explained calls for reciprocal treatment of the Japanese in America. Not surprisingly, the Service Committee's counsel was to "take the 'bumps' as they come and still 'keep up our chins.' "[25] In fact, according to the committee, *nisei* should expect the bumps, be grateful for the "fair and humane" treatment of their enemy alien parents, and be thankful that there was not further repression.

The committee admonished *nisei* to show their gratitude by being productive and not idle, participating in voluntary labor, buying defense bonds, donating blood, and scrupulously obeying military orders. It also warned *nisei* against speaking Japanese in public, wearing Japanese clothes and footwear, displaying Japanese signs, and congregating in large numbers. "We must not tolerate a half-way allegiance," advised the committee. "Those who waver or who we know are disloyal or whom we consider potentially dangerous must be exposed not only for the welfare of our country but for our own sake." The committee accordingly worked with and through Burns's Honolulu Police Department contact group.[26] The caveat, "remember that this is war and war is ruthless," seemed to guide committee members. "We must be willing to die, if necessary, to help America live," they declared; "winning this war is what counts, nothing else matters; for if America loses this war, what is there to live for?"[27]

The *nisei*, in reality, were driven to superpatriotism by racism and the anti-Japanese movement and were provoked to excesses by the military government. Lieutenant Colonel Charles Selby, speaking before the Conference of Americans of Japanese Ancestry organized by the committee in 1943, began condescendingly, "I presume that you have rejoiced at the good news from Italy," referring to the Italian surrender. He continued, "but have you stopped to realize that the Italian capitulation may actually be bad news for you?" Selby explained that America could henceforth concentrate on "the war of extermination against the Japs." As American casualties mounted and Japanese atrocities became widely known, the Japanese in Hawaii would inevitably suffer from the community reaction. "Therefore," he concluded, "you gentlemen cannot afford to be complacent or retrogress to the pre-war attitude but must redouble your efforts, lest you soon find the people of Japanese ancestry are more than ever on the spot."[28]

The colonel highlighted two things that antagonized whites and required correction: the use of Japanese by people able "to speak American," and the "cockiness" of the younger generation. "It has been said that this is merely an expression of a truly American trait; perhaps this is true," said Selby. "But that doesn't alter the fact that it is annoying and that it does cause criticism of your racial group." Selby summed up his lecture to the *nisei:* "Your problem requires immediate, aggressive, and continuing action to educate all people of Japanese ancestry in these Islands, so that there will be a minimum of criticism and a maximum contribution toward beating the hell out of the Japs."[29]

The fatuousness of Selby's call for "beating the hell out of the Japs" was proven by Hawaii's youth nearly half a world away. On September 12, 1943, the day the colonel spoke, *nisei* young men of the 100th Battalion in North Africa prepared for the invasion of Italy, which had capitulated but was still held by German troops. Ten days after Selby's indictment, they climbed down rope ladders from their transports onto landing barges. On September 28, through rain and mud, Company B set off through the village of Castelvetere toward higher ground near Chiusano. As the men rounded a bend in the road at about 10:00 A.M., three German machine guns raked the area while mortar and artillery shells zeroed in. Sergeant Shigeo Takata exposed himself to draw enemy fire and thereby locate their position. Takata was hit in the head by a piece of shrapnel; as he died, he revealed to his comrades the location of the German gunners. Engagement with the enemy on this front claimed two *nisei* lives and seven wounded, and Takata posthumously received the Distinguished Service Cross for his valor.[30]

Eliminating Cockiness

The Speak American Campaign was launched on October 12, 1942, with much fanfare in the white press. The Service Committee distributed and displayed posters and stickers admonishing the Japanese to "speak American," and committee members held community meetings to organize English-language classes for adults. In a radio address, Shigeo Yoshida explained the need to "speak American." To win the war, Hawaii's diverse population had to unite against the "ruthless enemies seeking to destroy our way of life." Use of one tongue, the "language of America," was unifying, as opposed to the "language of the enemy," which was divisive because it was "irritating" and "discourteous" to whites. Taking his argument one step further, Yoshida proposed that Japanese should "not only speak but think in the language of America." He thus proposed the motto "Speak, think and act American."[31]

Liquidating Japanese-language schools yielded more tangible results than the Speak American Campaign in that success could be measured by the number of schools closed. Members of the Service Committee on Oahu and their counterparts on the outer islands worked to effectuate the "voluntary" eradication of this source of irritation. The Kauai Morale Committee set a standard by dissolving not only all Japanese-language schools (twenty-two) and targeted associations (fourteen), but also most of the Japanese temples (thirteen of nineteen) on the island over a two-year period that began in October 1942. Further, the committee returned the property of the disbanded institutions to their former owners and disbursed their assets to civic and patriotic organizations such as the American Red Cross, YMCA, and Veteran's Trust Fund, and to sugar plantations and private landowners. Although most language schools and churches did not own real property, the estimated assets of fifteen language schools alone totaled $72,410.[32]

In January 1943, Takie and Umetaro Okumura sent letters to Hawaii's military and civilian leaders urging action "to prevent the reappearance of foreign language schools as separate institutions in [this] American community." They warned of a continuing desire among the Japanese to revive the language schools and advised that "every possible effort" be made at "a thorough Americanization" of Hawaii to make it "truly impregnable as an outpost of America in the Pacific. We do not want to see Hawaii become a victim of another treacherous attack."[33] Umetaro Okumura wrote to territorial Senator David Y. K. Akana, who had introduced Bill 104 restricting language-school attendance to those who had completed fourth grade or were over fifteen years of age: "Father and I want to express our thanks for your courage in leading the move to wipe out from this community the foreign language schools. Your proposed measure will place the language schools in such a condition that they can not possibly revive after the war."[34] Act 104 passed in 1943, but was later challenged by Chinese-language schools.

The Okumuras took their message to the planters, reminding them that they bore responsibility for the "Japanese problem" for having been the original importers of Asian labor. They asked for the removal of all Japanese-language schools and Buddhist temples from plantation property. In response, Kenneth B. Carney of the HSPA's public relations committee proposed that the planters finance a "broad educational campaign" to Americanize Hawaii's Japanese along "approved lines" of "culture appreciation" in the public schools.[35] Japanese morale committees, at the 1944 territorial conference held on Maui, declared their opposition to the reopening of Japanese-language schools because they were "a source of misunderstanding and suspicion" and recommended that foreign-language instruction be confined to the public schools and adult education classes be established to promote English and an appreciation of American history, institutions, and culture.[36]

In such an atmosphere, the *issei* feared venturing beyond their homes because their presence constituted an imposition on whites and an embarassment to the community. "We are afraid. We don't know what to do," testified one *issei*. "Even our own children don't let us go out. If we go out, we will be the focus of hate and revenge. So we stay in the house."[37] *Nisei*, too, were held hostage because of race. They were frequently reminded that they were "on the spot" and had to act in ways that would not irritate or offend whites.

During the 1942 elections on Kauai, Yutaka Hamamoto, Noboru Miyake, and Chris Watase sought reelection to the county board of supervisors, and a fourth Japanese, incumbent Wallace Otsuka, ran for his seat in the territorial House. During the primaries, the Republican campaign manager, S. W. Chang, proposed that Otsuka, a Republican, pull out of the race, following the example of two other Japanese incumbents in the House, Tom Ouye of Kauai and George Eguchi of Oahu. Despite the suggestion, all four Japanese incumbents on Kauai ran and won renomination.[38]

The result caused a national uproar. An editorial in the *New York Daily*

News, carried by the United Press and reprinted in most of its papers across the country, called attention to "old style imperialism": "We cannot afford the risk of having any applecarts upset in those islands by the present or former subjects of the Mikado, and if the Japanese in Hawaii don't like that attitude they had better go back where they or their ancestors came from." On October 10, the Kauai weekly, the *Garden Island*, ran an editorial, "Kauai Out on a Limb." Its author, Clarice B. Taylor, contrasted Kauai's election results with those on Hawaii where two of three Japanese incumbents were defeated, and urged the withdrawal of Hamamoto, Otsuka, and Watase as "their patriotic duty in this crisis for the good of the territory."[39] Before the next issue of the paper appeared, all four had withdrawn, whereupon the Kauai Republican county committee and Governor Ingram M. Stainback praised them for their "patriotism."

Nisei patriotism at times required some bending of the usual definitions of responsible citizenship. The Kauai Morale Committee admonished *nisei*: "We must quit insisting on our 'bill of rights' when we are on the spot."[40] Taylor's *Garden Island* editorial conceded that it was undemocratic to ask candidates to withdraw on the basis of their ancestry, and it was an invasion of the rights of Japanese citizens on the West Coast to remove and intern them, but right or wrong was not the question. The time for "pussyfooting" was past.[41]

Instead, the Kauai committee advocated that the Japanese be active, not passive, in proving their loyalty: "Join the Kiawe Korps [*sic*] willingly. Buy bonds as income makes possible. Give blood gladly. Give your time for other civilian defense duties. Be an all-out fighter for victory."[42] Civilian volunteers in the Kiawe Corps performed manual labor for the army during their days off from work. During some Sundays in January and February 1942, more than 1,200 turned out on Oahu to string barbed wire, cut brush, and construct trails, roads, and landing fields. On Kauai, most Corps workers were *issei*; over the course of two years, they labored an average three Sundays per month, for a total of over 58,000 man-days. Japanese women rolled bandages, volunteered in hospitals, and helped in clothing drives.[43]

Honolulu Mayor Lester Petrie typified the racist ideology that imposed "all-out Americanism" on Hawaii's Japanese. Petrie described the *issei* as "simple coolies whose mental equipment would not fit them for the role [of saboteurs] even if they were so inclined," and he placed the burden of proof on "the people of Japanese blood" as to "where their loyalty lies."[44]

Bicknell believed that a great majority of whites were racist and considered local Japanese to be their enemy. Whites, he wrote, were moved by "blind prejudices and racial discriminatory inclinations" that could not be swayed by reason. At the other pole were whites, termed "zealots" by Bicknell, who were blind to security concerns and campaigned against internment. The push and pull by both extremes was so intense, declared Bicknell, that "it often reached such proportions that officials charged with maintaining internal security felt the war was being waged against the Japanese elements of the population of Hawaii rather than the military forces of Imperial Japan."[45]

Constant Pressure

Unlike their West Coast kin, most of Hawaii's Japanese still lived in their own homes in the summer of 1942; they worked and received salaries, and retained some rights, yet they were just as surely contained. The military rulers circumscribed the Japanese by exerting constant pressure on them, foremost through the "ceaseless investigation of suspected subversive elements" and apprehension of those deemed dangerous to internal security.[46] The army also restricted place of residence and source of livelihood.

Evacuation and relocation, terms generally associated only with the West Coast Japanese, applied to a significant number of Japanese in the islands. Less than two weeks after Japan's attack, farmers in the West Loch area of Pearl Harbor were given two days to pack up and leave their farms, although they were permitted back during daylight hours to move their livestock and harvest their crops. Many were forced to double up with friends and relatives on Ewa plantation, and because several farmers had borrowed "considerable money" and invested "practically all of their life's savings" to establish their farms, they suffered "heavy losses."[47] A week later, the military police ordered 1,500 Japanese residents in the Iwilei district near Honolulu harbor and the railroad terminal to move out by morning or they would be shot. The displaced people worried over "disposal of furniture and other belongings, care of the aged and ill, and the handling of pets." Those with nowhere to go found temporary shelter at Kaiulani School. Some eventually settled in a low-cost housing project, but a year later, others were still homeless.[48]

The rights of liberty and property for Hawaii's Japanese were also decided on an individual basis. One pig farmer, Makaru Okuma of Waialua, apparently offended his neighbor, the army, by raising pigs, and the farmer was the subject of an investigation and interview to determine his loyalty. Lieutenant Kanemi Kanazawa of G-2 reported on Okuma: "Subject is an illeterate [sic] laborer of below average intelligence. He does not speak English and has a poor knowledge of Japanese. He is unable to read even the Japanese newspapers intelligently. Subject has no idea who is the Governor of Hawaii, but was conscious of the fact that a war between Japan and the United States exists. Subject's home is dirty and untidy and hasn't the slightest influence of culture." Although the lieutenant conceded that Okuma posed little danger to internal security, he recommended that the farmer and his pigs be removed and placed at the disposal of Waialua plantation. Ultimately, Okuma was saved by army headquarters because of the value of hogs for the territory's food supply and "to evacuate him would require that we take over his leasehold and reimburse him for damages."[49]

Squabbles over jurisdiction sometimes determined the fate of the Japanese. Generally, the navy sought the eviction of "pro-Axis sympathizers" and all Japanese from areas adjacent to naval bases; the army's concern over security was tempered by its responsibilities for maintaining production and overseeing relocation. In August 1942, the navy recommended the removal of all Japanese from the Kailua/Kaneohe Naval Air Station area on Oahu. The army complied by evicting a fraction of that population—"13 Jap aliens and 23 citizens of Jap ancestry"—and assigning armed patrols to secure the area. The navy acknowledged the army's action, but expanded its security zone to include all of Kaneohe Bay from the Pali to Kailua and repeated its original demand that "all pro-axis sympathizers and persons of Japanese ancestry must be evacuated from this area."[50]

The navy's insistence prompted a more studied reply by the army's G-2 head, Kendall J. Fielder: "It has long been realized that from a security standpoint it would be desirable to remove all persons of Japanese extraction from the Territory of Hawaii." However preferable that measure was, it was impractical because of the limited number of transport ships to take 160,000 Japanese to the mainland and because of its potential disruption on the economy. To bolster his contention, Fielder cited occupational statistics to verify the economy's dependence on Japanese workers. The

Japanese supplied 17,000 (24 percent) agricultural laborers, 11,000 (45 percent) in manufacturing and industry, 8,000 (56 percent) in domestic and personal service, 4,980 (45 percent) in trades, and 3,200 (30 percent) in transportation and commerce. Additionally, the Japanese operated over 90 percent of the truck farms on Oahu and made up 80 percent of all dairy employees and food handlers and over 60 percent of Oahu Railway's workers. "We have a delicate situation on our hands," concluded Fielder, "and must avoid mass discrimination against the Japanese residents, and any move which will alienate what loyalty that exists." In the light of that reality, Fielder proposed, the army's policy of custodial detention and periodic searches was adequate: "This also keeps the pressure on— tends to command respect of authorities." [51] Because the army's rationale prevailed, the 2,998 Japanese living in the Kaneohe Bay area were spared forcible removal.

The need for Japanese labor moderated the army's approach to security. In the words of the military governor, "An idle Jap with a family to feed is more dangerous than one under supervision and working with other races." [52] Lieutenant General Delos C. Emmons, Short's replacement on December 17, 1941, was particularly eager to see displaced *issei* farmers put to work producing food.[53] Indeed, Emmons's ideal of full employment was more than an expressed desire; it was required of the entire population.

In 1942, the Honolulu Police Department assisted the provost marshal's office by organizing a "vagrancy detail" whose purpose was to round up unemployed adults, called "deserters" and "loafers and drifters" by the military. During its first year, the squad arrested 328; in 1943, it arrested 1,311.[54] Provost courts usually sentenced the arrested to imprisonment and hard labor.[55] Newspapers published the court proceedings: "Having disregarded repeated warnings to return to her . . . job . . . Miss Sueko Helen Nakahira, 19, Waialua, was sentenced Wednesday to 30 days in jail, on an absenteeism charge. She told Lt. Col. Moe D. Baroff, provost judge, that she still is unwilling to work at the laundry." [56] The vagaries of martial law were undemocratic in that Japanese unemployment and protests over wages or conditions raised questions not only of a labor dispute but also of patriotism and subversion.

Japanese workers faced other barriers. Military and civilian intelligence saw Japanese fishermen and their sampans as security threats long before Pearl Harbor. The Justice Department in February 1941 impounded vessels of the tuna fleet for alleged violations of the law that forbade alien registration of ships or *nisei* registrations for the benefit of *issei*.[57] Before war broke out, the FBI charged forty Japanese fishermen with venturing beyond the defensive zones at the entrance to Pearl Harbor and Kaneone Bay.[58] The strafing by American patrol planes of Japanese sampan fishermen out at sea immediately after Japan's attack occurred against that prewar backdrop of suspicion and harassment. In two instances, sampans were actually escorted back to harbor waving white flags, in accordance with instructions given them, when they were set afire by navy planes. When the shooting stopped, at least six fishermen had been killed and an undetermined number treated for injuries. Seven of the wounded taken to Queen's Hospital in Honolulu were treated as prisoners of war and held under guard.[59]

The military excluded all *issei* and some *nisei* from certain jobs, such as war project and dock work, fishing, transportation, photography, and teaching; private employers discriminated against the Japanese in hiring practices.[60] Conditions sometimes compelled both generations to take undesirable jobs. As a result, the Japanese did not participate as fully as the rest of Hawaii's people in the wartime economic boom.[61]

Racism in the workplace further stifled dissent. "With the advent of the war," reported a union observer, "the preponderantly Japanese membership of local 135 was confused and dispirited, and fearful of activity. Being of Japanese extraction, whether citizens or not . . . they were not only made to feel suspect, but were in fact suspected, and in many cases, openly so."[62] In April 1942, the army arrested and confined Ichiro Izuka, president of a Kauai longshoremen's local. His interrogators included plantation mangers, who quizzed him during the three months he was held without charge about his union activities. Izuka had led a July 1940 strike of mainly Japanese longshoremen at Port Allen, Kauai, in support of a strike by largely Filipino longshoremen at nearby Ahukini Landing that was directed at the Lihue plantation and lasted nearly a year.[63]

The army apparently also tried to intimidate plantation workers near Hilo by employing Antone B. Pacheco, described in a union memorandum as "a professional informer" for G-2. Pacheco, the document claimed, showed his military intelligence credentials to employees of the Hilo Sugar Company, attempted to dissuade them from joining unions, and warned Japanese workers that union activity was "subversive of the war effort." The local military intelligence officer and brother of a plantation manager on the island of Hawaii, Major Lester W. Bryan, publicly commended Pacheco for his services: "I have only the highest praise for the work done by Mr. Pacheco." [64]

While some areas of employment were off-limits to the Japanese, others, such as agriculture, welcomed them. Farms and plantations, in fact, represented the greatest concentration of Japanese laborers, constituting 10,397, or nearly 31 percent of the 1942 plantation workforce.[65] That pattern of job clustering was discriminatory—84 percent of plantation workers were Filipino and Japanese—in that ordinarily they could not leave the plantations, and their wages were substantially lower than non-plantation rates. In 1942, field laborers averaged 34.3 cents per hour in cash or 42.5 cents an hour including bonuses and perquisites on one plantation, while an equivalent worker made 65 cents an hour off the plantation.[66]

Planters engaged in labor contracting during the war because of the widespread labor shortage and the military's need for manpower. Under the "loaned labor" agreement, planters supplied workers to the army. Workers received standard plantation salaries and perquisites; the planters recovered all their labor costs plus 10 percent for administering the program and an additional 8 percent of the total.[67] The agreement enabled the planters to control their labor force (which could have been impounded under martial law) and to turn a profit; it gave the military access to a ready labor supply at a cheaper rate than standard wages paid to defense workers. The magnitude of the loaned-labor relationship can best be seen in the reported figure of 514,130 man-days of plantation labor supplied to the army from 1941 to 1944.[68]

Both the police and the territorial Employment Bureau, places to which unemployed workers reported, provided lists of unemployed persons to the HSPA for plantation recruitment.[69] The basis for the cooperation between the military and planters was laid before the war when Green and his assistants, Morrison and Hanley, toured Ewa plantation and were impressed with its "astute labor policies." Later, as an executive in the Office of Military Governor, Green invited J. Douglas Bond, Ewa plantation manager, to direct the army's Section of Labor Control and appointed plantation managers to help plan and administer the program of labor control. The group coordinated and regulated labor to maximize production for the war effort until March 10, 1943, when the army reluctantly relinquished control over nonmilitary labor to the War Manpower Commission. Still, the army was critical of the commission and accused the civilians of failing to "appreciate or understand the scope and complexity of the operations involved." As a result, effective August 21, 1944, the army, navy, and commission established the Manpower Priorities Committee to work together on an integrated labor-control program.[70]

The military's control of labor depended heavily on the disposition of Japanese union members. According to army estimates, the Japanese constituted 80 percent of carpenters and bartenders, 75 percent of dairy workers, 70 percent of street, railway, brewery, and agricultural workers, 30 percent of drydock laborers, and 17 percent of longshoremen—all union members.[71] The August 21, 1943, walkout of Theo. H. Davies workers, of whom seventy of the ninety-four were Japanese, led the military to believe that a new "radical" element within the union leadership was responsible for manipulating Japanese workers "along racial lines" to further its goal of ending military control of labor. That attack on military control of labor, radioed Morrison, was an assault on martial law.[72]

The repressive period of military rule gave rise to the postwar unionization movement that mobilized and politicized workers to resist the hegemony of the planters or the Big Five.[73] During the war, worker protest led to the army's consideration of a way to end martial law, as revealed in a memorandum dated January 27, 1944, from Hawaiian commander Lieutenant General Robert C. Richardson, Jr., to Assistant Secretary of War John J. McCloy: "For your very confidential information, I am studying the local situation with a view to proposing the elimination of martial law provided that my office can be given, by executive decree, the necessary power to conduct the war effort and insure the security of the Territory." He added: "Some sort of control of labor would appear to be necessary in the prosecution of the Army and Navy contracts, particularly the operations at Pearl Harbor."[74]

The context of Richardson's "study of the local situation" was a slowdown by transportation workers in Honolulu on July 1, 1943, the Theo. H. Davies strike, and unrest in the local dairy industry, which prompted editorials in the *Honolulu Advertiser* objecting to the participation of Japanese in trade unions. J. S. Daves, secretary of the Building and Construction Trades Council, wrote to Richardson and charged that "radical" union leaders Arthur A. Rutledge of the Central Labor Council and John Reinecke of the territorial Department of Education "have instigated a plot of planting unrest in the minds of the Japanese workers in the Territory and particularly the Island of Oahu" by calling attention to "the so-called pitiful plight of the Japanese workers . . . to the point where they assume an arrogant attitude and employers are finding it increasingly difficult to deal with their employee problems." Rutledge and Reinecke's "control" of Japanese workers was "a threat to the internal security of the Islands."[75]

Word of labor unrest in the islands reached Congress largely through representatives of the Labor Department in Hawaii, who submitted a report that was harshly critical of army rule, stimulating interest in a federal investigation into charges of "rapidly disintegrating" labor relations in the territory. The report painted a grim picture of unrestrained abuse by the army and the Big Five, such as use of Selective Service and prisons to punish and coerce people, so that workers were "virtual 'slaves' of private individuals." The net result, claimed the report, was that "bad feelings" existed between civilians and the military, resulting in a "serious malutilization of manpower."[76]

The report's criticism of army rule was seconded by several AFL locals in their "Memorandum on Military Control of Hawaiian Labor," dated March 27, 1944, which was notable not only for its courage in challenging an autocratic and oppressive system but also for its antiracist stand in defending Japanese workers. According to the document, the Japanese "were in many instances too frightened to display [union] activity of any sort." In calling for an end to "this illegal military control over patriotic citizens," the memorandum alleged that the army's antilabor bias mirrored and, in fact, arose from historical attitudes and practices of Hawaii's planters, a small group of Anglo-Saxons. This group exercised almost exclusive economic control over workers, who were overwhelmingly non-European, about one-third of whom were Japanese. Unionization was thus depicted as a racial, rather than a class, struggle—as a movement directed against white supremacy.[77]

A *Christian Science Monitor* correspondent confirmed labor's memorandum on the merging of military and business interests in the matter of white supremacy. Military officials, he wrote, were "inclined to discourage the growing momentum of trade unions among the Japanese here." Businessmen supported the army's efforts to break the unionizing of Japanese workers because they saw it "as posing a serious long-term problem which might jeopardize the strong controls which local white residents have long exercised."[78]

Search and Intern

The army's Counter Intelligence Corps (CIC) was created on January 1, 1942, in Hawaii to detect and prevent espionage and sabotage, and to uncover "treason, sedition, subversive activity and disaffection." CIC replaced G-2's contact office in Honolulu, which, like the FBI's staff in the territory, had expanded during the months preceding Pearl Harbor, and absorbed the army's Corps of Intelligence Police. In February 1942, CIC maintained a staff of thirty-three agents; a year later, it had eighty-one agents; two years later, it reached its peak with ninety-seven agents. A month after its founding, CIC formalized a delimitation agreement with ONI and FBI, making it the sole agency responsible for the islands' internal security.[79] Even after the end of martial law, CIC carried out the program of investigation and apprehension considered by the military to be a cornerstone of its strategy of constantly pressuring the Japanese.

CIC agents spread out from their headquarters in Honolulu to branch offices on the islands of Kauai, Maui, Hawaii, and Molokai. The Japanese subsection was the most active of all CIC units, although other subsections added to the mountain of information on Hawaii's Japanese. By September 1945, CIC had investigated about 6,000 army volunteers and draftees of Japanese descent. Those probes, testing for loyalty, employed an elaborate point system to determine fitness for service to America. A Japanese enlistee received one point for each of the following: if he used an Anglicized first name, was a registered voter, had married an American citizen, had attended an American high school or college, or was an agricultural worker. An enlistee lost one point if he used his Japanese given name, married a citizen of Japan, had ever attended a Japanese-language school, or was a fisherman.[80] CIC records filling two file cabinets and 25 index-card drawers at the start of the war later filled a record room with seventy-five file cabinets containing at least 60,000 files and more than 148 index-card drawers holding 20,000 names.[81]

CIC's companion agency in the program of investigation and apprehension was the Alien Processing Center, established on December 15, 1941. Its first head, Major Edward E. Walker, had been assigned to the post just two days earlier and was presented with several hundred people already in custody. His task was to establish a procedure for hearing cases and "processing" suspects, aliens and citizens, through civilian hearing boards, each consisting of three civilians, one of whom was an attorney, and an army officer. The boards advised the military governor on each detainee, recommending internment (generally for the war's duration), release on parole (release into the custody of a loyal sponsor), or release. Walker set up shop at the immigration station next to the barracks that housed internees destined for Sand Island.[82] He organized prehearing boards on the outer islands, which screened cases that were finally decided in Honolulu.

At the hearing, an attorney could represent the accused, at the latter's expense, and detainees could call witnesses. The Processing Center, according to Walker, was "a beehive of activity"; "the waiting room was filled up with witnesses of all sorts ready to testify for various internees."[83] The hearing board sent its recommendations to an intelligence reviewing board composed of the heads of CIC, ONI, and FBI; and the military governor's legal section studied and ruled on the case. During their first six months, from January 1 to July 1, 1942, hearing boards reviewed 971 cases, recommending 867 for internment, 77 for release on parole, and 27 for release.[84]

Internee case files revealed more of the hearing boards' prejudices than any danger posed by the accused. Frequently the government's case consisted of allegations made by informers or unsubstantiated impressions and statements, for example: neighbor reported subject to be "the most rabid haole hater the informant has ever run across"; "when questioned relative to his desire as to the outcome of the war . . . he stated he preferred not to answer and seemed reticent about talking about the war"; and in the instance of a dual citizen who did not know the name of the mayor of Honolulu or the meaning of the Constitution, "he has made no particular effort to inform himself of the principles of American citizenship and loyalty, or the English language, and while he claims he wants America to win it is believed that his genuine loyalty to the United States is so highly improbable as to be negligible."[85]

Detainees were presumed guilty unless proven otherwise. As mandated by Major Louis F. Springer, former commandant at Sand Island and Walker's successor, "an alien does not owe loyalty in a strict sense to the United States, but it is felt that an alien owes a temporary loyalty, or must prove by his actions or expressions that he is not inimical to the interest of this country."[86] Noted a manual for inspectors: "Determination of loyalty is a difficult procedure; it cannot be made by use of mathematical formulae." For suspect Japanese, however, the determination was simplified, "as a practical matter," by creating a class of disloyals that included "individuals whose background is strongly Japanese, but who have demonstrated no positive pro-Japanese sentiments." Because that upbringing caused a person to react "in a Japanese manner," according to the manual, investigators needed only to establish the "strongly Japanese" character of an individual to determine his or her fitness for internment.[87]

Selective treatment of the Japanese was shown in another way. Although called an "alien" Processing Center, the center processed alien Germans and Italians but both alien and citizen Japanese. The indiscriminate lumping of the Japanese necessitated a wording change on the arrest warrant from "alien enemies" to "persons deemed inimical to the security of the Nation."[88]

Under these circumstances, the Japanese accused had very little hope for acquittal. For example, in an appeal to Emmons dated April 10, 1942, a *nisei* son argued on behalf of his interned *issei* father, who was a prominent businessman, married to a *nisei*, had nine children, did not own property in Japan, and never attended or contributed to Japanese consulate functions or receptions for visiting Japanese naval officers. The father had resigned from the Japanese Chamber of Commerce to join the predominantly white Honolulu Chamber of Commerce and had contributed rare specimens to the Bishop Museum. He and his company purchased U.S. savings and war bonds, his brother was a member of the Territorial Guard and Varsity Victory Volunteers, his sons served in the Kiawe Corps, and he purchased a funeral plot for himself and his family in a Honolulu cemetery. Prominent whites were among those willing to testify on his behalf, and the *nisei* letter writer ended with the fervent hope for "the utter defeat of Japan and the rest of the Axis Nations." Executive Green, for the military governor, signed the single-sentence response: "Your recent request for reconsideration . . . has had our most careful attention, but I regret to inform you that we are unable to take any action that will effect his release from custody at this time."[89]

Honouliuli

After March 1, 1943, a concentration camp built amid cane fields at Honouliuli gulch, near Ewa on Oahu, replaced the camp at Sand Island. Honouliuli anchored a chain of camps extending from Kalaheo on Kauai, to

Molokai and Lanai, to Haiku on Maui, and to Waiakea on Hawaii. "I have made two visits to the camp in its new location [at Honouliuli]," reported the Swedish vice-consul, Gustaf W. Olson. "I found its population of about 250 housed in frame cottages each holding eight to ten occupants and equipped with double-deck beds. The cottages have good air circulation and ample daylight." He gave a glowing account of the Japanese section of the camp, noting its medical dispensary and hospital, dental clinic, canteen, and modern kitchen.

On his second visit, in May 1943, Olson observed that electricity had been installed and that "cottage occupants had busied themselves with planting of trees and shrubs, arranging flower beds with rock borders and otherwise embellishing their surroundings with the materials at hand." The 84 *issei* and 154 *nisei* internees were "generally well content with conditions in the camp and no complaints were registered." They "appreciatively acknowledged" the "humane treatment" of camp guards and "especially complimented" the camp commander. Olson's periodic reports of Honouliuli and the other camps were uniformly laudatory.[90] In his September 1943 commentary, Olson wrote of Maui's Haiku Camp: "It is a most delightful place, and being on vacation at the time of my visit I would rather have stayed there than return to the hotel in Wailuku."[91]

Japanese internees did not share Olson's preference for life behind barbed wire. Dan Nishikawa recalled his anger over being interned. He credited his interest in crafts with stopping him from going mad. He recalled how white internees received fresh fruit and vegetables and even pumpkin pie for Thanksgiving; the Japanese, during the first three months at Honouliuli, were given canned items, mainly pork and beans and chili con carne. Only after Nishikawa protested did they get eggs and fresh fruit and vegetables. American fliers, he testified, practiced bombing raids on the concentration camp, buzzing the internees' "shacks." When he complained, Nishikawa was told that in the event of another attack by Japan, American planes would bomb the camp first.[92]

Another Honouliuli internee, Umeno Harada, pleaded for clemency after having been confined for twenty-two months. One of the few women in the camp, Harada described her state as "a mother in deepest distress whose heart is bleeding and can't take the suffering much longer. I am in my nerves, I lost more than 30 pounds. I have been patiently waiting to be united to my children again who are waiting every hour for the mother to come home."[93] Despite the fact that an MID investigation of the

Niihau incident had revealed that Harada played no part in the escape of the downed Japanese pilot, the review board denied her application for release. Harada was finally released in June 1944.

Writing to his superior in Honolulu, the army commander of Hawaii district described the Waiakea camp: "The Waiakea Prison Camp is the most convenient and practicable institution for confinement at hard labor on Hawaii. The county jail is a rest house [in comparison]." Waiakea internees, he reported, were employed on defense work at Hilo airport "where hard labor means just that."[94] According to the camp's Prison Report, a sentence of one month at hard labor was given for using profane and obscene language, three months at hard labor for being a "disorderly person," six months for being a "common nuisance," and one year for "possession of excessive amount of currency" and unlawful possession of a Japanese flag.[95] Waiakea's internees shared the camp with such civil offenders as rapists and burglars.

Conflicts between the interned Japanese arose from the pro-Japanese or pro-American labels forced on the Japanese by Hawaii's rulers. The nuances of being favorably disposed to either Japan or America could not be tolerated by the stark categories of *inu* (i.e., "dog," pro-American) or "Jap" (pro-Japanese). Thus, antifascists were deemed anti-Japanese because Japan was an Axis nation; similarly, those who wished to "repatriate" to Japan were considered anti-American. At Honouliuli, about two months before Japan's surrender, an *issei* accused of being anti-Japanese was physically assaulted by a group of five *kibei*. Apparently the *issei* man, an outspoken critic of Japan's militarists and a member of the communist Nippon Kai Kaku, had refused to retract his assertion that Japan was losing the war. According to one account, "the group . . . began to make threatening gestures at [the *issei* man], and . . . fearing that he was to be beaten ran out of the barracks yelling for the guards." The confrontation ended quickly, and the *kibei* men were placed in solitary confinement and put on a bread-and-water diet.[96]

Sam Nishimura, comparing Sand Island with Honouliuli, explained that the latter camp was better because it was "family type internment," with nine men sharing a barracks. Several of Nishimura's roommates worked in the kitchen. In the evening they returned with pastries and coffee for snacks before the lights went out at 9:00 o'clock. Still, Honouliuli was regimented: internees lined up for morning and evening rollcalls, and made beds and cleaned their rooms for unannounced inspections. Also, confinement at Honouliuli was stressful, recalled Nishimura; some broke down and "lost their minds." He described an internee who ceaselessly rolled what began as a four-inch-square rock until it formed "a perfect baseball." On being asked what he planned to do with it, he answered, "I'm going to give this to my sweetheart." The man, said Nishimura, was "just going at it everyday. Nothing else. Nobody talked to him." [97]

"Roei No Uta" (Bivouac Song)

Before World War I, the territory's National Guard had launched a vigorous recruitment campaign for all volunteers except the Japanese, who "were not much wanted." [98] Despite that sentiment, Japanese volunteered and formed Company D of the guard's 1st Regiment during World War I. They did not see combat, and during the interwar period, *nisei* enlistment was again discouraged. In October 1940, forty Japanese were in the National Guard when it was federalized and divided into two regiments— the 298th and 299th Infantry—that underwent training at Schofield Barracks. Of the Japanese in those regiments, Hawaiian commander Herron observed: "In the training camp they were remarkably diligent and obedient to orders. When 4 o'clock came, after a long hard day, and others turned to rest or recreation, the Japanese kept right on at drill or study. There were no malingerers among them and they were quick to learn." [99] Selective Service inductions increased during the months leading up to Pearl Harbor, and by December 1941, 1,500 *nisei* recruits were serving in integrated units of the 298th and 299th.

"Roll call—rifle and ammo issued—set to dig trenches, guard details," recalled a *nisei* soldier about the day of Japan's attack; for the next three days, the soldiers dug trenches. But on December 10, the soldier continued, "our rifles, ammo, and bayonets were taken from all us AJAS [Americans of Japanese ancestry] with orders to stay in quarters—not even to go for a 'shi-shi' [meaning "to urinate"] break! MGS [military guards] ringed our area. [The military guards apparently hemmed in the *nisei* encampment with machine guns.] Then two days later, rifles, etc. were returned, no questions asked, no answers given. Detailed out to guard duty—sent to guard the Schofield Fire Station—on the alert for sabotage!" [100] Over the next six months, the men of the 298th strung barbed wire, patroled the beaches, and constructed and manned machine-gun emplacements.

Meanwhile, the army deliberated the fate of the *nisei* soldiers. An in-

credulous colonel inspecting the regiment's outpost asked the commander of the 298th, "You sleep here where these Japs can slit your throat?"[101]
Skepticism of *nisei* loyalty prompted Emmons to expel the 317 Japanese
volunteers serving in the Territorial Guard in January 1942, while granting official recognition to the white (and white-Hawaiian) Businessmen's
Military Training Corps "to watch the local Japanese."[102] Ted Tsukiyama
described his reaction to being put on a truck and taken to the University
of Hawaii where he and other *nisei* were discharged from the Territorial
Guard: "That morning, when they threw us out was just the lowest point
in my life. . . . Just, you know, frustration, anguish, disappointment, the
feeling of rejection. And the impact of the reality of what was happening
to us . . . that you are being distrusted by your own country and all the
fine things you learned about democracy."[103] About a week after they had
been informed that their "services were no longer needed," those ma-
ligned *nisei* wrote to Emmons, expressing their disappointment but still
offering their devotion: "Hawaii is our home; the United States, our country," they declared. "We wish to do our part as loyal Americans in every
way possible and we hereby offer ourselves for whatever service you may
see fit to use us."[104] The military governor accepted that offer and put the
nisei to work in a labor battalion.

The military attached them as civilian laborers to the 34th Combat Engineers Regiment at Schofield Barracks and designated them the Corps of
Engineers Auxiliary, but the *nisei* called themselves the "Varsity Victory
Volunteers" (vvv). In the words of a prominent vvv member, those young
men, most of whom were students at the University of Hawaii, "set out
to fight a twofold fight for tolerance and justice."[105] The men, about 170
in all, were organized into twelve labor gangs under the direction of non-
Japanese army staff. They typically worked six days a week from 7:30 A.M.
to 4:30 P.M., were paid $90 per month, and during the eleven months of
vvv's existence constructed six warehouses, strung several miles of barbed
wire, quarried several tons of rocks, completed one road and began work
on two others, and built and repaired furniture. They made three visits to
the blood bank and bought war bonds totaling $27,850.[106] The vvv asked
to be disbanded in January 1943 after it became possible to volunteer for
combat duty in their country's military.

Nisei soldiers serving in the 298th and 299th Infantry continued to be objects of suspicion and scrutiny. On February 1, 1942, the War Department
proposed to discharge or transfer all Japanese in the military. Emmons

replied that a troop shortage necessitated keeping the 298th and 299th intact until the arrival of mainland reinforcements. The military governor suggested that eventually the dismissed *nisei* soldiers could be reorganized into a labor corps, like the recently formed vvv, to relieve plantation workers from stringing barbed wire and clearing bushes. Use of plantation laborers was proving costly, reported Emmons, because it interrupted sugar production.[107]

Throughout March and April 1942, army officers in Hawaii worried that *nisei* soldiers might become "a potential force in our midst completely armed and equipped for organized resistance" and attempted to weed out "undesirables" from the 298th and have them assigned to labor battalions. "Although in some cases the suspicion is slight and has not yet been borne out by further developments," an investigator admitted, "it is felt that no exceptions should be made."[108] At the end of March, on orders from the War Department, new enlistments of Japanese recruits were discontinued except in special cases; in mid-May, Emmons recommended that a segregated unit be created composed of *nisei* from the 298th and 299th and that it be removed from Hawaii.[109] General George C. Marshall, army chief of staff, responded to the department commander's suggestion on May 28, 1942, and authorized formation of the proposed battalion.

Nisei soldiers throughout the territory were brought, without notice or fanfare, to Schofield Barracks where they were housed in tents at some distance from the regular troops. Their rifles were taken away, and their camp was surrounded by barbed wire. On June 5, they were designated the Hawaiian Provisional Battalion and were taken by train and transport to Honolulu's Pier 31. In the early afternoon, they were placed in the hold of the *Maui*. Later that evening, in the company of naval escort vessels and other transport ships loaded with the wives and children of army and navy personnel—refugees fleeing Hawaii—the *Maui* set sail, carrying 1,432 men of the Provisional Battalion. One man, peering portside, described the departure: "The moon was out and smiling this night as we glided past Aloha Tower and through the harbor *Destination Unknown*." Perhaps men to the starboard caught sight of the dark shapes on Sand Island. For too many, this would be their last glimpses of their island home. "Before we had any chance to bid goodbye to our loved ones," recalled Spark M. Matsunaga, "we found ourselves on board a troopship sailing for God-knew-where. Speculation was rife that we were headed for a concentration camp."[110] Like their fathers, who had preceded them on the *Ulysses Grant* three months earlier, these *nisei* sons sailed eastward for San Francisco Bay.

The journey would take the Provisional Battalion—granted a degree of permanence with its redesignation as the 100th Infantry Battalion on arrival in Oakland—to the snows of Camp McCoy in Wisconsin, to Camp Shelby in Mississippi, Camp Claiborne in Louisiana, and to the glaring sun of Oran, Algeria. During their fierce battle to take the hilltop fortress of Cassino, the men of the 100th composed and sang "*Roei no uta*," "Bivouac Song," destined to become the anthem of Company B. The lyrics were composed by Yukio Takaki; the melody was a Japanese tune popular in Hawaii at the time. The song recalled the various places and battles of the war, each stanza ending with the descriptive phrases:

> Steaming with blood and salt, the 100th Bn
> Bursting with pride, the 100th Bn
> We never give up, the 100th Bn
> Spirits soaring, the 100th Bn
> Blossomed fully, the 100th Bn
> Chins up, the 100th Bn
> and Dripping with blood and sweat, the 100th Bn.[111]

"*Roei no uta*" was more than an anthem; it was an apt symbol of the men who adopted it. Like them, the song was a harmonious coming together, in melody and words, of past and present, of the lands of their ancestry and of their birth.

Chapter 11

In Morning Sunlight

Koko Head nears,
And now Diamond Head!
How bright the sea is
Shining in morning sunlight!
—Sojin Takei

Penned Cargo

Two ships left Honolulu harbor during the early months of the war: the *Ulysses Grant*, departing on February 20, 1942, with 172 Japanese *issei* and *nisei* "troublemakers"; and the *Maui*, setting sail on June 5, 1942, with 1,432 *nisei* men of the Provisional Battalion. Although both ships headed for America, the *Ulysses Grant* discharged its hold at Angel Island on the north side of San Francisco Bay. (During World War II, Angel Island served as a prisoner-of-war camp; in an earlier period, the island had confined Asian migrants seeking Gold Mountain.)[1] The *Maui* unloaded its store, as if embarrassed by the contents, under the cover of darkness on the east side of the bay, at Oakland. From here, the paths of the two groups diverged. The elders were placed into concentration camps; the youth were herded to training fields in preparation for their "blood sacrifice." Despite that branching, both fathers and sons—in the *Ulysses Grant* and *Maui*—were penned cargo and the victims of Hawaii's anti-Japanese movement.

Before military trucks and armed jeep escorts sped the internees through the streets of Honolulu to the waiting *Ulysses Grant*, the Japanese were subjected to a final, humiliating body search. Kaetsu Furuya recounted how they were stripped and branded before boarding the ship: "We had to be stark naked . . . on the bed and then we had our nose, mouth, hands, feet . . . anus, genitals, everything was examined carefully and then we had numbers written on our bodies. In red ink. Mine was '13.'"[2] Once on board the *Ulysses Grant,* the human cargo was confined below deck for the duration of the ten-day crossing to the mainland. According to one of the men, their keepers instructed them on the use of life vests, but locked the door to the hold in which the Japanese were kept. "What is the use of life jackets if our door is locked?" he asked. "Unless someone came to unlock the door first, our lives had to go with the life of the boat."[3]

On board, the food was apparently "delicious," plentiful, and served three times a day. But there was little water for washing, none for bathing, and the door was unlocked only every three hours to permit use of the bathroom. As a result, there were long lines whenever toilet time came, and for those who could not wait, a garbage can in the corridor served the purpose. Suikei Furuya and thirteen other men were separated from the rest of the group and placed "in a small room in the bottom of the boat" that was kept in semidarkness. There was nothing for the men to do. "I like to travel by . . . boat," he recalled, "but I'd never had such an unpleasant trip by a boat in my life." Perhaps the greatest torment was administered not to the body but to the mind by the suggestion of their guards that enemy submarines lurked in the vicinity and that the *Ulysses Grant* could be torpedoed at any moment.[4]

On arriving at Angel Island, there was the usual body inspection: "We were kept naked. Then we dropped down on all fours and our anuses were checked," recalled Furuya. "My first impression of the mainland was really bad."[5] The island was a transit stop en route to Camp McCoy, where they arrived on March 9, 1942. Although Furuya described the camp commander, Lieutenant Colonel Horace I. Rogers, as "a warm hearted person" who "tried to give us as much freedom as he could within the limit of the military law," camp conditions were stressful, especially with regard to food. "We weren't sure why we were always hungry," wrote Furuya. Internees received a potato and two slices of bread for lunch, and dumpling soup and two slices of bread for dinner. "The rumor began to spread that our mess officer was stealing our share of food." The men complained to Rogers, and the situation improved. On May 25, the men were moved to Camp Forrest, Tennessee; a month later, those selected for repatriation were taken to New York for transportation aboard the *Gripsholm* for Japan.

The crossing of the *Maui* was also laden with meaning and symbolism. *Nisei* sons, uncommon patriots and warriors, were dispensable constitutents in this experiment in democracy; their fellow travelers, wives and children of Hawaii's whites, constituted precious cargo destined for a safe haven. The standard-bearers of the exiled race feared that they would suffer the same fate as their fathers. "Since we were already 'living on borrowed time' anyway," remembered a *nisei*, " 'go for broke' was the attitude. A dice game continued non-stop (for 5 days) in the hold of the *Maui* en route. I saw a $3,000 bet laid once, but did not stay to watch how it turned out. I think I heard that the guy made it!"[6] "Go for Broke" was not a declaration of patriotic zeal; instead, the motto of the 442nd Regimental Combat Team originated from a profound recognition of coercion, with little choice and even less to lose.

After five days, the convoy reached San Francisco Bay, sailed past Angel Island and on to the port of Oakland. White evacuees walked down the gangplank and headed for shelter and home; the *nisei* soldiers remained below deck until nightfall. Following a quick dockside inspection, guards hustled the men into three troop trains that had closed blinds and traveled on tracks laid by Chinese and Japanese. "Sailed right under the Golden Gate Bridge—first glimpse of 'America the Beautiful!' " exclaimed a *nisei* diarist. "Lay at anchor in Oakland until dusk. Hurry up and wait! Herded, hurried into waiting Pullman sleepers to 'Destination Unknown' again!"[7] The trains pushed into America's heartland, through the deserts of the southern rail, the mountains and plains of the central route, and the forests of the northern line. During the five-day journey, "card and dice games continued, and more money changed pockets—large wads of it."[8]

On the last day, as the train slowed and stopped, across the tracks lay a barbed-wire enclosure with guard towers at intervals along the fence. "For half an hour we sat silently in our seats, thinking only of the worst; many were pensive with grim and hollow faces," remembered a *nisei*. "Then, suddenly, as if to alleviate our pained thoughts, the train backed slowly out of the yard, switched to another track, and continued on."[9] All three trains eventually made their way to Camp McCoy: "Cases of beer were stacked plunk on the concrete lanai of the PX and the men just squatted down and sucked em up! Hamburgers and hot dogs, by the cases, went too! That was our initiation to Camp McCoy."[10] Situated in a corner of the military base was the concentration camp that the men had believed was intended for them; instead, it held their elders.

Speaking of his seven months at Camp McCoy, Spark Matsunaga said,

"We pictured ourselves as a battalion of forced laborers." The *nisei* labor battalion was subjected to further indignities, marching and training with wooden guns before being entrusted with arms for combat exercises.[11] The army believed that the Japanese "race" exuded a distinctive odor and that trained dogs could detect and thereby locate Japanese snipers in the dense jungles of the Pacific theater. In October, twenty-six men from Company B were assigned to a secret project on Cat Island in Mississippi where they wore heavy padded clothing and face guards and hid and waited, presumably emitting their peculiar "Jap" odor, for the "Americans" and their attack dogs in the semitropical vegetation of Cat Island.[12]

During their mainland sojourn, the men also encountered individual acts of kindness. Earl M. Finch, a Mississippi rancher, organized parties and dances, outings, and watermelon feasts for the *nisei* troops at nearby Camp Shelby. "He extended a helping hand to a lonely group of homesick soldiers, unwanted and suspected on the Mainland, when few others would," read a testimony.[13] Still, the experience for some exacted such a heavy toll that they resolved never to return to the mainland, if they survived to return.

Discarding

The mainland was a dumping ground for other discards from Hawaii. During deliberations by the Western Defense Command and the military and political establishment in Washington about the fate of West Coast Japanese, key participants, especially President Roosevelt and Navy Secretary Knox, questioned the adequacy of Hawaii's defense against internal subversion. Roosevelt was a long-standing critic of the Hawaiian Department's method of controlling the Japanese, and Knox favored the mass internment of *issei* on an island other than Oahu. As in the exchange between Hawaii and Washington on the Joint Defense Plan, the Hawaiian commander was asked to respond to Knox's proposal.

Emmons replied on January 11, 1942, in a radiogram: "Informed opinion is that there are as many dangerous elements among the citizens as among the aliens and that few could be trusted in event of invasion." Only a "wholesale evacuation of all Japanese and many others" would ensure the territory's security. At the same time, the removal of sizable numbers of

Japanese was "dangerous and highly impractical" because of the need for *nisei* loyalty and Japanese labor. Further, concentrating the *issei* in one area posed logistical problems of guarding, transporting, housing, and feeding them, taxing an already overburdened army. "However," concluded the military governor, "if evacuation is decided upon by War Department [I] strongly recommend that evacuation be to the mainland," beginning with the removal of currently interned Japanese and "any suspected Japanese who are now in confinement or who may be apprehended in the future."[14] Six days later, Washington authorized Emmons "to evacuate enemy aliens he deemed dangerous" to mainland camps.

Despite Washington's persistent pressure for mass internment and Hawaii's preference for selective detention, neither side advocated an antiracist position, and both sought to control the Japanese.[15] To Emmons, labor and security were inseparable; to the president, labor was dwarfed by national security. "I think that General Emmons should be told," Roosevelt instructed Secretary of War Henry L. Stimson, "that the only consideration is that of the safety of the Islands and that the labor situation is not only a secondary matter but should not be given any consideration whatsoever."[16]

Emmons had before him the tarnished careers of his predecessor, Short, and the navy commander Admiral Husband E. Kimmel, both victims of Japan's success at Pearl Harbor. He knew that his primary responsibility as department commander was "the safety of the Islands," but he also realized that labor was scarce, shipping and supplies short, and troop strength stretched to its limit. In a radiogram to the War Department on February 4, 1942, the military governor compromised: "It is desirable for health, supply and security reasons to evacuate as many Japanese as practicable and as soon as practicable." But that would mean a substantial loss of Japanese labor and a disruption of the local economy. "We can overcome all problems with respect to the Japanese," promised Emmons, "provided that our requisitions for troops, supplies and equipment on all islands be filled as soon as possible."

In underscoring his request for reinforcements, Emmons noted that he had dismissed *nisei* from the Territorial Guard, but was "compelled because of shortage of other troops to use the Japanese personnel in [the] National Guard." The situation was "critical," he warned, because the National Guard was the first line of defense for the outlying islands and was composed largely of *nisei* soldiers, who should be removed from the islands. "We can handle this evacuation problem," repeated the Hawaiian commander, referring to the removal of "as many Japanese as practicable" to mainland concentration camps, "provided our requisitions for troops, supplies and equipment on all islands be filled, and provided . . . suitable transportation is made available."[17]

Throughout February and March, Washington continued to press for the mass removal of Hawaii's Japanese as part of the plan for the mass removal and confinement of West Coast Japanese.[18] On March 8, 1942, the Joint Chiefs of Staff recommended that the Hawaiian Department send Japanese, both alien and citizen, to the mainland for internment. The plan was approved by Roosevelt with the modification that, for the moment, the removal should involve only those Japanese deemed dangerous to security.[19] Furthermore, the directive to Emmons showed that Washington had agreed to the terms of the Hawaiian commander: "Persons evacuated will be selected by you with due regard to your requirements for labor. Evacuation will be delayed until you have received your quota of reinforcing troops."[20] For his part, under the authority granted him in January, Emmons delivered the first shipment of Japanese with the departure of the *Ulysses Grant* the day after Roosevelt signed Executive Order 9066, authorizing the exclusion of Japanese from the Western Defense Command. The timing was critical for those implementing the exchange, because the West Coast was not under martial law. EO 9066, in their view, permitted the continued management of Hawaii's refuse once they stepped onto West Coast soil.

Not all the president's men were fully satisfied with the wisdom or legality of the arrangement. McCloy reflected on the situation and, as early as March 28, 1942, cautiously admitted that there were "some grave legal difficulties in placing American citizens, even of Japanese ancestry, in concentration camps." His superior, Stimson, was more to the point. "As the thing stands at present," the war secretary wrote, "a number of them have been arrested in Hawaii without very much evidence of disloyalty, have been shipped to the United States, and are interned there. McCloy and I are both agreed that this was contrary to law." Stimson characterized the affair as "the President's own attempt to imprison by internment some of the leaders of the Japanese in Hawaii against whom we have nothing but very grave suspicions." Stimson's solution was as unprincipled as the president's action when he informed Roosevelt that he was sending the American citizens "back to Hawaii which is under a state of martial law and where we can do what we please with them."[21]

Roosevelt and Knox nonetheless doggedly pursued their frustrated object of mass internment for Hawaii's Japanese. "Both the President and the Secretary of the Navy," wrote McCloy, "continuously refer to the desirability of moving Japanese from the Island of Oahu to some other Island rather than to bring any numbers of them to the United States." Opposing them were Stimson and the General Staff, who believed the difficulties involved outweighed the benefits. "However, the matter has not come to rest," sighed McCloy, "and the thought now is that if the number that were to be moved were to be rather limited, say, 10,000 or 15,000, the practicability of moving them to [the island of] Hawaii would be apparent."[22] The Hawaiian commander would not oblige; instead, he offered more already interned Japanese and eventually their families for mainland concentration camps under a fraudulant program of "voluntary evacuation and resettlement."

Between 1942 and 1943, six shiploads of 675 Japanese and 25 German and Italian internees, and four shiploads of 1,037 internees and their immediate family members made the crossing.[23] In deference to the "really difficult constitutional question" involved in that transfer of aliens and citizens to mainland concentration camps, the power to exclude under EO 9066 was extended to Emmons in Hawaii, and internees were given the choice of continued confinement in the islands or "voluntary evacuation" to the mainland. Besides the coercion implicit in that "choice," the military commander did not need to rely on the cooperation of the internees, as pointed out by General George C. Marshall, who assured Emmons: "You will have ample authority under Presidential Order and your status as Military Governor to order evacuation of any Japanese, citizen or alien, you deem potentially dangerous, and any attempt to coerce consent both unnecessary and undesirable."[24]

Written in the files of the "volunteers" was the phrase "elected evacuation as an alternative to continued internment in Hawaii for the duration [of the war]." To maintain the pretense of voluntary evacuation and thereby circumvent the Constitution, the internees were released from custody at the time of their departure from Hawaii in an action commonly referred to as a "gangplank release."[25] On arriving on the West Coast, the Western Defense Command, under its power to exclude, removed the Japanese from the military zone and passed them on to the War Relocation Authority (WRA) for "resettlement" in "relocation centers" in the American interior. The crucial distinction in the revised presidential order was that Hawaii's Japanese were being "excluded" and "relocated" from a military to a safe zone, instead of being transported for internment in concentration camps.[26] The difference was fictional because, as observed by Supreme Court Justice Owen Roberts in the *Korematsu* case, the exclusion order was "but a part of an over-all plan for forceable detention."[27]

Managing

Voluntary evacuation, claimed an army officer, gave the Japanese "an opportunity to establish their loyalty." Instead, many of Hawaii's Japanese answered "no–no" to the WRA's "loyalty questionnaire" shortly after their arrival in mainland camps. Approximately 275 of them indicated a desire to renounce their American citizenship. "The majority of them apparently did not desire to take advantage of any improved condition pointing towards establishing themselves as loyal Americans," concluded the officer.[28]

The internees were scattered across the American landscape and confined at Angel Island, Camp McCoy, Camp Forrest, Camp Livingstone (Louisiana), Camp Shelby (Mississippi), and Fort Sill (Oklahoma), administered by the army; Fort Missoula (Montana), Lordsburg and Santa Fe (New Mexico) and Crystal City and Seagoville (Texas), administered by the Justice Department; and Jerome (Arkansas), Topaz (Utah), and Tule Lake (California), administered by the WRA. Asked Keiho Soga:

> When the war is over
> And after we are gone
> Who will visit
> This lonely grave in the wild
> Where my friend lies buried?[29]

The odyssey of Suikei Furuya was perhaps representative of Hawaii's Japanese in that distant land. Among the first group sent from the territory, Furuya passed through Angel Island, Camp McCoy, and Camp Forrest. He wrote of conflicts among "mentally strained" men who shared a single barracks, of the joy of receiving letters from home, and of baseball games and an evening lecture series, the most popular activities at Camp McCoy. The "huts" at Camp Forrest, he remembered, "were makeshift and cracks were seen all over the place"; when it rained, the roof leaked and "our floors were always flooded." The bedding was dirty, and the authorities refused to provide clean sheets and covers. "I couldn't stand the smell of them," recalled Furuya. Meals at Camp Forrest, however, were good, and in the evening, "we saw the glow of fireflies here and there. I felt so relaxed that I forgot the hard conditions that I was placed [in]." Just as the men began to settle in, they were moved to Camp Livingstone, Louisiana.

Camp Livingstone was divided by wire fences that separated Hawaii and Canal Zone from mainland Japanese. With many highly educated people in the camp, wrote Furuya, internees were able to organize "cultural and academic classes" and a curriculum for "Internee College." On one occasion, the men refused to carry pine logs for a military airport being built outside the camp. "To help the authority meant to sell ourselves to the enemy," explained Furuya. The army responded with a general lockup and stationed at each gate guards who directed their machine guns toward the enclosed Japanese. The strike leaders "must have felt intimidated," speculated Furuya, and "they finally decided to compromise. We lost."

After eleven months in Louisiana, Furuya was sent to Fort Missoula where he joined Germans, Italians, and Peruvian Japanese. The excitement of greater freedoms in being allowed to play baseball and golf, go fishing, see movies, and take photographs in camp was surpassed by the fervor generated among the men with the entrance of forty women internees. That attention, however, was unrequited; in fact, "these internee women didn't seem to notice [the] existence of any males in the camp," reported Furuya. Christmas 1943 was memorable because of the gifts—books, green tea, *shoyu, miso,* medicines—sent by the Japanese Red Cross. "We were so grateful for their kindness," he recalled, "that we didn't know how to express [it] in words."

On April 3, 1944, Furuya left Montana for Santa Fe, where about 800 internees from Hawaii were gathered. "The four years of camp life," reflected Furuya, "were not after all in vain. We learned a lot. . . . We learned to appreciate our wives. . . . We found that those who were respected in our communities before turned out to be completely opposite of what we expected them to be, whereas there were others whom we thought idle but we found beautiful personalities among them." Still, Furuya longed for freedom beyond the barbed-wire fence. "I must have been mentally exhausted from constantly living together with a mass of people," he wrote. "I had a strong desire to be alone in a quiet atmosphere," and yet,

"I knew it was almost impossible to obtain. One day, to my surprise, I found a quiet grass field. . . . I began to go there in the evenings and looked at the endless view of Santa Fe Plateau."[30]

The poet Sojin Takei wrote of similar longings, of freedom, loneliness, and family. Here are two of his poems.

There is no fence
High up in the sky.
The evening crows
Fly up and disappear
Into the endless horizon.

My wife and children
Live in a far away land.
How lonely are the nights
Behind these barbed wire fences.[31]

Under the family reunification program, internees could request to have their spouses and children join them, or family members in Hawaii could be "voluntarily evacuated" to the mainland. Once on the mainland, however, family members were "relocated" to WRA camps, separated from their loved ones, who were generally interned in army or Justice Department camps. Although Seikaku Takesono was in Santa Fe, for example, his wife and children were transported to and held in Jerome for six months before they were reunited.[32] George Hoshida was taken away from his pregnant wife and three young children in Hilo. Their eldest daughter, left paralyzed by an automobile accident, had to be institutionalized by his wife, who had no means of support after Hoshida's internment. While left unattended at that facility, the child drowned in a bathtub. "Of course I heard it was best that she went," remembered Hoshida, "but not like that. Not like that." Three months after the birth of her fourth child, Hoshida's wife and children were "voluntarily evacuated" to Jerome in the middle of winter; one daughter contracted beri-beri, and the baby had diarrhea and nearly died. "So, actually," concluded Hoshida, "my wife suffered more; my family suffered more." Nearly a year passed before they were finally reunited in Lordsburg.[33]

The transfer register showed that 107 women, men, and children were removed from the Hawaiian Department to the WRA's Jerome concentration camp in the first shipment. The spoils of war included Fumi Ansai, six months' pregnant, and Takeshi, and their eleven-month-old son; Kachi and Joseph Araki and their eight children ranging in age from one to eleven; three single women; and forty-eight-year-old Saki Yamane and her seven children. The 443 family groups among the second transfer unit included Tsuruye Koide and her nineteen-month-old daughter; Tamotsu Aoki, who had a "severe deformity . . . of [the] lumbo-sacral region of [the] spinal column"; his wife, Mitsuko, their five children, and Mitsuko's seventy-one-year-old father and sixty-eight-year-old mother; and Yoshiko and Yukuma Hayashi, whose ten-month-old son required a special feeding formula.[34] Although the WRA privately admitted that those "volunteers" were "almost, but not quite, eligible for internment," it confined Hawaii's "evacuees" in concentration camps and even sought to separate them from mainland Japanese.[35]

Confinement and isolation in mainland camps, cabled McCloy, "would impose severe discrimination against Hawaiian Japanese to which others are not subjected." Perhaps more importantly, it "would require additional construction difficult to accomplish and delay in getting materials might postpone evacuation."[36] Indeed, the worry over who would bear the burden of housing, feeding, and controlling Hawaii's Japanese appeared to be a paramount concern among those who shared the responsibility for administering this exclusion program.[37] Most astonishingly, those in charge were uncertain about the official status of the "evacuees" after having sent three shiploads to the mainland. G-2's Bicknell assured the Western Defense Command: "You have received only our best grade of internees—those whom we consider dangerous or potentially dangerous while free in Hawaii." The intelligence officer then asked, almost parenthetically: "What is an evacuee—a citizen or resident moved for the benefit of the government but free to conduct his affairs as he wishes within the limits of his mobility, or a suspect whose actions should be somewhat controlled? Are our evacuees considered to be equal to yours, or does their previous internment make [them] suspects, if so, to what degree?"[38]

Resisting

In a February 27, 1943, letter, Dillon Myer, WRA head, informed McCloy of his agency's disenchantment with Hawaii's "best grade internees." "Our experience at Jerome, where the Hawaiian evacuees are located, has not been good," reported Myer. "They have proved to be unwilling workers and about half of them have answered no to the loyalty question. . . . They definitely are not the kind of people who should be scattered among the West Coast evacuees." Myer asked the War Department to dissuade Emmons from fulfilling his pledge to send several thousand more Japanese to the mainland.[39] In accord with the WRA director's desire, the Hawaiian commander promised to halt the evacuation program, except for suspects in excess of Hawaii's holding capacity, and asked that the WRA explain to Knox the problems involved in a mass removal. "I suggest that the reasons for deferring evacuation be given to the Secretary of the Navy," cabled Emmons, "who has publicly stated that he is in favor of additional Japanese evacuation from Hawaii in large numbers."[40]

Myer drafted, but apparently did not send, a letter to the navy secretary, asking that he "give renewed consideration to the necessity for further evacuation of persons of Japanese ancestry from the Territory of Hawaii to the Continental United States." Before the WRA director could act, responding to a note from the army's General Staff, Knox explained that his support of evacuation was solely "based upon the desire to segregate disloyal and dangerous elements" from the general population. Evacuation was unnecessary if segregation took place in Hawaii with all the disloyals confined to a single island.[41] Given that opening, McCloy wired Emmons on April 2, 1943: "You will suspend evacuation to mainland of all Japanese except those recommended by you for custodial detention in excess of your detention capacity and that there be no evacuation of those considered safe for release on mainland without first obtaining from WRA through this office an agreement to take them."[42]

Myer's casting of Hawaii's Japanese as troublemakers was very likely contrived. The day before he wrote to McCloy, Myer telephoned the Jerome camp asking for a statement from the camp director on the Hawaii contingent there, probably to use as evidence to support his request to stop the inflow of "evacuees" from Hawaii. The document provided by the camp's reports officer was sent to Myer on February 28, a day after the WRA director's letter to McCloy. Instead of confirming Myer's portrayal of "unwilling workers" and disloyals, the reports officer declared: "The 810 Hawaiian evacuees at this center have not presented any particular problem to date. With a few general exceptions they have conformed with the general behavior pattern which we have come to accept as typical of the other residents." The report continued: "The men especially were quick to seek employment in the center. . . . There has been no official complaint from any supervisor, Caucasian or Japanese, relative to the work habits, workmanship or attitude of these men." On the issue of loyalty and military service, the Jerome officer contradicted the WRA director by stating that "numerically their cooperation has been outstanding."[43]

Myer's singling out of Hawaii's Japanese was typical of WRA thinking, which classified the captive population by generation, education, and regions of origin, believing that *issei* and *kibei* were more "pro-Japan" than *nisei* and that Japanese from the Pacific Northwest were more accommodating than those from California.[44] Japanese from Hawaii were troublemakers, according to the WRA, because they came from a society where they rarely experienced discrimination and thus reacted more strenuously to perceived mistreatment than those who had endured it and come to expect racism. "The WRA itself feared those from Hawaii," observed Hawaii evacuee Iwao Kosaka. "They thought of us as willing to fight at the smallest incident. I think the Nisei from Hawaii had previously raised some hell beforehand. As a result, as soon as they heard of people from Hawaii, they thought of us as being troublemakers."[45]

The reality was more complex, and definitions of loyalty and disloyalty could not be reduced to responses on the loyalty questionnaire. For many, the injustice of their forcible removal and detention was the source and substance of their protest. "Prior to my internment in a concentration camp," wrote Fumio Kusunoki, "I was willing to swear allegiance and give my life for my country, the USA, but even tho' I swore allegiance to this country many times during my stay in their internment camp, I was not recognized by the government. I stayed in the internment camp for 10 months. It is very difficult for me to answer this question, yes or no." Hiroshi Miyahara answered no to question 28, adding, "because of the treatment which I was given in Hawaii where I was interned on Sand Island in spite of my willingness to swear loyalty to the U.S." His wife, Chiyoko, declared, "I can't answer until my husband's internment is clarified." Ichisaburo Nakamura explained:

I had long believed that I was an American citizen, loyal to the US and had taught my pupils at my language school according to this belief. I was, however, arrested without any proper reason as soon as the war broke out. After two and [a] half months the investigators of my case showed me the warrant of arrest in which they pointed out that I was an enemy alien. I asserted once again that I was loyal to this country, but in fact I had been treated as an enemy alien. The investigating authority sent me to Honolulu in order to intern me in the mainland. I had been kept at Sand Island Detention Camp for nine months. In addition, my internment for the duration of the war was ordered by the military governor of Hawaii on March 9, 1942. When I left Hawaii on 12-27-42 a note of release was given to me under the restriction that I was going to a relocation center in the mainland. Now I realized that the authority had not considered me as an American citizen. Because of the reason above I could not answer the questions 27 and 28.[46]

A recurrent phrase in the statements of Hawaii's Japanese, appended to questions 27 and 28, was "because of Sand Island" or "because of internment" despite repeated expressions of loyalty. Eighteen-year-old Sarah Okada wrote: "I don't know what loyalty means because of my father's internment without no reason, even though he is a citizen."[47]

The WRA saw those who questioned violations of their rights of citizenship as agitators. A WRA official described a prominent leader of the opposition: "From the time he was detained at Sand Island in Hawaii until he was finally sent to Leupp from Jerome he was a trouble-maker. . . . When he was evacuated from Hawaii, he was brought to Jerome Center, where he allegedly agitated trouble during the registration [loyalty questionnaire crisis] and was considered a general trouble-maker of the incorrigible type by officials at that project."[48] Another WRA case summary claimed: "Subject is extremely pro-Japanese and anti-American in his sentiments. He speaks little English and is Japanese in his attitude and reactions. He admits that he has been taught the Emperor is the Son of God and he should always be loyal to the Emperor of Japan."[49] WRA impressions of individuals and their answers to questions 27 and 28 constituted the bases for segregating the "loyals" from the "disloyals" and confining the latter in a single concentration camp—Tule Lake.[50] Tule Lake was the mainland equivalent of Knox's segregation plan for Molokai or some other island of the Hawaiian chain.

"Disloyal"
With papers so stamped
I am relocated to Tule Lake.
But for myself,
A clear conscience.[51]

An Accounting

Altogether, from 1942 to 1945, 1,875 Japanese from Hawaii made the crossing to mainland concentration camps. Of that total, 1,118 were confined in WRA camps and 757 in Department of Justice camps.[52] As a result of the 1943 segregation, the WRA designated 340 in their group from Hawaii as "disloyal" and sent them to Tule Lake.[53] In all, 1,466 Japanese were held in Hawaii's concentration camps.[54] The figures listed below suggest frequent movement among the camp population, and show a general decline as the war reached its close.[55]

Included among the territory's discards were some two dozen traded in a State Department-sponsored exchange program that swapped Japanese captives from the Americas for U.S. prisoners held by Japan.[56] The War Department did not favor the use of U.S. Japanese citizens and resident

Number of Japanese Confined in Hawaii's
Concentration Camps, 1942–1945

Year	Sand Island	Kauai	Maui	Molokai	Lanai	Hawaii	Total
1942							
Jan	190	41	51	4	2	85	373
Feb	292	53	56	4	3	110	518
Sept	319	9	9	—	—	6	343
1943	(Honouliuli)*						
June	238	—	—	—	—	—	238
Aug	229	1	4	—	—	—	234
Dec	169	—	1	—	—	—	170
1944							
Jan	324	—	—	—	—	—	324
June	184	2	—	—	—	2	188
Oct	117	—	—	—	—	—	117
1945							
Sept	25	—	—	—	—	—	25

*Those interned at Sand Island were sent to Honouliuli in 1943.

aliens as pawns in that traffic because it feared the "repatriates" would supply intelligence information to Japan's military. In the early months of the war, however, repatriates were among those who made the crossing to the mainland from Hawaii. On August 18, 1942, the *Republic* left Honolulu harbor with 133 repatriates, 37 women and 96 children. On board, the Miyao children, Takaomi, age nine, Junko, age six, and Masanori, age four, sailed without their parents because their mother, Yuki Miyao (of the "Y. Miyao" confusion by military authorities), had been interned with her husband in mainland camps. The *Republic* berthed in San Francisco, and the repatriates traveled by train across the continent to Asheville, North Carolina, where a State Department representative received delivery of the outcasts.[57]

One of the last groups of Japanese expelled from Hawaii for confinement in mainland camps were sixty-seven *nisei* transported from Hawaiian concentration camps to Tule Lake on November 9, 1944.[58] The lifting of martial law on October 24, 1944, made the arbitrary internment of citizens difficult at best, prompting the exclusion of *nisei* from the territory. Japan's decline and inevitable defeat eroded the argument of military necessity, and the legal challenges mounted against martial law in Hawaii, and the mass removal and detention on the mainland compelled a new strategy for the control of America's Japanese.[59] In anticipation of the eventual success of the pending *habeas corpus* cases in the U.S. Supreme Court, Washington's and Hawaii's military rulers hammered out a plan in the spring and summer of 1944 to "merely perpetuate security regulations" that were in effect under martial law without martial law.[60]

Washington proposed a presidential executive order, modeled after EO 9066, transferring the security function of government in Hawaii from the secretary of the interior to the secretary of war. Lieutenant General Robert C. Richardson, commander of the Central Pacific Area (inclusive of the former Hawaiian Department), compared the Western Defense Command's "evacuation of whole populations" with Hawaii's "more logical" management of Japanese, "utilizing their manpower but apprehending and interning individual Japanese who . . . were found to be potentially dangerous." Thus, explained the general, "many thousands of laborers, as well as skilled workers, have been available to work on necessary construction, while the cultivation of sugar and pineapples has continued, thereby preserving the agricultural economy of the community which would most certainly have failed completely if persons of Japanese ancestry had been evacuated from the Territory." The "continuing pressure" to intern both alien and citizen, not simple exclusion as authorized under EO 9066, however, had to be strictly applied to guarantee the good behavior of Hawaii's Japanese.[61]

McCloy radioed Richardson that both the Interior and Justice Departments were "firmly convinced of inadvisability, on grounds of policy together with serious doubts as to legality, of President, in a formal state paper such as an Executive Order, attempting to confer power to intern American citizens in Hawaii." Nevertheless, both departments agreed to withdraw their objections to the transfer of citizens from Hawaii and agreed to accept island *nisei* into Tule Lake concentration camp.[62] "With this concession by the Interior and Justice Departments," stated the general, "I am in a position to expel from the Territory citizens of Japanese ancestry and dual citizens disloyal or believed inimical to the security of the Territory. As a matter of fact, this power is to our advantage and I shall insist on the right to arrest and detain such citizens pending their expulsion and deportation, as now authorized in the proposed executive order."[63] Richardson retained those "rights" when Roosevelt signed Executive Order 9489 on October 18, 1944, authorizing the Pacific Ocean Areas commander to declare Hawaii a military area, to regulate travel and maintain press censorship, and to intern enemy aliens and exclude from the islands all those deemed dangerous to security. Consequently, although martial law ended in Hawaii six days after its signing, EO 9489 permitted a virtual business as usual at Iolani Palace.[64]

The War Years, 1941–1945

America's war with Japan, like the exclusionist Gentlemen's Agreement of 1908 and the worker resistance of 1909, marked another great divide in Hawaii's anti-Japanese movement. It was both a culmination and a new beginning. Labor controls and economic, political, and cultural hegemony during World War II followed decades of yellow peril hyperbole and military planning for Pacific dominance that gathered distillates of racism in martial law, concentration camps, and blood sacrifice. As a new beginning for Hawaii's Japanese, the war extinguished countless dreams, fortunes, and lives; it also gave birth to a battle-scarred generation confident in their claim to America and relentless in their pursuit of "full-fledged" manhood and equal opportunity.

White supremacy, as expressed in a concerted movement against the

"Japanese menace," was a unifying ideology and practice that held together the sometimes disparate interests of white workers, planters, the territorial government, and the military. White supremacy justified army control of the territory, which promoted the diversification and expansion of Hawaii's industries, especially in defense work. A few business and political leaders sought to restore civil government, and AFL locals took an antimilitary, antiracist stand in March 1944, but those efforts represented a minority position and came late in the war. The overwhelming sentiment of Hawaii's whites was articulated by the Honolulu Chamber of Commerce in a wire to President Roosevelt on December 27, 1942, expressing contentment with army rule and protesting attempts to reinstate constitutional government. That message prompted an Interior Department head to assert: "I was somewhat disturbed by the telegram from the Chamber of Commerce to the President which gave the impression that a large and responsible group of American businessmen had so far departed from normal American thinking as to prefer military control of all activities of civilian life . . . instead of the normal process of American government."[65] J. Garner Anthony, former territorial attorney general, pointedly declared: "In short, the Army deprived the citizen of his most cherished possession—the inheritance of free men—which the founders of this country had waged bloody battles to secure, and these were supinely exchanged for meat, butter, Kleenex, and liquor."[66]

The indispensable Japanese labor was the starting point of wartime social relations and military security, racist distractions such as those interjected by Roosevelt and Knox notwithstanding.[67] The islands' Japanese could not be interned as a matter of practical reality; mass confinement would be too costly to initiate and maintain and too destructive of Hawaii's economy. Hawaii's Japanese escaped the fate of their West Coast kin because of their labor utility and were forced to work at jobs assigned or approved by the military government or face punishment or expulsion under the army's program to remove indigents and nonproducers from Hawaii. Recalled George Hoshida: "All those ones on the welfare. We were on the welfare. We couldn't afford anything, so the military ordered them to evacuate—many of these people on welfare."[68] Hoshida's claim was affirmed by a territorial department head, who quoted the Hawaiian commander's description of the "voluntary evacuation" of Hawaii's Japanese to mainland concentration camps. The program, explained the military governor, was "a part of the general policy of removing from the

Territory as many persons as possible who are not productive or essential to the economy of the islands or whose presence in the islands during the war is considered undesirable from a security standpoint."[69]

The army rounded up "loafers" of all racial and ethnic groups under vagrancy codes, put them to work instead of imprisoning them, and called the movement of workers away from sugar and pineapple plantations "desertions" that deserved "serious consideration."[70] The Japanese were generally excluded from higher-paying defense work and were concentrated in lower-paying agricultural and service jobs, were harassed and intimidated in union activities, were impressed into labor battalions that donated their weekends to "voluntary" work, and were sentenced to hard labor for petty offenses. The planters relied on schoolchildren as a source of labor and exerted considerable pressure on the military rulers to delay the start of schools, to time vacations, and even to close schools to coincide with production schedules. That use of child labor was substantial: in July 1942, students furnished sugar plantations with 131,000 days of work and pineapple canneries with 153,000 days.[71]

The army's need for Japanese labor—reminiscent of Wyllie's "we are in much need of them"—was inseparably paired with the need to manipulate racism to justify the military order. The territory's security required an anti-Japanese movement that elicited Japanese labor but repressed Japanese culture and empowerment. Buddhist churches, Japanese-language schools, electoral politics, and "cockiness" fell by the wayside in the crusade against self that admonished *nisei* to "speak, think and act American." In many ways, the "new spokesmen" for the Japanese community succeeded overmuch in promoting "all-out Americanism"; even *issei*, former objects of filial respect, feared venturing beyond their thresholds or conversing in their native tongue.

Martial law, concentration camps, and a people held hostage through terror were extraordinary measures that departed from the continuities of migrant labor and dependency. Martial law, although blanketing everyone, was conceived and instituted specifically for one segment of the population; concentration camps, although holding European enemy aliens, confined mainly Japanese—alien *and* citizen—not because they were spies but because they were leaders of the community. Those exemplars of powerlessness, together with their harsh treatment at the hands of their captors, served mentally to imprison even those who remained outside the barbed-wire fence, having the same chilling effect as the 1889 lynching of Honokaa storekeeper Hiroshi Goto, who had raised his voice in defense of workers, or the 1929 execution of the sickly and impoverished Myles Yutaka Fukunaga, son of a former plantation worker, for the murder of ten-year-old Gill Jamieson, child of Frederick W. Jamieson, vice-president of the Hawaiian Trust Company.[72] The blood-soaked deeds of the "Go for Broke" and Military Intelligence Service (MIS) *nisei* soldiers were similarly extraordinary, dwarfing the misdeeds of those charged with upholding the Constitution, and supplied the key that unlocked the concentration camps' gates.[73]

Although extraordinary, neither oppression nor resistance during World War II arose situationally amid wartime hysteria, racism, or failure of political leadership.[74] It evolved from Hawaii's anti-Japanese movement through its stages of migrant labor and dependency. The origins and lineage of martial law and concentration camps can be precisely tracked through military intelligence records and war plans.

The army began focussing on the "Japanese problem" when Japanese migrants became settlers, constituting a permanent, populous community, and especially after Japanese workers organized a mass resistance movement that sought full participation in American life, in effect, advocating a democratic revolution to topple the oligarchy and the structures of white supremacy they had erected. In conspiring to repel the challenge, the military bolstered an antidemocratic, oligarchic order, making common cause with the planters and the territorial government. During the war, the army itself became an autocratic ruler.

The 1920 strike of Filipino and Japanese plantation workers mustered a comprehensive counterattack led by the planters and the territorial government that sought to isolate Hawaii's Japanese as a racial group that was subversive of national security, to centralize the sugar industry and institute more repressive measures to deal with worker unrest, and to eradicate Japanism and promote Americanism. That campaign, couched in the form of labor relief, drew national attention largely through the Hawaii Emergency Labor Commission. The "Japanese problem" became a military problem magnified many times over into a race war by the federal Hawaiian Labor Commission report. The imagery of the yellow peril, the "spectre of alien domination," argued for a military solution because of military necessity.

Military and civilian intelligence in Hawaii and on the mainland considered the "Japanese problem" their leading concern by 1922. But detailed plans for containing the "Japanese menace" arose in the territory, not on the mainland. The most obvious reasons for that development were geographic (Hawaii was nearer to Japan and could be readily cut off from the mainland), demographic (Hawaii's Japanese approached a plurality of the total population, but were an insignificant number on the West Coast), and economic (sugar, the mainstay of the islands' economy, and other major industries required Japanese labor). Although the intelligence services regularly surveyed the West Coast Japanese at least as early as World War I, it was not until 1940 that the navy sought to expel Japanese fishermen from Terminal Island in Los Angeles harbor and the FBI planned the internment of alien (including Japanese) "subversives."[75] In contrast, by 1923, the army's Hawaiian Department had planned the imposition of martial law, registration of all aliens, and internment of selected enemy aliens.

Apart from the Justice Department roundup of 2,295 enemy aliens, 1,291 of whom were Japanese (367 in Hawaii and 924 on the mainland), by December 10, 1941, the army's defense of the West Coast was confused and capricious, depending on the temper of its commander, John De Witt, and his associates. Headquarters declared the entire West Coast a "theater of operations" four days after Pearl Harbor, providing the legal mechanism for placing civilians under military control. Toward the end of January 1942, De Witt recommended the total exclusion of enemy aliens from highly restricted zones and a pass and permit system for all enemy aliens in less restricted zones. Military control was still exercised only over enemy aliens and not citizens, as announced on February 1, 1942, in a joint press release: "The Department of War and the Department of Justice are in agreement that the present military situation does not at this time require the removal of American citizens of the Japanese race."[76] The decision for mass removal of the West Coast Japanese was made by President Roosevelt on February 11, 1942, and the executive order authorizing the army to exclude "any and all persons" from designated areas under the auspices of "military necessity" was signed eight days later. Finally, the WRA resolved to intern, rather than relocate, Japanese only after an April 7, 1942, meeting with western governors, who objected to having their states become "California's dumping ground."[77]

Hawaii, in contrast, stood prepared. The MID in 1929 made no distinction between Japanese alien and citizen, spy and patriot, but simply marked leaders of the community for internment as "the most practicable

plan for controlling sabotage or other Japanese activities." Like the planters' scheme of the 1920s and 1930s, the army designed a sweeping strategy
for Japanese domestication, including a declaration of martial law, the internment of leaders even before actual hostilities, extraction of Japanese
labor, and the formation of a *nisei* counterpropaganda system directed
against ethnic identity and culture. Pearl Harbor merely triggered the
gun loading of the previous two decades, or, more correctly, of the anti-
Japanese movement that spanned the entire range of a people's history,
from plantation to concentration camp.

Morning Sunlight

The ashes of Hiroshima and Nagasaki brought home to Hawaii's shore
the remnants of the wartime diaspora—internees freed from camps in
Hawaii and on the mainland and the bodies of warrior heroes and their
surviving comrades—in a return passage that was for many a bittersweet
triumph. Despite Roosevelt's wartime forked rhetoric that "Americanism
is a matter of the mind and heart; Americanism is not, and never was, a
matter of race or ancestry," the uprooted knew that Americanism was a
matter of race and that equality would be wrested from Hawaii's political
and economic leaders only after much struggle. "We who by God's will
were permitted to return," stated Katsumi Kometani, a veteran and original member of the army's Emergency Service Committee, "and you who
are fortunate to be here have a challenge—an obligation to those who now
peacefully sleep under the white crosses in Italy and France—to build a
better Hawaii." Although showing some residue of self-blame, Kometani
was able to say with confidence, "By the blood and tears of our people
we have earned a place for ourselves in this community. . . . We have
helped win the war on the battlefront but we have not yet won the war
on the homefront. We shall have won only when we attain those things
for which our country is dedicated, namely, equality of opportunity and
the dignity of man."[78]

The irrefutable nature of that claim and demand, termed "cockiness"
by some, was impossible to deny. Even the popular writer Edgar Rice
Burroughs had admitted before the war ended, "As strongly as I feel both
we and the Japanese would be better off if there were none of them on our
soil, I cannot forget that there are thousands of them in Italy, fighting and

dying at the side of other Americans; and I cannot conceive of America repaying them by disenfranchisement and deportation."[79] Frank Midkiff, in response to Burroughs's inquiry ("Taking into consideration only the greatest good of the greatest number and a long time view which envisions the world in which our descendants will have to live, what would be the ideal solution of this problem?"), argued that America was, since its inception, multiethnic and yet united in a common love of freedom and individualism and a hatred of class distinctions. "Now, we have no objection to these various groups retaining their mores and customs," wrote the Honolulu Chamber of Commerce president, "so long as these customs are necessary in order to provide controls for rearing their children, but we expect all of them ultimately to become out and out American citizens." Americanization, he concluded, was "the ideal solution for the Japanese problem, and it is taking place in positive fashion in this Territory."[80]

Midkiff's reply, shaped after consultation with other prominent members of Hawaii's elite, revealed the direction that thinking would take during the postwar era. Not only did the power brokers have to contend with *nisei* veterans but also with a growing impatience among the second generation over persistent inequality, and with an electorate increasingly bearing the face of the Pacific enemy. As predicted, the Japanese eventually fulfilled the worst fears of military strategists by dominating the electoral process through Democratic party politics.[81] The *"aloha* spirit," a spontaneous, natural feeling of warmth for all people, emanating from the Hawaiians and infecting all who inhabited this melting pot of the Pacific, warded off "race thinking" and brought tourists to these shores, building a new industry that by the 1960s had surpassed the cultivation of cane. (The military had outstripped sugar and pineapple to become Hawaii's leading industry during the 1950s.)

Cane cultivation—organized according to capitalist principles—was both a point of departure and an entry in the saga of Hawaii's Japanese, providing a reason for their presence in the islands and defining their position within the social order. The anti-Japanese movement established the parameters of social relations, predicated foremost on the utility of Japanese labor for the maintenance of white economic and political dominance and racial supremacy. Human agency—Japanese resistance—strove to remove the barriers of class and racial oppression, thereby seeking a democratic transformation of an undemocratic order.

The *issei,* having gone through the cold night rain, looked to their children to rekindle the cane fires of human dignity set in countless fields across this loveliest fleet of islands. They would not be disappointed. Returning from mainland concentration camps, the exiled poet Sojin Takei peered across the ship's bow and, looking homeward, saw not only land but a fullness of possibilities, exclaiming, "How bright the sea is, shining in morning sunlight!"

Notes

Preface

1. Commission on Wartime Relocation and Internment of Civilians, *Personal Justice Denied* (Washington, D.C.: Government Printing Office, 1982), 261.

2. Romanzo Adams, "The Unorthodox Race Doctrine of Hawaii," in *Race and Culture Contacts*, ed. E. B. Reuter (New York: McGraw-Hill, 1934); and Andrew W. Lind, *Hawaii: The Last of the Magic Isles* (London: Oxford University Press, 1969). See John Mei Liu, "Cultivating Cane: Asian Labor and the Hawaiian Sugar Plantation System within the Capitalist World Economy, 1835–1920," doctoral dissertation, University of California, Los Angeles, 1985, for a critique of the Adams–Lind hypothesis.

3. Andrew W. Lind, *Hawaii's Japanese: An Experiment in Democracy* (Princeton: Princeton University Press, 1946), 62–63.

4. J. Garner Anthony, *Hawaii under Army Rule* (Stanford: Stanford University Press, 1955); preface of 1975 reprint.

5. Roger Daniels, *Concentration Camps: North America* (Malabar, Fla.: Robert E. Krieger, 1981), 2. See also Jacobus tenBroek et al., *Prejudice, War and the Constitution* (Berkeley: University of California Press, 1954), 11–67.

6. Lucie Cheng and Edna Bonacich, eds., *Labor Immigration under Capitalism: Asian Workers in the United States Before World War II* (Berkeley: University of California Press, 1984), makes a significant contribution toward conceptualizing Asian migration as labor migration; however, the book falters in its discussion of anti-Asianism and class struggle.

7. See, e.g., Gordon W. Prange, *At Dawn We Slept: The Untold Story of Pearl Harbor* (New York: McGraw-Hill, 1981), 402–406, 412–413, 586, 705–706, 729–731.

8. My interpretation of Hawaiian history is influenced by works such as Colin Bundy, *The Rise and Fall of the South African Peasantry* (Berkeley: University of California Press, 1979); Barry Hindess and Paul Q. Hirst, *Pre-Capitalist Modes of Production* (London: Routledge and Kegan Paul, 1975); and Shula Marks and Anthony Atmore, eds., *Economy and Society in Pre-industrial South Africa* (London: Longman, 1980). Their ideas of mode of production, social formation, and articulation of precapitalist with capitalist societies bear particular relevance to Hawaii before and after the arrival of Europeans. Theories of migrant labor, world-system and dependency, and internal colonialism, contained in books such as Stephen

Castles and Godula Kosack, *Immigrant Workers and Class Structure in Western Europe* (London: Oxford University Press, 1973); Immanuel Wallerstein, *The Modern World-System* (New York: Academic Press, 1974); and Robert Blauner, *Racial Oppression in America* (New York: Harper & Row, 1972), help to order and explain the history of Hawaii's sugar plantations, Asian migration to the islands, and racial and class oppression in the Hawaiian kingdom and territory. Victims of oppression, however, frequently resisted and thereby improved their condition and changed the course of history, as shown in such books as Herbert Aptheker, *American Negro Slave Revolts* (New York: Columbia University Press, 1944); and Gary Y. Okihiro, ed., *In Resistance: Studies in African, Caribbean, and Afro-American History* (Amherst: University of Massachusetts Press, 1986). I apply this idea to Hawaii's Japanese.

Chapter 1: So Much Charity, So Little Democracy

1. E.S.C. Handy and Mary Pukui, *The Polynesian Family System in Kau* (Honolulu: Charles E. Tuttle, 1972).

2. E.S.C. Handy and Elizabeth Green Handy, *Native Planters in Old Hawaii: Their Life, Lore, and Environment*, Bulletin no. 233 (Honolulu: Bishop Museum Press, 1972).

3. Edward D. Beechert, *Working in Hawaii: A Labor History* (Honolulu: University of Hawaii Press, 1985), 10–11.

4. Ibid., 19–20; and Gavan Daws, *Shoal of Time: A History of the Hawaiian Islands* (New York: Macmillan, 1968), 47.

5. Quoted in Noel J. Kent, *Hawaii: Islands under the Influence* (New York: Monthly Review Press, 1983), 28. See also Beechert, *Working*, 21–22.

6. Cited in Beechert, *Working*, 31.

7. Ibid., 21, 31.

8. Daws, *Shoal*, 127; and Beechert, *Working*, 33.

9. Quoted in Ronald Takaki, *Pau Hana: Plantation Life and Labor in Hawaii, 1835–1920* (Honolulu: University of Hawaii Press, 1983), 5.

10. Quoted in Daws, *Shoal*, 106.

11. Lawrence H. Fuchs, *Hawaii Pono: A Social History* (New York: Harcourt, Brace and World, 1961), 16–17.

12. Daws, *Shoal*, 108.

13. Fuchs, *Hawaii Pono*, 22–24.

14. Ralph S. Kuykendall, *The Hawaiian Kingdom, 1854–1874: Twenty Critical Years* (Honolulu: University of Hawaii Press, 1953), 142.

15. Ibid., 145–146.

16. Ibid., 131–133. Lunalilo, Kamehameha V's successor in 1872, abolished property qualifications for voting in the 1874 constitution, but retained the autocratic powers reinstated by Kamehameha V.

17. Cited in ibid., 225–226. See also Merze Tate, *Hawaii: Reciprocity or Annexation* (East Lansing: Michigan State University Press, 1968).

18. Kuykendall, *Hawaiian Kingdom*, 248–249.

19. Beechert, *Working*, 79–80.

20. Daws, *Shoal*, 240–252.

21. Ibid., 287–289; and Thomas J. Osborne, *"Empire Can Wait": American Opposition to Hawaiian Annexation, 1893–1898* (Kent, Ohio: Kent State University Press, 1981), 34–39.

22. Fuchs, *Hawaii Pono*, 35–36.

23. U.S. Congress, House, *Annexation of the Hawaiian Islands: Report of the Committee on Foreign Affairs*, 55th Cong., 2nd sess., 1898, 31.

24. Daws, *Shoal*, 294.

25. Fuchs, *Hawaii Pono*, 34.

26. Robert M. C. Littler, *The Governance of Hawaii: A Study in Territorial Administration* (Stanford: Stanford University Press, 1929), 67, 72, 74–81; Robert C. Schmitt, *Historical Statistics of Hawaii* (Honolulu: University of Hawaii Press, 1977), 607; Daws, *Shoal*, 294–297; and Fuchs, *Hawaii Pono*, 152–181.

27. See Norman Meller, "Centralization in Hawaii: Retrospect and Prospect," *American Political Science Review* 52, no. 1 (March 1958): 100–103.

28. John P. Frank, "Ex Parte Milligan v. the Five Companies: Martial Law in Hawaii," *Columbia Law Review* 44, no. 5 (September 1944): 644–645.

29. Littler, *Governance*, 31–38.

30. Fuchs, *Hawaii Pono*, 164–165.

31. Frank E. Midkiff, "The Economic Determinants of Education in Hawaii," doctoral dissertation, Yale University, 1935, 132.

32. Littler, *Governance*, 14.

33. Joseph Barber, Jr., *Hawaii: Restless Rampart* (Indianapolis: Bobbs-Merrill, 1941), 41–45. See also Daws, *Shoal*, 311–314; U.S. Congress, House, *Statehood for Hawaii: Hearings Before the Subcommittee of the Committee on the Territories*, 79 Cong., 2nd sess., 1946, 783–823; U.S. Congress, Senate, *Law Enforcement in the Territory of Hawaii*, S. Doc. 78, 72nd Cong., 1st sess., 1932, Exhibit 6; James H. Shoemaker, *Labor in the Territory of Hawaii, 1939* (Washington, D.C.: Government Printing Office, 1940), 26–31; and "Hawaii: Sugar-Coated Fort," *Fortune* 22, no. 2 (August 1940): 31–37, 78, 81–82.

34. George Cooper and Gavan Daws, *Land and Power in Hawaii: The Democratic Years* (Honolulu: Benchmark Books, 1985), 3.

35. Fuchs, *Hawaii Pono*, 153.

36. Beechert, *Working*, 34–36.

37. Ibid., 41–57.

38. Hilary Conroy, *The Japanese Frontier in Hawaii, 1868–1898* (Berkeley: University of California Press, 1953), 8, 10.

39. Ibid., 11–14; and Beechert, *Working*, 59–78.

40. "Notes on the History of the Sugar Industry of the Hawaii Islands," *Thrum's Hawaiian Annual, 1875,* 34–42. See also Tin-Yuke Char, ed., *The Sandalwood Mountains: Readings and Stories of the Early Chinese in Hawaii* (Honolulu: University Press of Hawaii, 1975), 54–57.

41. Takaki, *Pau Hana,* 12–13. See also Char, *Sandalwood Mountains,* 54–55; and Beechert, *Working,* 63.

42. Char, *Sandalwood Mountains,* 62.

43. Ibid., 64; and Edward C. Lydon, *The Anti-Chinese Movement in the Hawaiian Kingdom, 1852–1886* (San Francisco: R and E Research Associates, 1975), 16.

44. U.S. Congress, House, *Statehood for Hawaii,* 784.

45. Ibid. See also Ray Stannard Baker, "Human Nature in Hawaii," *American Magazine* 73, no. 3 (January 1912): 328–339.

46. Cited in Julius W. Pratt, "The Ideology of American Expansion," in *Essays in Honor of William E. Dodd,* ed. Avery O. Craven (Chicago: University of Chicago Press, 1935), 335–353.

47. John M. Liu offers the best explication of the incorporation of Hawaii within the world-system in "Cultivating Cane" and "Race, Ethnicity, and the Sugar Plantation System: Asian Labor in Hawaii, 1850–1900," in Cheng and Bonacich, *Labor Immigration,* 186–210.

Chapter 2: *Hole Hole Bushi*

1. Quoted in Masaji Marumoto, "'First Year' Immigrants to Hawaii and Eugene Van Reed," in *East Across the Pacific: Historical and Sociological Studies of Japanese Immigration and Assimilation,* ed. Hilary Conroy and T. Scott Miyakawa (Santa Barbara, Calif: ABC-Clio, 1972), 8.

2. Ibid., 12; and Conroy, *Japanese Frontier,* 19.

3. In a letter dated March 30, 1867, cited in Marumoto, "'First Year' Immigrants," 14.

4. Ralph S. Kuykendall, *The Earliest Japanese Labor Immigration to Hawaii,* University of Hawaii, Occasional Papers, no. 25 (Honolulu: Advertiser Publishing, 1935), 6–7; Marumoto, "'First Year' Immigrants," 14; and Conroy, *Japanese Frontier,* 16.

5. Conroy, *Japanese Frontier,* 20; and Kuykendall, *Earliest Japanese,* 9–10.

6. On the Japanese government's refusal to grant permission for the *Scioto's* departure, see Kuykendall, *Earliest Japanese,* 10–13, 16–24; Marumoto, "'First Year' Immigrants," 16–22; and Conroy, *Japanese Frontier,* 22–27.

7. Conroy, *Japanese Frontier,* 21, 27; and Franklin Odo and Kazuko Sinoto, *A Pictorial History of the Japanese in Hawaii, 1885–1924* (Honolulu: Bishop Museum Press, 1985), 16.

8. Conroy, *Japanese Frontier*, 27; and Ernest K. Wakukawa, *A History of the Japanese People in Hawaii* (Honolulu: Toyo Shoin, 1938), 28–29.

9. Marumoto, " 'First Year' Immigrants," 21–22; and Conroy, *Japanese Frontier*, 27–28. Saiki states that Wakichi died of beri-beri, aggravated because of the lack of fresh fruits and vegetables. Patsy Sumie Saiki, *Japanese Women in Hawaii: The First 100 Years* (Honolulu: Kisaku, 1985), 19–20.

10. Conroy, *Japanese Frontier*, 28–29; and Saiki, *Japanese Women*, 17–23.

11. Quoted in Marumoto, " 'First Year' Immigrants," 24.

12. These Nuuanu plantation rules were for the year 1866, as reported in Conroy, *Japanese Frontier*, 29–30. Cf. Takaki, *Pau Hana*, 67–68; and Beechert, *Working*, 71–73.

13. Marumoto, " 'First Year' Immigrants," 24–25; Conroy, *Japanese Frontier*, 30; and Kuykendall, *Earliest Japanese*, 14.

14. Wakukawa, *History*, 36–40; and Beechert, *Working*, 69. See also Y. Baron Goto, *Children of Gan-nen-mono: The First-Year Men* (Honolulu: Bishop Museum Press, 1968). It is true, however, that Japan offered to pay return passage for only forty *gannenmono*. Conroy, *Japanese Frontier*, 36.

15. Marumoto, " 'First Year' Immigrants," 36; and Goto, *Children*.

16. Wakukawa, *History*, p. 40.

17. Romanzo Adams, *The Japanese in Hawaii: A Statistical Study Bearing on the Future Number and Voting Strength and on the Economic and Social Character of the Hawaiian Japanese* (New York: National Committee on American Japanese Relations, 1924), 14–15; Andrew W. Lind, *Hawaii's People* (Honolulu: University of Hawaii Press, 1967), 75; and Conroy, *Japanese Frontier*, 54–55. See also Lydon, *Anti-Chinese Movement*.

18. Yukiko Irwin and Hilary Conroy, "Robert Walker Irwin and Systematic Immigration to Hawaii," in Conroy and Miyakawa, *East Across the Pacific*, 46–47; Alan Takeo Moriyama, *Imingaisha: Japanese Emigration Companies and Hawaii, 1894–1908* (Honolulu: University of Hawaii Press, 1985), 15–16; and Roland Kotani, *The Japanese in Hawaii: A Century of Struggle* (Honolulu: Hawaii Hochi, 1985), 11.

19. Irwin and Conroy, "Robert Walker Irwin," 47; and Odo and Sinoto, *Pictorial History*, 21.

20. Kotani, *Japanese*, 11; and Conroy, *Japanese Frontier*, 65–66, 87. Cf. Irwin and Conroy, "Robert Walker Irwin," 40–55, for a more generous treatment of Irwin's economic motives.

21. Quoted in Kotani, *Japanese*, 3.

22. For more on Kalakaua's grand strategy for Japan and Japanese migrants, see Conroy, *Japanese Frontier*, 54–64; and Kotani, *Japanese*, 6–8.

23. Conroy, *Japanese Frontier*, 66–67; and Wakukawa, *Japanese*, 47–48.

24. Conroy, *Japanese Frontier*, 70.

25. Ibid., 71–72.

26. Kotani, *Japanese*, 23; and Conroy, *Japanese Frontier*, 77–78.

27. Cited in James H. Okahata, ed., *A History of Japanese in Hawaii* (Honolulu: United Japanese Society of Hawaii, 1971), 125–126.

28. Franklin S. Odo and Harry Minoru Urata, "Hole Hole Bushi: Songs of Hawaii's Japanese Immigrants," *Mana* (Hawaii ed.) 6, no. 1 (1981): 72. The epigraph to this chapter is also from this article.

29. Conroy, *Japanese Frontier*, 78–79.

30. Ibid., 76–77.

31. Quoted in Moriyama, *Imingaisha*, 75.

32. U.S. Bureau of Labor Statistics, *Third Report of the Commissioner of Labor on Hawaii, 1905* (Washington, D.C.: Government Printing Office, 1906), 148–153; and Moriyama, *Imingaisha*, 81, 84–87.

33. Moriyama, *Imingaisha*, 126. See also Bureau of Labor Statistics, *Third Report*, 150–152.

34. Quoted in Kazuo Ito, *Issei: A History of Japanese Immigrants in North America*, trans. Shinichiro Nakamura and Jean S. Gerard (Seattle: Japanese Community Service, 1973), 20–21.

35. Moriyama, *Imingaisha*, 127–128; Wakukawa, *History*, 146–159; and Bureau of Labor Statistics, *Third Report*, 153.

36. Odo and Urata, "Hole Hole Bushi."

37. I am grateful to Franklin Odo for sharing with me these unpublished *hole hole bushi*, which will be included in a forthcoming book on *issei* literature.

38. Song composed by Nae Nakasone, published in Ethnic Studies Oral History Project and United Okinawan Association of Hawaii, *Uchinanchu: A History of Okinawans in Hawaii* (Honolulu: Ethnic Studies Program, University of Hawaii at Manoa, 1981), xi.

39. Wray Taylor, "Labor in Hawaii," reprinted in Char, *Sandalwood Mountains*, 82–85.

40. Baishiro Tamashiro, n.d., oral history interview, published in Ethnic Studies Oral History Project, *Uchinanchu*, 360.

41. Under the *hapai ko* contract system, workers were paid by the load. Noriyu Koga remembered being paid 50 cents for filling a train boxcar with cane stalks. Dorothy Ochiai Hazama and Jane Okamoto Komeiji, *Okage Sama De: The Japanese in Hawai'i, 1885–1985* (Honolulu: Bess Press, 1986), 42.

42. Haruno Nunogawa Sato, November 4, 1984, interview, published in Hazama and Komeiji, *Okage Sama De*, 34.

43. See 37.

44. Kame Kakazu, September 1, 1974, oral history interview, in author's possession.

45. Tsuru Yamauchi, n.d., oral history interview, published in Ethnic Studies Oral History Project, *Uchinanchu*, 488.

46. Ibid., 497.

47. Ibid., 495.

48. See note 37.

49. Yamauchi, oral history, 489.

50. Choki Oshiro, untitled autobiography written in 1978, published in Ethnic Studies Oral History Project, *Uchinanchu*, 415.

51. Ito, *Issei*, 21.

52. Ibid., 24.

53. Odo and Urata, "Hole Hole Bushi," 73; and Odo and Sinoto, *Pictorial History*, 76.

54. See, e.g., LeRoi Jones, *Blues People: The Negro Experience in White America and the Music That Developed from It* (New York: Morrow, 1963).

55. Beechert, *Working*, 52–57.

56. Yamauchi, oral history, 494–495.

57. Odo and Urata, "Hole Hole Bushi," 72.

58. Reproduced in Beechert, *Working*, 72; and Takaki, *Pau Hana*, 67.

59. Beechert, *Working*, 112–113. Cases involving runaways rose from 2,099 in 1876 to 5,876 in 1898. Ibid., 48.

60. Ibid., 122.

61. Okahata, *History*, 126–127; and Beechert, *Working*, 115. Okahata explained that the suspects were apprehended only after persistent investigative efforts by Eiji Takumi. See also Karl Yoneda, "A Brief History of U.S. Asian Labor," *Political Affairs*, September 1976, where Goto is referred to as "Katsu Goto, ex-Honokaa sugar worker."

62. Beechert, *Working*, 133.

63. Ibid., 133–134.

64. Cited in Takaki, *Pau Hana*, 141–142.

65. Beechert, *Working*, 132. Cf. Takaki, *Pau Hana*, 141, who estimated that by 1907, 40,000 Japanese had left Hawaii for the West Coast. See also Moriyama, *Imingaisha*, 133.

66. Beechert, *Working*, 132.

67. Bureau of Labor Statistics, *Third Report*, 41–42.

68. Takaki, *Pau Hana*, 140–145; Beechert, *Working*, 132; Moriyama, *Imingaisha*, 132–137; and Curtis Cosmos Aller, Jr., "Evolution of Hawaiian Labor Relations: From Benevolent Paternalism to Mature Collective Bargaining," doctoral dissertation, Harvard University, 1958, 171–174.

69. Bureau of Labor Statistics, *Third Report*, 45.

70. U.S. Bureau of Labor Statistics, *Fourth Report of the Commissioner of Labor on Hawaii, 1910* (Washington, D.C.: Government Printing Office, 1911), 60.

71. John E. Reinecke, *Feigned Necessity: Hawaii's Attempt to Obtain Chinese Contract Labor, 1921–23* (San Francisco: Chinese Materials Center, 1979), 26–27.

72. W. F. Frear to Secretary of the Interior, January 24, 1908, National Archives, Record Group 126, Department of Interior, Hawaii (henceforth RG 126 Interior), Box 603. See also William Loeb, Jr. (President's secretary), to James Rudolph Garfield (Interior Secretary), February 7, 1908; Loeb, Jr., to Garfield, February 10, 1908; Frear to Garfield, February 28, 1908; and Frear to Garfield, August 26, 1908, RG 126 Interior, Box 603; and Frank F. Chuman, *The Bamboo People: The Law and Japanese-Americans* (Del Mar, Calif.: Publisher's Inc., 1976), 33–37.

73. Chuman, *Bamboo*, 35–36.

74. From Japanese consular records, in Okahata, *History*, 111. Cf. Moriyama, *Imingaisha*, 52, 139; and Yamato Ichihashi, *Japanese in the United States: A Critical Study of the Problems of the Japanese Immigrants and Their Children* (Stanford: Stanford University Press, 1932), 27–30.

75. Moriyama, *Imingaisha*, 139; and Adams, *Japanese in Hawaii*, 8–9.

76. Ichihashi, *Japanese*, 31–32; and Adams, *Japanese in Hawaii*, 16–20.

77. Quoted in Moriyama, *Imingaisha*, 140.

78. Quoted in Beechert, *Working*, 138.

79. Mary Dorita Clifford, "The Hawaiian Sugar Planters Association and Filipino Exclusion," in *Letters in Exile: An Introductory Reader on the History of Filipinos in America*, ed. Jesse Quinsaat (Los Angeles: UCLA Asian American Studies Center, 1976), 76–77.

80. Andrew W. Lind, *An Island Community: Ecological Succession in Hawaii* (Chicago: University of Chicago Press, 1938), 233.

81. Ibid., 236.

82. Quoted in ibid., 238–239.

83. Ibid., 214.

84. Herbert Blumer, "Paternalism in Industry," *Social Process in Hawaii* 15 (1951): 26–31; Kiyoshi Ikeda, "Unionization and the Plantation," *Social Process in Hawaii* 15 (1951): 14–25; and Aller, "Evolution of Hawaiian Labor Relations," 182–184.

85. Okahata, *History*, 127.

Chapter 3: With the Force of Wildfire

1. See, e.g., Takaki, *Pau Hana*, 127–145; and Aptheker, *American Negro Slave Revolts*.

2. John E. Reinecke, *Labor Disturbances in Hawaii, 1890–1925: A Summary* (Honolulu: University of Hawaii Industrial Relations Center, 1966).

3. Beechert, *Working*, 162.

4. U.S. Department of Labor, *Report of the Commissioner of Labor on Hawaii, 1901* (Washington, D.C.: Government Printing Office, 1902), 254–257.

5. Ibid., 112–113.

6. Bureau of Labor Statistics, *Third Report*, 136–137.

7. Wakukawa, *History*, 129–132; and Okahata, *History*, 170–171.

8. Quoted in Aller, "Evolution of Hawaiian Labor Relations," 187–188.

9. Beechert, *Working*, 163–166; and Bureau of Labor Statistics, *Third Report*, 137–139.

10. Wakukawa, *History*, 131–132, 134; Beechert, *Working*, 166–167; and Takaki, *Pau Hana*, 150.

11. Bureau of Labor Statistics, *Third Report*, 141.

12. Ibid., 141–142.

13. Okahata, *History*, 171–172.

14. Bureau of Labor Statistics, *Fourth Report*, 63–64.

15. Okahata, *History*, 173–174.

16. Wakukawa, *History*, 170–172; Okahata, *History*, 173–176; and Bureau of Labor Statistics, *Fourth Report*, 63–64.

17. Bureau of Labor Statistics, *Fourth Report*, 64; Wakukawa, *History*, 172; and Okahata, *History*, 174.

18. Quoted in Takaki, *Pau Hana*, 154.

19. Bureau of Labor Statistics, *Fourth Report*, 65–75.

20. Ibid., 74–75.

21. Ibid., 84–86.

22. Okahata, *History*, 175.

23. Beechert, *Working*, 172.

24. Bureau of Labor Statistics, *Fourth Report*, 79–82.

25. Takaki, *Pau Hana*, 154.

26. Okahata, *History*, 176–177; Wakukawa, *History*, 179; and Beechert, *Working*, 172.

27. Wakukawa, *History*, 180–182.

28. Okahata, *History*, 177; and Wakukawa, *History*, 180.

29. Okahata, *History*, 178.

30. Quoted in Takaki, *Pau Hana*, 160.

31. Okahata, *History*, 177. See Beechert, *Working*, 171–172, on the inefficiency of strikebreakers and the planters' preference for the regular workforce.

32. Okahata, *History*, 181.

33. William Henry (High Sheriff, Territory of Hawaii) to C. R. Hemenway (Attorney General, Territory of Hawaii), June 21, 1909, Hawaii State Archives, Official Files of the Governors of Hawaii, Walter Francis Frear, General Files, U.S. Departments, Interior Department.

34. Ibid.

35. Aller, "Evolution of Hawaiian Labor Relations," 193; and Bureau of Labor Statistics, *Fourth Report*, 89–90.

36. Takaki, *Pau Hana*, 163–164.

37. Bureau of Labor Statistics, *Fourth Report*, 87–89.

38. Aller, "Evolution of Hawaiian Labor Relations," 192; and Edward Johannessen, *The Hawaiian Labor Movement: A Brief History* (Boston: Bruce Humphries, 1956), 65.

39. Kotani, *Japanese*, 33; Moriyama, *Imingaisha*, 97; Bureau of Labor Statistics, *Fourth Report*, 23; and Liu, "Cultivating Cane," 198.

40. Quoted in Takaki, *Pau Hana*, 162. See also, Clifford, "Hawaiian Sugar Planters Association," 76–81; Mary Dorita Clifford, "Filipino Immigration to Hawaii," master's thesis, University of Hawaii, 1954; and Bruno Lasker, *Filipino Immigration to Continental United States and to Hawaii* (Chicago: University of Chicago Press, 1931), 28–32, 159–168, 203–211.

41. U.S. Bureau of Labor Statistics, *Labor Conditions in Hawaii* (Washington, D.C.: Government Printing Office, 1916), 18; U.S. Immigration Commission, *Reports of the Immigration Commission* (Washington, D.C.: Government Printing Office, 1911), 1:715; and Okahata, *History*, 185.

42. Bureau of Labor Statistics, *Fourth Report*, 75–78.

43. Cf. previous accounts of the 1909 strike that point to the involvement of only the Japanese as a defect and cause of the strike's failure, paralleling the planters' charge of "blood unionism." Alan Moriyama, "The 1909 and 1920 Strikes of Japanese Sugar Plantation Workers in Hawaii," in *Counterpoint: Perspectives on Asian America*, ed. Emma Gee (Los Angeles: Asian American Studies Center, UCLA, 1976), 172–173; and Takaki, *Pau Hana*, 164.

44. Takaki, *Pau Hana*, 162.

45. Ibid., 164. See, Liu, "Cultivating Cane," 195–203, for a critique of the "blood unionism" charge.

46. Walter Frear to Secretary of the Interior, November 14, 1911, Files of the Governors, Frear, General Files.

47. Kent, *Hawaii*, 35.

48. Daws, *Shoal*, 251–252.

49. Lind, *Hawaii's People*, 28; and Daws, *Shoal*, 285.

50. Kent, *Hawaii*, 60–61.

51. See, e.g., Castles and Kosack, *Immigrant Workers*; Cheng and Bonacich, *Labor Immigration*; and Gary Y. Okihiro, "Migrant Labor and the 'Poverty' of Asian American Studies," *Amerasia Journal* 14, no. 1 (1988): 129–136.

52. Odo, manuscript.

53. Theo. H. Davies & Co. to C. McLennan, June 2, 1890, reproduced in Hazama and Komeiji, *Okage Sama De*, 24. See also Ronald Takaki, *Strangers from a Different Shore: A History of Asian Americans* (Boston: Little, Brown, 1989), 24–25.

54. Beechert, *Working*, 93–95.

55. Takaki, *Pau Hana*, 28; Lind, *Hawaii's People*, 75; and Moriyama, *Imingaisha*, 97.

56. Beechert, *Working*, 109. See also Bureau of Labor Statistics, *Fourth Report*,

24–25, on the drop in wages between 1902 and 1905 "principally because labor became more plentiful with the great influx of Japanese."

Chapter 4: Cane Fires

1. Beechert, *Working*, 196.
2. Okahata, *History*, 186–187.
3. Ibid., 168–169.
4. Ibid., 166–167.
5. Odo and Sinoto, *Pictorial History*, 208–209.
6. Wakukawa, *History*, 231–232.
7. Ibid., 232–235.
8. Ibid., 235.
9. Reinecke, *Labor Disturbances*, 15.
10. Takaki, *Pau Hana*, 165. See also Wakukawa, *History*, 236; and Beechert, *Working*, 197–198.
11. Okahata, *History*, 187. See also Yayoi Kurita, "Labor Movements among the Japanese Plantation Workers in Hawaii," n.d., seminar paper, University of Hawaii, Hamilton Library, Special Collections, 22–23; and Takaki, *Pau Hana*, 165.
12. Beechert, *Working*, 197.
13. Ibid.
14. Ibid., 199. In early December 1919, newspapers reported a membership of 24,000 in the federation. These included 8,000 on the island of Hawaii, 6,000 on Oahu, 6,000 on Maui, and 4,000 on Kauai. Richard Alan Liebes, "Labor Organization in Hawaii: A Study of the Efforts of Labor to Obtain Security through Organization," master's thesis, University of Hawaii, 1938, 33.
15. Wakukawa, *History*, 240–242.
16. Ibid., 242–244.
17. Ibid., 244.
18. Ibid., 244–245. See also Okahata, *History*, 189.
19. Beechert, *Working*, 201.
20. Ibid., 201–202.
21. Ibid., 202.
22. Hawaii Laborers' Association, "Facts About the Strike on Sugar Plantations in Hawaii," Honolulu, July 1920, pamphlet reprinted in U.S. Congress, House, *Labor Problems in Hawaii: Hearings Before the Committee on Immigration and Naturalization*, 67th Cong., 1st sess., 1921, 833.
23. Beechert, *Working*, 202.
24. U.S. Congress, House, *Labor Problems: Hearings*, 833–834. See also Wakukawa, *History*, 246–247.
25. Takaki, *Pau Hana*, 166.

26. Takashi Tsutsumi, "History of Hawaii Laborers' Movement," trans. Umetaro Okumura, University of Hawaii, Hamilton Library, 234.

27. Beechert, *Working*, 203; Takaki, *Pau Hana*, 170; Wakukawa, *History*, 249–250; Moriyama, "1909 and 1920 Strikes," 175; and Fuchs, *Hawaii Pono*, 217–218.

28. Quoted in Moriyama, "1909 and 1920 Strikes," 175; Beechert, *Working*, 203; and Takaki, *Pau Hana*, 170.

29. Cited in Johannessen, *Hawaiian Labor Movement*, 69.

30. Moriyama, "1909 and 1920 Strikes," 175. According to Moriyama, Portuguese and Hawaiians were paid $4 a day, and Chinese and Koreans $3 per day. Cf. Beechert, *Working*, 204–205.

31. John E. Reinecke, "The Big Lie of 1920," University of Hawaii, Hamilton Library, Special Collections, chap. 21, p. 3. See also Wakukawa, *History*, 251–252.

32. Reinecke, "Big Lie," chap. 22, p. 1. See also U.S. Congress, House, *Labor Problems: Hearings*, 834–835; and Okahata, *History*, 190.

33. Reinecke, "Big Lie," chap. 21, p. 1.

34. Ibid., chap. 22, pp. 2–3. See also Moriyama, "1909 and 1920 Strikes," 180 n. 62, for a discussion on the range of figures on the numbers who died from the epidemic.

35. U.S. Congress, House, *Labor Problems: Hearings*, 835.

36. Beechert, *Working*, 206.

37. U.S. Congress, House, *Labor Problems: Hearings*, 839; and Wakukawa, *History*, 255–256.

38. Beechert, *Working*, 206; and Henry Pelling, *American Labor* (Chicago: University of Chicago Press, 1960), 141.

39. U.S. Congress, House, *Labor Problems: Hearings*, 839; and Wakukawa, *History*, 257.

40. Fuchs, *Hawaii Pono*, 222–223; and Reinecke, *Feigned Necessity*, 122–124.

41. Okahata, *History*, 191.

42. Ibid., 192; and Reinecke, "Big Lie," chap. 25, p. 3.

43. Reinecke, "Big Lie," chap. 25, pp. 3–4.

44. *Nippu Jiji*, April 21, 1920.

45. U.S. Congress, House, *Labor Problems: Hearings*, 840; and Fuchs, *Hawaii Pono*, 223.

46. "Minutes of a Meeting of a Certain Group of Japanese Laborers Called by Mr. Isobe to Meet with Mr. John Waterhouse, President of the H.S.P.A.," Hawaii State Archives, Official Files of the Governors of Hawaii, Charles James McCarthy, Miscellaneous File, Strike Data, 1920.

47. U.S. Congress, House, *Labor Problems: Hearings*, 840–841.

48. Beechert, *Working*, 208. Cf. Okahata, *History*, 193; and Moriyama, "1909 and 1920 Strikes," 176.

49. U.S. Congress, House, *Labor Problems: Hearings*, 841.

50. Quoted in Fuchs, *Hawaii Pono*, 224.

51. Lt. Col. George M. Brooke to Director, Military Intelligence, General Staff, December 12, 1919, Files of the Governors, McCarthy, General Files, U.S. Departments, Army (Hawaiian Department), Confidential Letters.

52. Fuchs, *Hawaii Pono*, 220. Political pressure on Iaukea to exercise the military solution was particularly intense following the cane fires set on McBryde plantation on the island of Kauai, February 14 to 15, 1920. Reinecke, *Feigned Necessity*, 113 n. 63.

53. Beechert, *Working*, 205.

54. Tsutsumi, "History," 3.

55. Ibid., preface.

56. *Pacific Commercial Advertiser*, February 6, 1920.

57. See Kurita, "Labor Movements," 37–59; Takaki, *Pau Hana*, 172; and Fuchs, *Hawaii Pono*, 216–217.

58. As quoted in Wakukawa, *History*, 248–249.

59. Quoted in Fuchs, *Hawaii Pono*, 220.

60. Curtis P. Iaukea to H. H. Miyazawa, February 26, 1920, Files of the Governors, McCarthy, Miscellaneous File, Strike Data, 1920.

61. *Pacific Commercial Advertiser*, January 27, 1920.

62. Takaki, *Pau Hana*, 174; and Aller, "Evolution of Hawaiian Labor Relations," 198.

63. Beechert, *Working*, 193, 195.

Chapter 5: In the National Defense

1. Liebes, "Labor Organization," 38; and Reinecke, *Feigned Necessity*, 165–168.

2. Hawaii Emergency Labor Commission to The President, May 19, 1921, National Archives, Record Group 174, General Records of the Department of Labor (henceforth RG 174 Labor Department), File No. 165/342, 1–2.

3. Quoted in Reinecke, *Feigned Necessity*, 163.

4. Ibid., 183.

5. Walter F. Dillingham to C. J. McCarthy, June 13, 1921, Files of the Governors, McCarthy, General Files, Territorial Departments, Labor Commission, Hawaii Emergency. For the brief given to Harding, see Hawaiian Emergency Labor Commission to the President, May 19, 1921, RG 174 Labor Department, File No. 165/342.

6. U.S. Congress, House, *Labor Problems: Hearings*, 215.

7. Ibid., 231.

8. Ibid., 228–229.

9. Reinecke, *Feigned Necessity*, 184, 187.

10. Ibid., 188.

11. "Hawaii and the Japanese," Hawaii State Archives, Official Files of the Governors of Hawaii, Wallace Rider Farrington, General Files, Territorial Departments, Labor Commission, Hawaii Emergency. See also Reinecke, *Feigned Necessity*, 187–191.

12. Reference to Tsutsumi's (secretary, Federation of Japanese Labor) oft-quoted remark to workers at Ewa plantation during the 1920 strike: "Don't worry. A Japanese cruiser is coming to take you home. Why deny that the Japanese Government is back of the labor question? Don't deny it. It will surely scare the Americans." See Reinecke, "Big Lie," chap. 17, pp. 1–3.

13. Hawaii's Governor Charles J. McCarthy had made this same point earlier about the threat of *nisei* control of the ballot, in testimony before the Senate Committee on Immigration in 1920. See U.S. Congress, Senate, *Japanese in Hawaii: Hearings Before the Committee on Immigration*, 66th Cong., 2nd sess., 1920, 19.

14. Quoted in Reinecke, *Feigned Necessity*, 213.

15. U.S. Congress, House, *Labor Problems: Hearings*, 317.

16. Ibid., 316.

17. Minutes of a Meeting of the Hawaii Emergency Labor Commission, September 29, 1921, Files of the Governors, Farrington, General Files, Territorial Departments, Labor Commission, Hawaii Emergency.

18. Ibid.

19. Reinecke, *Feigned Necessity*, 339–344. For a list of organizations in Hawaii endorsing the commission's resolution, see ibid., Appendix 8.

20. Walter F. Dillingham to Wallace R. Farrington, August 23, 1921, Files of the Governors, Farrington, General Files, Territorial Departments, Labor Commission, Hawaii Emergency.

21. Quoted in Reinecke, *Feigned Necessity*, 344–345 n. 25.

22. *San Jose Mercury*, August 29, 1919.

23. Reinecke, *Feigned Necessity*, 370–371 n. 86.

24. Ibid., 368–370.

25. Ibid., 178.

26. Ibid., 259–263, 281.

27. See, e.g., Wakukawa, *History*, 262–263.

28. Reinecke, *Feigned Necessity*, 182.

29. Ibid., 260.

30. Johnson's remark is quoted in ibid., 421; De Witt's version, in testimony before the House Naval Affairs Committee meeting in San Francisco, was carried by Associated Press dispatches on April 13, 1943, and published in West Coast papers the following day.

31. Reinecke, *Feigned Necessity*, 435.

32. Ibid., 437.

33. Wire, Retlaw to Farrington, June 19, 1922, Files of the Governors, Farrington, General Files, Territorial Departments, Labor Commission, Hawaii Emergency, April to June 1922.

34. Wallace Rider Farrington to The President, June 21, 1922, Files of the Governors, Farrington, General Files, Territorial Departments, Labor Commission, Hawaii Emergency, April to June 1922.

35. Reinecke, *Feigned Necessity*, 453–454.

36. "Report of the Hawaiian Labor Commission, 1923, Synopsis of Findings and Recommendations," RG 174 Labor Department, File No. 16/125, pt. II, sec. VII, exhibit B.

37. Reinecke, *Feigned Necessity*, 454–455.

38. "Report of Hawaiian Labor Commission," pt. I.

39. Reinecke, *Feigned Necessity*, 458–459.

40. Ibid., 462.

41. "Report of Hawaiian Labor Commission," pt. I, p. 2.

42. Ibid., p. 4.

43. Ibid., pt. II, sec. VII, p. 3.

44. Ibid., pp. 3–4.

45. Ibid., pt. I, pp. 3–4.

46. Ibid., pt. II, sec. VII, p. 5.

47. Ibid., pp. 4–5.

48. Ibid., p. 6.

49. Ibid., p. 2.

50. Reinecke, *Feigned Necessity*, 464.

51. Charles E. Hughes to James J. Davis, February 6, 1923, "Report of Hawaiian Labor Commission," section titled "Correspondence between Secretary of State and Secretary of Labor."

52. Reinecke, *Feigned Necessity*, 467.

53. Ibid., 482.

54. Ibid., 483.

55. Quoted in ibid., 494.

56. Beechert, *Working*, 211.

57. Liebes, "Labor Organization," Appendix D; and Beechert, *Working*, 214–215.

58. Liebes, "Labor Organization," Appendix D; and Beechert, *Working*, 215.

59. Ibid.

60. Beechert, *Working*, 215.

61. Liebes, "Labor Organization," Appendix D.

62. Ibid., 81–82.

63. Tsutsumi, "History," 315, 316. See also Federation of Japanese Labor in Hawaii, *The Voice of Labor in Hawaii* (pamphlet, Microfilm no. 290, Hamilton

Library, University of Hawaii, Honolulu, 1920).

64. U.S. Congress, House, *Labor Problems in Hawaii: Report of the Committee on Immigration and Naturalization*, 67th Cong., 4th sess., 1923, 9.

Chapter 6: Race War

1. National Archives, Record Group 165, War Department, General Staff, Military Intelligence Division (henceforth RG 165 MID), File No. 9679-91.

2. Col. Stephen O. Fuqua (Assistant Chief of Staff, G-2, Hawaiian Department) to Major Kingman (War Plans Division, General Staff), July 5, 1922, RG 165 MID, File No. 9679-79/2.

3. [Unsigned], "The Increase of Japanese Population in the Hawaiian Islands and What It Means," May 6, 1918, RG 165 MID, File No. 10520-22/1. See also Col. H. C. Merriam (Intelligence Officer, Hawaiian Department) to Director, MID (General Staff), September 6, 1918, RG 165 MID, File No. 1766-782.

4. Aid for Information (U.S. Naval Station, Honolulu) to Director of Naval Intelligence (Washington, D.C.), June 20, 1918, RG 165 MID, File No. 10520-22/5.

5. Office of Naval Intelligence (Washington, D.C.) to State Department, Operations, and Military Intelligence Division, August 14, 1918, RG 165 MID, File No. 1052-37/1.

6. Office of Naval Intelligence (Washington, D.C.) to State Department, Operations, and Military Intelligence Division, September 26, 1918, RG 165 MID, File No. 10520-22/6. See also H. C. Merriam to Director, Military Intelligence (General Staff), September 5, 1918, RG 165 MID, File No. 9605-50/1.

7. Capt. Philip E. Spalding (Assistant Military Censor, Honolulu Postal Censorship Station), "Japanese in Hawaii," n.d., RG 165 MID, File No. 1766-927/1.

8. Office of Naval Intelligence (Washington, D.C.) to State Department, Military Intelligence Division, Labor Department, and Interior Department, n.d., RG 165 MID, File No. 1766-957/2.

9. C. J. McCarthy to Secretary of Interior, January 31, 1921, Files of the Governors, McCarthy, General Files, U.S. Departments, Interior Department, Re. Japanese Language Schools.

10. A. A. Hopkins, "Confidential Survey: Territory of Hawaii, Japanese Activities," January 31, 1921, RG 165 MID, File No. 1766-S-97/1.

11. Ibid.

12. Ibid.

13. Ibid.

14. Ibid.; and Beechert, *Working*, 213.

15. George M. Brooke (Intelligence Director, Hawaiian Department), to Military Intelligence, General Staff, November 22, 1919, RG 165 MID, File No. 1766-S-

28/1; and George M. Brooke to Military Intelligence, General Staff, November 24, 1919, RG 165 MID, File No. 1766-S-29/1.

16. George M. Brooke (Assistant Chief of Staff, G-2, Hawaiian Department), to Director, Military Intelligence, General Staff, April 7, 1920, RG 165 MID, File No. 165/1766-S-72.

17. George M. Brooke, "Estimate of the Japanese Situation as It Affects the Territory of Hawaii, From the Military Point of View," October 11, 1920, RG 165 MID, File No. 1766-S-87; also Assistant Chief of Staff, G-2 (Hawaiian Department), "Situation Survey for Week Ending March 20, 1920," RG 165 MID, File No. 255-I-1/28.

18. Brooke, "Estimate of Japanese Situation."

19. Ibid. See also George M. Brooke, "Summary of Important Racial, National and Political Movements in the Territory of Hawaii," February 12, 1921, RG 165 MID, File No. 255-I-16.

20. Capt. S. A. Wood, Jr. (Acting Assistant Chief of Staff for Military Intelligence, Hawaiian Department), to Director, Military Intelligence Division, General Staff, July 29, 1921, RG 165 MID, File No. 1766-S-111/4.

21. S. A. Wood, Jr., "The Japanese Situation in Hawaii," July 27, 1921, RG 165 MID, File No. 1766-S-111/3.

22. Ibid.

23. Ibid.

24. Ibid.

25. J. E. Hoover (Special Assistant to Attorney General), to Brig. General C. E. Nolan (Director, MID, War Department), October 19, 1920, RG 165 MID, File No. 10405-28.

26. Hopkins, "Confidential Survey." The Eighth Division was a Bureau of Investigation service region headquartered in Los Angeles and covering California, Nevada, and Utah. The Ninth Corps Area was an army service region headquartered in San Francisco.

27. Hopkins, "Confidential Survey."

28. Ibid.

29. Director, MID to Assistant Chief of Staff, MID, Ninth Corps Area, November 4, 1920, RG 165 MID, File No. 1766-Z-189/5. For an example of interagency cooperation, see RG 165 MID, File No. 2327-H-23/2–9.

30. "Japanese Situation," RG 165 MID, File Nos. 1766-S-115/1–8. See also "Resume Report on General Intelligence Activities, Eighth Division," National Archives, Investigative Files of the Bureau of Investigation, File B.S. 202600-5, Reels 46–47. During the 1920s, the bureau maintained these "Resume Reports" on division activities. In these, Japanese were simply one of a number of groups being watched, including labor organizations, blacks, and radicals. The "Japanese Situation" reports thus marked a clear departure for the bureau in raising the "Japanese problem" to that level of prominence.

31. Ralph H. Colvin, "Japanese Situation" (for week ending August 27, 1921), RG 165 MID, File No. 1766-S-115/3.

32. Ralph H. Colvin and Frank M. Sturgis, "Japanese Situation" (for week ending September 24, 1921), RG 165 MID, File No. 1766-S-115/5. See also Yuji Ichioka, "'Attorney for the Defense': Yamato Ichihashi and Japanese Immigration," *Pacific Historical Review* 55, no. 2 (1986): 192–225.

33. Ralph H. Colvin and Frank M. Sturgis, "Japanese Situation" (for week ending October 8, 1921), RG 165 MID, File No. 1766-S-115/6.

34. See, e.g., Roger Daniels, *The Politics of Prejudice* (New York: Atheneum, 1970); and John J. Stephan, *Hawaii under the Rising Sun: Japan's Plans for Conquest After Pearl Harbor* (Honolulu: University of Hawaii Press, 1984), 55–59.

35. "Resume Report," Bureau of Investigation, File B.S. 202600-5, Reel 47.

36. That fear of a Japanese–black alliance continued through 1941. See Bob Kumamoto, "The Search for Spies: American Counterintelligence and the Japanese American Community, 1931–1942," *Amerasia Journal* 6, no. 2 (Fall 1979): 54–55; and "Japanese Intelligence and Propaganda in the United States During 1941," December 4, 1941, National Archives, Record Group 38, Chief of Naval Operations, Office of Naval Intelligence (henceforth RG 38 ONI), Security Classified Administrative Correspondence, 1942–1946, Box 222, A8-5EF 37/EG.

37. See, e.g., A. A. Hopkins, "Japanese Situation," RG 165 MID, File Nos. 1766-Z-417/1 to 1766-Z-417/15.

38. A. A. Hopkins, "Japanese Situation" (for week ending March 18, 1922), RG 165 MID, File No. 1766-Z-417/7. An identification of individual Japanese by the intelligence community that predates Hopkins's list can be found in the "Weekly Report of Japanese Activities," March 21, 1921, emanating from the Commandant, 12th Naval District. These San Francisco Japanese community leaders, identified as being "pro-Japanese," included the Japanese consul, an officer of the Japanese Association, and five businessmen. RG 165 MID, File No. 1766-Z-289/4; and RG 165 MID, File No. 1766-Z-289/2. An early listing of Buddhist churches in California, complete with their addresses, was compiled by MID in 1921. See F. D. Griffith, Jr. (Assistant Chief of Staff, Military Intelligence) to Director, MID, General Staff, January 24, 1921, RG 165 MID, File No. 1766-Z-255.

39. Maj. John J. Kingman (General Staff, War Department) to Assistant Chief of Staff, G-2, War Department, July 24, 1922, RG 165 MID, File No. 9679-79/2.

40. Fuqua to Kingman, July 5, 1922, RG 165 MID, File No. 9679-79/2.

41. Ibid.

42. "Summary of Data on Factors Bearing on the Japanese Situation in Relation to Our Military Problem," RG 165 MID, 1917–1941, File No. 1766-S-131 (henceforth Summerall Report), 42.

43. Ibid., 4–10.

44. Ibid., 12–13.

45. Ibid., 14.
46. Ibid., 16.
47. Ibid., 17.
48. Ibid., 24–25.
49. Ibid., 27. Republican Wise had been backed by the planters and the press. Reinecke, *Feigned Necessity*, 441.
50. Summerall Report, 27.
51. Ibid., 28.
52. Ibid.
53. Ibid., 29.
54. Ibid., 31.
55. Ibid., 32.
56. Ibid., 46.
57. Ibid., 37.
58. Ibid., 40–42.
59. Ibid., 41–42.
60. Ibid., 47. The report made a clear distinction between assimilation and Americanization. The former meant complete absorption (with a presumption of loyalty), while the latter simply referred to culture or learned behavior (without, necessarily, a presumption of loyalty).
61. Assistant Chief of Staff for Military Intelligence (Hawaiian Department), "A Survey of the Hawaiian-born Japanese in the Territory of Hawaii," June 1, 1926, RG 165 MID, File No. 1766-S-132/3. See also various studies titled "Strategic Estimate of the Situation: Hawaiian Islands," filed on January 1, 1926, 1927, 1928, and 1930 by the head of the department's G-2. RG 165 MID, File Nos. 255-I-82/5, 255-I-82/2, 255-I-82/6, and 255-I-82/3.
62. Assistant Chief of Staff for Military Intelligence (Hawaiian Department), "A Survey of the Japanese in the Territory of Hawaii," October 1929, RG 165 MID, File No. 9605-97/2. For interim reports on selected subjects, see Maj. T. K. P. Stilwell (Assistant Chief of Staff, G-2, Hawaiian Department) to Assistant Chief of Staff, G-2, War Department, October 21, 1927 and December 30, 1927, RG 165 MID, File No. 2657-Z-19; and RG 165 MID, File Nos. 2277-Z-1/2 to 2277-Z-1/4.
63. See also Fuqua to Kingman, July 5, 1922, RG 165 MID, File No. 9679-79/2. Fuqua called Umetaro Okumura "a reliable Japanese agent" who provided G-2 with information on the Americanization movement. In fact, Okumura had served as an informant for ONI since at least 1918. Office of Naval Intelligence (Washington, D.C.) to State Department, Naval Operations, and MID, August 14, 1918, RG 165 MID, File No. 1052-37/1.
64. Maurice Matloff and Edwin M. Snell, *Strategic Planning For Coalition Warfare, 1941–1942* (Washington, D.C.: Government Printing Office, 1953), 1.
65. "Project For the Defense of Oahu," (revised to January 1, 1923), National

Archives, Record Group 165, War Department, General Staff, War Plans Division, Numerical File, 1920-42 (henceforth RG 165 WPD), File No. 986/10.

66. Col. J. L. De Witt (Acting Assistant Chief of Staff, WPD) to Judge Advocate General, May 21, 1923, RG 165 WPD, File No. 986/14.

67. W. A. Bethel (Judge Advocate General) to Acting Assistant Chief of Staff, WPD, General Staff, June 28, 1923, RG 165 WPD, File No. 986/14. Reference to General Andrew Jackson's defense of New Orleans against the British in 1814–1815 when he declared martial law in the city.

68. Memorandum, Brig. Gen. B. H. Wells (Assistant Chief of Staff, WPD), July 20, 1923, RG 165 WPD, File No. 986/14; and Memorandum for Adjutant General, "Subject: Project for the Defense of Oahu—Editions of 1921 and 1923," RG 165 WPD, File No. 986/14.

69. Maj. Gen. E. M. Lewis (Commander, Hawaiian Department) to Adjutant General (War Department), May 13, 1925, RG 165 WPD, File No. 1031-11.

70. Brig. Gen. LeRoy Eltinge (Assistant Chief of Staff, WPD) to Chief of Staff, February 3, 1925, RG 165 WPD, File No. 1901.

71. "Resume Report," Bureau of Investigation, File B.S. 202600-5, Reel 47.

72. Ibid.

Chapter 7: Extinguishing the Dawn

1. Lind, *Hawaii's People*, 28.

2. Louise H. Hunter, *Buddhism in Hawaii: Its Impact on a Yankee Community* (Honolulu: University of Hawaii Press, 1971), 121–122. Shiro Sokabe was a leading Japanese Christian minister on the islands of Hawaii and Maui and, along with Takie Okumura, was a major proponent of the Americanization movement. See Reinecke, *Feigned Necessity*, 118–119 n. 76; and Jiro Nakano, *Samurai Missionary: The Reverend Shiro Sokabe* (Honolulu: Hawaii Conference of the United Church of Christ, 1984).

3. *Honolulu Star-Bulletin*, January 24, 1920; and *Pacific Commercial Advertiser*, February 5, 1920, and March 1, 1920.

4. U.S. Department of the Interior, Bureau of Education, *A Survey of Education in Hawaii*, Bulletin no. 16 (Washington, D.C.: Government Printing Office, 1920), 111.

5. Hunter, *Buddhism*, 129.

6. Takie Okumura and Umetaro Okumura, *Hawaii's American–Japanese Problem* (Honolulu: n.p., 1923), 5–12; and Takie Okumura, *Seventy Years of Divine Blessings* (Honolulu: n.p., 1939), 130.

7. Okumura and Okumura, *Hawaii's Problem*, 10.

8. Okumura, *Seventy Years*, 128–129.

9. Ibid., 130.

10. Okumura and Okumura, *Hawaii's Problem*, 13–14.

11. Ibid., 19.

12. Ibid.

13. Ibid., 22–23. See also Nakano, *Samurai*, 92–93.

14. Hunter, *Buddhism*, 149. According to army intelligence, the Okumuras had the financial support of "missionary and Christian business elements" in Hawaii. Fuqua to Kingman, July 5, 1922, RG 165 MID, File No. 9679-79/2.

15. Okumura, *Seventy Years*, 133; and Hunter, *Buddhism*, 138.

16. Quoted in Hunter, *Buddhism*, 159.

17. Vaughan MacCaughey, "Some Outstanding Educational Problems," *Paradise of the Pacific* 32 (July 1919): 29.

18. Department of Interior, *Survey of Education*, 9.

19. Ibid., 44.

20. Ibid., 113.

21. Ibid., 121.

22. Ibid., 134.

23. Ibid., 134–137.

24. Ibid., 139–142.

25. Quoted in *Advertiser*, November 25, 1919. See also John N. Hawkins, "Politics, Education, and Language Policy: The Case of Japanese Language Schools in Hawaii," *Amerasia Journal* 5, no. 1 (1978): 39–56.

26. Quoted in *Advertiser*, November 10, 1919.

27. Okahata, *History*, 217–220; and Wakukawa, *History*, 276–279.

28. Wakukawa, *History*, 279–281; and Daniel Erwin Weinberg, "The Movement to 'Americanize' the Japanese Community in Hawaii: An Analysis of One Hundred Percent Americanization Activity in the Territory of Hawaii as Expressed in the Caucasian Press, 1919–1923," master's thesis, University of Hawaii, 1967, 115–117, Appendix B.

29. Weinberg, "Movement," 116–117.

30. Wakukawa, *History*, 281–283; and Okahata, *History*, 221. Also see *A Brief Survey of the Foreign Language School Question* (Honolulu: Japanese Educational Association of Hawaii, 1923).

31. Milton M. Gordon, *Assimilation in American Life: The Role of Race, Religion, and National Origins* (New York: Oxford University Press, 1964).

32. William Carlson Smith, *Americans in Process: A Study of Our Citizens of Oriental Ancestry* (Ann Arbor, Mich.: Edwards Brothers, 1937), 62. See also Isaac B. Berkson, *Theories of Americanization: A Critical Study With Special Reference to the Jewish Group* (New York: Columbia University, 1920).

33. Department of Interior, *Survey of Education*, 4.

34. Ibid., 35.

35. Ibid.

36. Ibid., 32.

37. Quoted in Ralph Kant Stueber, "Hawaii: A Case Study in Development Education 1778–1960," doctoral dissertation, University of Wisconsin, 1964, 243.

38. Ibid., 249. See also Fuchs, *Hawaii Pono*, 276–279; and Amy Agbayani and David Takeuchi, "English Standard Schools: A Policy Analysis," in *Issues in Asian and Pacific American Education*, ed. Nobuya Tsuchida (Minneapolis: Asian/Pacific American Learning Resource Center, 1986), 36–38. Admission to the standard schools was based on a subjective assessment by an evaluator of the applicant's speech patterns in conversation; even after passing the examination, only a select number were permitted entrance. According to Agbayani and Takeuchi, the selection procedures and small number of schools created a "closed system" from which Filipinos and Japanese were "systematically excluded."

39. Stueber, "Hawaii," 250. See also Agbayani and Takeuchi, "English Standard Schools," 30–47.

40. Stueber, "Hawaii," 255.

41. Quoted in Fuchs, *Hawaii Pono*, 263.

42. Vaughan MacCaughey, "The Public Schools of Hawaii: 1919," *Hawaii Educational Review* 8, no. 1 (1919): 8. See also Fuchs, *Hawaii Pono*, 281, 291–294.

43. Department of Interior, *Survey of Education*, 4.

44. Fuchs, *Hawaii Pono*, 269–270. See also *Americanization Institute Papers* (Honolulu: Citizenship Education Committee, 1919).

45. Fuchs, *Hawaii Pono*, 280. See also Stueber, "Hawaii," 286–290.

46. Stueber, "Hawaii," 202. See also Fuchs, *Hawaii Pono*, 295–297.

47. Jisoo Sanjume, "An Analysis of the New Americans Conference from 1927 to 1938," master's thesis, University of Hawaii, 1939, 15.

48. Okumura, *Seventy Years*, 152–153. For an interpretive history of the New Americans Conference, see Gail M. Nomura, "The Debate Over the Role of Nisei in Prewar Hawaii: The New Americans Conference, 1927–1941," *Journal of Ethnic Studies* 15, no. 1 (Spring 1987): 95–115.

49. Sanjume, "Analysis," 17.

50. Ibid., 27, 34.

51. First Annual Conference of New Americans, *Proceedings*, August 1–6, 1927, 1–2.

52. Sixth Annual Conference of New Americans, *Proceedings*, July 21–27, 1932, 7–10.

53. New Americans (1927), *Proceedings*, 6–7.

54. Ibid., 11.

55. Fourth Annual Conference of New Americans, *Proceedings*, July 30–August 5, 1930, 30.

56. Second Annual Conference of New Americans, *Proceedings*, August 1–7, 1928, 22.

57. Fifth Annual Conference of New Americans, *Proceedings*, July 13–18, 1931, 8–10.

58. New Americans (1932), *Proceedings*, 31–33.

59. New Americans (1927), *Proceedings*, 27.

60. Tenth Annual New Americans Conference, *Proceedings*, July 13–18, 1936, 58. See also Seventh Annual New Americans Conference, *Proceedings*, June 19–24, 1933, 32–34.

61. Third Annual Conference of New Americans, *Proceedings*, July 29–August 3, 1929, 5–6.

62. New Americans (1932), *Proceedings*, 3–4.

63. Eighth Annual New Americans Conference, *Proceedings*, June 18–23, 1934, 8–9.

64. New Americans (1928), *Proceedings*, 2.

65. New Americans (1930), *Proceedings*, 17–18.

66. New Americans (1933), *Proceedings*, 8–9.

67. Thirteenth New Americans Conference, *Proceedings*, July 17–23, 1939, 9–12. See also New Americans (1939), *Proceedings*, 49–51.

68. Fourteenth New Americans Conference, *Proceedings*, July 15–21, 1940, 17–18.

69. Fifteenth New Americans Conference, *Proceedings*, July 15–21, 1941, 10–13.

70. New Americans (1930), *Proceedings*, 19.

71. New Americans (1940), *Proceedings*, 19. See also New Americans (1941), *Proceedings*, 13.

72. New Americans (1934), *Proceedings*, 43. Cf. the 1940 Japanese American Citizens League creed, quoted in Daniels, *Concentration Camps*, 24–25.

73. Ninth Annual New Americans Conference, *Proceedings*, July 15–20, 1935, 46.

74. Hunter, *Buddhism*, 162–163. Cf. Buddhist adaptations on the mainland and the debate on the extent and meaning of these changes in Robert Spencer, "Japanese Buddhism in the United States, 1940–1946: A Study in Acculturation," doctoral dissertation, University of California, Berkeley, 1946; Isao Horinouchi, "Americanized Buddhism: A Sociological Analysis of a Protestantized Japanese Religion," doctoral dissertation, University of California, Davis, 1973; and Tetsuden Kashima, *Buddhism in America: The Social Organization of an Ethnic Religious Institution* (Westport, Conn.: Greenwood Press, 1977).

75. Quoted in Hunter, *Buddhism*, 131. See also Okahata, *History*, 230.

76. Hunter, *Buddhism*, 167.

77. Ibid., 166.

78. Ibid., 172, 178.

79. Okahata, *History*, 230. See also Hunter, *Buddhism*, 172. For a similar analy-

sis of Buddhism on the mainland, see Shigeo H. Kanda, "Recovering Cultural Symbols: A Case for Buddhism in the Japanese American Communities," *Journal of the American Academy of Religion* 44, no. 4 (December 1978): 445–475.

80. Quoted in Wakukawa, *History*, 286–287. A group of Japanese community leaders, under the direction of Consul General Keiichi Yamasaki, bowed to the pressure being applied by the governor and adopted a resolution declaring their loyalty and, in effect, blaming themselves for anti-Japanese hostility. The text and signatories of the resolution can be found in ibid., 288.

81. Ibid., 289–290.

82. Okahata, *History*, 222; Wakukawa, *History*, 290–294; and Weinberg, "Movement," 117–120.

83. Quoted in Wakukawa, *History*, 296–298; Okahata, *History*, 223; and Stueber, "Hawaii," 272.

84. Wakukawa, *History*, 298–300.

85. Okahata, *History*, 224.

86. Hunter, *Buddhism*, 168; and Koichi Glenn Harada, "A Survey of the Japanese Language Schools in Hawaii," master's thesis, University of Hawaii, 1934, 56.

87. Harada, "Survey," 57.

88. Hunter, *Buddhism*, 169; and Harada, "Survey," 119.

89. Hunter, *Buddhism*, 169. See also Harada, "Survey," 58.

90. Okahata, *History*, 225; Harada, "Survey," 53; and Stueber, "Hawaii," 276.

91. Cited in Fuchs, *Hawaii Pono*, 288–289.

92. Adams, *Japanese in Hawaii*, 23.

93. Romanzo Adams and Dan Kane-Zo Kai, *The Education of the Boys of Hawaii and Their Economic Outlook*, Research Publications no. 4 (Honolulu: University of Hawaii, 1928), 30, 46. See also, J. M. Lydgate, "Hawaii's Labor Problems," *Hawaii Educational Review* 8, no. 2 (1919): 15–18.

94. Fuchs, *Hawaii Pono*, 287.

95. Stueber, "Hawaii," 290.

96. Fuchs, *Hawaii Pono*, 292. See also Beechert, *Working*, 241–244.

97. Stueber, "Hawaii," 303–304.

98. Midkiff, "Economic Determinants," 233.

99. Ibid., 334.

100. Ibid., 336.

101. Fuchs, *Hawaii Pono*, 296; and Stueber, "Hawaii," 298.

102. Midkiff, "Economic Determinants," 261.

103. U.S. Congress, Senate, *Japanese in Hawaii: Hearings*, 40.

104. Okumura and Okumura, *Hawaii's Problem*, 11.

105. New Americans (1936), *Proceedings*, 48–53.

106. Lind, *Hawaii's People*, 75.

107. Cited in Okahata, *History*, 249.

108. Beechert, *Working*, 253.

109. The nature of plantation work also changed, accounting for the increase in women's employment. Beechert, *Working*, 254.

110. Okahata, *History*, 247–250.

111. Department of Interior, *Survey of Education*, 19, 20.

112. Quoted in Wakukawa, *History*, 362–364.

Chapter 8: Dark Designs

1. Brig. Gen. George S. Simonds (Assistant Chief of Staff, WPD) to Judge Advocate General, April 14, 1931, RG 165 WPD, File No. 3535.

2. Col. A. W. Brown (Acting Judge Advocate) to Assistant Chief of Staff, WPD, July 6, 1931, RG 165 WPD, File No. 3535.

3. George S. Simonds (Assistant Chief of Staff, WPD) to Chief of Staff, July 29, 1931, RG 165 WPD, File No. 3535.

4. Brig. Gen. C. E. Kilbourne (Assistant Chief of Staff, WPD) to Assistant Chief of Staff, G-2, April 5, 1933, RG 165 MID, File No. 242-12/133.

5. Col. Alfred T. Smith (Assistant Chief of Staff, G-2) to Adjutant General, April 12, 1933, RG 165 MID, File No. 242-12/133.

6. "Estimate of the Situation—Japanese Population in Hawaii," RG 165 MID, File Nos. 242-12/133 and 242-12/133A.

7. C. E. Kilbourne (Assistant Chief of Staff, WPD) to Chief of Staff, July 19, 1933, RG 165 WPD, File No. 3535.

8. Brig. Gen. L. T. Gerow (Acting Assistant Chief of Staff, WPD) to Chief of Staff, November 20, 1940, RG 165 WPD, File No. 3535.

9. L. T. Gerow (Acting Assistant Chief of Staff, WPD) to Chief of Staff, June 20, 1941, RG 165 WPD, File No. 3535.

10. Henry L. Stimson (Secretary of War) to Senator Robert R. Reynolds (Chair, Committee on Military Affairs), October 30, 1941, RG 165 WPD, File No. 3535.

11. Lt. Col. Sherman Miles (General Staff) to Assistant Chief of Staff, WPD, October 22, 1934, RG 165 WPD, File No. 3675.

12. C. E. Kilbourne (Assistant Chief of Staff, WPD) to Commanding General, Hawaiian Department, November 13, 1934, RG 165 WPD, File No. 3675.

13. Miles to Assistant Chief of Staff, WPD, October 22, 1934.

14. Kilbourne to Commanding General, Hawaiian Department, November 13, 1934.

15. Maj. Gen. Halstead Dorey (Commander, Hawaiian Department) to WPD, January 30, 1935, RG 165 WPD, File No. 3675.

16. B. H. Wells (Commander, Hawaiian Department) to Adjutant General, March 14, 1933, RG 165 MID, File No. 1766-S-146/2; and FBI, "Memorandum on

Pearl Harbor Attack and Bureau's Activities Before and After," December 6, 1945, 1:2, which states that the bureau's Honolulu Field Division originally opened in April 1931 and closed in May 1934, reopened in August 1937 and closed April 30, 1938, due to a lack of funds. I am indebted to Michael Gordon, Bob Kumamoto, and Gail M. Nomura for calling to my attention this internal report. See also J. Edgar Hoover to E. R. W. McCabe (Assistant Chief of Staff, MID), June 21, 1938, RG 165 MID, File No. 9794-197/6.

17. J. P. Mac Farland (Bureau of Investigation), "A Survey of the Japanese Situation in Hawaii," June 7, 1933, RG 165 MID, File No. 1766-S-146/8.

18. J. P. Mac Farland, "A Survey of the Japanese Situation in Hawaii," October 31, 1933, RG 165 MID, File No. 1766-S-146/9.

19. Maj. James I. Muir (Assistant Chief of Staff, G-2, Hawaiian Department) to Assistant Chief of Staff, G-2, War Department, February 5, 1934, RG 165 MID, File No. 1766-S-152.

20. James I. Muir to Assistant Chief of Staff, G-2, War Department, July 19, 1934, RG 165 MID, File No. 1766-S-153/1. On this "shift" in Japanese mass sentiment, see the report of Lt. Commander T. M. Leovy (ONI, Pearl Harbor), December 11, 1934, RG 165 MID, File No. 1766-S-153/2.

21. Cited in Kumamoto, "Search for Spies," 47–49. By the end of the decade, ONI reported a "very noticeable increase" in Japanese "anti-American propaganda" aimed at the *nisei*, but also at *issei* and white Americans. See, e.g., RG 38 ONI, Box 218, A8-5/EF 37.

22. Kumamoto, "Search for Spies," 49–50. See also the report of Lt. Col. H. R. Oldfield, head of G-2, Ninth Corps Area, on alleged Japanese espionage in California. Oldfield to War Department, January 22, 1938, RG 165 MID, File No. 1766-Z-629/1.

23. MID (General Staff), "Estimate of the Situation Orange," October 1935, RG 165 MID, File No. 242-12-147.

24. Col. F. H. Lincoln (Assistant Chief of Staff, G-2, General Staff) to Assistant Chief of Staff, WPD, December 24, 1935, RG 165 MID, File No. 242-12-147.

25. Admiral W. H. Standley (Joint Board) to Secretary of War, May 19, 1936, RG 165 MID, File No. 242-12-155.

26. F.D.R. to Chief of Operations, August 10, 1936, RG 165 WPD, File No. 3675.

27. W. H. Standley (Chief of Naval Operations) to Chief of Staff, August 24, 1936, RG 165 WPD, File No. 3675.

28. Harry H. Woodring (Acting Secretary of War) to The President, August 29, 1936, RG 165 MID, File No. 242-12-159.

29. W. H. Standley (Joint Board) to Secretary of War, October 14, 1936, RG 165 MID, File No. 242-12-160.

30. See Commander W. F. Towle to the Commandant, October 20, 1937, RG 165 MID, File No. 242-12-170d.

31. Brig. Gen. W. Krueger (Assistant Chief of Staff, General Staff) to Assistant Chief of Staff, G-2, June 14, 1937, RG 165 MID, File No. 242-12-170a.

32. Michael Slackman, historian at Pearl Harbor's USS *Arizona* Memorial, discovered this document at the National Archives, in Record Group 338, Hawaiian Department, Adjutant General's Office, Emergency Defense and Mobilization Plans, 1940–1941, Box 3. Slackman reported his find in "The Orange Race: George S. Patton, Jr.'s Japanese-American Hostage Plan," *Biography* 7, no. 1 (Winter 1984): 1–49, and published a photocopy of the entire plan as an appendix to that article.

33. Ibid., 18.

34. See, e.g., ibid., 12, 14.

35. Minutes of Joint Conference, May 31, 1940, RG 165 MID, File No. 9794-186A/2. Military intelligence had anticipated the FBI's involvement in Hawaii. See Col. E. R. W. McCabe (Assistant Chief of Staff, G-2) to J. Edgar Hoover (Director, FBI), January 7, 1939, RG 165 MID, File No. 242-101/3.

36. "Proposal for Coordination of FBI, ONI and MID," June 5, 1940, RG 165 MID, 9794-186A/4. See also Kumamoto, "Search for Spies," 51–53.

37. Minutes of Joint Conference, June 18, 1940, RG 165 MID, File No. 9794-186A/5.

38. Minutes of Joint Conference, July 26, 1940, RG 165 MID, File No. 9794-186A/12. On the other hand, Hoover strenuously objected to what he perceived as MID usurpation of FBI prerogatives in civilian counterintelligence operations. See Kumamoto, "Search for Spies," 53.

39. John Edgar Hoover (Director, FBI) to Brig. Gen. Sherman Miles (Assistant Chief of Staff, G-2), July 5, 1940, RG 165 MID, File No. 9794-212/15. See also Minutes of Joint Conference, June 25, 1940, RG 165 MID, File No. 9794-186A/3.

40. Memorandum of Interview with Lt. Col. Byron M. Meurlott, March 9, 1945, National Archives, Record Group 338, Military Government of Hawaii, Research and Historical Section, (henceforth RG 338 Military Government), Box 894.

41. Lt. Col. George W. Bicknell (Head, Contact Office), "Security Measures in Hawaii During World War II," Microfilm Reel 54, Item 5, Hamilton Library, University of Hawaii. Despite the delimitation agreement, the FBI continued to rely on the ONI and MID for intelligence on the civilian Japanese population because the bureau was a novice in this field. FBI, "Memorandum on Pearl Harbor Attack," 1:102–108.

42. J. H. Polkinhorn (FBI agent, Honolulu), "Japanese Activities in the United States," March 4, 1940, RG 165 MID, File No. 1766-S-163/1.

43. N. J. Alaga (FBI agent, Honolulu), "Japanese Activities in the Territory of Hawaii," September 27, 1940, RG 165 MID, File No. 1766-S-163/2.

44. N. J. Alaga, Intelligence Survey of Oahu, December 9, 1940, RG 165 MID, File No. 2327-H-60/2; D. M. Douglas (FBI agent), Intelligence Survey of Hawaii,

December 15, 1940, RG 165 MID, File No. 2327-H-60/3; F. G. Tillman (FBI agent), Intelligence Survey of Maui, December 16, 1940, RG 165 MID, File No. 2327-H-60/4; and R. L. Moore (FBI agent), Intelligence Survey of Kauai, January 6, 1941, RG 165 MID, File No. 2327-H-60/5.

45. [Unsigned], Memorandum, November 15, 1940, RG 165 MID, File No. 2327-H-60. FBI director Hoover passed the memorandum to Adolf A. Berle, Jr., assistant secretary of state, Rear Admiral Walter S. Anderson, director of naval intelligence, and Sherman Miles, head of the War Department's G-2.

46. This latest concern over Japan's "persistent propaganda campaign" might have been stimulated, in part, by the MAGIC intercepts of the Japanese government's secret, coded transmissions. Beginning in the fall of 1940, American intelligence cryptanalysts succeeded in breaking the code, giving the U.S. access to Japanese diplomatic messages. Some of these MAGIC documents spoke of Japan's intention to formulate a plan for political and cultural "propaganda" in America. U.S. Department of Defense, *The "Magic" Background of Pearl Harbor*, vol. 1 (Washington, D.C.: Government Printing Office, 1977), documents 112–115, p. 119. But those same documents indicated that Japan's "propaganda" effort was poorly funded and that it sought to undo U.S. "propaganda" unfavorable to Japan rather than seek to attract *nisei*, blacks, or radicals to Japan's cause. See John A. Herzig, "Japanese Americans and MAGIC," *Amerasia Journal* 11, no. 2 (1984): 47–65.

47. Bicknell, "Security," 12.

48. Ibid., 13. See also Blake Clark, *Hawaii, the 49th State* (Garden City, N.Y.: Doubleday, 1947), 115–116.

49. Bicknell, "Security," 15.

50. Ibid., 18. Cf. Japan's view of Hawaii's *issei* and especially *nisei* as "Americanized," requiring cultural restoration/revitalization. Stephan, *Hawaii*, 161–166.

51. Bicknell, "Security," 18.

52. Clark, *Hawaii*, 118–119; and Robert L. Shivers, *Cooperation of the Various Racial Groups with Each Other and with the Constituted Authorities Before and After December 7, 1941* (Honolulu: Chamber of Commerce of Honolulu, 1946), 4.

53. Clark, *Hawaii*, 120.

54. Ibid., 123.

55. Liu, "Cultivating Cane," 198; and Lind, *Hawaii's People*, 75.

56. ELN to Secretary of State, February 2, 1923, Microfilm 2501, University of Hawaii, Hamilton Library (from National Archives, Record Group 59, Department of State Decimal File, 1910–1929, Labor Problems in Hawaii).

57. Quoted in Takaki, *Pau Hana*, 65.

58. Liu, "Cultivating Cane," 135–136; Moriyama, *Imingaisha*, 97; and Okahata, *History*, 200–201.

59. Bureau of Labor Statistics, *Fourth Report*, 23, 26. Portuguese *lunas* received, on average, $42.90 per month.

60. Shoemaker, *Labor in Hawaii, 1939*, 53–55.

61. U.S. Congress, House, *Labor Problems: Hearings*, 313.

62. Reinecke, *Feigned Necessity*, 272.

63. Nakano, *Samurai*, 92–93. See also *A Collection of Sermons by the Rev. Takie Okumura* (Honolulu: Makiki Christian Church, 1974), 44, in which Okumura recounted his conversation with a Buddhist priest, Gakuo Okabe, who said: "You are very fortunate because you are put up at the manager's house when you make your rounds. As for me, I am given lodging in a corner of the laborers' quarters."

64. Takie and Umetaro Okumura, Report no. 5 [plantation tours], Okumura Papers, Hawaiian Mission Children's Society Library.

Chapter 9: Into the Cold Night Rain

1. Gwenfread Allen, *Hawaii's War Years* (Honolulu: University of Hawaii Press, 1950), 65–66; and HSPA, "The War Record of Civilian and Industrial Hawaii," manuscript, 1945, University of Hawaii, Hamilton Library, Special Collections, 14–19.

2. Stanley D. Porteus, *And Blow Not the Trumpet: A Prelude to Peril* (Palo Alto: Pacific Books, 1947), 100.

3. Allen, *Hawaii's War*, 68; and Porteus, *Blow Not*, 113. A "home guard" force was permitted only under Public Law 214 passed by Congress in August 1941, about a year after Hawaii had established its Provisional Police. See Hawaii State Archives, Official Files of the Governors of Hawaii, Joseph Boyd Poindexter, General Files, War File, Home Guard Organization.

4. Porteus, *Blow Not*, 123; and HSPA, "War Record," 11–14, 56–67.

5. Allen, *Hawaii's War*, 68; and Defense Volunteer Organizations, Maui Volunteers (Lahaina), University of Hawaii, War Records Depository, File No. 20.06. Cf. Porteus, *Blow Not*, 124.

6. John A. Burns Oral History Project, 1975–1976, University of Hawaii, Hamilton Library, Special Collections, Tapes 2 and 4. See also Allen, *Hawaii's War*, 82; and Clark, *Hawaii*, 121.

7. Allen, *Hawaii's War*, 70.

8. Ibid., 71.

9. Department Maneuvers, 1940, April 13, 1940, RG 338 Military Government, Box 2.

10. I cannot explain why Japan is herein designated RED, the color normally assigned to Britain. On an accompanying field order, however, the warring nation is identified as ORANGE, or Japan. Operations Orders, Hawaiian Division, Field Order No. 1 W, RG 338 Military Government, Box 2.

11. Research and Historical Section: Drafts, Correspondence, and Note Cards

on a History of the Military Government of Hawaii, RG 338 Military Government, Box 891.

12. Allen, *Hawaii's War*, 79–80.

13. Ibid., 80; and Anthony, *Hawaii under Army*, 4.

14. Allen, *Hawaii's War*, 36; and Research and Historical Section, RG 338 Military Government, Box 891.

15. Quoted in Anthony, *Hawaii under Army*, 4.

16. Anthony, *Hawaii under Army*, 5–9; J. Garner Anthony, "Hawaiian Martial Law in the Supreme Court," *Yale Law Review* 57, no. 27 (November 1947): 27–31; and Allen, *Hawaii's War*, 35–36.

17. *Final Report of the Emergency Service Committee*, Honolulu, May 1946, 2.

18. Included in the printed program of the rally, Shunzo Sakamaki Papers, University Archives, University of Hawaii at Manoa. Accompanying that printed program in the Sakamaki Papers were congratulatory messages from Hawaii's army commander, Walter Short, and navy commandant, C. C. Bloch, and Secretary of War Henry Stimson, Secretary of the Navy Frank Knox, and FBI Director J. Edgar Hoover. In expressing his gratitude over the resolution, Hoover hastened to add, "I would like to suggest that should information regarding violations of the espionage, sabotage or related laws come to your attention it be reported immediately to Mr. R. L. Shivers." J. E. Hoover to Shunzo Sakamaki, July 21, 1941, Sakamaki Papers.

19. Quoted in Tetsuo Toyama, *Eighty Years in Hawaii* (Tokyo: Tosho Printing, n.d.), 61–62. See also Stephan, *Hawaii*, 39–40, on the effect of necessary patriotism on the Japanese press.

20. Clark, *Hawaii*, 123–124, stated that Ching formed this committee with the encouragement of FBI head Shivers.

21. Shivers, *Cooperation*, 5–8.

22. B. H. Wells, HSPA Secretary, to Plantation Managers, November 1, 1940, in Sakamaki Papers. Japan had amended its Nationality Act in 1916 and 1924 to allow *nisei* to renounce their Japanese citizenship. See Yuji Ichioka, *The Issei: The World of the First Generation Japanese Immigrants, 1885–1924* (New York: Free Press, 1988), 204, 206. The procedure was complicated, however, and involved delays and correspondence. A major problem for applicants was securing witnesses to establish the place and date of their birth.

23. Typescript of speech in Sakamaki Papers.

24. *Honolulu Advertiser*, February 12, 1941.

25. Lt. Gen. C. D. Herron to Shunzo Sakamaki, December 21, 1940, Sakamaki Papers.

26. Lt. Gen. Walter C. Short to Adjutant General, May 15, 1941, National Archives, Record Group 319, Records of the Army Staff (henceforth RG 319 Army Staff), Adjutant General's Office, Emergency Defense and Mobilization Plans, 1940–1941, Box 3.

27. Short to War Plans Division, July 21, 1941, RG 319 Army Staff, Office of Assistant Chief of Staff, G-2, Records Relating to the Attack on Pearl Harbor and to Sabotage Activities, c. 1937–1947, Box 1. Short was arguing against the proposed arrest and prosecution of Japanese consular agents under the Espionage Act of 1917. (The FBI had been conducting an intensive investigation of consular agents since the passage of the Foreign Agents Registration Act of 1940 with the aim of prosecuting them under the act.) Short's defense of "fair play," nonetheless, was based on his belief that "prosecution at this time would unduly alarm entire population and jeopardize success [in] our current campaign to secure loyalty [of] Japanese population."

28. "Recommendations of Representatives of the War Department and of the Department of Justice for Cooperation Respecting Internment of Alien Enemies," March 26, 1941, Japanese Internment and Relocation: The Hawaii Experience, University of Hawaii, Hamilton Library, Special Collections [henceforth JIR], Box 3, Item 4. (JIR was a research project headed by Dennis M. Ogawa that collected archival and oral history materials on the Japanese wartime experience in Hawaii. JIR has amassed a valuable body of documentary evidence. However, some of the materials collected from the National Archives are not fully identified as to their location in the archives. I have thus had to use the JIR listing instead of the original archival entry.) The formal agreement was signed by the secretaries of war and justice on July 18, 1941. JIR, Box 3, Item 14.

29. Short to Adjutant General, April 18, 1941, JIR, Box 3, Item 6.

30. Short to Adjutant General, July 3, 1941, JIR, Box 3, Item 13.

31. Allen, *Hawaii's War,* 65–72, 85.

32. FBI, "Memorandum on Pearl Harbor Attack," 1:ii, 2.

33. Ibid., 300.

34. Ibid., 2–3.

35. Ibid., iii–v. As indicated in note 27, Short intervened to prevent these arrests.

36. FBI, "Memorandum on Pearl Harbor Attack," 1:213. See also "Memorandum of Interview with Lt. Col. Byron M. Meurlott," March 9, 1945, RG 338 Military Government, Box 894.

37. FBI, "Memorandum on Pearl Harbor Attack," 1:214–216; and Lt. Col. M. W. Marston (Assistant Chief of Staff, G-2, Hawaiian Department) to MID, G-2 (Washington, D.C.), July 5, 1941, RG 165 MID, File No. 10110-2833/37.

38. W. O. Cogswell, Interview with Joseph B. Poindexter, February 17, 1945, RG 338 Military Government, Box 894.

39. FBI, "Memorandum on Pearl Harbor Attack," 1:218.

40. "Memorandum of Interview . . . Meurlott."

41. Ibid.; and "Memorandum of Interview with Maj. Edward E. Walker," March 9, 1945, RG 338 Military Government, Box 894. Likewise, the army arrested Japanese civilians before the declaration of martial law. Office of the Chief

of Military History, United States Army Forces Middle Pacific and Predecessor Commands During World War II, 7 December 1941–2 September 1945: History of G-2 Section, Historical Manuscript File, vol. 10, pt. 2, p. 23.

42. Burns Oral History Project, Tape 4.

43. Allen, *Hawaii's War*, 35–36.

44. Much has been written on the legality of martial law in Hawaii. See, e.g., Anthony, *Hawaii Under Army*; "Hawaiian Martial Law"; "Martial Law in Hawaii," *California Law Review* 30, no. 4 (May 1942): 371–396; and "Martial Law, Military Government and the Writ of Habeas Corpus in Hawaii," *California Law Review* 31, no. 5 (December 1943): 477–514; John P. Frank, "Ex Parte Milligan v. The Five Companies: Martial Law in Hawaii," *Columbia Law Review* 44, no. 5 (September 1944): 639–668; Archibald King, "The Legality of Martial Law in Hawaii," *California Law Review* 30, no. 6 (September 1942): 599–633; Robert S. Rankin, "Hawaii Under Martial Law," *Journal of Politics* 5, no. 3 (August 1943): 270–290; and J. W. Brabner Smith, "Martial Law and the Writ of Habeas Corpus," *Georgetown Law Journal* 30, no. 8 (June 1942): 697–704.

45. FBI, "Memorandum on Pearl Harbor Attack," 1:218–219. Cf. Allen, *Hawaii's War*, 39, where the numbers of internees on December 8, 1941 are given as 370 Japanese, 98 Germans, and 14 Italians. According to Bicknell, the pickup of Japanese suspects was delayed for several hours because of a shortage of trucks and military police. Prange, *At Dawn*, 562.

46. "Memorandum of Interview . . . Meurlott."

47. FBI, "Memorandum on Pearl Harbor Attack," 1:203–206.

48. Ibid., 206–209.

49. Yukiko Kimura, "Some Effects of the War Situation upon the Alien Japanese in Hawaii," *Social Process in Hawaii* 8 (November 1943): 18.

50. Office of the Chief of Military History, United States Forces Middle Pacific and Predecessor Commands During World War II, 7 December 1941–2 September 1945: History of Provost Marshal's Office, Historical Manuscript File, vol. 24, pt. 2, pp. 198–199. See also Michael John Gordon, "Suspects in Paradise: Looking for Japanese 'Subversives' in the Territory of Hawaii, 1939–1945," master's thesis, University of Iowa, 1983, 78–81, 83.

51. Poem by Risuke Yasui, included in a collection of *waka* poems by Jikai Yamazato, *Koji wa Harukaze* (1951), trans. Yumiko Iwahara, JIR, Box 2, T-1.

52. Soga's account is taken from his *My Life in Barbed Wire* (1948), JIR, Box 2, T-12. I have not used information from Kazuo Miyamoto's *Hawaii: End of the Rainbow* (Rutland, Vt.: Charles E. Tuttle, 1964) and Patsy Sumie Saiki's *Ganbare! An Example of Japanese Spirit* (Honolulu: Kisaku, 1982) because these are embellished accounts that, while based on historical data and filled with personal insight, make it impossible to separate fact from fiction.

53. Suikei Furuya, *Haisho Ten-ten* (1964), JIR, Box 2, T-6.

54. Soga, *My Life.*

55. J. H. Linson (Medical Director, Chief Quarantine Officer) to The Surgeon General (U.S. Public Health Service), December 20, 1941, JIR, Box 3.

56. Office of Chief of Military History, United States Army, Provost Marshal's, vol. 24, pt. 2, pp. 188–189.

57. Soga, *My Life.*

58. S. Furuya, *Haisho Ten-ten.* Soga described a Buddhist priest who chanted continually, an internee who claimed to represent the Japanese military, and a man who believed himself to be the reincarnation of Charles Hasebe, an internee who was supposedly shot by the guards. Keiho (Yasutaro) Soga, *Tessaku seikatsu* (Honolulu: Hawaii Times, 1948), JIR, Box 2, T-13.

59. Soga, *My Life.* See also Hunter, *Buddhism,* 189–190, on the reactions of priests to confinement.

60. Soga, *My Life.*

61. S. Furuya, *Haisho Ten-ten.*

62. Maj. Louis F. Springer, "Treatment of Japanese Civilian Internees at Sand Island," JIR, Box 3, S-27.

63. Soga, *My Life.* In little acts of defiance, internees replied "poisoner" or "pissoner" instead of the prescribed "prisoner." Kotani, *Japanese in Hawaii,* 80.

64. Minosuke Hanabusa, February 11, 1982, oral history interview, JIR, Box 2.

65. Soga, *My Life.*

66. Hanabusa, oral history.

67. Soga, *My Life.* In another version, Soga's account is translated "bread and water." Soga, *Tessaku seikatsu.* Dan Nishikawa, a former Sand Island internee, recalled that one night, soldiers rounded up all the Japanese when the air raid siren went off, jammed them into the cafeteria, bolted the doors, and stood inside facing them with machine guns. Beverly Creamer, "Memories That Remain Interned Forever," *Honolulu Advertiser,* September 9, 1981.

68. Soga, *My Life.*

69. Kaetsu Furuya, n.d., oral history interview, JIR, Box 2. Cf. Soga, *Tessaku seikatsu.*

70. Jukichi and Haruko Inouye, n.d., oral history interview, JIR, Box 2.

71. Myoshu Sasai, n.d., oral history interview, JIR, Box 2. For a police report on the arrest and detention of Japanese on the Big Island, see "The Hawaii Police Department and World War II (A Summary of the Period from Dec. 7, 1941 to June 30, 1943)," University of Hawaii, War Records Depository, File No. 31.02; and on Maui, see *Annual Report,* Police Department, County of Maui, 1941, University of Hawaii, War Records Depository, File No. 31.04.

72. Hisashi Fukuhara, n.d., oral history interview, JIR, Box 2.

73. Sasai, oral history.

74. Soga, *Tessaku seikatsu;* and Soga, *My Life.*

75. For accounts of the Niihau Incident, see Allan Beekman, *The Niihau Incident* (Honolulu: Heritage Press of Pacific, 1982); and Burl Burlingame's four-part series in the *Honolulu Star-Bulletin*, December 7–10, 1986.

76. K. Furuya, oral history.

77. Soga, *My Life*.

78. S. Furuya, *Haisho Ten-ten*.

79. Soga, *My Life*.; and S. Furuya, *Haisho Ten-ten*.

80. Soga, *Tessaku seikatsu*.

81. Soga, *My Life*.

82. Ibid. Apparently, later groups of Sand Island internees were permitted to eat the vegetables grown in the camp garden. Sam Nishimura, oral history interview, July 12, 1976, in Ethnic Studies Oral History Project, *Waialua and Haleiwa: The People Tell Their Story*, University of Hawaii at Manoa, 1977, 6:381–382.

83. Soga, *My Life*.

84. Ibid.; Inouye, oral history; and Sasai, oral history.

Chapter 10: Bivouac Song

1. Anthony, *Hawaii under Army*, 35.

2. Allen, *Hawaii's War*, 107–130.

3. Office of Chief of Military History, United States Army, Provost Marshal's, vol. 24, pt. 1, p. 18. On measures directed specifically at the Japanese, see Territorial Office of Defense, Health and Welfare Services, "The Japanese Population of the Territory of Hawaii—Its Relationship to the War Effort," May 21, 1942, JIR, Box 1, RG 210–1.

4. Office of Chief of Military History, United States Army, Provost Marshal's, vol. 24, pt. 1, p. 19; and General Orders No. 5, December 8, 1941, University of Hawaii, War Records Depository, File No. 30.06.

5. Central Identification Bureau, RG 338 Military Government, Boxes 383–401; and *Final Report of Emergency Service Committee*, 36–37. Even returned *nisei* veterans received distinctive badges from the Office of Internal Security.

6. Frank E. Midkiff (Chair, Evacuation Committee) to Frank H. Locey (Director, Office of Civilian Defense), May 8, 1942, University of Hawaii, War Records Depository, File No. 27.02.

7. Tim Klass, *World War II on Kauai* (Lihue: Kauai Historical Society, n.d.), University of Hawaii, War Records Depository, File No. 37.

8. Sherman Miles (Acting Assistant Chief of Staff, G-2, Washington, D.C.), "Japanese Potentialities with Respect to Hawaii," December 17, 1941, JIR, Box 1.

9. As Stephan, *Hawaii*, has shown, Miles was incorrect in that Japan, from

December 9, 1941, to mid 1942, planned the conquest of Hawaii; however, as demonstrated by Miles's memorandum and in the absence of other evidence, the U.S. military was ignorant of Japan's intentions.

   10. Quoted in FBI, "Memorandum on Pearl Harbor Attack," 2:1048. See also Allen, *Hawaii's War*, 47–56.

   11. Col. Archer L. Lerch (Deputy Provost Marshal General) to Adjutant General, January 10, 1942, JIR, Box 3.

   12. Daniels, *Concentration Camps*, 73.

   13. Shigeo Yoshida, "A Plan to Meet the Japanese Problem in Hawaii," May 5, 1942, attached to letter from Charles F. Loomis to John A. Hamilton, October 31, 1942, University of Hawaii, War Records Depository, Martial Law Files, no. 26.

   14. Kimie Kawahara and Yuriko Hatanaka, "The Impact of War on an Immigrant Culture," *Social Process in Hawaii* 8 (November 1943): 38.

   15. Ibid., 37–38; and Klass, *World War II*, 59.

   16. Klass, *World War II*, 57; and Kimura, "Some Effects," 19–20.

   17. Interview of Rev. Ernest H. Hunt, n.d., University of Hawaii, War Records Depository, File No. 60.05; Hunter, *Buddhism*, 187; and Klass, *World War II*, 57. Hunt reported that FBI agents, during a raid on a home, ordered the occupant to destroy his family shrine, or *butsudan*. Hunter, *Buddhism*, 193.

   18. Col. Wm. R. C. Morrison (Executive, OMG) to Office of Representative of Military Governor, Maui District, April 24, 1944, RG 338 Military Government, Box 63. See correspondence and investigations prompted by the request of Hatsuno Mihara to resume services at the Paia (Maui) Buddhist Church. RG 338 Military Government, Box 63.

   19. Kawahara and Hatanaka, "Impact of War," 43; Hunt, interview; and Klass, *World War II*, 57.

   20. Kawahara and Hatanaka, "Impact of War," 43.

   21. Kimura, "Some Effects," 21; and Kawahara and Hatanaka, "Impact of War," 40–41, 44. See RG 338 Military Government, Box 53, for examples of military regulation of funerals, birthdays, and weddings at which *issei* were present.

   22. Katsumi Kometani, "The Nisei and the Future," *Nisei in Hawaii and the Pacific* 6, no. 1 (1952): 10, reprinted in *Kodomo no tame ni: The Japanese American Experience in Hawaii*, ed. Dennis M. Ogawa (Honolulu: University Press of Hawaii, 1978), 364–365.

   23. Jim Andrew Richstad, "The Press and the Courts under Martial Rule in Hawaii During World War II—From Pearl Harbor to Duncan v. Kahanamoku," doctoral dissertation, University of Minnesota, 1967, 119–171.

   24. *Final Report of Emergency Service Committee*, 2.

   25. Ibid., 11–12.

   26. Ibid., 9. According to a contact group member, "Some of our own people called us *inu*, dogs, and held us in suspicion. They misunderstood our purpose."

Quoted in Tom Coffman, *Catch a Wave: A Case Study of Hawaii's New Politics* (Honolulu: University Press of Hawaii, 1973), 15.

27. *Final Report of Emergency Service Committee*, 14–15.

28. Lt. Col. Charles Selby, "Problems of People of Japanese Ancestry in Hawaii as Seen From the Military Point of View," in Report of Conference of Americans of Japanese Ancestry, Honolulu, September 12, 1943, University of Hawaii, War Records Depository, File No. 45.01.

29. Ibid.

30. Thomas D. Murphy, *Ambassadors in Arms* (Honolulu: University of Hawaii Press, 1954), 125–128; and Harry Katahara et al., *The Boys of Company "B"* (Honolulu: Hawaii Hochi, 1981), 36–37.

31. Shigeo Yoshida, "Speak American," *Hawaii Educational Review*, 31 (1942): 106, reprinted in Ogawa, *Kodomo*, 329–331. See also Allen, *Hawaii's War*, 145.

32. *Final Report of the Kauai Morale Committee*, September 30, 1945, University of Hawaii, War Records Depository, File No. 37, 37–42. Of the 166 Japanese-language schools in 1941, only 42 remained undissolved in 1945, 5 on Kauai, 14 on Oahu, 11 on Maui, and 12 on Hawaii. *Report of Second Oahu Conference of Americans of Japanese Ancestry*, Nuuanu YMCA, Honolulu, January 28, 1945.

33. Quoted in, Hunter, *Buddhism*, 191.

34. Ibid., 192.

35. Ibid.

36. Morale and Emergency Service Committees, *Report of the Second Territorial Conference*, Kahului, Maui, July 21–23, 1944, University of Hawaii, War Records Depository, File No. 45.01, 43–51. See also Hawaii Conference, Hawaii Morale Group, AJA Committee, Hilo, Hawaii, December 3, 1944, University of Hawaii, War Records Depository, File No. 45.

37. Cited in Kimura, "Some Effects," 18.

38. Klass, *World War II*, 59; and *Final Report of Kauai Morale Committee*, 27.

39. *Final Report of Kauai Morale Committee*, 28, Appendix 3; Klass, *World War II*, 60–61; and Allen, *Hawaii's War*, 145. Speaking generally, John Burns noted that "a very real effort" was made during the war to exclude Japanese from politics. Burns Oral History Project, Tape 5.

40. *Final Report of Kauai Morale Committee*, Appendix 6.

41. Ibid., 30.

42. Ibid., Appendix 6; *Final Report of Emergency Service Committee*, 18–20; and for lists of persons donating blood or purchasing bonds, see RG 338 Military Government, Box 140.

43. Allen, *Hawaii's War*, 91, 350; Klass, *World War II*, 31–32; *Final Report of Kauai Morale Committee*, 14–15; and John A. Hamilton to Leslie A. Hicks, March 27, 1942, University of Hawaii, War Records Depository, File No. 22.

44. Lester Petrie, "The New Honolulu," *Collier's*, March 21, 1942, 30.

45. Bicknell, "Security Measures," 84–85. The army dealt with both war fronts, in the Pacific and in Hawaii, as if they were one as operationalized by the Department's G-2 Section. See, e.g., Office of Chief of Military History, United States Army, G-2 Section, vol. 10, pts. 1–2, JIR, Box 2, CH-7, CH-8.

46. Office of Chief of Military History, United States Army, G-2 Section, vol. 10, pt. 2, p. 19. Those listed "I-A" were picked up and interned on December 7, 1941; those listed "I-B" were put under surveillance.

47. Allen, *Hawaii's War*, 109.

48. Ibid., 109–110.

49. Lt. Kanemi Kanazawa to Officer in Charge, April 21, 1942; and response by Maj. F. A. Stacy to Commanding General, n.d., RG 338 Military Government, Box 54.

50. The Commandant (14th Naval District) to Commanding General (Hawaiian Department), August 24, 1942; Maj. Gen. Henry T. Burgin to Commandant (14th Naval District), September 12, 1942; The Commandant (14th Naval District) to Commanding General (Hawaiian Department), December 9, 1942; and Office of Military Governor inter-staff routing slip, December 12, 1942, RG 338 Military Government, Box 54.

51. K.J.F., December 14, 1942, RG 338 Military Government, Box 54. Other contested areas between army and navy included, on the island of Oahu, the Waianae area, Ewa Junction, Pearl City peninsula, and the perimeter of Pearl Harbor. See RG 338 Military Government, Box 54, File "Evacuation and Restricted Area."

52. Emmons to Adjutant General, February 11, 1942, JIR, Box 3, A-8.

53. Brig. Gen. Thomas H. Green (Executive, OMG) to Will N. King (Chair, USDA War Board), September 28, 1942, RG 338 Military Government, Box 48.

54. Paul R. Van Zwalenburg, "Hawaiian Labor Unions under Military Government," master's thesis, University of Hawaii, 1961, 39; and "Procurement and Utilization of Manpower," pt. 6, RG 338 Military Government, Box 89. For a complete listing of provost court prosecutions for violation of labor laws, see RG 338 Military Government, Boxes 509–510, 527–538. Between June 1942 and August 1944, there were, from my count, a total of 1,349 such cases; of these, only 143 involved Japanese.

55. See, e.g., the prison report of Waiakea Prison, RG 338 Military Government, Box 557. On full employment and punishment for infractions, see General Orders No. 56 and No. 91.

56. *Honolulu Star-Bulletin*, July 22, 1943.

57. Allen, *Hawaii's War*, 74; and Samuel Wilder King to Harold L. Ickes, June 18, 1941, RG 126 Territories/Hawaii, Box 723.

58. FBI, "Memorandum on Pearl Harbor Attack," 1:406.

59. Allen, *Hawaii's War*, 41.

60. Territorial Office of Defence, "Japanese Population," 8–9; and Navy Yard

Order 14–42, "Employment of Japanese by Naval Activities and Naval Personnel," May 23, 1942, Naval Historical Center, Operational Archives, Wallin Papers.

61. Territorial Office of Defence, "Japanese Population," 8–9; and Yukiko Kimura, "Social Effects of Increased Income of Defense Workers of Oriental Ancestry in Hawaii," *Social Process in Hawaii* 7 (November 1941): 46–55. Cf. Beechert, *Working*, 287, in which a union representative reported that Japanese earned more money working on nonmilitary construction jobs.

62. Quoted in Beechert, *Working*, 288. For military views of Japanese unionism, see RG 338 Military Government, Box 61.

63. Beechert, *Working*, 277–279, 287–288. On the acquiescence of labor generally, see Anthony, *Hawaii*, 41–45.

64. "Memorandum on Military Control of Hawaiian Labor," March 27, 1944, University of Hawaii, War Records Depository, File No. 38.08, 8–11.

65. Lind, *Hawaii's People*, 75.

66. Van Zwalenburg, "Hawaiian Labor Unions," 32, 34. See "Procurement and Utilization," pt. 6, RG 338 Military Government, Box 891, for the concern of both the military and planters over the high rate of plantation labor "desertions" during the early weeks of the war.

67. Van Zwalenburg, "Hawaiian Labor Unions," 33; Beechert, *Working*, 287; and various correspondence/draft agreements contained in RG 338 Military Government, Box 17.

68. HSPA, "War Record," 24.

69. Chauncey B. Wightman (HSPA assistant secretary) to Trustees, January 24, 1942, RG 338 Military Government, Box 459.

70. Research and Historical Section: Drafts, Correspondence, and Note Cards on a History of the Military Government of Hawaii, RG 338 Military Government, Box 891, Pt. 6. See also series of radiograms between McCloy (War Department) and Emmons (Hawaiian Department), January 1943, RG 338 Military Government, Box 61.

71. Wm. R. C. Morrison, August 25, 1943, RG 338 Military Government, Box 61.

72. Wm. R. C. Morrison to Chief of Staff (Washington, D.C.), December 17, 1943, RG 338 Military Government, Box 61.

73. Burns Oral History Project, Tape 5; and James H. Shoemaker, *The Economy of Hawaii in 1947*, Department of Labor Bulletin no. 926, 26.

74. Lt. Gen. Robert C. Richardson, Jr. to John J. McCloy, January 27, 1944, RG 338 Military Government, Box 61.

75. J. S. Daves to Robert C. Richardson, Jr., August 30, 1943, RG 338 Military Government, Box 61. See Arthur A. Rutledge to Robert C. Richardson, Jr., September 25, 1943, RG 338 Military Government, Box 61; and Bernard W. Stern, *Rutledge Unionism: Labor Relations in the Honolulu Transit Industry* (Honolulu: University of Hawaii, Center for Labor Education and Research, 1986), on the intraunion split

and on refuting the "race issue" of Japanese activities in unions.

76. James P. Mitchell (Director, Industrial Personnel Division) to Gen. Edmond H. Leavey (War Department), December 7, 1943, RG 338 Military Government, Box 61.

77. "Memorandum on Military Control."

78. Gordon Walker, in the *Christian Science Monitor*, September 16, 1943, quoted in "Memorandum on Military Control," 9.

79. Office of Chief of Military History, United States Army, G-2 Section, vol. 10, pt. 2, pp. 13–14, 23–24. ONI still managed subversion on naval bases and among navy personnel.

80. "Analysis Chart of Special Questionnaire Relating to Citizens of Japanese Ancestry Who Make Application for Voluntary Induction into the Army of the United States for Service with the Combat Team," JIR, Box 3.

81. Office of Chief of Military History, United States Army, G-2 Section, vol. 10, pt. 2, p. 34.

82. APC appeared to be relatively unimportant judged by the difficulties Walker faced in just getting started. For instance, Bicknell assigned him three small rooms in CIC's Dillingham Building, Eifler refused to house him on Sand Island, and he had to fend for himself in finally securing adequate space at the immigration station. "Memorandum of Interview . . . Walker." It seems that in the OMG scheme of things, civilian hearing boards presented a semblance, without the substance, of a trial by peers.

83. "Memorandum of Interview . . . Walker."

84. Capt. Robert I. Freund (assistant director, APC) to Brig. Gen. Thomas H. Green (executive, OMG), July 20, 1942, RG 338 Military Government, Box 893.

85. Internee case files are contained in RG 338 Military Government, Boxes 143–289. For hearing board procedures, see "A Partial Account of Lahaina's Part in World War II," University of Hawaii, War Records Depository, File No. 20.06.

86. "Hawaiian Department Alien Processing Center," RG 338 Military Government, Box 893.

87. "Factors to Be Considered in Investigations of Japanese Subjects," Office of Chief of Military History, United States Army, Provost Marshal's, vol. 24, pt. 5, Appendix A.

88. "Memorandum of Interview . . . Walker."

89. Letter and response included in RG 338 Military Government, Box 79.

90. Gustaf W. Olson to Col. Erik de Laval (Swedish Legation, Washington, D.C.), June 19, 1943, JIR, Box 2. See also *Revue Internationale de la Croix-Rouge* 291 (March 1943): 210–213; and Brig. Gen. B. M. Bryan (director, Aliens Division, War Department) to Office of Military Governor, March 31, 1943, JIR, Box 3, S-23.

91. Gustaf W. Olson to Col. Erik de Laval, September 23, 1943, JIR, Box 2.

92. Creamer, "Memories That Remain."

93. Irene Harada to Lt. Col. Eugene V. Slattery (OMG), October 23, 1943, RG

338 Military Government, Box 163.

94. Lt. Col. V. S. Burton to Col. Thomas H. Green, January 26, 1942, RG 338 Military Government, Box 557.

95. "Prison Report (Waiakea Prison)," RG 338 Military Government, Box 557.

96. Basil A. Thomas (special agent, CIC), "Disturbance among Civilian Internees at Honouliuli on 28 June 1945," June 30, 1945, RG 338 Military Government, Box 24.

97. Nishimura, oral history, 378, 380, 383.

98. Murphy, *Ambassadors*, 41.

99. Ibid., 43.

100. *Boys of Company "B"*, 8–9; and Murphy, *Ambassadors*, 45.

101. Murphy, *Ambassadors*, 45.

102. Ibid., 52–53. The Hawaii Territorial Guard was hastily formed on December 7, 1941 with University of Hawaii ROTC members as its nucleus. The Territorial Guard was primarily an antisabotage unit.

103. From oral history, quoted in Franklin Odo, "No Flags to Burn; No Swords to Bury: Nisei Elite in WWII," paper presented at the 79th Annual Meeting of the Pacific Coast Branch, American Historical Association, Honolulu, August 13–17, 1986, 22–23.

104. Letter, January 30, 1942, reproduced in Yutaka Nakahata and Ralph Toyota, "Varsity Victory Volunteers: A Social Movement," *Social Process in Hawaii* 8 (November 1943): 30.

105. Ibid., 31.

106. Ibid., 31–33.

107. Murphy, *Ambassadors*, 58–59.

108. Maj. Gen. Maxwell Murray (25th Infantry Division) to Emmons, March 23, 1942; and Col. Thos. B. Burgess (General Staff Corps, Chief of Staff) to Emmons, April 2, 1942, RG 338 Military Government, Box 5. I am indebted to Michael Slackman for bringing these documents to my attention.

109. Murphy, *Ambassadors*, 59. One of Emmons's concerns, according to Fielder, was the safety of *nisei* troops who might be mistakenly shot by white defenders in the event of a Japanese invasion. Ibid., 60; and Masayo Umezawa Duus, *Unlikely Liberators: The Men of the 100th and 442nd* (Honolulu: University of Hawaii Press, 1987), 20.

110. Quoted in Bill Hosokawa, *Nisei: The Quiet Americans* (New York: Morrow, 1969), 401. About the same time, *nisei* linguists from the mainland were being sent west to serve in the Pacific theater in translating, interrogating, and intelligence work; others were training at the Military Intelligence Service Language School at Camp Savage, Minnesota. Ibid., 394–400.

111. A group of Company B veterans composed this version of *"Roei no uta"* in 1981, because, except for two stanzas, the words to the original song had been

forgotten. *Boys of Company "B"*, 48–53. Although most of the men of the 100th Battalion were Japanese, the unit included *hapas*, Japanese-Hawaiian, Japanese-Chinese, Japanese-Filipino, Japanese-Portuguese, and a Korean.

Chapter 11: In Morning Sunlight

1. See, e.g., Connie Young Yu, "Rediscovered Voices: Chinese Immigrants and Angel Island," *Amerasia Journal* 4, no. 2 (1977): 123–139; and Him Mark Lai, Genny Lim, and Judy Yung, *Island: Poetry and History of Chinese Immigrants on Angel Island, 1910–1940* (San Francisco: Hoc Doi Project, San Francisco Study Center, 1980).

2. K. Furuya, oral history.

3. Soga, *Tessaku seikatsu*; Soga, *My Life*; and S. Furuya, *Haisho Ten-ten*.

4. S. Furuya, *Haisho Ten-ten*. See also Soga, *Tessaku seikatsu*; and Soga, *My Life*.

5. S. Furuya, *Haisho Ten-ten*.

6. *Boys of Company "B"*, 12.

7. Ibid.

8. Murphy, *Ambassadors*, 71.

9. Quoted in ibid. See also Duus, *Unlikely*, 22–23.

10. *Boys of Company "B"*, 13.

11. Cited in Hosokawa, *Nisei*, 401.

12. Murphy, *Ambassadors*, 92–93; and Duus, *Unlikely*, 47–49.

13. Lawrence H. Sakamoto, *Hawaii's Own: Picture Story of 442nd Regiment, 100th Battalion and Interpreters* (Honolulu: n.p., 1946), 86–87.

14. Emmons to Adjutant General, January 11, 1942, JIR, Box 3.

15. Cf. *Personal Justice Denied*, 268–274, for another interpretation of Emmons's motives.

16. Quoted in ibid., 274.

17. Emmons to Adjutant General, February 4, 1942, JIR, Box 3.

18. See, e.g., Maj. Gen. Allen W. Gullion (Provost Marshal General) to Chief of Administrative Service, SOS, March 22, 1942, JIR, Box 3.

19. In his memorandum approving the recommendation of the Joint Chiefs of Staff, March 13, 1942, Roosevelt discriminated between citizens of non-Japanese and Japanese ancestry. Non-Japanese, directed the President, were not to be removed to the mainland despite posing a security risk, while Japanese, up to 15,000 persons, could be transferred to the mainland for custody by the War Relocation Authority (WRA), the civilian agency that administered the mainland concentration camps. Roosevelt's memorandum is quoted in a radiogram, Marshall to Commanding General (Hawaiian Department), July 20, 1942, JIR, Box 3, A-15.

20. Maj. Gen. Dwight D. Eisenhower (Assistant Chief of Staff, War Plans Divi-

sion) to John J. McCloy, n.d., JIR, Box 3; and Eisenhower to McCloy, April 3, 1942, JIR, Box 3.

21. Quoted in *Personal Justice Denied*, 271–272. See also radiograms, Emmons to Adjutant General, March 1, 1942; and n.a. to Hawaiian Department, March 3, 1942, RG 338 Military Government, Box 59.

22. McCloy to Emmons, May 18, 1942, JIR, Box 1.

23. Office of Chief of Military History, United States Army, Provost Marshal's, vol. 24, pt. 2, pp. 202–203; Transfer Register, Transfer Units 1–4, November 12, 1942, December 27, 1942, January 25, 1943, March 2, 1943 (departure dates), RG 338 Military Government, Box 5; and Soga, *Tessaku seikatsu*.

24. Marshall to Emmons, October 8, 1942, RG 338 Military Government, Box 54. See also JIR, Box 3, A-16.

25. Capt. Stanley D. Arnold, "Memorandum for Colonel Claude B. Washburne, Officer in Charge, Civil Affairs Division, Western Defense Command," May 29, 1945, JIR, Box 3, A-39.

26. Reproduced in Col. J. R. Deane (secretary, General Staff) to John J. McCloy, July 17, 1942, JIR, Box 3, A-15; and radio, Marshall to Commanding General, July 20, 1942, JIR, Box 3, A-15.

27. Chuman, *Bamboo People*, 193–194. The *Korematsu* case was one of the three landmark test cases of the mass removal and confinement of West Coast Japanese heard by the Supreme Court during 1943–1944. Justice Roberts had led the investigative Pearl Harbor commission that issued in 1942 the Roberts report that alleged Japanese espionage in Hawaii.

28. Arnold, "Memorandum." The WRA administered the loyalty questionnaire in the fall of 1943 in preparation for their segregation program, designed to separate the disloyals from the loyals. Question 27 asked internees if they were willing to foreswear allegiance to Japan, and Question 28 asked if they were willing to serve in the U.S. armed forces. On the vagaries of the questionnaire, see Daniels, *Concentration Camps*, 104–129.

29. Included in a collection of *tanka* poems edited by Jiro Nakano and Kay Nakano, *Poets Behind Barbed Wire* (Honolulu: Bamboo Ridge Press, 1983), 64; reprinted here with permission.

30. S. Furuya, *Haisho Ten-ten*.

31. In Nakano and Nakano, *Poets Behind*, 44; reprinted here with permission.

32. Seikaku Takesono, March 11, 1982, oral history interview, JIR, Box 4.

33. George Hoshida, October 5, 1981, oral history interview, JIR, Box 4.

34. Transfer Register, Transfer Units 1 and 2.

35. John H. Provinse (acting director, WRA) to Dillon S. Myer (director, WRA), October 6, 1942, National Archives, Record Group 210, Records of the War Relocation Authority (henceforth RG 210 WRA), Subject-Classified General Files, Box 280, File No. 39.034, no. 1.

36. McCloy to Emmons, December 30, 1942, JIR, Box 3, A-23.

37. See, e.g., Provinse to Myer, October 6, 1942; and Dillon S. Myer, "Memorandum for the Files," November 2, 1942, RG 210 WRA, Subject-Classified General Files, Box 280, File No. 39.034, no. 1.

38. Bicknell to Col. Karl R. Bendetsen (assistant chief of staff, Civil Affairs Division, Wartime Civil Control Administration), February 11, 1943, RG 338 Military Government, Box 12.

39. Myer to McCloy, February 27, 1943, RG 210 WRA, Subject-Classified General Files, Box 280, File No. 39.034, no. 1.

40. Col. William P. Scobey (executive, General Staff), to Myer, March 11, 1943, RG 210 WRA, Subject-Classified General Files, Box 280, File No. 39.034, no. 1.

41. Myer to Secretary of the Navy, n.d.; and Scobey to Naval Intelligence, March 11, 1943, RG 210 WRA, Subject-Classified General Files, Box 280, File No. 39.034, no. 1; and Capt. E. M. Zacharias (acting director, Naval Intelligence) to Scobey, March 31, 1943, JIR, Box 3, A-24.

42. McCloy to Emmons, April 2, 1943, JIR, Box 3, A-24.

43. "Hawaiian Evacuees," attached to letter from Paul A. Taylor (director, Jerome Relocation Center) to Myer, February 28, 1943, RG 210 WRA, Subject-Classified General Files, Box 280, File No. 39.034, no. 1. In his cover letter, Taylor downplayed the favorable report. "Generally speaking," he wrote, "the remarks that have been made in Staff Meetings concerning the evacuees from Hawaii are much less favorable than this report would indicate."

44. See, e.g., Gary Y. Okihiro, "Japanese Resistance in America's Concentration Camps: A Re-evaluation," *Amerasia Journal* 2 (Fall 1973): 20–34; Arthur A. Hansen and David A. Hacker, "The Manzanar Riot: An Ethnic Perspective," *Amerasia Journal* 2, no. 2 (Fall 1974): 112–157; and Gary Y. Okihiro, "Tule Lake under Martial Law: A Study in Japanese Resistance," *Journal of Ethnic Studies* 5, no. 3 (1977): 71–85.

45. Iwao Kosaka, n.d., oral history interview, JIR, Box 4.

46. WRA, "Summaries of the Activities of Persons of Japanese Ancestry [*sic*], Since Arriving on the Mainland After Evacuation From Hawaii, Who Are Not Residing at Tule Lake Center, Newell, California," April 24, 1945, RG 210 WRA, Subject-Classified General Files, Box 280, File No. 39.034A; and WRA, "Summaries of the Activities of Persons of Japanese Ancestry, Since Arriving on the Mainland After Evacuation From Hawaii; Who Are Now Residing at Tule Lake Center, Newell, California," July 2, 1945, RG 210 WRA, Subject-Classified General Files, Box 280, File No. 39.034, no. 1.

47. WRA, "Summaries of Activities," July 2, 1945.

48. Ibid.

49. WRA, "Summaries of the Activities of Persons of Japanese Ancestry, Since Arriving on the Mainland After Evacuation From Hawaii: Who Are Now Residing at the Tule Lake Center, Newell, California," May 10, 1945, RG 210 WRA, Box 280, File No. 39.034A.

50. For an account of the WRA's segregation program and a history of Tule Lake, see Dorothy S. Thomas and Richard Nishimoto, *The Spoilage: Japanese-American Evacuation and Resettlement During World War II* (Berkeley: University of California Press, 1969).

51. *Tanka* by Muin Ozaki, in Nakano and Nakano, *Poets Behind*, 59; reprinted here with permission.

52. Allen, *Hawaii's War*, 141. See also Myer to Joseph R. Farrington (territorial delegate to Congress), May 12, 1945, RG 210 WRA, Subject-Classified General Files, Box 280, File No. 39.034A.

53. Myer to Farrington, November 22, 1943, RG 210 WRA, Subject-Classified General Files, Box 280, File No. 39.034, no. 1.

54. Office of Chief of Military History, United States Army, G-2 Section, vol. 10, pt. 2, p. 26. Cf. Allen, *Hawaii's War*, 134.

55. Bendetsen to Assistant Chief of Staff, War Plans Division, January 30, 1942, JIR, Box 3, 407–40; Headquarters Hawaiian Department to Adjutant General, February 8, 1942; JIR, Box 3, 407–39; Brig. Gen. B. M. Bryan (director, aliens division, War Department) to Office of Military Governor, March 31, 1943, JIR, Box 3, S-23; Olson to de Laval, June 19, 1943; Olson to de Laval, September 23, 1943; Maj. Louis F. Springer, Weekly Reports, RG 338 Military Government, Box 59, File "Internee and Prisoner of War Statistical Report"; "Civilian Internees and Prisoners of War Held within the Central Pacific Area," JIR, Box 3, S-28; Office of Chief of Military History, United States Army, Provost Marshal's, vol. 24, pt. 2, pp. 203–204; and Office of Chief of Military History, United States Army, G-2 Section, vol. 10, pt. 2, p. 26.

56. On the wartime "repatriation" program, see C. Harvey Gardiner, *Pawns in a Triangle of Hate: The Peruvian Japanese and the United States* (Seattle: University of Washington Press, 1981).

57. Col. Kendall J. Fielder to Chief, Military Intelligence Service, August 17, 1942; and attached documents, JIR, Box 1. These repatriates were not consular officials of Japan, but Japanese Americans.

58. Office of Chief of Military History, United States Army, Provost Marshal's, vol. 24, pt. 2, p. 203.

59. Anthony, *Hawaii under Army*; Chuman, *Bamboo People*, 182–197; and Peter Irons, *Justice at War: The Story of the Japanese American Internment Cases* (New York: Oxford University Press, 1983).

60. Robert C. Richardson, Jr. (commanding general, Pacific Ocean Areas) to McCloy, August 19, 1944; and attached documents, JIR, Box 1.

61. Richardson, "Memorandum on Proposed Presidential Executive Orders," June 16, 1944, RG 338 Military Government, Box 54, Folder "Proposed Executive Order, File No. 1."

62. McCloy to Richardson, September 2, 1944, RG 338 Military Government, Box 54, Folder "Proposed Executive Order, File No. 2."

63. Richardson to Commander in Chief (Pacific Ocean Areas, Pearl Harbor), September 3, 1944, RG 338 Military Government, Box 54, Folder "Proposed Executive Order, File No. 2."

64. In fact, during his tour of Hawaii, Roosevelt warned the governor that the ending of martial law placed added responsibility in the hands of civil authority. "I told them that at the least sign of any change in the situation for the worse," reported the president, "I would promptly re-establish martial law." Roosevelt to Secretaries of War and the Navy, August 15, 1944, RG 338 Military Government, Box 55.

65. Fuchs, *Hawaii Pono*, 300–301.

66. Anthony, *Hawaii under Army*, 108.

67. See also J. A. Balch, *Shall the Japanese Be Allowed to Dominate Hawaii?* (n.p., 1942), for a racist statement from a member of the white elite.

68. Hoshida, oral history.

69. John H. Wilson (Director, Department of Public Welfare) to Agents & Supervisors, February 26, 1943, University of Hawaii, War Records Depository, File No. 27.01. See also *Personal Justice Denied*, 273–274.

70. "Procurement and Utilization," pt. 6, RG 338 Military Government, Box 891.

71. Ibid.

72. See, e.g., Kotani, *Japanese*, 59–65.

73. On the role of Hawaiian *nisei* in MIS, see Tad Ichinokuchi, ed., *John Aiso and the M.I.S.: Japanese-American Soldiers in the Military Intelligence Service, World War II* (Los Angeles: Military Intelligence Service Club of Southern California, 1988).

74. Paraphrased from the findings of the congressional commission in identifying the causes for the mainland internment of primarily Japanese Americans, in *Personal Justice Denied*.

75. Kumamoto, "Search for Spies," 58–60.

76. Daniels, *Concentration Camps*, 55.

77. Ibid., 92–96.

78. Quoted in Murphy, *Ambassadors*, 280–281.

79. Edgar Rice Burroughs, "Our Japanese Problem," *Hawaii* 5, no. 11 (June 30, 1944): 13. At least 187 of Hawaii's Japanese, however, renounced their U.S. citizenship while under confinement during the war, and many were probably among the 1,116 renunciants "repatriated" to Japan. "Hawaiian Evacuees Who Have Renounced Their American Citizenship," JIR, Box 3, 389–9; and Chuman, *Bamboo People*, 276–277.

80. Frank E. Midkiff to Edgar Rice Burroughs, December 16, 1943, University of Hawaii, War Records Depository, File No. 15.05.

81. See, e.g., Fuchs, *Hawaii Pono*, 308–322.

Index

Reinecke, John, 83, 242, 243
Republican party, 13, 14, 117, 235, 236
resistance: collective forms of, 41–43,
  53, 98–99, 153–156, 185, 190, 275;
  individual acts of, 41, 156–157, 190;
  women's, 41, 43. *See also* strikes
Richardson, Robert C., Jr., 242,
  268, 269
Roosevelt, Franklin D., 162, 173, 174,
  175, 177, 191, 208, 210, 224, 256, 257,
  258, 259, 269, 270, 273, 274
Roosevelt, Theodore, 12, 37, 38, 66
Rutledge, Arthur A., 242, 243

Saito, Miki, 28, 38, 60
Sakamaki, Shunzo, 184, 185, 203
Sasai, Myoshu, 219–220
Selby, Charles, 232, 233
Shiba, Sometaro, 46, 47, 52, 53
Shibusawa, Eiichi, 132, 133, 159
Shigeta, Ko, 28, 32–33
Shivers, Robert L., 178, 203, 208, 209
Short, Walter C., 199, 201, 204, 205,
  206, 210, 239, 257
Soga, Yasutaro, 47, 49, 50, 52, 53, 54,
  56, 212, 213, 214, 215, 216, 217, 218,
  221, 222, 223, 224
Sokabe, Shiro, 131, 188
Standley, W. H., 173, 174, 175
Stevens, John L., 11, 57
Stimson, Henry L., 168, 257, 258, 259
Stirling, Yates, Jr., 143, 161–162
strikes: pre-annexation, 41–42; of 1900,
  42, 43; of 1904 (Waipahu and Waialua), 43–45; of 1905 (Lahaina), 45; of
  1909 (Oahu), 45–53, 60, 65, 185, 186,
  189, 269; of 1920 (Oahu), 66–81, 86,
  90, 91, 93, 94, 98, 100, 109, 112, 113,
  115, 120, 121, 122, 130, 131, 134, 139,
  160, 185, 187, 188, 189, 190, 272
Summerall report. *See* military, Summerall report

Takei, Sojin, 262, 276
Thompson, Frank, 71, 178
Thurston, Lorrin A., 11, 137–138
Toyama, Tetsuo, 202, 213
traders, 4, 7–8, 17, 18
Tsutsumi, Takashi, 71, 77–78, 100–
  101, 115

Van Reed, Eugene M., 19, 20, 21, 23
Varsity Victory Volunteers, 246,
  250, 251

Walker, Edward E., 244, 245
War Relocation Authority, 259, 260,
  263, 264, 265, 266, 267, 273. *See also*
  Myer, Dillon
Watase, Chris, 235, 236
Waterhouse, John, 72, 75, 76, 78, 178
Wells, Briant H., 148, 165
West Coast: anti-Asian movement on,
  37, 86, 87, 89, 90, 110, 132; Asian
  laborers on, 84, 87; Japanese menace
  on, 172, 175, 237, 258, 259, 260, 264,
  273; migration to, 36–37
white supremacy, 17, 56, 57, 80, 91, 98,
  103, 117, 159, 166, 167, 191, 269, 272,
  275. *See also* racism; whites
whites: early influence of, 6–7; labor,
  83, 90, 91, 187, 270; number of, 57,
  104, 135; and oligarchy, 7–12, 14, 58,
  86, 88, 101, 127, 129, 186, 188, 196,
  229, 270, 272; as planters, 8, 14, 34,
  36, 38, 39, 40, 41, 44, 49, 50, 52, 53,
  54, 55, 56, 57, 69, 70, 78, 80, 81, 82,
  89–90, 101, 105, 126, 127, 131, 160,
  162, 185, 186, 187, 188, 189, 190,
  191, 196, 241, 242, 243, 270, 272;
  women, 96
Wilcox, Robert W., 11, 13
women (Japanese): and childbirth
  and children, 30, 31–32, 72; within
  the household, 48, 230–231; as in-